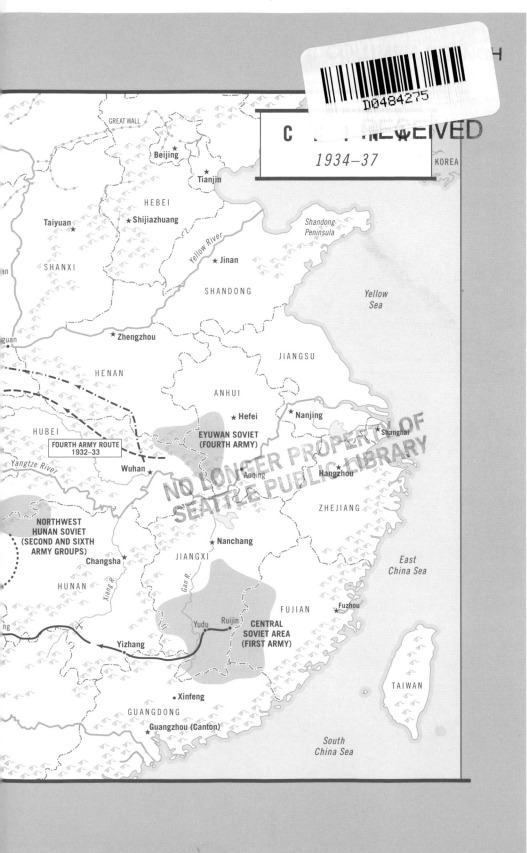

C   RECEIVED

1934–37

KOREA

GREAT WALL

★ Beijing

★ Tianjin

HEBEI

Taiyuan ★   ★ Shijiazhuang

SHANXI

Yellow River

★ Jinan

SHANDONG

Shandong
Peninsula

Yellow
Sea

guan

★ Zhengzhou

HENAN

JIANGSU

ANHUI

★ Hefei   ★ Nanjing

Shanghai

HUBEI

FOURTH ARMY ROUTE
1932–33

EYUWAN SOVIET
(FOURTH ARMY)

Yangtze River   Wuhan ★

Anqing   Hangzhou

ZHEJIANG

NORTHWEST
HUNAN SOVIET
(SECOND AND SIXTH
ARMY GROUPS)

★ Nanchang

East
China Sea

Changsha ★

JIANGXI

Gan R.

HUNAN

Xiang R.

FUJIAN

Fuzhou ★

ng

X

Yudu Ruijin

CENTRAL
SOVIET AREA
(FIRST ARMY)

Yizhang

TAIWAN

• Xinfeng

GUANGDONG

★ Guangzhou (Canton)

South
China Sea

UNBOUND

Also by Dean King

AUTHOR

Skeletons on the Zahara

Patrick O'Brian: A Life Revealed

A Sea of Words

Harbors and High Seas

EDITOR

*Every Man Will Do His Duty: An Anthology of
Firsthand Accounts from the Age of Nelson, 1793–1815*

UNBOUND

A True Story
of War, Love, and Survival

Dean King

Little, Brown and Company

NEW YORK   BOSTON   LONDON

Little, Brown and Company
Hachette Book Group
237 Park Avenue, New York, NY 10017
www.hachettebookgroup.com

First Edition: March 2010

Little, Brown and Company is a division of Hachette Book Group, Inc.
The Little, Brown name and logo are trademarks of Hachette Book Group, Inc.

L. Tom Perry Special Collections, Harold B. Lee Library, Brigham Young University. Provo, Utah:
#2737 (p. 10); #2627 (p. 27); #2638 (p. 32); #3260 (p. 38); #2254 (p. 41);
#2768 (p. 51); #3979 (p. 52, top); #3982 (p. 52, bottom); #2647 (p. 105); #2649
(p. 271, top); #2264 (p. 271, bottom); #2265 (p. 293); #2753 (p. 294); #2635 (p. 323,
top left); #2642 (p. 323, top right); #3237 (p. 323, bottom left); #2634 (p. 323,
bottom right); #2629 (p. 324). *Elly Zhen* (p. 24). *Xiao Yun* (pp. 192, 329). *Lawrence Gray*
(pp. 204, 257). *Andy Smith* (pp. 194, 210, 223, 231, 234, 241, 339).

Library of Congress Cataloging-in-Publication Data
King, Dean.
  Unbound : a true story of war, love, and survival / Dean King. — 1st ed.
    p. cm.
  Includes bibliographical references.
  ISBN 978-0-316-16708-6
  1. China — History — Long March, 1934–1935.   2. China — History — Long March,
1934–1935 — Biography.   I. Title.
  DS777.5134.K565 2010
  951.04'2 — dc22   2009024843

10   9   8   7   6   5   4   3   2   1

RRD-IN

Maps by Jeffrey L. Ward
Book design by Fearn Cutler de Vicq

Printed in the United States of America

This book is dedicated to my third daughter, Willa (she has waited patiently), and many other females who have inspired me: Jessica, Betsey, Helen, Mary, Hazel, Grace, Nora, Amy, Liza, Sarah, Betsey, Liz, Anna, Ellie, Meg, Daphne, Daisy, Ann, Isabella, Olivia, Varena, Bonnie, Rachel, Frances, Hannah, Charlotte, Sally, Alix, Coco, Chloe, Priscilla, Jody, Mrs. Carver, and Mrs. McGrath.

CONTENTS

Contents

PRONUNCIATION GUIDE

I have used the *pinyin* (literally "spell, sound") system of transliterating most of the Chinese words and names in this book. Under this system, developed by the People's Republic of China in 1958 and the most commonly used today, the old Mao Tse-tung is now Mao Zedong (although I have kept the more familiar Chiang Kaishek and Sun Yatsen from the Wade-Giles system).

Leaving aside an explanation of the four tones, here is a rough guide to pronunciation of Mandarin Chinese:

consonants
c: *ts,* as in *hats*
q: *ch,* as in *cheat*
x: *sh,* as in *sheet*
z: *ds,* as in *words*
zh: *j* as in *jam*
other letters: similar to English

vowels
ai: "eye"
an: "ahn"
ang: "ahng"
e after c/ch, s/sh, z/zh: "uh"

ei: *ay* as in *hay*

en: "uh"

eng: *ung* as in *hung*

i after c/ch, s/sh, z/zh: "uh"

ia: "ya"

ian: "yen"

iang: "yeeahng"

ie: "yeah"

iu: "ooh"

ian: "yen"

ou: "oh"

ua: "wa"

uai: "why"

uan: "won"

uang: "oo-ang"

ui: "way"

uo: "wa"

yan: "yen"

yi: "ee"

examples

Cai Chang: "tsai chahng"

Deng Liujin: "duhng layooh-jeein"

Deng Yingchao: "duhng yehng-chow"

He Zizhen: "huh dsuh-juhn"

Jiangxi: "jeeahng-she"

Jin Weiying: "jeein way-yehng"

Kang Keqing: "kahng kuuh-cheng"

Li Bozhao: "lee boah-jow"

Li Jianzhen: "lee jyen-juhn"

Liu Ying: "layooh yehng"

Ma Yixiang: "mah ee-sheeahng"

tongyangxi: "tohng-yahng-she"

Wang Quanyuan: "wahng choowen-yoowen"
Wang Xinlan: "wahng sheein-lahn"
Wei Xiuying: "way sheeyo-yehng"
Wu Zhonglian: "woo juhng-leean"
xuanchuan: "shoowen-chwan"
Zhang Qinqiu: "jahng cheein-choh"
Zhou Shaolan: "joe sha-oh-lahn"

PRINCIPAL WOMEN
OF THIS ACCOUNT OF
THE LONG MARCH

> The following cast of characters can be found in slightly abridged
> form on the detachable bookmark at the back of this book.

A note about Chinese names: The first name, almost always one syllable,
is the surname, and the second name is the given or chosen name. It
was not unusual, especially among the revolutionaries, for a person to
change his or her chosen name as an adult to reflect personal charac-
teristics or aspirations.

Note on the dates used here and throughout the book: Birth and other personal dates are often known only by the year, so age references, given
here at the time of the Long March, are roughly accurate but could be
off by a matter of months.

    Cai Chang, age 34. From a distinguished family of gentry heavily
involved in revolutionary politics in Hunan province, Cai studied in
France in 1919 and helped establish the French branch of the Chinese
Communist Party in 1921. She and her brother Cai Hesen were close
friends of Mao Zedong's. In 1923, she joined the Chinese Communist
Party and married Li Fuchun. She was elected to the Central Committee in 1928. In Yanan, Cai served in the Central Committee organization. On the Long March, she was a favorite among the women
for her humor and high spirits. In 1945, she was elected to the Central

Committee and served as the only woman member. She was elected the first president of the All-China Democratic Women's Federation in 1949 and held that position for thirty years. She was denounced in the Cultural Revolution, primarily for being the wife of Li Fuchun, but was later rehabilitated and elected vice-chair of the standing committee of the National People's Assembly.[1]

Deng Yingchao, age 30. Born to an impoverished family of gentry in Guangxi province, she was educated in Beijing and Tianjin. During the May Fourth Movement in 1919, she met Zhou Enlai, whom she married in 1925. She traveled with Zhou to Moscow in 1928 and served in a number of high-level positions first for the Nationalist Party before it split with the Communist Party and then for the Communists. During the Long March, she suffered from tuberculosis and had to be carried on a litter over much of the route. She was elected an alternate member of the Central Committee in 1945 and a member in 1949. She held many high-level positions until the Cultural Revolution. In 1978, she became a full member of the Politburo and until her death was considered one of the Eight Elders consulted by the Party leadership, a remarkable position of stature for a woman in China.

He Zizhen, age 24. Born in Jiangxi province to a family of gentry, He joined the Youth League when she was fifteen and the Communist Party the following year. In 1928, at age eighteen, she met Mao Zedong on Jingangshan and is said to have saved him and Zhu De when they were trapped behind enemy lines. Riding a horse and wielding two pistols, she led enemy soldiers on a ten-mile chase that allowed the two to escape. She and Mao married that year but became increasingly estranged during the Long March. When it was over, he sent her to Russia and ended up divorcing her. She returned to China in 1948 and lived a largely secluded life in southern China.

Jin "Ah Jin" Weiying, age 30. From a progressive family in Zhejiang province, Jin attended primary school and teacher's college. She started out as a teacher but, after moving to Shanghai, became active in the labor movement and joined the Chinese Communist Party at age twenty-two. She rose precipitously to a position on the executive committee of the Central Soviet in Jiangxi. She married Deng Xiaoping, who would one day succeed Mao as China's top leader, but they were divorced before the Long March. Jin then married Li Weihan. When she reached Yanan, she worked for the Central Committee and the Anti-Japanese University. In 1938, ill and separated from her husband, she was sent to Russia, where she is believed to have been killed in a German bombing raid.

Kang Keqing, age 23. The daughter of a fisherman and his wife, Kang was given away to a family with no children and raised in a village in western Jiangxi province. By the age of fourteen, she began working for the Communist underground. She met Zhu De on Jingangshan and married him in 1929. She joined the Communist Party when she was twenty. Despite her passion for military life, Kang was eventually channeled to women's affairs. Though childless, she headed organizations dealing with children's welfare and joined the executive committee of the All-China Women's Federation, where she was elected deputy chair in 1957. Disgraced during the Cultural Revolution, she was raised to the Central Committee in 1977.

Li Bozhao, age 23. From an impoverished intellectual-gentry family in the Sichuan province city of Chongqing, Li studied at a women's teachers' college that was also a hotbed of revolutionary activity and controversy. She joined the CYL at fourteen and was expelled from the college. At the age of fifteen, she traveled to Moscow via Shanghai and studied at the precursor to Sun Yatsen University. There she met Cai Chang and Zhou Enlai and, at the age of eighteen, married Yang Shangkun, future deputy director of the CCP Political Department. Back in China, Li taught and worked in propaganda. Moving to Jiangxi province, she edited a newspaper and directed and wrote for a theater troupe. During the Long March, her songs, dances, and living newspaper and theater acts were primary tools for entertaining and boosting troop morale and spreading the Red Party message to locals.

After the march, Li had a flourishing career as a playwright, story writer, and novelist and wrote two operas, *The Long March* and *Northward,* about the epic journey she had experienced. Given her profession, it is not surprising that she was a primary target of the Cultural Revolution. Publicly disparaged and brutalized, Li was forced to clean the toilets of a six-story building. Branded a traitor in 1966, Yang Shangkun fared even worse, spending a dozen years in prison.

Li Jianzhen, age 28. From a Guangdong peasant family, Li was sold by her mother for eight copper coins when she was an infant. She learned to read at the window of the village school when she dropped off the sons of her new family. Though of the merchant class, this family embraced the revolution, and Jianzhen joined the Communist Youth League in 1926. She lost her husband in 1930 and left an infant behind when the Party moved her to Fujian, where she met Mao Zedong, Zhou Enlai, and Deng Yingchao, who transferred her to Jiangxi. As head of the Women's Department, she supervised the making of food sacks, straw shoes, and clothing for the Red Army. Along with Wang Quanyuan, Li Guiying, and Deng Liujiun, she was one of the best singers among the Long March women, who were often asked to entertain. In 1938, Li and her second husband relocated to the southeast, where he was killed in 1943. In 1949, she was elected to the executive council of the All-China Women's Federation. She eventually served as Guangdong's Party secretary, a rare achievement for a woman.

Liu "Little Sparrow" Ying, age 29. From Hunan gentry, Liu attended private school. At the age of twenty, she joined the Chinese Communist Party and quickly rose to head the Hunan Women's Department. She may have had a baby by Lin Wei, a French-educated revolutionary, who was killed in 1927. Liu studied at the Central Workers' University in Moscow. From 1932 to 1934, she worked with the Communist Youth League. During the Long March, she served as a political fighter, often traveling with her friend Cai Chang. In May 1935, she succeeded Deng Xiaoping as a secretary for the Central

Committee and married Central Committee general secretary Zhang Wentian. From 1950 to 1954, Liu was in charge of Party affairs in Moscow while Zhang Wentian served as ambassador to the Soviet Union. In 1959, Zhang was branded a "rightist opportunist," foreshadowing the couple's six-year exile in Guangdong during the Cultural Revolution, which Zhang did not survive.

Ma Yixiang, age 11. Ma came from a poor farming family that lived in the remote mountains of western Hunan. The youngest of four children, she was the only one to survive childhood. Even so, her parents had a hard time providing for her and sold her as a *tongyangxi*. Ma joined the Red Army to escape the abuse of her in-law family and was assigned to the Second Army Group.

Wang Quanyuan, age 21. Born to a peasant family in Jiangxi province, Wang joined the Communist Youth League at age seventeen and the Chinese Communist Party four years later. During the Long March, she was assigned to the Fourth Army and found herself separated from her friends. Placed in charge of the Women's Regiment, she crossed the Yellow River with the ill-fated West Route Army. She was enslaved by Ma Muslim horsemen, escaping after two years in captivity. Upon her return, the Communists rejected her because of her lengthy absence. She traveled back to Jiangxi but was still accused of being a traitor. More than four decades and several husbands later, she was accepted back into the Party and lived near Jinggangshan in Jiangxi until her death in 2009.

Wang Xinlan, age 10. One of six daughters of a wealthy Sichuanese family, Wang grew up in a large house surrounded by fruit orchards and rose gardens. Her two brothers played soccer in the courtyard. Her father, the only person from their village to study at the Imperial College in the Qing Dynasty, valued education and hired a tutor to teach his daughters Chinese. He later sent them to the primary school, where Wang learned to read and write and received "revolutionary enlightenment." Though wealthy, the family sided with the Communists and held secret organizational meetings on their estate.

Wei "Shorty" Xiuying, age 22. From a peasant family in Ruijin, in Jiangxi, Shorty ran off with the Red Army in 1930 after men from her village encouraged her to escape the abuse of her adoptive family. She joined the Party in 1932. During the Long March she was a political fighter, who often filled in carrying the litters. Afterward, she worked in the Women's Bureau, and after a stint of guerrilla fighting in Jiangzi-Guangdong, she studied at the Marx-Lenin School and the Party School in Yanan.

Wu Zhonglian, age 26. From Hunan, Wu grew up poor but excelled in school, joined the Communist Party at the age of nineteen, and became active in the underground. Finding her way to Jingang-shan, she worked in the Communist Youth League. She moved to Ruijin, where she acted as a guerrilla fighter and taught at the Red Army School. Literate and capable, she served as a secretary of her Cadres unit on the Long March, each night scratching out sheaves of marching orders for the following day. After 1949, she and her second husband settled in Hangzhou with her son, who was born on the trail and went by the nickname Long March Wu. She became president of the Zhejiang People's High Court and served on the executive committee of the All-China Women's Federation. She was persecuted to death during the Cultural Revolution.

Zhang Qinqiu, age 30. From Hangzhou province, Zhang Qinqiu moved to Shanghai to study at the age of eight and met Shen Zemin, the man who introduced her to the revolution. She became one of the first female Party members in 1924 and the following year married Shen and moved to Moscow, where they both studied at Sun Yatsen University. Later they moved to the Eyuwan Soviet base. During the Long March, Zhang briefly became head of the Fourth Army Political Department, the highest position held by any Communist woman during this period. She led the Fourth Army's Women's Independent

Regiment, a combat force and the first of its kind. With the West
Route Army, she gave birth to a baby on the Gobi Desert. In later
years, she served as Deputy Minister of the Textile Industry. She was
persecuted to death during the Cultural Revolution.

Zhou "Young Orchid" Shaolan, age 17. Zhou left her life as
a *tongyangxi* to join the revolution and become a nurse in the Twenty-
fifth Army. Though young, she was bold and refused to be left behind
when the army tried to send her and her fellow nurses home. She
nursed General Xu Haidong after he suffered a serious head wound
and eventually married him, changing her name to Zhou Dongping.

USEFUL TERMS

I have used some Chinese terms that have no corollary in English. These include:

dabanjia The big house moving.

datuhao The "smashing" of landlords and tyrants and the confiscation of their property, a portion of which was usually distributed to the peasants as part of the Reds' show of beneficence to the masses. Most landlords fled when they heard of the approach of the Red Army. Those who did not were often publicly humiliated, beaten, or executed.

guanxi An all-important concept in China since ancient times, *guanxi* is influence and status determined by family, friend, and work connections; political and military power; and wealth.

jin A unit of weight equaling 1.1 pounds.

kang A fire-heated mud-brick platform that served as a bed in some parts of China.

li A unit of distance equaling 0.31 miles but also subject at times to the degree of difficulty. Thus, it might be said that a mountain is thirty *li* up but only ten *li* down.

tongyangxi Commonly translated as "child bride," a *tongyangxi* might be given away or sold. Frequently, there was no apparent husband, so the *tongyangxi* was a servant. In cases in which the *tongyangxi* was betrothed, the male was often younger by several years, and the girl was expected to help raise her future husband.

xuanchuan Often unsatisfactorily translated as "propaganda," *xuanchuan* was the promotion and advocacy of Communist ideology, usually in the form of songs, slogans, and performances—often dovetailing with recruitment—and morale work, especially in the face of danger and during times of hardship. In modern corporate terms, *xuanchuan* teams were responsible for human resources, internal communications, and public relations.

AUTHOR'S NOTE

I n 1934, thirty women set out with Mao Zedong's Red Army on an epic journey. The Chinese Nationalists under Chiang Kaishek had vowed to exterminate them and to destroy the Jiangxi Soviet, their remote southeastern China enclave where several million people lived under Communist rule. Having surrounded the enclave with thousands of heavily armed blockhouses, the Nationalist Army bombed its towns to rubble and launched a massive invasion with more than a million troops.

The women fled with Mao's army not only to save their lives but also to continue pursuing their dream — a dream of freedom from the servitude and destitution that were the legacy of their ancient society. In it, women were bound to the house and the field; poor families remained perpetually on the brink of starvation; and by some social perversion, a woman's beauty and worthiness were considered inverse to the size of her feet. For many, this meant having the bones in their feet crushed in childhood and their feet bound so that they could wear three-inch slippers.

Now the Communists had to find a new place to start their experimental society all over again. Along with Mao's force of 86,000 men, the thirty women would march a vast distance on foot — four thousand miles in a single year — in search of their new home.

Harried by Nationalist forces and their American-made fighter-bombers, the Reds would cross southern China from east to west and then head north up the daunting Tibetan Plateau. In the remote forests of the south, on the ice-capped peaks in the west, and across the bitter swamps of the northwest, they marched at a blistering pace and fought when they had to. Bullets, fever, exposure, and starvation decimated their ranks, but still they carried on.

By the time they stopped in north-central China, they had participated in one of the great military odysseys of any age. Only a fraction of the men remained. All of the women were still alive, though not all had reached their final destination. The astonishing trek became known throughout China and the world as the Long March.

At first, the women did not fully comprehend the extent of what they had undertaken. "If one had a strong body, the Long March was not very difficult," Li Jianzhen told the American journalist Helen Foster Snow not long afterward. "I carried a gun, my own blanket, and fifteen *jin* of food on the way."[1] Li's nonchalance, typical of the female marchers, belied the fact that she and her comrades had just participated in a shockingly grueling ordeal and one of modern China's defining moments.

In addition to Mao's First Army, three other Red Armies—the Fourth Army, the Second Army (originally the Second and Sixth army groups), and the Twenty-fifth Army—would undergo similar Long Marches from different parts of China to finally join forces all in one place. These armies also had women contingents.

This is the story of the women who marched with Mao, and to a lesser extent that of their compatriots who marched in the other Red Armies. Although their paths were often extremely bitter, their struggles were suffused with a certain restrained joy. They were the chosen, *unbound* both metaphorically and in some cases literally. While Mao's version of Communism would eventually bring its own voluminous troubles to China, they marched to advance the plight of the poor and of women, which had remained essentially unchanged since the Dark Ages.

In this, these courageous women were successful, leaving behind an enduring lesson in perseverance and fortitude.

Author's Note

DURING THE PAST FIVE YEARS, I have driven and walked the Long March route in many provinces, talked to Long March survivors and historians across China, and examined histories and accounts of the journey, some of which have emerged in the more open periods of the post-Mao era and others of which had never been translated into English before.

I also met with Beijing scholar Guo Chen, who created the first comprehensive work focusing on the Long March women in the 1970s and 1980s; with Stanford scholar Helen Praeger Young, who interviewed many of the surviving women from 1986 to 1989; and with British adventurers Ed Jocelyn and Andy McEwen, who retraced the entire Long March on foot in 2002. Jocelyn led my trek in Sichuan and Gansu provinces in 2009 and around the proverbial campfire enlightened me on Long March geography, politics, and little-known details.

These sources and experiences and many others have contributed to my effort to dig beneath the polemics and misinformation that have so often tainted modern Chinese history — especially that of the Long March, a favorite subject of Mao's propagandists — and to reach for the enduring human story that lies within.

Thousands of years before today,
Women were not treated like people, ayo!
We were beaten up and tortured.
Joining the Red Army for the revolution,
We women started over, ayo!
Follow the Red Party with heart and soul.
How glorious to be a heroine, ayo!

—*A women's song on the Long March*

To be a revolutionary is to go and look for a good place.

—*Ma Yixiang*

PART ONE

THE MARCH TO THE WEST

chapter 1

A Flowering

In the globally and even cosmically tumultuous year of 1910, little could have seemed less significant than the birth of a peasant girl in the far reaches of southeastern China. That year, the Great Fire wiped out a vast swath of northwestern U.S. woodlands, the flooding Seine swamped the Paris Métro, and the earth passed through the tail of Halley's comet. Mexico erupted in revolution, Japan annexed Korea, and Egypt's first native prime minister was assassinated. So disturbing was the changing world that the Vatican demanded that its new priests renounce Modernism.

But the most stunning and epochal convulsion of all was unfolding in China, the world's oldest continuous civilization, where the Qing dynasty had entered its death throes. Two thousand years of dynastic rule in Asia's largest and most populous nation were crashing onto the shores of the twentieth century, launching what was to be four decades of upheaval and civil war and, on the tide of world wars, reshaping the global order.[1]

Only months prior to the fall of the last Chinese dynasty, the peasant girl was born in the obscure village of Yeping to the Wei family. In traditional China, the birth of a boy was called *jieguo,* "the bearing of fruit," and was considered a boon to the family. The birth of a girl was called *kaihua,* "a flowering"—though visually pleasing, ultimately unrewarding because only her eventual in-laws would prosper from her labor and offspring.[2]

The little girl had entered a world of rigid gender and birth-order politics, a realm of oppressive spirits, ancestral ghosts, and Daoist, Confucian, Buddhist, and cultural traditions that would weigh on her like the blanket of bamboo smoke that hovered over a village house. She could quite possibly live her life within a one-mile radius. Befitting her status as a daughter in traditional China, the little Wei girl in Yeping was given no name. But she was lucky in two regards: First, some peasants too poor to feed their families drowned newborn daughters in their night soil buckets. Though destitute, this girl's parents had let her live. Second, her family could not afford to bind her feet to produce the "three-inch lilies" that would make her an attractive bride but would also require crushing the bones at the end of her feet, bending her toes under to her heels, and securing them with strips of cloth. She did not have the luxury of being permanently deformed and housebound. She was needed in the fields.

Yeping would eventually find itself at the hub of Chinese Communism, but for now the sleepy village in southern Jiangxi province was a mountainous backwater so remote that no roads reached it from the north. Camphor trees here had growth rings of more than five hundred years, and change came slowly to the village. The isolated inhabitants—about forty families in all—spoke with a thick southern accent, frequently interjecting "*ha*," "*sa*," and "*bo*" to emphasize their points, while also using expressions dating back to ancient Chinese. The local dialect differed greatly not only from the predominant Mandarin but also from that of villages only a few miles away.

In rural Jiangxi, an archipelago of remote homesteads and villages each steeped in the past and its own superstitions, the women worshipped the white-robed female bodhisattva Guan Yin, who brought them sons and saved them from both deadly fires and drowning.[3] In each village, humble roadside stone shrines to the villagers' own bearded earth deity brought protection from drought and famine. Villagers, mostly tenant farmers, lived in mud-brick huts with dirt and pebble floors that turned liquid during spring's subtropical rainfalls.

Most of these huts had only two rooms: a kitchen and a bedroom, where the whole family slept.

Abundant rice — two or even three crops per year — was a blessing of the region and so central to life that in both Mandarin (the principal Chinese dialect) and Cantonese (the language of Guangdong), the term meaning "to eat," *chi fan,* literally means "to eat cooked rice." But the Wei family tasted little of its harvest. All of their rice crop went to the landlord. Instead, they ate the same small fibrous sweet potatoes that they fed to their pigs.

The family cooked in large metal woks on a wood-burning mud-brick stove. They ate yam congee or pumpkin soup for breakfast, lunch, and dinner, at a wooden table with a drawer for bowls and chopsticks and benches on either side. Stacks of pumpkins occupied one corner of the kitchen, where ducks and chickens roamed, fouling the floor and necessitating constant sweeping.

Outside, the yard was thick with animal and human odors. Near the outhouse — a collection of boards around a hole with brick foot pads on either side — sat the pigsty with a breeding pair, whose sucklings were sold to the local butcher. The waste of both humans and beasts was collected in pits only a little farther away, to be held for use as fertilizer for the crops.

Around Yeping, crops grew year-round, but for the peasant farmers fall was the busiest time. After bringing in the rice, they harvested yams, which they peeled, cubed, and dried on rooftops or in communal courtyards. Pumpkins, some of which had been culled in summer while green and tasting like zucchini, also were harvested now, orange and sweet. After long workdays, villagers sat in bamboo chairs around the courtyard, where laundry dried on poles and naked children and rawboned dogs (a selection of the latter to end up on a spit come winter) produced a din among the prodigious flies. Children from the same clan ran in a pack, calling one another "brother" and "sister."

Although the baby girl born to the Wei family in 1910 had her share of good luck, it only went so far. Six months after her birth, her mother died.

HUNDREDS OF MILES TO THE NORTH, in the great capital city of Beijing, as the Qing dynasty teetered, old and new powers clashed over the fate of the nation. At their height, the Qing, from Manchuria, had reshaped China, suppressing warlords, pushing into Tibet, and taking Taiwan from the Dutch. But their rule had been in a steady decline as China was rocked by the Opium Wars (1839–1842 and 1856–1860) and the loss of Hong Kong to Britain, by the bloody civil war known as the Taiping Rebellion (1850–1864), and by the Sino-Japanese War (1894–1895), which had cost it Taiwan. With the abdication of the last emperor, a mere child, in 1912, the dynasty finally collapsed.

Sun Yatsen, a reformer and unifier later considered the father of modern China, emerged as the provisional president of the newly founded Republic of China. A visionary, Sun asserted that the country belonged to all its historic peoples, including the Hui (Chinese Sunni Muslims of Turkic descent), Man (Manchus), Meng (Mongols), and Zang (Tibetans), not just the predominant Han. His enlightened reign was all too brief, however. In 1912, a former Qing military commander pushed Sun aside, taking the presidency and declaring himself emperor, dealing democracy a mortal blow. When he died in 1916, China again plunged into chaos.

THAT SAME YEAR, the girl in Yeping, now six, was sold by her father as a *tongyangxi,* or child bride, to a family in another village. This was not an uncommon practice. The husband-to-be might be much older or younger, perhaps an infant himself, in which case she was expected to raise him while serving in his parents' household. Often the acquiring family had no son at all for the girl to marry, in which case she simply became a servant.[4]

As the girl had grown older, though not that much larger, the villagers had begun to call her "Shorty." When Shorty was told that she should prepare to depart for her new home, she surreptitiously collected stones and hid them in the bedroom. When two men came to get her the next day, she attacked them with her stockpile. After she had hurled all her rocks at them, she grabbed a sickle and swung it at them. One of them tugged the weapon out of her small hands and hoisted her over his shoulder like a sack of rice. But Shorty was not finished. Furiously pounding the man's backside, she clenched one of his ears in her teeth. The man dropped her, and the two men bolted without the girl they called a "pint-sized demon."

Shorty's respite was brief. Her family summoned an older cousin to come for her. In rural China, where children might just as easily eat or sleep in the homes of their aunts and uncles as in their own, cousins were like siblings, and she was fond of this one. He successfully coaxed her into letting him take her to her new home, and as unceremoniously as that, Shorty's childhood was over.

Henceforth, she spent her days fetching water, chopping wood, doing laundry, and cooking. The *tongyangxi* was expected to make pig fodder and to collect the night soil and pig waste for the fertilizer pit. When Shorty made mistakes, her in-laws chastised or beat her and sometimes refused to feed her. Like millions of peasant girls across China, she did little but work. She was paid in welts and bruises across her small body and in near-ceaseless scorn.

FOLLOWING WORLD WAR I, when the Treaty of Versailles transferred China's Shandong Peninsula to its enemy Japan, the Chinese, who had contributed workers to assist the Allies in France, erupted in anger. On May 4, 1919, students demonstrated in Tiananmen Square and then began a strike, which spread around the country and took root particularly in Shanghai. Journalists, merchants, and workers also mobilized. Among the more radical voices to emerge from the turmoil of the so-called May Fourth Movement was that of a twenty-five-year-old Hunan student. In his start-up weekly *Xiang River Review,* he proclaimed: "Today we must change our old attitudes.... Question the unquestionable. Dare to do the unthinkable." He favored the establishment of a democracy, but above all he could not tolerate a new government that preserved the old system, which virtually enslaved the common people. There could be, the student believed, no compromise with the forces that had for so long repressed China's potential. "We are awakened!" he boldly declared. "The world is ours, the state is ours, society is ours!"[5] His name was Mao Zedong.

Two heavyweight reformers emerged from the turmoil: the Nationalist (Guomindang) Party, a moderate democratic socialist organization cofounded by Sun Yatsen, and the Chinese Communist Party (CCP), founded by Li Dazhao and Chen Duxiu in 1921. (Mao Zedong attended the Party's 1st congress in Shanghai in July of that year.) Modeled after and advised by its counterpart in the Soviet Union, the Party rose meteorically. By 1927, 60,000 Party members had organized millions of peasant farmers and urban laborers under the Red banner. Broken into myriad secret cells scattered throughout the vast country, it had become the largest Communist party in the world.

For a time, the Nationalists and Communists were allied against the regional warlords. After Western governments refused to support the alliance, the Nationalists used Soviet funding to establish a military academy in Guangzhou (then Canton), the capital of Guangdong province. They set up a soldier named Chiang Kaishek as principal of the school, whose mission it was to prepare soldiers for a campaign to unite China.[6]

In the spring of 1925, Sun Yatsen died, and the uneasy partnership between the Nationalists and Communists imploded. Right-leaning Chiang Kaishek took command of the National Revolutionary Army and in 1927 united with rightist militias to attack their former allies, killing 5,000 labor organizers and Communists in Shanghai and initiating what became known as the White Terror. In poor rural Jiangxi, peasant farmers suspected of being Communist sympathizers were gunned down in their fields. Others, including pregnant women, were rounded up during the day and executed en masse at night. Many were beaten and tortured in order to get them to betray the hiding places of their comrades. According to one Jiangxi woman, "Some were stripped naked and burned at the stake."[7]

On August 1, 1927, Communist soldiers in Nanchang, the capital of Jiangxi province, rose up against their former Nationalist allies and held the city for five days in what is considered the first battle of the Chinese Civil War. The Communists, under Zhou Enlai, He Long, Liu Bocheng, Lin Biao, and Zhu De, captured thousands of small arms and a vast quantity of ammunition before being driven out. A month later, Mao Zedong led the Autumn Harvest Uprising in Hunan. The rebellion, like other Communist outbreaks, was viciously suppressed, and the Communists fled from the cities, where they were subject to immediate execution.

The Sixth Chinese Communist Party Congress in 1928 was held in the safety of Moscow. At the congress, the Party embraced the enormous potential of peasant women in a society that had long oppressed and abused them. Echoing sentiments espoused by Mao earlier, delegates declared that it was of the "greatest importance to absorb . . . peasant women into . . . the revolutionary movement." These women, the group recognized, were a core element of village economies, held sway in family life, and had a crucial influence on the peasant troops. In past movements, the delegates stated, peasant women had proven to be brave fighters. In this regard, history provided a legendary role model in Queen Mother Xin. The Shang dynasty warrior, wife of King Wu Ding, had led an army of 13,000 men, enormous in its day (thirteen centuries before the Christian Era), in defeating four hostile states attacking the Shang's northwestern frontier. As a sign of her heroism, Xin had been buried with dozens of bronze-bladed dagger-axes with turquoise-inlaid handles.[8]

Even before the Moscow gathering, the Chinese Communists had initiated a number of revolutionary practices regarding women. They had denounced arranged marriages, and they had condemned the practice of foot-binding. They had created real educational and leadership opportunities.

To WITHSTAND THE LOSSES they had sustained in the White Terror, the Communists launched a wave of recruiting and reorganization. In the fall of 1930, Red Army troops arrived in Shorty Wei's village.

Deng Fa, Cai Shufan, and Hu Di in Yeping, in the late fall of 1931. *(Helen Foster Snow Archives. This and all photos from the Helen Foster Snow Archives come from the L. Tom Perry Special Collections, Harold B. Lee Library, Brigham Young University.)*

They had already begun to transform her rural county of 230,000 residents, which, until now, had changed little since its founding in the third century. The Red Army's brand of transformation was swift and shocking: They swept into a village, executing landlords (though most fled ahead of them), seizing their land, destroying deeds and boundary markers, and banning religion. They then redistributed what they had taken, including temple property, among the peasants. They set up schools to teach the peasants how to read, established peasant-led Party rule, and recruited the young and able, men and women, to help carry the revolution to the next village. It was a progressive and merciless, sometimes ferocious, radical reconception.[9]

Shorty, still unmarried and nameless, joined a group of field hands to listen to what the Communist recruiters had to say. The only female in the audience, she liked what she heard, and even more, she liked the idea of escaping her in-laws' house. She had little to lose, and although she stood less than four and a half feet tall, the feisty girl with thick eyebrows and wide cheeks was unintimidated. She stepped forward and volunteered to be a soldier.

chapter 2

The Struggle

Three years before setting up camp in Yeping, following Mao's Autumn Harvest Uprising and other failed revolts, the Communists had fled from urban areas and established bases in the rural countryside. One contingent had created a soviet—an autonomous region governed by a Communist council—called Eyuwan in the remote borderlands of Hubei, Henan, and Anhui provinces in east-central China.[1] Mao had sought refuge on Jinggangshan, a mountain on the Hunan-Jiangxi border in southeastern China, about a hundred miles south-southwest of Nanchang. Here he had united with groups of miners and rebel bandits, the latter dispossessed peasants who had been preying on wealthy landowners, and with a small local Communist force to form an army of several thousand.

A fortress of a mountain with a plateau on top, accessible only through a few narrow passes, Jinggangshan became a revolutionary hotbed under the leadership of Mao, who was a rousing visionary, and Zhu De, a former Nationalist public security chief and officers training corps commandant who had defected with about 1,000 men.[2] Zhu, who dressed and talked like a common soldier and went by the nickname "Chief Cook" (he had once escaped arrest during a Nationalist raid by claiming to be a kitchen hand), had a devoted following of men. The mountaintop became the center of a sprawling soviet that would produce some of the steeliest Red Army soldiers and leaders.

More than a hundred women found their way to this redoubt. Like the men, they helped spread Mao's message of agrarian revolution to the local peasants and helped expand and transform the military base into an actual ministate. Doing this meant recruiting both men and women in villages throughout the region.

Ouyang Quanyuan, like Shorty Wei, was only sixteen when she fell under the spell of Red recruiters. She had gone to the market in her village, in the hills along the middle Gan River, to trade eggs for salt. A major tributary of the Yangtze, the Gan was an important trade artery in southeastern China, flowing north the entire length of the province and through the capital of Nanchang.

At the market, Ouyang encountered an amazing thing: a gregarious band of strangers had flooded the streets, waving red flags, banging on drums, and sounding gongs. Eventually, the locals assembled, sweeping her up in the crush. *Baodong,* or "rebellion," was on their lips. The strangers made confusing speeches. "We poor are liberated," they proclaimed. "Join the revolution!" Ouyang was not sure what liberation was, but she felt a thrill at the news that her life had possibilities she had never considered.

When Ouyang was eleven, her father had betrothed her to a man of twenty-seven. She had been allowed to remain in her parents' home, however, walking the three miles to and from her in-laws' house each day to work in the fields at harvesttime. After witnessing the rally, she could not wait to tell both families about the exciting things she had seen and heard. Practical and hardworking, she had always worn her hair twisted into a bun and held in place by a wooden hairpin. Now, taking up Communist ways, she cut her hair short and encouraged the women around her to cut their hair and to reject foot-binding.

Soon her mother-in-law, afraid that she would lose her daughter-in-law to this new force in their lives, demanded that the marriage be made and consummated. Ouyang took her husband's family name, as was the local custom. It would be one of Wang Quanyuan's last overtly traditional acts.[3]

IN 1929, the Nationalists forced Mao Zedong's contingent to flee to even remoter country more than a hundred miles to the southeast, in the low, densely forested peaks of the Wuyi Mountains. There the Communists put down roots on a bend in the Mian (Cotton) River.

Ruijin had taken its name, meaning "auspicious gold," in AD 904, when a discovery of the precious metal had led to a prospecting boom. Now the red clay yielded little but stains, and one Communist soldier described the town as "ancient and withered."

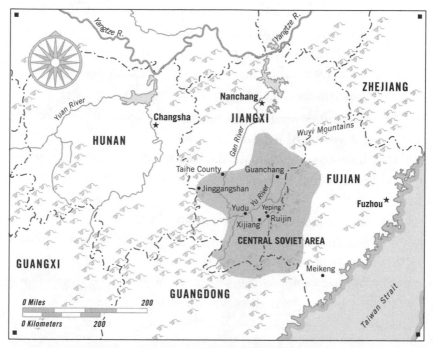

Central Soviet Republic, 1934

The protracted White Terror was taking a severe toll on the Communists across China. Chiang Kaishek's forces had annihilated the ranks of their previously swelling farm and labor organizations and by some counts would slay four out of every five Party members.[4] As Shanghai, the center of Chinese Communist activism, increasingly became a death zone, the Communists fled. A few were lucky enough to escape abroad to study. Others furtively made their way to the various soviets in remote parts of remote provinces. Most of the leaders sought refuge in Mao's burgeoning soviet, which buzzed with activity.

It was here that the Communists were most successful in their efforts to implement their agrarian revolution and to reorganize society. They soon built a bureaucracy to govern the region's three million rural inhabitants, and by 1930 Jiangxi had become the "Central Soviet Republic" and Ruijin the headquarters of the Chinese Communist Party, with the top leaders establishing themselves just north of Ruijin—in Yeping, Shorty Wei's no-longer-sleepy hometown. Beneath thick canopies of trees, the Communists built meeting halls and wooden houses that provided the leadership with shelter. Catch basins in paved courtyards collected the copious rainfall from the rooftops and provided water for household use. In one gargantuan hollowed-out camphor tree, Mao found a quiet reading spot.

In the fall of 1931, a time of year normally taken up with the harvest, representatives from the other Communist strongholds in south and central China came to Yeping to discuss strategy. Twenty-year-old Li Bozhao was among the many new arrivals. Outgoing and energetic, she was a model of the new assertive woman. The daughter of a noted scholar, she had studied under the Communist firebrand and rising leader Zhang Wentian (also known as Luo Fu)[5] in a Sichuan school before being expelled for staging a school play depicting the abuse of women. Although she was just fifteen at the time, the Communists had sent her to Moscow, where she studied mechanics, warfare, and drama and met a number of the higher-ranking comrades.

In Jiangxi, Li led a school for artists and actors and directed the education department. She also made history by editing the first issue of the Communist newspaper *Red China*. Li and her staff lived and worked in Yeping's farm huts, sleeping on straw beds atop dirt floors. By the smoky light of oil lamps, they wrote and revised, their eyes turning puffy and red, cranking out 12,000 words a day.[6]

The Nationalists had relocated the nation's capital from Beijing to Nanjing in 1928. Nanjing had served as the original capital during the Ming dynasty (1368–1644), the last period of ethnic Han rule, an era when the nation was one of the richest and most powerful in the world. Chiang Kaishek saw himself as the one who would return China to such glory.

Getting to the Communists, however, would not be easy: there were few paved roads and fewer railroads. Then, like a lightbulb going off overhead, the solution came to Chiang. He arranged to buy American warplanes—thirty-two Vought Corsair fighter-bombers—with the approval of President Herbert Hoover. Chiang soon hired a former U.S. Army pilot, Douglas Aircraft representative Floyd Shumaker, to purchase more American airplanes and create a fleet of long-range bombers and attackers. Over the next several years, Chiang would use both air and ground forces in an attempt to overwhelm the Reds.

Using hit-and-run guerrilla tactics, Mao, who was the chairman of the Central Soviet, managed to fend off two "encirclement and extermination" campaigns, the second against a force of 200,000 men and Chiang's increasingly proficient air force. Chiang's third attempt, with 300,000 troops, withered in the fall of 1931, after Japan, with its eye on China's internal travails, invaded Manchuria and set up the puppet state of Manchukuo. In early 1932, Japanese airplanes bombed Shanghai, and Japanese ships bombarded Nanjing from the Yangtze.[7]

Like a bulldog, Chiang continued to ramp up his air force. Americans not only advised, trained, and supplied the Nationalists but also, led by Shumaker, flew combat missions, bombing and strafing the "local bandits," as Chiang called the Communists. An American flier, U.S. Army Reserve pilot Robert Short, died fighting for the Nationalists when he single-handedly attempted to thwart a Japanese bombing raid on the lower Yangtze River.[8] Soon twenty new state-of-the-art Douglas fighters with Browning and Lewis machine guns prowled the Chinese skies and, in the spring of 1933, zeroed in on Yeping, forcing the Communist leaders to abandon their enclave and reinstall themselves three miles away in another village.

Now mustering half a million men, Chiang aimed his Fourth Encirclement and Extermination Campaign at the sprawling Eyuwan Soviet. He was able to overrun it, forcing the soviet's influential leader, Zhang Guotao, who like Mao had attended the First Congress of the CCP, to flee west with his men. Turning his attention again to the south, Chiang agreed to a treaty with the Japanese, a move that infuriated the Chinese people and incited massive student riots but that bought him time to focus on snuffing out the Central Soviet.

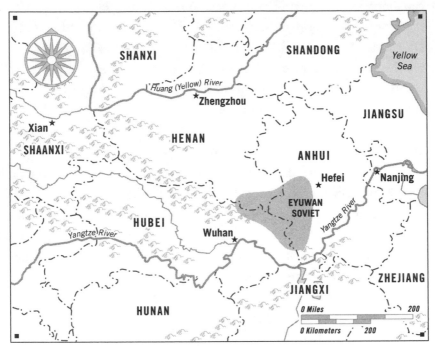

The Eyuwan Soviet, 1932–1933

Guided by General Hans von Seeckt and other advisers on loan from Hitler's Germany, Chiang ordered his forces in the fall of 1933 to encircle the Jiangxi Soviet with concrete-and-stone blockhouses, each manned by a company of fifty or more men and armed with machine guns. Constructing three thousand of these lethal bunkers in an ever-tightening spiral, the Nationalists blockaded the interior, methodically starving it of provisions, medicine, fuel, metal, and ammunition and ratcheting up the pressure on the Communist nerve center.

Mao, who was still officially the soviet's chairman, had effectively been ousted from power in the fall of 1932, placed on sick leave, and shunted aside by the influential group of Russian-educated Chinese Communist leaders known as the Twenty-eight Bolsheviks. Now led by a trio—Bo Gu (originally Qin Bangxian), distinctive in his thick black-framed glasses; Zhou Enlai, a military instructor and tactful power broker; and the German Otto Braun, a Comintern military adviser called Li De by the Chinese—the Central Red Army preferred conventional military tactics to Mao's wily guerrilla ways.[9] In April 1934, as Chiang pressed the fight, the Red Army, following Braun's advice, dug in and defended its northernmost stronghold in the Jiangxi Soviet, the town of Guangchang. In a series of deft counterattacks, the Communists hammered the Nationalists, cutting down 20,000 men.

Facing this setback, Chiang turned to his greatest strength: his air force. Chiang's bombers leveled Guangchang, killing a thousand Red fighters. Without planes of their own, the Reds could only counter with potshots from the ground. Having lost around 5,000 men during seventeen days of fighting, the Communists were forced to fall back, leaving open a route to Ruijin. Braun's strategy of digging in had cost too many lives, and it infuriated some of the Red Army commanders.[10]

Nationalist bombers.

A month later, Chiang—whose air force, with its growing infrastructure of landing strips, could now penetrate nearly any part of China, no matter how remote—launched his Fifth Encirclement and

Extermination Campaign. Supported by intensive air strikes, one million Nationalist soldiers marched into Jiangxi from the north, south, and west. Their aim was to crush all vestiges of the Communist central government and wipe out the Red Army officers and Chinese Communist Party leadership.

chapter 3

The Chosen

EARLY OCTOBER 1934

As cormorants fished in the Cotton River and bats feasted on the fall mosquito hatch, the upheaval of war and the long blockade took a grim toll on the Jiangxi Soviet. Salt and cooking oil had disappeared from the people's diet, and now rice, the staple of life, had to be strictly rationed. The denizens of Ruijin ate asparagus leaves seasoned with flakes of saltpeter (used elsewhere in fireworks and fertilizer), which they scraped from whitewashed walls. Diseases, including typhoid fever — with its headaches, dehydration, and inflammation — ran rampant among the weakened citizens of the Central Soviet. There was little medicine for treatment, and even festering foot sores had turned deadly.

Caught in the pincers of war for more than five years, the Jiangxi peasant masses had yielded nearly half a million men between the ages of fifteen and forty-five to the Red Army, but many of these recruits had been killed in battle. The women left behind struggled in the fields to feed their families as well as the army. Now, in the fall of 1934, they were all under heavy siege and more than 50,000 Red Army soldiers, many of them raw recruits, had fallen in the latest onslaught.[1]

The previous spring, Communist leaders had foreseen the possible fall of the Central Soviet. With the Comintern's blessing, they had secretly planned an escape in case things grew truly desperate. But they were no longer simply a mobile guerrilla army. Out of the wilderness, they had created the infrastructure of a Red nation, including ministry headquarters, educational institutions, hospitals, manufacturing operations, and a state mint that produced gold coins. They were not prepared to abandon all of this and had quietly been readying for a massive exodus, assembling personnel and supplies. If the day arrived, they hoped to move nearly 100,000 soldiers, cadres, and porters—laden with munitions, rations, and necessities—through the siege lines and rings of blockhouses. To finesse these perils and to avoid carnage from the sky, they knew they would have to act with all possible stealth. The plan was enormously risky, justifiable only by utter desperation.

Now that desperate day had arrived.

WHEN WORD PASSED URGENTLY through Jiangxi that the women should report to headquarters—indeed, that they should rush there without finishing up current assignments—many were in remote villages still recruiting soldiers and laborers. Most of these spiritual descendants of Queen Mother Xin already knew each other well. They had lived and worked together in one capacity or another since 1931 in Ruijin or in the nearby villages and towns, where they had gone to escape the Nationalists' bombs. Some had met even before that, at Jinggangshan or in the dismal textile mills of Shanghai, where they had served as Communist organizers. Since moving to Jiangxi, they had recruited soldiers, organized female laborers, educated villagers, and collected rice and other food. They had manned and helped run the sixty theatrical troupes that roamed from village to village and to the front to entertain and inform peasants and soldiers. They had felt the loss of innumerable friends and comrades killed.

Liu Ying, known as "Little Sparrow," was one of their best. She had entered the Communist ranks through a Hunan teachers school founded by Xu Teli, a Communist recently returned from France. Xu's message had astounded her: "You are equal to males," he had insisted. Such declarations were a large part of the Party's appeal. Most Chinese had little interest in complex theories of labor and capital. Instead, they were drawn to the movement by its advocacy of equality and the promise of escape from poverty.[2]

Little Sparrow went on to become the leader of the school's clandestine Communist cell. At night, she and her fellow adherents printed flyers, and in the early mornings they passed them out and gave impassioned speeches on busy streets before vanishing into the crowd. Little Sparrow had been one of just two girls among eighty young activists in two provinces chosen to attend a new academy to train cadres, the Party's elite workhorses. The next year, she had organized in Hunan's labor unions. At age twenty-one, she fell in love with and married the Moscow-educated general secretary of Hunan. That spring, however, he had been killed in a Nationalist raid on a Shanghai-area farmhouse, where he was organizing an uprising. The Party had sent her to Moscow for two years to keep her out of harm's way.

Now, exhorting the locals to fight the Nationalists in order to save their land, Little Sparrow's Red Recruitment Shock Brigade had surpassed its goal by 50 percent in half the allotted time. To encourage enlistments, she and her team of ten had been authorized to promise a number of benefits to the recruits' families, including first dibs on provisions, tools, and other necessities at army stores — payable in crops, if necessary — land-tax reductions, and the labor of civilian peasant men, who were required to work on the farms of soldiers for up to ten days a month. Businessmen and factory workers were required to pay extra taxes to compensate for not serving in the military. A June edition of *Red China* lauded Little Sparrow's accomplishment (2,200 able-bodied recruits), and she and her team were rewarded with hats, books, towels, and soap.[3]

One day in early October, to Little Sparrow's great surprise, Mao Zedong showed up in the local Youth League offices. The ousted leader was recovering from a bout of malaria, but he strode vigorously and deliberately toward her and took her aside. Little Sparrow was under five feet tall, round-faced, and, with her short dark hair, a boyish beauty. "Stop what you're doing," he told her, "and get to Ruijin immediately. There's a special plan."

Stunned by this suggestion, she looked up at Mao, a gaunt fellow Hunanese, who — though only five feet nine himself — towered over her, and replied that she had not yet reached her new quota of recruits. Although Mao was chairman of the Jiangxi Soviet, he was not her direct superior. "Liu Ying, you must go," he responded. "It's a unique situation." Soon afterward, she received a phone call from her superior, who confirmed the instructions and told her to leave as soon as possible.

With few possessions and no attachments, Little Sparrow mounted a horse and set out immediately, eager to find out what the urgent matter was. Though relieved to abandon her unachievable recruiting task, she felt uneasy. She and her guard hurried through a landscape of volcanic peaks and caves, past peasant shacks where pumpkins dried on rooftops, and covered the sixty miles to Ruijin in a day.

Arriving in the early evening, Little Sparrow glimpsed the nine-tiered Dragon Pearl Pagoda, marking the Cotton River's entrance into town from the southwest. Dragons were considered the gods of rain and floods, so the three-century-old pagoda, appropriately dedicated and aligned following the principles of feng shui — literally, "wind, water," referring to the flow of energy — served to preserve the river's equilibrium. Also known as the Pen of a Scholar, the six-sided Ming dynasty structure, a white ghost in the dim light, represented Ruijin's renown for culture and academics.

As Little Sparrow rode through the bomb-pocked streets to the Youth League headquarters, she recalled her first visit to Ruijin. Fifteen months earlier, she had arrived from Moscow after a six-month journey by ship, train, and — for the last month and several hundred miles — foot. Life in Ruijin had been hard compared to Moscow, where as a student at the Comintern's radio school, she had slept on a mattress and used a pillow for the first time. She had met students from the United States and Britain, among other places, and had been given a new coat, uniform, and leather shoes. No such luxuries had been handed out in Ruijin, yet it had quickly become the home she had never had. She had rekindled relationships with those she had known in Shanghai and Moscow, and she had met Mao and joined an inner circle of educated young women. During a tumultuous decade of strikes and upheaval, these women had proven capable in important roles: organizing, provisioning, recruiting, clerking in government ministries, practicing *xuanchuan* (often translated as "propaganda" work, but in this case more akin to evangelism), and even teaching military tactics. They were worldly to a degree that Chinese common women never had been.

For them, and for the men as well, life in the soviet power clique was heady. There were long meals; outdoor Ping-Pong games punctuated by juicy gossip, singing, and cavorting; mischief and pranks. Spouses were moving targets. One of Little Sparrow's friends, Jin Weiying (called "Ah Jin"), had left her husband, Deng Xiaoping (a future leader of China), for another high-ranking Communist. Another friend, married to a Chinese Communist still in Moscow, had lived with another man in Ruijin while her husband was away. Little Sparrow fit right in. In January, she had hastily married a Red Army School instructor and then divorced him after two days.[4] Such behavior would have been unthinkable a few years earlier — and many of those who sided with the Communists still found it shocking — yet it seemed to go almost unnoticed by the leaders. Following her impulsive marriage, Little Sparrow was promoted in the Youth League, where she served as a role model.

Shortly after Little Sparrow had arrived at the Youth League headquarters, a courier reached Wang Quanyuan in the countryside. "Wang Quanyuan: Please come back tonight, urgent matter," said the note, signed by Little Sparrow. Wang grabbed a bite to eat, packed her blanket and her few possessions, and set out alone over the mountain roads.[5]

Like Little Sparrow, Wang had been dispatched to recruit soldiers, only to find a lack of men between the ages of fifteen and forty-five in her area. One night, eavesdropping through an open window, Wang had heard women inside talking: "Look, it's raining now. It's so cold in the mountains. . . . He could be sick or freezing." She came to learn that the local Party head had been double-crossing the Red Army and secretly sending army-age men to hide in the hills before her visits. Wang reported the news to her superiors, who told her to assemble the villagers and put the local Party head on trial. "If the masses say execute him," they told Wang, "then execute him." They did.

Ruijin's Longzhu Dragon Pearl Pagoda.
(Elly Zhen)

Wang, never one to disobey orders, pushed on deliberately, covering the thirty miles to Ruijin virtually nonstop. It was after ten at night when she arrived. Everyone was asleep, but Wang reported as instructed to Little Sparrow, knocking on her door. Wiping sleep from her eyes, Little Sparrow looked surprised. "You came back this late?" she said.

"You told me to come right away," Wang responded.

Little Sparrow handed Wang a form to fill out regarding her personal history and told her, "Tomorrow morning after breakfast, go to the hospital for a physical exam."

THE HUNDRED OR SO WOMEN summoned to town for the chance to be included in the mysterious upcoming operation reported to a hospital housed in one of Ruijin's traditional brick homes. This was a watershed moment in their lives; undoubtedly more of them understood this than would later let on. Peasant women across Jiangxi had been busy for months making rice sacks and straw sandals to equip soldiers on the go. Without specifics, they knew what was planned. There were other hints that a strenuous march lay ahead: for one, the officers were eating their ducks. Every Chinese peasant knew that you harvested only the ducklings and preserved the breeders. It was clear that the officers were betting that whatever lay ahead, it was best that they eat whatever they could before their departure.[6]

The women were all cadres — Youth League or Party members — and they had all cut their hair short, marking them as revolutionaries in the defiant fashion pioneered by women's movement organizer Xiang Jingyu, who had been gagged and shot in the head during the White Terror. Waiting in the hospital, Wang Quanyuan wore a blue Lenin suit, characterized by its large lapels and breast pockets. Others wore Sun Yatsen suits, short tunics with stand-up collars and center buttons (based on a style worn by Chinese expatriate men in Japan). The best suits made were of fine wool; the women's were made of a thin cotton weave.

As their names were called, the women went into the examining room. For most, it was the first medical exam in their lives, and their nervousness only increased after word spread that the doctor, a man, was going to look them over — everywhere.

As they waited, the women chatted anxiously. They speculated on the nature of the operation that was about to take place. Some said they were going to the front. Others believed they were going to fight the Japanese in the north. Most of them assumed that no matter what the operation was, they would be back in a month or two. Certainly, it was agreed, it was better to be picked to go with the leaders than to be left behind. All of them desperately wanted to be selected, and they knew that the doctors were looking for reasons to disqualify them.

Some of those reasons were easy to find. Most of the women were gaunt, and those who looked weak were quickly disqualified. Also eliminated was anyone injured, wounded, or ill with any of the myriad diseases that plagued the soviet, from pneumonia to malaria to dysentery, against which the Communists had few remedies.

At last it was Wang's turn. Her given name, Quanyuan, or "Bubbling-Up Beauty," was apt: she was tall, graceful, and pretty. She had grown up roaming the hills around her village and practicing daily stretching, which was commonly known to have many salubrious effects. She was confident of her fitness. Still, she was nervous. Who knew exactly what the doctors were looking for — or what they might find? The doctor listened to her breathe through a stethoscope. Then he measured her chest with a tape. He tested her hearing with a ticking watch, her eyesight with colored paper, and her reflexes with a wooden mallet. He pushed on her legs while she resisted as instructed.

Afterward, she and the other women waited anxiously outside the hospital for news. When the results were finally announced, everyone was stunned. Of the hundred women examined, only a fifth had been selected. Shouts of joy were quickly drowned out by the groans and wails of those who had been passed over. A few flew into fits of rage, but it did them little good, no matter who they were. For some the fall was greater than for others: a number of key organizers as well as the wives of several prominent leaders had been excluded. But among those who had passed was Wang Quanyuan.

Those who had been chosen were not the only women who would be allowed to join the special operation. Those with *guanxi* — the influence of family and political connections, still a factor even in Communist China — such as Li Jianzhen, head of the Women's Department, and nine colleagues who worked in the central government, were exempted from the physical. Among those nine were Li Bozhao and Little Sparrow.[7]

Another woman had a special job to perform. Twenty-one-year-old Xiao Yuehua was tall, pretty, and quiet. She had been reduced to pushing a janitor's broom during a Party purge in which her husband, the secretary of the Fujian Youth League, had been branded a traitor to the cause and executed. The attractive southerner had eventually been transferred to the Ruijin Youth League headquarters. Li Jianzhen, who had been asked to find a "wife" for the blond-haired, blue-eyed German military adviser Otto Braun, chose Xiao, who was relatively big-boned and, Li thought, would be a good match for the large European.

WITH THE SELECTION process complete, the Red Army moved into high gear. For three furious days, as Nationalist bombers strafed the streets and dropped their payloads to soften up the interior of the Central Soviet for invasion, Red officers and cadres, including the women, scrambled madly around Ruijin and its satellite enclaves preparing to abandon the Jiangxi Soviet.

Li Jianzhen, a leader among the women. *(Helen Foster Snow Archives, Brigham Young University)*

Although it was customary to convalesce after childbirth for thirty days (a practice called "doing the month"), twenty-one-year-old Xie Xiaomei, who worked at the Central Party School, had abruptly left her hospital bed after just a few days and passed her physical. As commanded, she began to dispatch or reassign the student body with the exception of the three hundred young men who had been appointed to a military unit. In the frantic final days of the Ruijin government, Xie arranged for the packing of school documents in metal trunks and even the butchering of the cafeteria pigs. She also performed a task of a more personal nature: finding a home for her tiny daughter. She had barely had time to get to know the child, and now she had to leave her behind.

Troops loaded up rice bags and ammunition pouches and checked weapons. After a prolonged stretch of recruiting, the army had swollen to 86,000 soldiers and support staff, more than half of them under the age of twenty-four and so green that Dr. Nelson Fu estimated that 90 percent were virgins.[8] By contrast, the thirty women who would accompany the force had all been Party or Youth League members for years; each was specially trained for important noncombatant tasks; and, though the youngest was just nineteen, all were sexually experienced. In some ways, they were already more liberated than many of the men with whom they would set out.

Among the chosen women, the exhilaration and agitation were palpable. "We were all working women," Wang would say, "and good friends."[9] Yet they would be leaving other comrades, friends, and family members behind. Their attachment to the Party was deep and complex. Most had absorbed its ethos in their teens, and it had become more than a political system: it was a way of life, a religion even, to which they were totally committed, despite the fact that its ways sometimes baffled them. The Party had raised the women out of unbearably cruel peasant lives and given them freedoms they never could have dreamed of in traditional Confucian villages. Conversely, they were acutely aware of the summary penalties that could result from failure to perform as Party officials required. They had seen much retribution and brutality within the Red community.

Among those who had been accepted for the operation, no one understood this better than Zhong Yuelin, an ideal Red soldier, an ardent convert at the age of fifteen. For her, the Communists offered an irresistible vision of unity and idealism. But just before she was due to take her oath at a clandestine Youth League meeting, her recruiter had abruptly disappeared. Each subsequent day, she had watched as, one by one, members of the group mysteriously vanished. The terrified teenager had learned just how swiftly and finally the Party could pass judgment on its own members.

A quiet girl with an oval face, Zhong would soon walk a fine line of her own.

chapter 4

Leaving Jiangxi

OCTOBER 1934

Early on the morning of October 10, most of the thirty chosen women of the Red First Army were called to a meeting. The Communists were surrounded by more than a million Nationalist troops, Luo Mai, one of the senior leaders, informed them and explained that they had no choice but to attempt to break out of this encirclement. After the meeting, they were to finish gathering their gear and make their way to a village ten miles south of Ruijin. Once they had all assembled at the various departure points, they would set out at night, silently, to avoid arousing suspicion on the ground or being detected by Nationalist reconnaissance planes. Luo did not say where they were going or how far.[1]

Now in survival mode, the Reds were abandoning the cumbersome, including 26,000 wounded soldiers; 6,000 elderly, impaired, or otherwise undesirable soldiers; all the children; and nearly all the women. A few invalids, though unfit for rapid travel, were considered too accomplished or knowledgeable to leave behind. They were collected in what would be called the cadre convalescent company.[2] Many of the women had been assigned to a unit called the women's work group within the convalescent company. Among other tasks, they were to look after about a hundred men and a few women requiring special medical and transport attention.

In the remaining hours before departure, husbands and wives bade farewell to each other. Mothers and fathers reassured their children

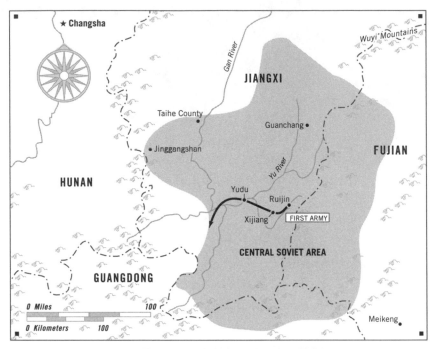

The First Army Mobilizes, October 1934

that they would be back soon. Parents staying behind embraced departing sons and wished them a speedy return. Those staying had no illusions about their precarious position. Chiang's bombers had not relented, and hundreds of his "White Devil" soldiers were moving relentlessly closer, tightening the noose. Little did the marchers know that most of them would never return. And for many of those left behind, this would be their graveyard.

IN JULY 1934, after being found again by Chiang's bombers, the Communist leadership had relocated to the village of Meikeng, next to Cloud Stone Mountain. There, on a densely wooded hillside, up a zigzagging trail, a Buddhist temple had served as Mao's home, while the mountain's granite caves had served as bomb shelters.[3]

Among the women now gathered in Meikeng, Zhong Yuelin, the youngest of the bunch, was hanging on by the thinnest thread. After passing her physical, she had suddenly become sick with dysentery, a potentially lethal illness and one that was hard to hide. Housed together, the women slept in close quarters. The night before they were to set out from Ruijin, Zhong's bunkmate had noticed that she rose many times to go outside. In the morning, she had reported Zhong to their superior officer. Suddenly, her selection had been at risk. Dong Biwu, an early, influential Party member, had grilled her about her symptoms and told her she could not go. She had protested vehemently, swearing that she would not be a burden and that she would rather die on the trail than stay behind. Her determination convinced a doctor to give her two small packets of "Western" medicine, which she gratefully swallowed. Dong relented and allowed Zhong to join her comrades.[4]

Each soldier — other than the porters, all were considered soldiers, whether toting guns or doing political or medical work — had been told to pack a blanket and a bag of rice to last ten days. They were to carry the barest necessities in their knapsacks — a change of clothes, a second pair of straw sandals, a comb, soap, and a flashlight and batteries if they had been lucky enough to get them. They had each been issued one enamel cup per person to be strapped to their backpacks or belts and a small towel and a toothbrush. (Having pioneered toothbrushing — with twigs — and toothpaste in ancient times, the Chinese had gone on to invent the bristled toothbrush in the 1500s, using the neck hairs of cold-climate pigs. Americans did not become regular tooth brushers until GIs brought home the practice after World War II.)

The soldiers were instructed to wrap their possessions tightly so that they would not make noise on the trail. They were to talk as quietly as possible, and if they got lost, to look for discreet signs along the trail left by those who had preceded them.

The women's work group would be directly responsible for five litters, made of cloth, canvas, or cotton netting. Each could be carried by two to four people and was equipped with long bamboo or wooden poles for smoother riding. One would be occupied by Deng Feng, a major general with a soft-nosed lead slug in his body from the third encirclement campaign, and another by a colonel without legs. Among the other comrades the women would look after were He Zizhen, Mao's pregnant wife, and Deng Yingchao, Zhou Enlai's wife, who was suffering from tuberculosis. (Both of these women had separate horses and litters at their disposal.)

left: Deng Yingchao, a Party organizer and the wife of Zhou Enlai. *(Helen Foster Snow Archives, Brigham Young University) right:* Deng Yingchao and Zhou Enlai in Guangdong province in 1926.

Dong Biwu would lead the convalescent company, including its staff and invalids, and most of the women would be under his supervision.[5] At age forty-eight already considered an elder statesman, Dong was a good man for the job. He was an educator, scholarly and sympathetic. He was also familiar to most of the women. Wang Quanyuan had studied military tactics under him. Despite Dong's *guanxi,* his own wife, who was frail and underweight, had failed her physical. As the two hugged and cried, she gave him a flashlight as a parting gift. Years later, Dong would learn the painful news that she had been captured by Nationalist troops and executed.

As dusk brought the hour of final departure, Party security chief

Deng Fa addressed the group in Cantonese-accented Mandarin, atypically opting for a light touch. Deng had a special reason to take interest in the convalescent company: his wife, Chen Huiqing, twenty-five and pregnant, would be a ward of the unit. "This is a great company," Deng told the women. "We have musicians, actors, and writers. If we want to put on a show, we have all we need!"[6] In fact, the Communists had discovered that such shows were crucial to getting their message to the masses, most of whom were not literate, and they had determined to carry with them costumes, scenery, and makeup.

As the light in the sky faded over Ruijin, Deng Fa launched the marchers on the path to Yudu, fifty-six miles away, where additional soldiers had gathered.[7] Advance troops had posted stars painted on paper along the route to guide them.

While almost no two accounts of the Reds' departure from the Jiangxi Soviet are alike, one thing is certain: the massive group of evacuees moved with almost uncanny stealth. At varying times, from numerous towns and encampments, more than 80,000 soldiers, political leaders, and support personnel slipped away. It would take three weeks for Chiang Kaishek to realize that the various troop movements registered by his forces were actually a mass exodus.

Clad in her blue Lenin jacket and an eight-cornered Red Army cap, Wang Quanyuan churned along with the rest of the women's work group, repositioning the Mauser pistol tucked into her belt and the enamel washbasin clanging against the buckles on the outside of her pack as necessary. (These basins would prove invaluable for boiling drinking water, cooking, and soaking feet and, when not otherwise in use, as a dry place to sit.) Shorty Wei and other women wore leaves in their hair as camouflage.

As the women walked, their hearts were filled with foreboding. The moon rose in the sky, and they began softly singing folk tunes with improvised revolutionary lyrics. Jiangxi province was not just the central Red bastion; it had become their home and was the birthplace of many of the women, including Shorty and Wang Quanyuan. Now they were leaving it behind, perhaps for the last time, with very little sense of the world beyond their provincial borders.

Young friends at the Chinese Soviet Representatives meeting in Ruijin in March 1932, the only known photograph of a group of First Army Long March women together prior to the Long March. Standing are twenty-year-old Kang Keqing, twenty-seven-year-old Qian Xijun, Zhou Yuelin, and twenty-one-year-old He Zizhen, all of whom would join the Long March. Zeng Biyi and Peng Ru, both seated, would not.

The music helped ease the pain of departure. Earlier that day, He Zizhen had handed over her beloved two-year-old Xiao (Little) Mao to her sister and her sister's husband, Mao's brother Zetan, who were staying behind. Giving a small bundle of clothes to her sister, He hugged Xiao Mao and placed him on the saddle of the couple's horse. "You're going with Auntie and Uncle," she told the toddler. "Be good. I'll be back as soon as I can."[8] She would never see any of them again.

Likewise, Xie Xiaomei had turned her newborn daughter over to a family staying behind. Although this was not an unusual practice among the Communist women, who had to be ready to relocate without children at the drop of a command, the weight of it was as heavy as her breasts with their now useless milk. The march had just begun, and she was already struggling to keep up, her body exhausted from childbirth and the endless preparations for departure.

In Jiangxi, the women had taken to mothering the motherless *tongyangxi*. The eminent Cai Chang, for one, a former member of the CCP's Central Committee, had fed and mentored Shorty and, speaking with a soft lisp through perfect teeth, had taught her how to read — two new characters each day. Encouraged by her new comrades, Shorty had at long last taken a name. With an endearing combination of moxie, naiveté, and — it would turn out — foresight, she had chosen to call herself Xiuying: "Excellent Hero."

Now swept up in the excitement of their departure, Shorty and Wang Quanyuan reveled in the beautiful moonlight. Qian Xijun, however, walked in silence, stunned by the sudden uprooting. She knew nothing of her husband's whereabouts or if he was coming to wherever it was they were headed. Even for one used to living in a besieged rebel state, this personal uncertainty was disturbing.

With so many people setting out from so many locations, departures were staggered. The streams took many paths, but the river flowed in one direction. Some marchers experienced a miserable trudge through pouring rain, the feet of thousands of heavily burdened travelers thrashing the muddy path until it was nearly impassable. Marchers repeatedly slipped and fell. As the porters bogged down, at times to a standstill, so did those behind them. Standing still, they sank into the mud, saturating their straw sandals, which were often sucked off their feet when they moved again. For reasons of stealth, no one was allowed to use a flashlight or torch, making navigation even more difficult. Among those making their way through the muck were the impish Liao Siguang and Liu Qunxian. Liu, who feared dogs, and Liao, who was afraid of snakes, formed the perfect walking tandem: Liu walked in front with a stick in her hand to ward off serpents, while Liao shooed away the dogs that sometimes approached stealthily from behind.

The Red columns slowly progressed through forests of pine, camphor, and bamboo, all casting over the trail resiny fragrances. These mixed with the pungent odor of recently harvested rice paddies, whose

left: Jin Weiying.

The arsenal in Yudu.

moist, flat bottoms were just beginning to crack. Treading carefully, the marchers began to get to know their loads and the tender spots on their feet and joints.

The group reached the village of Xijiang, about fifteen miles to the southwest of Ruijin and twenty-five miles southeast of Yudu, late at night. They crossed the Yu River on the village's floating bridge in the early-morning hours of the next day and then collapsed beneath the stars for a modest rest before setting off again. So it began.

KANG KEQING, a political instructor and director of the guard regiment of the all-male military headquarters, and a maverick by nature, traveled alongside her husband, First Army commander in chief Zhu De. Kang, a *tongyangxi* born on a Gan River fishing boat, had enlisted when she was sixteen and marched off to Jinggangshan, where she had met Zhu and his newlywed wife, Wu Yulan. Wu, a quiet but deft penner of Red slogans, had gone down the mountain one day and been captured by Nationalist soldiers. They had decapitated her and paraded her head through the streets.[9]

A few months after Wu's death, Zhu married Kang. Then a serious-minded eighteen-year-old with almond-shaped pale brown eyes, a soft round face, and symmetrical features, she was his fourth wife and less than half his age. She was not in love with him at first, she later said, but they were always "the best of comrades." He was a soldier's soldier, and she respected that. And they had a bond that to Kang was more important than love — devotion to the cause. To her, things were very clear. "We were not just fighting for ourselves," she would later say. "We were fighting for our country, for the people, to liberate our land from oppressive rule."[10]

Now Kang felt lost and empty inside, "floating in the air without a place to land." She was still reeling from her final days in Ruijin, when she had helped hunt down a military headquarters guard who had run off with a local landlord's wife. The man had fought furiously when found. Kang could still hear the gunshots when they stormed his hideout and see him lying in a pool of blood. The bullet that had taken his life was his own. The man had been a respected comrade entrusted with the leaders' lives. What had made him crack at a time when he was most needed?[11]

Kang, Zhu De, and his coterie caught up with the leaders on the banks of the Yu River at Yudu about forty miles from Ruijin. The Yu was a substantial river, though not deep in this season, with a hundred yards between its leafy banks, and in front of Kang it now twinkled with lantern light. A confusion of troops had descended on the river

Kang Keqing and
Zhu De.

He Zizhen and Mao
Zedong. *(Helen Foster
Snow Archives, Brigham
Young University)*

crossings—slim angular men, southerners, rice-eaters—with few
needs and fewer expectations. "Though you might not think it to look
at him," Peter Fleming, a special correspondent to the *London Times* (and
brother of Ian Fleming), who journeyed through China in 1933, noted of
the Chinese soldier, "he has great strength and endurance. He can live on
next to nothing. He is often a man of courage and resource, and he will
be loyal to a good master." About half of the troops had been recruited
in the past several months. Others were veteran hands, even in their

relative youth, wandering warriors who had killed and seen friends killed for years. Among these crack troops, American military attaché Captain Evans Carlson, stationed in China as a military observer shortly after the Long March, found a remarkable level of political training, appreciation for battle maneuvers, and voluntary discipline. Their strength lay not in a rigid military hierarchy—though they tended to revere their leaders—but in a democratic structure that made the troops feel responsible for their own and their comrades' actions. He called them the "most self-restrained, self-disciplined army I have ever seen."[12]

The best soldiers wore new uniforms. A brace of grenades dangled like medals on their chests, and a pair of bulging ten-pound rice bags sat on their shoulders. Bamboo hats hung on the backs of their standard-issue packs. They carried rifles with bayonets, knives, and clubs; some even held spears.

Among these troops were thousands of porters bearing artillery, munitions, and arsenal machinery. Others carried everything from the Red state's documents and office equipment to generators and an X-ray machine, plus tons of communications gear—phones, radios, and spools of telephone wire—medicine, and provisions, including (most vital of all) mounds of rice. Feeding the army while moving, usually through desolate backwaters, would be a challenge. Under the watchful eyes of Qian Xijun's husband, Mao Zemin, Mao Zedong's youngest brother and president of the national bank, another team carried hundreds of cases loaded with Mexican dollars, gold bars, Chinese Soviet currency, plates for making money, and a printing press made of lead. They crossed the Yu River, reflected in the dim rippling light, like a horde of migrating phantoms.[13]

The man who would most affect their fate, Mao Zedong, had delayed his departure, remaining in Yudu to discuss the situation with Party members being left behind. Mao was not one to fall in line as others might wish but always seemed to be carving his own parallel path. Finally, Mao, still suffering from the effects of malaria, mounted his favorite dun horse, captured in battle years before, and entered the Red slipstream. He crossed the Yu with Nelson Fu, a Western-trained doctor who had done his best to make Mao travel-worthy.

On the banks of the wide, dark Yu, hundreds of dim red-paper lanterns lit a path to a temporary bridge, a floating boardwalk held aloft on a string of wooden boats, which could be retracted and hidden from air reconnaissance in the reeds on the riverbank during the day. On the bow and stern of each boat hung a lantern casting shards of golden light on the water.

Thousands of locals had gathered to bid the soldiers farewell with gifts of sunflower seeds, peanuts, and eggs. Regiments converged on the bridge, creating bottlenecks as they strained to listen to the instructions of officers directing traffic. As Zhu De and his coterie arrived at the crossing, the chaotic sea of people seemed to part. Traffic officers stopped the lines of soldiers heading onto the rocking bridge to let the commander pass. Kang Keqing walked by her husband's side, and well-wishers stuffed her pockets with food and gifts. "Comrades, avenge us: beat the White Dogs!" she heard them calling. "Be safe, and come home victorious!"[4]

"Don't worry, brothers," the soldiers responded, "we'll destroy those White Dogs!"

The mobilized First Army included five army groups. The First Army Group, 17,000 men under Lin "the Eagle" Biao—including 15,000 combat troops—and the Third Army Group, 15,000 soldiers and support troops under Peng "the Lion" Dehuai, were the principal assault troops leading the formation.[5] The Ninth and the newly formed Eighth army groups followed close behind with 12,000 and 10,000 men respectively. The Fifth, with 11,000 men, covered the rear. These forces, each with thousands of rifles and machine guns (though far from enough to equip all of their soldiers) and three dozen small mortars, formed a protective sheath around the central column, the Red brain trust and leadership coterie, including the Central Committee, the Military Commission, and various groups of Party and central government officials, totaling 14,000 men and women. Among them were intelligence and engineering battalions, an elite guard, crack troops, an antiaircraft company, a field hospital, and the largest group among them, the heavily burdened porters, who were also considered reserve troops.

For a mobile army, the overall numbers were staggering: 86,000 men and only thirty women (thirty-two started, but two, their names

Kang Keqing in the Army, ca. 1936–38. *(Helen Foster Snow Archives, Brigham Young University)*

lost to posterity, abandoned the march in its early stages). They had 338 horses, 1,800,000 rifle and machine-gun cartridges, 76,000 grenades, and 38 mortars.[16]

Ahead were Communist allies—among them the Fourth Army and its corps of 2,000 fighting women in Sichuan to the northwest, forces in Hunan to the west that would eventually form the Second Army, and another contingent in Henan in east-central China. These forces awaited the chance to embark on their own journeys to link up with the First Army, in the hopes that they would find safety, stability, strength in numbers, and, if they were lucky, a chance to strike back.

Now, on what would later be called the Night March, the thirty women trod forward. It was not an easy task. No detailed maps existed, and asking directions from local peasants, whose world often did not extend much beyond their fields, could be maddening.[17] Although they could not have known it, they would soon discover that these initial miles would be among the easiest.

chapter 5

No Tears

Most of the women thought they were on their way to attack the rear of the enemy. Nevertheless, as they trudged through the darkness, it was hard to ignore the sheer amount of possessions being hauled along. The marchers had stripped Ruijin and Yudu of nearly everything of value, including livestock. Rumors that the Red state was in fact relocating began to spread, and the great migration quickly gained a nickname: *dabanjia,* or "the big house moving."[1]

It was the time of the rapeseed harvest when He Long's Second Army Group entered Yongshui, the Tujia mountain village of eleven-year-old Ma Yixiang.[2] Sangzhi County, in the north Wuling Range of rural northwestern Hunan, was a spectacular borderland of narrow valleys, jagged peaks, and dense forests inhabited by macaques, wolves, clouded leopards, and nimble South China tigers. A highland people, the Tujia grew rice, corn, wheat, and potatoes and raised pigs and sheep on the mountainsides, which rose up to 4,500 feet above sea level. They had their own spoken language, similar to Tibetan and Burmese, with no written words, and they worshipped ancestors, gods, and totems of white tigers. The women were skilled at handicrafts and favored costumes of bright red brocade.

From the shadows of their homes, the villagers eyed the passing soldiers warily, fearful of losing their remaining crops, not to mention

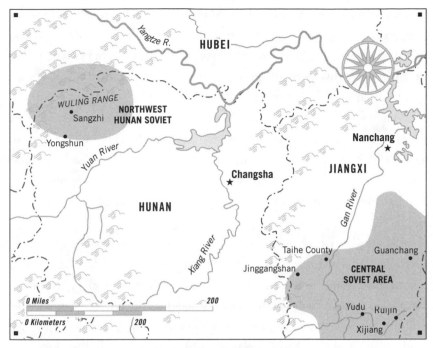

In the Northwest Hunan Soviet

their remaining sons. Several months earlier, the Nationalists had paid them a visit, saying that they had come to "rid them of bandits." Instead, the army had pillaged and conscripted. The hungry troops had taken their fruit and vegetables, their chickens, and even their dogs. Families had learned quickly to hide their daughters so that they would not be raped. With the arrival of this new army, many of the villagers fled into the nearby hills.

Malnourished, sickly, and naturally small, Ma was so short that she could not see over the windowsill of her parents' house. She stood on a stool and watched wide-eyed as the rain fell on the bedraggled soldiers marching by on the raised paths between the paddies. Although bamboo torches lit their way, many of the weary men slipped and fell in the mud. There was something grand about these drenched souls, and something pathetic, too. Locals could not even be certain that this was the Red Army. These men had no uniforms; instead, they wore trousers of blue, brown, or black and a hodgepodge of jackets, though many did have red stars on their long-billed caps and red stripes on their collars. "Some were even in old women's clothes," Ma recalled. "Whatever they got, that's what they wore." The marchers bivouacked on the nearby threshing grounds, their chaff fires wafting dank smoke and their songs echoing in the wet sky.

When she was eight years old, Ma had been sold as a *tongyangxi* to another family. Life in her new home was harsh. Her mother-in-law assigned her the most demeaning household tasks. "She used to make me carry the dog upstairs to eat the boy's feces," Ma later reported. "When the dog got too big for me to hold in my arms, I carried it on my back."

Ma's in-laws had many colorful epithets for her, such as Stupid Little Sister, Bad-Luck Girl, Short-Lived Devil, One Who Bears One Thousand Lashes, and One Who Is on the Road to Hell. No matter how hard she worked, no matter how hard she tried, her new family responded with abuse, some of it physical. Indeed, not long before the soldiers arrived, Ma had been beaten black-and-blue by her mother-in-law.[3]

Not surprisingly, Ma frequently escaped back to her parents' house, on a small patch of arable land in a narrow river valley between two mountains. Each time, Ma—unschooled, illiterate, hair in a long traditional braid—knelt before her mother and begged to be allowed to stay at home. But her parents, who survived mainly on mush and wild herbs, had little to offer her and inevitably sent her back. Superstition also played a role. Ma's mother was a hard woman, who had come to believe that Ma had the devil in her. Why else, she reasoned, had Ma's brother and sister died when she was one while Ma lived on to plague her? Now there was another baby boy, and she did not want to lose him, too.

This last time, however, she considered letting the newly returned Ma stay. She was obviously not well, and it was harvesttime, so there was momentarily enough food for one extra mouth. Besides, the girl worked hard collecting firewood and gathering rice husks and grass for pig fodder. Taking a chance, Ma's mother decided not to send her daughter back immediately, even though it would reflect badly on her.

As the ragtag marchers slept, rumors ran rife. The Nationalists had told the villagers that the Red general He Long was human only during the day and at night turned into a man-eating dragon. Some claimed that when he walked into a room, it glowed with his light. Others said that He Long was a friend of the peasants, his men stealing from the rich and giving to the poor.

Ma's father and uncles did not want to be dragged off by any army, but they believed the good things they had heard about the Communists. They went to the camp to explore and found the soldiers resting in the fields. Some Reds returned with them to use the family stove, and unlike the Nationalists, they paid for the wood they used. Later, a mess officer came to see if Ma's family had any rice. He did not have any money but gave them some dark blue fabric and told them that if he did not return in a week to repay them, they could keep the cloth for the rice they gave him.

Twelve days later, when the soldier still had not reappeared, Ma's mother made new clothes. Shortly thereafter, several Communists arrived with a warning: Chiang's men were coming. The Reds advised Ma's parents to send their children away, and she and her baby brother were taken to an uncle's house in the nearby mountains.

Awaiting the Nationalist assault, the Reds hid in pairs in the rice marshes, crouching behind the heaps of stalks left over from the harvest, and in the elbows of the mountains that pinched the small valley. Commandeering strategically located homes, they built defenses in rooms throughout the village, including one right in Ma's parents' kitchen.

As the Nationalists entered the town that night, the Communists ambushed them. While the fight raged, Ma, her brother, and a cousin hid under a slatted bed at her uncle's place, listening to gunshots and explosions.

At dawn, villagers emerged to discover an eerie silence. He Long's men were nowhere to be seen, but they were far from gone. Some quietly came to Ma's uncle's door looking for a guide, and he led them away. After he returned, Ma climbed a tree and listened as the Red soldiers reemerged to hunt down the remaining Nationalists. The Communists would try to convert Chiang's foot soldiers, medical men, and officers with special technical skills. Those who did not fit into these categories would be killed.

Consolidating their victory, He Long's Second Army Group established a headquarters in Ma's village, where they would stay for a year before departing to catch up with Mao and his much larger group. Meanwhile, Ma's aunt Peng became head of the local branch of the Women's Union, a Party organization, and she invited her niece to their meetings. Ma did not understand the politics, but she did respond to the kindness and caring of the other women. "Since I was a *tongyangxi,* they all sympathized with me," she later recalled. "And they all liked me because I wasn't naughty."

Ma had little knowledge of the world outside her village, but she began to see that the Communist women wore the same clothes as the men and, like them, worked at meaningful jobs. Just a child, she could not comprehend the complexities of Marxist doctrine, and some of what she admired most about the Communists was trivial or superficial, like the leather belts they wore around their waists. But on a profound level, the little girl realized that these visitors and their movement offered her some things she had never known before, namely a sense of belonging and a sense of mission. Ma begged her mother to let her join the Red Army. "If I go back to my mother-in-law's family," she pleaded, "they will beat me to death."

Bound by her agreement with her daughter's in-laws, Ma's mother refused. But her little girl now had a mind of her own.

chapter 6

Into Hunan
and Guangdong

OCTOBER–NOVEMBER 1934

K ang Keqing spent her nights with Zhu De. During the day, they
had their own work to do. She did not tend to the general or cook
for him. He had men to do that. When she could, she walked close
to Little Sparrow and Cai Chang, whose chatter and laughter helped
while away the long hours of walking. They had been abroad, and they
talked of exotic places and food that made her mouth water.[1]

Four or five months pregnant, twenty-three-year-old Liao Siguang
had reluctantly accepted being separated from her husband and rel-
egated to the slow-moving convalescent company. This was frustrating for many reasons, among them the fact that she was by nature
anything but a laggard.

Among the straw-sandaled, Liao, who was known for her mischie-
vousness, fiery temper, and fear of snakes, stood out even more for her
rubber-soled shoes, embroidered with flowers, than for the bulge in
her stomach. She had bought the shoes in Hong Kong, where she had
moved at age eighteen to pose as the wife of the Communist Youth
League chief. The bachelor Kai Feng would attract less suspicion as a
married man, but the acting lasted only a brief time: the two fell in
love and married for real. Their honeymoon was briefer still, coming
to an abrupt halt when a traitor fingered them. Expelled from Hong
Kong, they relocated to Shanghai, where Liao took her revolutionary
name Siguang, meaning "light of dawn."[2]

So far, however, the revolution had brought Liao mostly darkness. In the summer of 1933, the Nationalists had destroyed the offices in Shanghai where she and Kai Feng worked. Having just given birth, she had been forced to leave the baby at a missionary hospital and flee to Ruijin. Now here she was, a little more than a year later, pregnant and on the run again, heading in the direction of the village where she was born, a place she had had plenty of reason to leave. But Liao was not a complainer, and she kept up.

It was 150 miles from Yudu to the perimeter of Jiangxi where Red territory ended. The First Army reached this border after about a week of constant night marching. To cross over, they would have to break through the Nationalists' siege lines, a spine of concrete-and-steel, stone, or brick blockhouses with mounted machine guns, linked by barbed wire fences. These ominous fortifications occupied strategic positions along highways and mountain passes. The Red juggernaut had targeted what it considered to be the network's weakest section, but even these outposts possessed deadly firepower.

Encountering their first "turtle," as the soldiers nicknamed the blockhouses, just before dawn after an all-night trek, the Reds took an unexpected blow. As their combat troops attacked a fortified ridge manned by several hundred local forces and flanked by Nationalist troops, shrapnel from a round fired from the blockhouse hit their division commander. Within a matter of minutes, the Communists had defeated the Nationalists and locals, but their leader lay dead.

Shocked into silence, the Red columns hurried on with adrenaline-driven steps. Up and down the line the only sounds were the crunch of straw sandals on the ground and the trilling of the river. Once the sun rose, the encouraging songs of the *xuanchuan* team broke out, as the marchers moved on steadily. They had entered northeastern Guangdong, no longer in their sphere of influence, and the Nanling Mountains, the southernmost of China's three major east-west ranges. In this physical and psychological divide between central and southern China, between the cooler north and the tropical south, between Mandarin speakers and Cantonese speakers, large predator cats stalked forests of pine, cork, and catalpa trees for macaques and sambars. Now the marchers would see whether the challenging terrain could cloak their own advance.

Liao Siguang was back in her native province, the heart of an ancient kingdom that until annexed by the Qing dynasty in the nineteenth century had included parts of Guangxi, Yunnan, and northern Vietnam. She had endured hard times here as a child. Her parents had called her Jiao, or "Pampered," a sign of their best intentions for their daughter, but Liao's father had died when she was four, and her mother had been forced to sell her as a *tongyangxi*.[3]

By tradition — a tradition the Communists condemned as "feudal" though still alive today in remote areas of China — the day and hour of birth had a bearing on a child's fate. Before a marriage, a fortune-teller studied the *bazi* (eight important dates and times) of the bride and groom to see if they were compatible. If they were not, the parents either broke off the engagement or, more often, paid the seer to perform a corrective ritual, sometimes nothing more than the changing of a character in a name. If misfortune struck, especially if a husband or a member of his family died, the new wife was often considered to be the source of the bad luck.

When Liao was sixteen, a plague ravaged the village where she lived with her in-laws, infecting her and killing two of the three boys in the family, including her betrothed. The villagers blamed the calamity on Liao's inauspicious birthday. She became the scapegoat of the family's grief and lived in shame. When the Reds arrived, seventeen-year-old Liao, who was quick and open-minded, embraced their message — and the opportunity to escape her misery.

Now, in the town of Shuikou, where the convalescent company stopped for several days, the women held meetings and rallies and conducted *datuhao*. Here Liao Siguang and her comrades put their writing skills to use. On a wall of one house, they painted the slogan "Oppose imperialism and the occupation of Chinese lands," and on another they scrawled, "Brothers of the Guangdong Army, do not help the militia landlords attack your Red Army brothers. We are peasant brothers!" The women also hired porters and collected food, Liao later recalled, taking what they needed and giving the rest to the locals.

On October 26, the Red Army commanders told the troops that they had made a pact with Chen Jitang, the Guangdong governor, for safe passage west. Though powerful and in possession of American-made bombers, the autonomous Guangdong Army, like other provincial armies, did not relish a head-on collision with the Communists. Indeed, it was more interested in ushering them along than in halting their progress and giving Chiang Kaishek a pretext to enter the province. Likewise, the Reds hoped to make converts and allies, not enemies, as they traveled. Thus, while the Red soldiers were ordered to remain alert, they were also instructed not to take provincial soldiers hostage. They had received medical supplies and intelligence in addition to safe passage. Upon meeting, the two forces fired sham volleys into the air and hastily departed.[4]

SET AT EASE by the apparent success of his latest campaign against the Jiangxi Red Army bandits, Chiang Kaishek had headed north with his glamorous wife, Soong Meiling, in early October for meetings in Wuhan, the capital of Hubei province, and Xian, the capital of Shaanxi. They took the imperial train. In Xian, all four hundred of the city's automobiles were employed in their entourage. They bathed in hot springs, threw feasts for orphans, and the American-educated Meiling impressed the Christian missionaries with her well-heeled English. Feeling expansive, they flew north on a whim to spread their charm in backward Gansu province, a place never visited by any Chinese national leader. They visited Ninxia province, Mongolia, and Shanxi province. "On their travels," according to Chiang's biographer Jonathan Fenby, "the Chiangs were provided with the finest linen, silk eiderdowns, and perfumed pillows. Streets were cleaned and houses painted for their arrival."[5]

When the Chiangs finally returned to Nanking and Chiang Kaishek learned of the stunning movements of the Jiangxi Red Army, he was shocked into action. At the time of his departure, the Reds had been within his grasp, and now they were slipping through his fingers. On the other hand, forced to flee from their base, they were even more

Chiang Kaishek. *(Helen Foster Snow Archives, Brigham Young University)*

vulnerable now. A natural barrier, a substantial river, lay in front of them. Chiang knew the lessons of military history. He ordered fifteen divisions to mobilize and cut off the First Army at the Xiang River.

As the Communists moved farther from their former safe haven, the journey became slower and messier. To avoid being bombed by the Nationalists, they continued to march at night. They rested during the day, and if it was safe, the women boiled water to soak their bruised and abraded feet. Foot bathing was common among Chinese women, partly owing to the practice of foot-binding. Considered a gem when contained in a tiny silk slipper, the naked bound foot, never exposed to men, was a phantasmagoria of dead and festering flesh and abrasions caused by toenails growing into flesh. Boiling water purified the wounds and softened the skin and nails for trimming. Though none

The three Soong sisters — Ailing, Qingling, and Meiling — visit a hospital.
(Helen Foster Snow Archives, Brigham Young University)

Chiang Kaishek and Soong Meiling. *(Helen Foster Snow Archives, Brigham Young University)*

of the marchers still had bound feet, foot bathing was an ingrained cultural practice.

The marchers arose from uneasy daytime slumber at around four o'clock in the afternoon, cooked dinner in communal pots around open fires, and awaited the 5:30 p.m. bugle muster. Before they set off, officers rallied the troops and warned them not to fall behind.[6]

As they marched, their ranks stretching out over a long distance, soldiers chatted with one another, told stories to stay awake, or chastened one another to hurry up. When there was no moon and no sign of enemy airplanes, they illuminated their path with torches made of either kerosene-filled branches, green and freshly cut so as not to incinerate too quickly, or dry-bamboo fagots. Scattered across the hills, the torches lit the column like an undulating caravan to the stars.

The marchers had already trod more than two hundred miles from their base, and their straw sandals were falling apart. Many now shuffled along with rags wrapped around their feet, fantasizing about sumptuous meals and warm beds to curl up on. Inevitably, some fell asleep, unconsciously drifting along in the crowded ranks before stumbling, further abusing their blistered, bruised feet.

All night, the women supervised the carrying of stretcher-bound patients, filling in as porters when needed. Lugging the stretchers required uncommon concentration, for the paths were rocky and treacherous. It also required a nearly inhuman ability to ignore aching arms, legs, shoulders, backs, and joints. Some of the porters broke down in tears and begged to be allowed to return to their villages. Many simply ran away, and daily the women had to search for replacements.

As soon as the bugles signaled the end of a night's march, the soldiers found flat places beneath the camphor trees, alders, and pines. They shed their gear, joined a mess group to wolf down hot rice gruel, and then collapsed in exhausted slumber. For the women, however, rest had to wait while they tended to the sick and wounded. Wang Quanyuan was in charge of a large man who was blind in one eye and crazed by headaches from shrapnel still lodged inside his skull. The same bomb had shredded one of his legs.

Wang squatted by his stretcher with a bowl of rice and tried to coax him to eat. He clamped his eyes shut and turned away, and then, as she persisted, he swatted the bowl out of her hands. She caught it in the air. Dazed and tired, Wang cursed her luck. Hearing the commotion, Deng Yingchao, sick herself with tuberculosis, came over. "If you don't want to eat this good rice," she asked the man in a gentle voice, "what do you want?"

"Sister Deng, I'm so badly wounded," he mumbled, "I'll never heal. A big guy like me who has to be carried is a heavy burden. There's no reason for me to keep going." He struggled to sit up but couldn't.

"You'll heal," Deng consoled him. "When we reach our destination, the shrapnel will be removed, and you'll be fine." She nodded to Wang, who passed him the bowl again. This time, he took it. Wang returned to the rice pot with her own enamelware cup, but there was only boiling water left. She began to cry.

Sitting by a tree, Li Guiying—a former *tongyangxi* whose mother-in-law had beaten her so severely that the Communists had paraded the woman around town in a tall hat, making her shout, "Don't abuse *tongyangxi!*"—called Wang over. Li shared the rice she was eating, and together the two women scraped their cups and dried their tears.[7]

After everyone was fed, the women carried pots of hot water to the convalescents and the porters so that they could soak their battered feet. Li told Wang to take her time and finish eating while she began the task. After the porters and the wounded fell asleep, Li and Wang made beds of dry grass and shut their eyes. The next day they would do it all again.

MEETINGS WERE A STAPLE of Communist life, a vehicle for instruction, for boosting morale and unity, and for reinforcing the Red gospel. One afternoon, Shorty joined the others on a mountain plateau for one such gathering. As Dong Biwu, the women's leader, stood in front of a small audience exhorting them, the squeal of a plane suddenly broke the spell. The aircraft swooped down, but Dong, a veteran of the 1911 revolution, stood his ground. Following Dong's lead, the crowd remained in place as the plane unloaded its deadly cargo. A bomb hit the ground so close by that the impact showered them with dirt and stones. Still, the war-hardened Dong never moved. After their cries died down, Dong glared at the small crater, where the unexploded bomb sat still intact. Some later claimed that he looked skyward, raised an arm, grinned, and declared, "Comrade Marx is confounding the enemy."[8]

ON NOVEMBER 9, the *New York Times* reported that an estimated 40,000 Communists were "migrating westward . . . looting the territory in their path toward Szechwan, where they planned to establish Soviets." The newspaper's sources said that the Communists were "being harassed by soldiers who penned them in an area approximately 100 miles long and 12 miles wide . . . along the Hunan border." Four Nationalist divisions with a total of 20,000 men and 30,000 Guangdong soldiers were tracking the First Army.

By then, however, the Communists had already overrun more blockhouses and penetrated Hunan province just north of the Guangdong border. Chiang Kaishek railed against the so far ineffectual Hunanese warlord and provincial governor He Jian and the Guangdong strongman Chen Jitang, and thus chastened, they sprang into action.

He Jian already had Red blood on his hands, having captured and executed Mao's first wife, Yang Kaihui, and his sister in Changsha in 1930.[9] In the last days of October, his troops attacked the Communists. He Jian claimed that his forces killed hundreds of Reds and captured dozens of prisoners, but whether they sent the marchers fleeing, as he asserted, is hard to know, especially since they never intended to stay. Later, the Guangdong forces claimed to have killed five hundred Red soldiers and taken hundreds of weapons. But such numbers tended to be wildly exaggerated, and in any case, it was not enough to stop the marchers from pushing forward.

Marching on, the Communists overran several towns in northern Guangdong before reaching Reshui, a village built over copious hot springs, on a market day. Red soldiers disguised as hawkers infiltrated the teeming village, then scared away the local militia with a strate-gically adept barrage of grenades. Reshui thus secured, the central column occupied the town and proceeded to purchase pork, chicken, mutton, beef, rice, vegetables, grain, alcohol, and tobacco. In short order, the marchers swept the market stalls clean.[10]

In Chengkou, just south of the Hunan-Guangdong line, the Reds seized ammunition and thousands of tins of valuable kerosene for cooking and lighting torches and lanterns. After the local Nationalist commander fled, they scrubbed their grimy bodies in his personal hot spring, a brief sweet respite from the rigors of the march.[11]

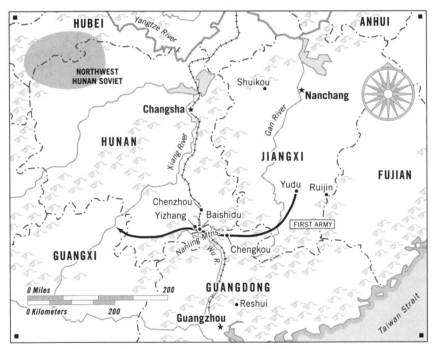

The First Army Breaks Out of Jiangxi Province

Throughout their journey, the Communists were expected to adhere to the Three Regulations—always obey orders; don't take a single needle or piece of thread from the masses; turn in everything captured—and the Eight Essential Rules:

1. Replace all doors when you leave a house.
2. Return and roll up straw mats.
3. Be courteous, polite, and helpful to the masses.
4. Return anything borrowed.
5. Fix or replace anything broken.
6. Be honest in transactions with peasants.
7. Pay for all articles taken.
8. Be sanitary and build latrines at a safe distance from houses.

These regulations and rules were reinforced over and over in chants, slogans, songs, and skits. Although transgressions occurred, the women were particularly inclined to maintain the rules — partly from the inherited habit of obeying male masters but also because they believed that such guidelines helped convert skeptical Chinese to the Communist cause.[12]

BACK ON THE TRAIL again, Kang Keqing had put the early days of her departure and the headquarters guard's suicide behind her. The dazzle and majesty of the Yu River crossing were also well behind her. Now she rued the tedium, the surging and stalling, the frequent rest breaks of the long column. Some 10,000 porters shared more than a thousand loads, often awkward objects — heavy machinery, combat gear, printing presses, sewing machines, medical equipment — that in some cases had to be hoisted by up to eight strong men working together. The porters were perpetually sweaty, out of breath, and testy. Stopping often to shift the weight from shoulder to shoulder, they backed up the traffic and created long delays. The slower the column moved, the closer enemy machine-gun and cannon fire came, and the edgier Kang grew.[13]

Continuing to push west, the Reds made for the Hunanese border town of Yizhang, crossing rivers and hills in dreary, rainy weather. Among other gear, the printing presses with their heavy lead type were left by the wayside as porters eager to return to their homes disappeared into the gloom. For those who stayed, the strains — physical and emotional—increased. More and more, they lagged behind the soldiers, moving awkwardly in teams over narrow paths and slick roads. Fear rose, and morale and discipline sank.

Crossing a hill in Hunan, the Fujian peasant Wu Fulian, a member of the women's work group, experienced just the type of situation Kang feared. Hemmed in by their own troops in front and horses and baggage behind, Wu and others with the stretcher teams, who were mostly unarmed, were suddenly attacked. The women scrambled into the brush to stow the wounded on their stretchers before climbing trees in a desperate attempt to hide. Fortunately for Wu and the others, help came, and the attackers were driven off, but it was clear that they could easily be trapped again. If caught, they could expect no mercy.

On NOVEMBER 10, only days after Chiang Kaishek had figured out that a wholesale migration of the Red nation was in progress, the Nationalists took Ruijin and went on a murderous rampage. The First Army commander in chief would later put the number killed in the hundreds of thousands.[14]

A few of the Reds left behind in Ruijin, such as the pregnant widow Huang Changjiao, escaped. She, three other women, and a newborn crossed the mountains on the Jiangxi-Fujian border and after a terrible ordeal were collected by Red partisans. But most did not get away. Tang Yizhen was about a month pregnant when the *dabanjia* started and had been left behind. According to Li Jianzhen, "The ruthless enemy sliced open her abdomen and speared her chest, pulling out her heart. Tang was only twenty-five years old" (p. 72). Among the most prominent of the Nationalist prizes was Mao Zedong's brother Mao Zetan, who was keeping Mao Zedong and He Zizhen's son, Xiao Mao. Mao Zetan's corpse was displayed in Ruijin as a trophy and a warning of what would happen to those who joined the Communists.

A week later, Yudu fell. Some of the 30,000 Red Army troops and personnel who had been left behind there fled into neighboring provinces or went into hiding in the nearby forests and mountains. Others

The third blockade, at Yizhang, Hunan.

died in battle or were executed by the Nationalists. "The record of the dead is a Who's Who of the revolutionary movement," journalist Harrison Salisbury later wrote. "More prominent Communists died among those left behind than in any other period of the struggle."[15]

For Chiang Kaishek, things were finally moving in the right direction. Air reconnaissance put the mobilized main Red forces at some 50,000 men, with 10,000 flanking each side and 10,000 protecting the rear, all moving west toward the three-hundred-foot-wide Xiang River. Now, like pincers, 90,000 Nationalist troops and irregular militia prepared to close in on the probable river ford.

On November 15, the Red Army took Yizhang, a key town on the Yuehan Railroad (an important piece of China's north-south rail system then under construction) beneath towering peaks near Hunan's southern border.[16] Yizhang, founded in the year AD 617, was the first county seat to fall to the Reds on the *dabanjia,* and they swiftly executed local landlords and wealthy residents and emptied the prison. They also confiscated clothing and food to distribute among the 3,000 people who gathered for a mass rally, recruiting dozens of new soldiers at the same time.

Meanwhile, following a fierce rain, other Red forces crossed the

5,200-foot Great King Mountain (Dawangshan) in the mud and dark, tying white rags to their packs so that they could see one another. After crossing Five Kings Mountain (Wuwangshan), they took Baishidu, a market town of about 2,000 households, twenty shops, and several brothels.

The marchers took advantage of some sunshine to wash their clothes, blankets, and dusty provision bags in the Wu River, one of the area's six major rivers, now shallow enough in most places to be crossed on foot with pants rolled up. They spread their wet things out to dry and set about bathing and scrubbing their feet, which had been stained ocher by the mud. Finally, they cleaned and polished their weapons.

Like Yizhang, Baishidu lay on the nearly completed 980-mile Yue-han Railroad, begun thirty-five years earlier to connect the capitals of Guangdong and Hubei. The Red soldiers, most of whom had never seen a train before, were excited to be out of the mountains and near the amenities of a thriving town. Four thousand underpaid Hunanese laborers toiled here in squalid conditions. Teams of workers stayed in small thatched-roof sheds — up to thirty men in each — and were ruled by overseers. Over the course of two days, Red soldiers distributed grain, pork, and clothes to the railroad workers remaining in Baishidu. In and around the sheds, Communist *xuanchuan* workers sang, gave speeches, and successfully persuaded four hundred of the Hunanese to don armbands of red rags and enlist.

A day later, the marchers moved on. They had no time to spare. Spurred on by Chiang and aided by air reconnaissance, various regional and Nationalist armies were descending upon them. The Reds had passed through the first circle of hell.

chapter 7

Xiang River Debacle

Anticipating the Communists' move to northwestern Hunan to join up with their comrades, Chiang mobilized his forces. If he could position enough troops along the Reds' anticipated route and use the rivers that crossed it to slow them down, he believed he could at last bottle up his enemies and destroy them.

The Communist military leaders understood this, at least to a degree, and they ordered the central column to jettison some of its heavy burden and pick up the pace. More machinery, baggage, books, and documents hit the wayside. Li Bozhao's theater group shed costumes, props, and makeup.

In the unceasing rain—a mixed blessing since it grounded the Nationalists' planes but at the same time left the marchers drenched and their path treacherous—the central column walked day and night, four hours on and four hours off, covering seventy miles on slick roads in forty-eight hours. To keep up the pace and decrease accidents, many made walking sticks from the roadside bamboo. The toll on knees, hip joints, and especially poorly clad feet was severe. "Comrades, we must ignore the pain!" the *xuanchuan* workers shouted. "We'll reach a city soon. Daozhou has good food to eat.... Keep moving!" Still, at rest breaks the women supplied Vaseline to groaning men for their blistered and raw feet.[1]

Cannon and machine-gun blasts echoed across the land, ricocheting from hill to hill and swirling around the marchers at all times from all directions, it seemed to Kang Keqing. Ahead, frontline Red Army soldiers carved a path, while those in the rear fought to delay their pursuers. To the right and left, more soldiers formed a protective corridor for those within. The women guided their stretchers, filling in as porters when shorthanded, sometimes working two to an end. He Zizhen, whose "belly was in danger," as Wang Quanyuan put it, was among those carried.[2] Her condition served as a reminder of what could happen if a woman broke the army rule against having sex. Few would be carried like Mao's wife.

Still, that rule was not always easy to adhere to. One night the marchers camped in a small village at dusk. There were few houses in the village, and the marchers were crammed into tight spaces. Wang found herself in a room with men and women crowded into two beds, heads to feet. Zhu Liangcai, the powerful Health Department commissar, approached her and shamelessly asked her to "marry" him. He meant to have sex.

"I won't consider it," she told him. "I don't want to get married. You forget about it too." But Zhu, who was a decade older than Wang, insisted. She resisted, and he grabbed her hair. This made Wang mad. "You old cow, don't think about eating fresh grass!" she scolded him loudly, for all to hear. "I don't want to!" Zhu backed off, but he would not forget the affront.[3]

The following day, the marchers climbed a high hill and descended toward a village. As the clouds broke and the sun emerged, they came upon some men in long cotton robes and short coats, carrying loads in bamboo baskets hanging from bamboo poles. The Reds stopped to share cigarettes with the men and asked them the best way to enter Daozhou, the walled town to which they were headed. The men told them that they must cross a river on a floating bridge of small boats fastened together with chains at a wharf on the shore opposite the city. They would have to seize the bridge before the local defenders discovered their approach and withdrew it.

The Reds passed rapidly through the village. Those with money bought peanuts, yams, and sugarcane to eat while walking. Hundreds of curious villagers came out to watch. "Where did this big army come from?" some asked. "Look how fast they walk!" others noted. "They don't even stop to rest." Some of the villagers served tea to the thirsty soldiers. In turn, the Reds handed out cigarettes and chatted with the locals to show goodwill and to get more information. All the while, the column never came to a halt.

They managed twenty-five miles that day and reached the banks of the Daoxian River after dark. The bridge the villagers had spoken of had been retracted. At dawn, some of the Reds swam across the river to the town's wharf. With the help of sympathetic local boatmen, they constructed a floating bridge of boats in less than half an hour. They then stormed the south gate of the city, only to discover that the defenders had already fled. The easy victory was soon tempered. As the Reds flooded into Daozhou, an air-raid warning sounded. The marchers scrambled for cover under trees and in houses and shops, emptying the streets. An airplane circled the city and flew away without attacking. However, the pilot was not fooled. Soon two more planes arrived and dropped bombs. Missing their marks, they killed only a horse tender and two horses. Another plane flew in low, guns blazing. The Reds responded with machine-gun fire from the city walls. Suddenly, a rooster tail of flames and black smoke burst from the plane's fuselage. Sinking from the sky, the fighter crash-landed on a farm outside town. The Reds raced to the site. They captured the two pilots alive and snatched a pair of machine guns and 5,000 rounds of ammunition before the aircraft burned up.

IN THE LAST WEEK OF NOVEMBER, the Red Army, in varying degrees of discipline and disarray, approached the Xiang River. In China, major rivers are defined by their mythology. The broad Xiang was said to be protected by the goddesses Ehuang and Nuying, empress sisters and wives of the mythical Great Shun, who reigned in ancient China for half a century in the twenty-third and twenty-second centuries BC. Unable to bear the pain of their husband's death at age

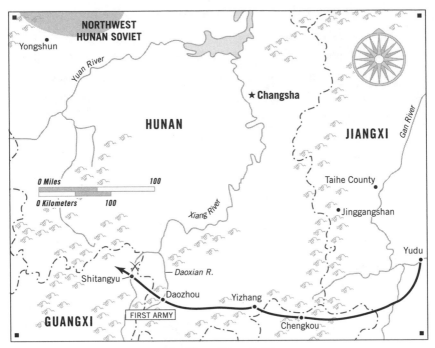

The Xiang River Battle

one hundred, the two sisters committed suicide in the river. Unusual teardrop-shaped spots on the bamboo growing along the shore were said to be the marks of their tears.

Chiang Kaishek bet he could assemble a force on the riverbanks strong enough to wipe out the Communists. Nationalist and Hunan forces converged on the Reds' flanks and rear, trying to box them in. Aircraft alternately dropped bombs and leaflets. Some offered a reward to those who defected with their guns, and others taunted the marchers: "Communist bandits, we have waited a long time for you. Please hurry! We have arranged nets above and snares below!"

As with their passage through Guangdong, the Reds negotiated with some of Chiang's paper allies, warlords who wanted both Communist and Nationalist troops out of their territory as soon as possible. In China, this was standard operating procedure. "For every one Chinese battle that is won by strategy and tactics, nine are won by a particularly unscrupulous form of commercial diplomacy," Peter

Chiang Kaishek (in the light uniform in the middle) and Nationalist officers in December 1934.

Fleming pointed out in his 1934 Chinese travelogue *One's Company* (p. 247).

A vanguard of 2,000 Red soldiers reached the bamboo-lined Xiang on November 27 and crossed it without a fight, gaining the town of Shitangyu. Ten thousand more crossed the following day. Together they would hold the river crossing for more than a week, waiting for the others to catch up.

Kang Keqing was with the political and military leaders fifty miles away when news arrived that the vanguard had crossed the river. After more than a month of marching, the weary ranks had slowed even more. It would take the porters carrying the stretchers and heavy equipment several more days in the highlands to reach the Xiang.

By the time the rest of the marchers reached the riverbanks, the Nationalists had responded. In a confusing swirl of battles in villages around the area, both sides claimed victories. The Nationalists reported Red deserters, and the Communists claimed new recruits. As important as the number of men lost was the weapons tally; each commander reported guns taken or forfeited alongside numbers of casualties and prisoners. The Nationalists were much better armed with machine guns, grenades, and bullets. The Red Army was so short of bullets that the soldiers were instructed not to fire until a hit was certain. What they lacked in weaponry, they made up for in desperation and determination, but these were not always enough. At one point, the Nationalist West Route Army surrounded and decimated a contingent of Red troops, killing or capturing up to 10,000 soldiers but confiscating only 6,000 rifles. Four in ten of the Communists had been unarmed.[4]

The rainy season on the Xiang River lasts from April to June, with the water level beginning to recede in July. In some places, the Xiang was now only about waist-deep, and for most soldiers, crossing it was a minor impediment as long as they were not fired on while defenseless in midstream.

Nationalist artillery and small arms had a bead on the wide river, making a daylight crossing impossible. When the trailing Communists finally made their move, it was accompanied by heavy fire. The flowing water quickly clouded with blood. In the darkness, men with pack animals waded through the cold current, while ferries hastily punted from shore to shore, disgorging the weary and the wounded along with the weaponry and baggage.

For the women, many of whom were quite small, the current was even more difficult, and the challenge was often emotional as well as physical. Since leaving the Jiangxi Soviet, Li Bozhao had lugged scripts that she needed for putting on productions. Now she had to abandon the last of them at the river's edge.

Through songs, dances, skits, and her incessant exhortations, Li had accomplished her main task during the trek: to raise morale. Yet her own was now tested. Li was so small that she struggled dangerously while trying to wade through the water. In places, she sank in over her head, and the swift current threatened to carry her away. Seeing her difficulties, Liu Bocheng, the Red Army chief of staff, who had lost an eye at the Battle of Fengdu County in Sichuan in 1916 and was known as "the One-Eyed General," let her clutch the tail of his mule and be towed across while she paddled to stay afloat.[5]

For her part, Wang Quanyuan crossed on a wooden bridge in a lull in the gunfire. Once on the other side, as the fighting heated up again, she was called into service as a medic. Wang had little training and few resources. She could wrap shredded cloth around a mangled limb or apply pressure to a wound to stop the bleeding. For the severely injured, however, she could do little more than console them as they died.[6]

While boats ferried supplies and personnel, Kang Keqing worried about the long file of those behind her. In fact, many porters did not reach the river, having deserted or been killed in the fighting. Those who made it often found that the burdens they had lugged so far had to be unceremoniously dumped. There was no way they could get them across in time, and they piled up like typhoon wreckage along the east bank.

By the morning of December 1, Kang and the political and military leadership had crossed the Xiang. Nationalist forces surrounded the corridor to the river formed by the Red Army forces and poured in gunfire. The Red troops fought furiously to push them back. Shot in the abdomen, twenty-nine-year-old division commander Chen Shuxiang continued to hold the line, directing his men from a stretcher. While the Red cadres remained largely intact and the thirty women made it across unscathed, Chen's division and many others were shredded. Captured in the last hours of fighting, Chen refused to be the ranking prize for the Nationalists. On an enemy stretcher, he pulled his intestines out of his bleeding wound. Nevertheless, the Nationalists were able to make an example of him by hanging his severed head on a city gate.

The crossing cost the Communists a staggering 30,000 lives. Moreover, now that they were outside the Jiangxi Soviet, they could no longer count on the support or easy conversion of the villagers they came into contact with, not even of the peasants whom they championed. Quite a few now fled before them, leaving empty houses and bare cupboards. The marchers were strangers in a wary land.

Attached to the medical group, the Taiwan-born Long March chronicler Cai Xiaoqian noted the deep, if not desperate, longing for home and family he witnessed in those around him. Many marchers, expecting to swiftly shatter the blockade and return home again, had brought along money to buy salt and tobacco for their families. It had now become clear that they would not be returning anytime soon.

Spirits plummeted, and the discipline on which the Red Army prided itself began to erode. "Mao Zedong was either oblivious or unconcerned about these issues," recalled Cai, who in 1945 would be sent to his native Taiwan to reestablish the Communist Party there but would defect to the Nationalists in 1949. In his memoir, which offers a rare account from a Long Marcher outside Mao's sphere of influence, Cai recounts harshly that Mao "did little other than sit on his stretcher and read *Journey to the West* and *Romance of the Three Kingdoms.*"[7]

The fact that Mao chose to read classic Chinese folk novels to pass the time characterizes both his cool demeanor and his appreciation for homegrown wisdom. *Journey to the West* perhaps spoke to the current crisis more than Cai knew. To redeem himself, the novel's protagonist, a magical monkey, must assist a Buddhist holy man in his westward pilgrimage. Monkey, a clever adversary and hero, faces his toughest challenges at the rivers they cross, which are inhabited by monsters. Even with his magical powers, Monkey must employ diplomacy and guile to succeed. Likewise, rivers held monsters for the migrating Reds.

✶

IN MULTIPLE THEATERS ACROSS CHINA, things looked similarly grim for the Communists, especially for the fledgling Twenty-fifth Army in the old Eyuwan Soviet. The Twenty-fifth had been formed from the remnants of the Fourth Army when it fled west to Sichuan to escape Chiang Kaishek's Third Encirclement Campaign in 1932, that is, largely from the orphans and children left behind. According to a 1936 Comintern document, the Twenty-fifth contained almost no soldiers over the age of eighteen. "In terrible conditions," noted the document, "they created a guerrilla force, which in turn became 'the Children's Army.'"[8]

Under the fierce commander Xu Haidong, nicknamed "Tiger Xu," they had fought and rallied partisans in the area for two more years, with some stunning underdog successes, earning Xu a price on his head of 100,000 silver coins. (By comparison, for Mao or Zhu De, the Nationalists would pay 250,000 silver coins.)[9] The Nationalists had responded with a ferocious campaign of destroying villages, executing suspected Reds, and selling the women and children they captured into prostitution or slavery as factory workers. Tens of thousands of men, women, and children were killed, and Xu's wife was sold as a concubine. In Hubei, villagers took Xu to see the bodies of seventeen women who had been raped, murdered, and left in the sun. "The White troops had evidently been in a great hurry," he later told the American journalist Edgar Snow. "They had taken the time to pull off only one leg of a girl's trousers."[10]

In the middle of a November night in 1934, Xu's remarkable force, including seven female nurses, all of whom had once had their feet bound, fled its mountain stronghold in southern Henan. At dawn, the Twenty-fifth stopped beside the Beijing–Hankou railroad tracks, where the hospital commissar assembled the nurses. Zeng Jilan was the eldest and thus considered the wisest; Young Orchid (Zhou Shaolan), just seventeen, was the boldest. "The enemy is both ahead of us and pursuing us," the commissar told them grimly. "It's too dangerous for you to accompany the troops. You must go home now and hide." He handed them each eight silver dollars. Clutching the coins, the women burst into tears.[11]

They had in fact struggled to maintain the pace on their misshapen feet. Still, they were determined not to be left behind. Finding the chief of staff, who had issued the order, the nurses threw down the coins. "I left my home to join the revolution," Young Orchid declared. "Now you want to send me back — back to be a tongyangxi again? You have no right to push the women out of the army!"

"The Red Army is our family. If we leave, we'll have no home," insisted eighteen-year-old Dai Juemin. This was true for Dai. Her father, a teacher who had participated in the May Fourth Movement, had become a county Party general secretary and was later killed by a Nationalist bomb. Her older brother, who had helped establish the Eyuwan Soviet, was subsequently executed in a Party purge, leaving the family totally bereft.

As the nurses protested, Xu Haidong happened to ride up. "They want to stay with the army," the chief of staff told him.

"Just these girls?" asked Xu, a thirty-four-year-old former master

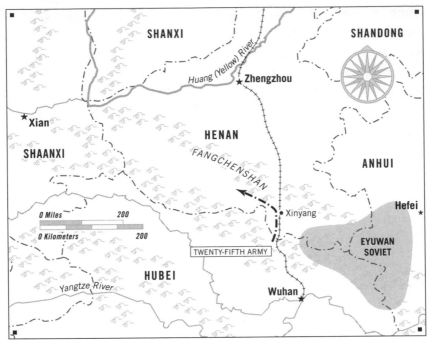

The Twenty-fifth Army Sets Out

potter who had become a political organizer before commanding an army. He looked them over. "Okay," he said softly, addressing them. "Why don't you come with us? As long as it's your choice." Seeing their relief, Xu cautioned, "The chief of staff has good reason to tell you to leave. We don't know where we're headed. We don't know how long we'll march each day. We do know that the coming weeks will be very difficult. You should be prepared for this."

"We've been prepared," Young Orchid said. "Whatever the men do, we can do. We will not lag behind."

On the night of November 17, after forty-eight straight hours of walking, the Twenty-fifth approached the city of Xinyang, an agricultural center bounded by mountains on the west and south. It is here, in an area rich in Daoist and Buddhist temples, that Pangu, creator of the universe in Chinese mythology, is said to have originated. Hatched from an egg, he separated heaven and earth by pushing them apart with his hands and feet. After fatally succumbing to exhaustion, his eyes became the sun and the moon and his body parts rivers, mountains, and forests.

The region is checkered with mountain streams and made even tougher to traverse because of its treacherous weather. Knowing that the uprooted Communists were now more vulnerable than ever, Nationalist forces tracked them relentlessly through this wilderness. With no time to pause, the nurses walked in a daze at times, nearly asleep on their feet. In the dark of night, on the rain-slick mountain trails, they sometimes roped themselves together.

Despite their promises, the women once again lagged behind the troops. They were given a horse to lighten their loads and to use if one of them was sick, hurt, or especially tired. The Supply Department had given them shoes too big for their stunted feet, so they had poked holes on both sides of the shoes and pulled them tight with string. Each morning, they wrapped their feet in rags, and during the day they stopped often to rewrap them. Even so, the shoes chafed their feet and made their ankles swell.

Ten days after setting out, the Twenty-fifth bivouacked in southwestern Henan on the side of 2,500-foot Fangchenshan, described in ancient texts as having "treacherous cliffs that even apes cannot scale." As the Reds crossed the road through the mountain pass there, Nationalist troops suddenly appeared through the cold mist. The Red soldiers yanked their guns from their shoulders and with stiff fingers fumbled to operate their rifle bolts. They fell back, but the Nationalists charged forward.

The two sides fought fiercely as the Nationalists tried to envelop the Reds. Young Orchid and the other nurses administered to the wounded and gathered the rifles and ammunition of the fallen. Eventually, they joined in the fight and helped to repel the attackers who finally disappeared behind a veil of mist and smoke.

The Twenty-fifth had escaped this time, but the young soldiers were shaken. They were a small, inexperienced force, wandering far from the place that had hidden them from their powerful enemies and provided for their needs. And like their comrades in the much larger groups of marchers elsewhere on the road, they had uncountable miles still to go.

PART TWO

CROSSING SOUTHERN CHINA

chapter 8

Thundergod Cliff

DECEMBER 1934

The Red Army was used to the loss of life even outside of battle. Prisoners were tortured and killed; notables were beheaded and their severed heads put on display. Both sides of the conflict demonstrated a high degree of callousness, returning acts of brutality in kind. Still, the number of lives lost in and around the Xiang River was devastating. Nobody knew exactly how many men remained in the First Army's shattered ranks, but the best guess was somewhere around 30,000. This meant that although the core of Party leaders and cadres in the central column had survived intact, the rest of the First Army had been reduced by more than half.[1]

Chiang's air force continued to dog the marchers, dropping bombs and strafing the battered columns, giving them no easy passage and no time to heal their bruised and bloody feet, let alone an opportunity for serious battle wounds and rifts in the leadership to mend. While the Party leaders prepared for an internal showdown over tactics and direction, the convalescent company and the women in it did their best to keep the parade of bloodstained stretchers and walking wounded moving.

In the waning days of 1934, as the world at large focused on fascist aggression—Hitler illegally establishing a German air force, Mussolini sending troops to Ethiopia, and Hirohito abandoning naval treaties with the West—the First Army raced to the cover of the foothills of the Yuechengling Mountains, part of a treacherous range separating Hunan and Guangxi. The Western press barely noticed.

The sharp inclines of the Yuechenglings were but one of the perils now facing the marchers. The range was inhabited by the potentially dangerous Yao, Miao, and Dong tribes. These ethnic communities did not speak Mandarin, and over the centuries the dominant Han Chinese had forced them onto ever higher, less fertile plots. ("Crows have no trees to rest on," a Han saying went, "and Miaos have no place to sleep.") The Miao were said to be so poor that their "bare feet are shoes," and in some places teenage boys and girls walked around naked.[2] Most of these tribes feared and hated the Han, especially their armies—all of their armies. But even more ominous for the Reds who were trying to move an army through this sparse country was the lack of food sources. This was desolate country, a land of peaks and bones.

The imperative was to move faster, and it was decided, according to Kang Keqing, to discard the "cans and jars and other useless things" that the overburdened marchers still carried. Eager to set an example, Kang searched her tent for things to get rid of. Her austere life had not accustomed her to many possessions. She tied up some clothes, mosquito netting, and supplies in a duck-down comforter and handed the bundle to her husband's bodyguard, Pan Kaiwen, to give to some villagers. Pan was taken aback. These appeared to him to be essential items, especially for the leaders. "The weather is turning cold," he pointed out. "You and General Zhu have horses to carry the load. You should bring these things with you."[3]

"The general asked us to bring only what we need," Kang insisted, putting her hand on the bundle. "If you won't take it, I will." Pan delivered the bundle. Others also gave their things to the locals, who in return yielded up vegetables and other provisions. Overtaxed, oppressed, and brutalized, the Miao and Yao received the goods—and the Red message of change for the poor—with guarded enthusiasm.

As they pushed hard into the Yuechenglings, the wilderness home of South China tigers and black bears, the Communists entered dense forests of sixty-foot Nan bamboo, Chinese fir, pine, oak, and azalea.

Kang, like the others, felt relieved that Chiang's troops were not in close pursuit, and in the narrow valleys and canted mountainsides, on paths the Communists described as winding like "sheep intestines," Nationalist airplanes could not easily reach them.[4]

Still, as a precaution, the Reds continued to travel mostly in darkness, when the mountains were often crusted in rime and fogged in. The trail was narrow, sheer, uneven, and overgrown. The column inched forward, sometimes moving no more than three miles a night. Ascending precarious switchbacks, they cleared and widened the way with sickles and axes, amputated branches sometimes tumbling off the edge and plummeting hundreds of feet into the deadly crevices and mountain folds below. Making the going even more difficult was the need to be on the lookout for venomous snakes. The brush was infested with vipers the locals called *wubu,* "five steps," because their bite was so toxic a victim went no farther. Small, triangle-headed snakes, jade-colored and known as "bamboo greens," coiled around bamboo, as still as stone until they struck.[5]

Malnourished pack animals, hooves worn raw, fell on the trail or tumbled from it. They were butchered on the spot for food and hides, which the Reds would later use to make sandals. When conditions grew even worse, they would eat those sandals.[6]

Once the column's torches flamed out, which they inevitably did after several hours, the marchers could not see their fingers in front of their faces, Kang later recalled. From then on, they had to feel their way in the dark. A moment of walking slumber could be deadly. When it rained, walking on the ridges became next to impossible. In one torrent, a porter fell on a slick path, gashing his right calf. "The flesh even burst forth," Wang Quanyuan recalled. "I found some medicinal herbs, chewed the leaves, and put them on the wound."[7] Then she wrapped his leg in leaves, secured them with a puttee, and took over his position carrying a stretcher. Nothing more could be done.

Even those who had followed orders to shed their burdens found the going increasingly tough as they approached the 7,000-foot Buddhist holy mountain Laoshanjie. Known locally as Cat Mountain, its summit was famous for exhibiting a rainbow halo at dawn and dusk, the result of cold, damp clouds meeting the warmer mountainside or, as some believed, of divine artifice.[8]

At the foot of Cat Mountain, the central column stopped in the afternoon at the Temple of a Thousand Houses, where they cooked and ate dinner, contemplating the climb ahead and the village's tragic tale. When a visiting Ming official had claimed a beautiful local as his concubine, she had fled to the mountaintop and, with a lover, leaped to her death. Her brothers had murdered the official, and the emperor had avenged the death by razing the village and killing all its inhabitants. The temple had been built by newcomers to appease the ghosts of the dead.

After the meal, bugles blew and the soldiers fell into formation. Li Bozhao, who was little more than five feet tall but strong, carried an officer named Lin Kai, who had been wasted away by a liver illness, on her back.[9]

Three miles up the trail, through forests of hemlock and silver pine, they reached a still smaller village of just half a dozen families. The villagers told them that the ascent was ninety *li,* about thirty miles, and the descent thirty *li,* ten miles—the *li* being the world's only known effort-sensitive unit of measure, a useful thing in such a mountainous place, where one *li* on level ground can be doubled going up or halved going down. The villagers further warned them that in another forty *li,* they would come to a very difficult section of the trail, called Thundergod Cliff, a dangerous, nearly vertical face thirty *li* up and fifty *li* down.

To make torches for a climb that would stretch into the night, the marchers stripped the trailside groves of dry bamboo. But it was not enough. The Yao houses and fences were made of bamboo, and even though the *xuanchuan* teams attached notices on fences and walls with rice glue telling the troops not to remove the bamboo from any structures, they took it anyway.

As the marchers climbed rocky switchbacks, night blanketed the mountain. The soldiers lit their torches and carried on, looking to some like a magnificent undulating fire serpent.

The path soon grew more difficult. Diminishing in width to two feet, it quickly jammed with troops, mules, and horses. The ranks ground to a halt. After a while, the tired soldiers sat down on the narrow trail. One medical worker dozed off and fell over the side. All of the marchers struggled to stay awake. Every so often, they got up and advanced again, then stopped and waited until the next lurch forward. Around two in the morning, word spread down the line that they had reached Thundergod Cliff. Everyone was ordered to stop and sleep right where they were.

A bone-chilling wind rushed across the top of the mountain. On the edge of a pitch-black abyss, the marchers wrapped themselves in their blankets, lay down, and, utterly exhausted, most fell asleep. Those who were too cold to sleep built small fires and gathered together to stay warm and chat in the faint glow of the embers.[10]

At dawn, the cooks sent pots of rice gruel down the line. The marchers rose and moved forward at a halting, tedious pace toward the stupendous stone face of Thundergod Cliff, a fitting aerie for the winged and eagle-beaked god who patrols the skies, banging a hammer and chisel to make thunder, hunting down and slaying wicked men. It all combined to give this a feeling of judgment day.

The path transformed into foot-wide shelves carved into the cliff, ending in a narrow, difficult cleft. Failure to negotiate the cleft meant a plummet of thousands of feet. Horses and livestock piled up at the edge of the precipice waiting their turn, as groups of soldiers — men and women — passed chests, machinery, backpacks, and guns up the line. Their own gear followed. The convalescent company had to release even the most critically ill and wounded to crawl up on their own. There was no other way. A legless officer crabbed along on his hands.

Finally, wranglers pulled and shoved the donkeys and horses up. Some of the animals stumbled and broke their legs or plummeted over the edge of the cliff, on occasion taking their handlers with them.

"After everyone passed the infamous Thundergod Cliff," Kang Keqing later recalled somewhat wistfully, "we congratulated each other, saying: 'It was as if we had passed through the gates of hell'" (p. 129). And soon it would seem as if they were inside.

THE WEATHER DETERIORATED. It rained for days, and while straw hats and straw or oilcloth raingear protected the marchers at first, they became thoroughly soaked. Muddy paths now ruined their reserve pairs of sandals. More and more, barefoot walkers slipped and fell. Sitting on their washbasins whenever they halted, the women took respite around small fires, but there was never enough time to dry off.

Unusual among her peers, Kang Keqing, who was called "Director" or "Little Commander" by the men, worked as a sweeper, alert to those who could not—or would not—keep up. Midway through each day's trek, she fell back and gathered the laggards, helping them carry their guns or other loads. Kang's harsh childhood had toughened her body and inured her to fatigue. She relished the active role of a soldier.

After Cat Mountain, the Reds continued along the northern Guangxi border, making strategic gifts to the local Yao, Miao, and Dong tribes as they marched. The Yao, who along with the other tribes had lived in the isolated mountain area for ages, were known for their dark complexion, powerful legs, and habit of going barefoot. Though they lived a relatively primitive life, they were strong and united, and the Reds did not want to have to fight them.[11]

The First Army passed through the area rapidly, but because of a lack of trading partners, it was forced to take whatever it could find for food, which was not much. Most of the locals had fled, either hiding or taking their supplies with them. Not only had they cached their unmilled grain, but they had also dismantled their water mills and hidden their stone mortars and tools to prevent the Communists from using them. In a few cases, the marchers uncovered heaps of concealed grain, which they husked by hand, pounding it with stones, bottles, or sticks and then separating the husks—in the absence of the locals' bellows—by blowing on them. It took an hour to mill a pound of rice in such a manner, and afterward their hands were cramped and bloody. It was a desperate trade-off: they could hardly spare the time and effort in the face of the Nationalists' pursuit, yet without anything to eat, they were doomed.[12]

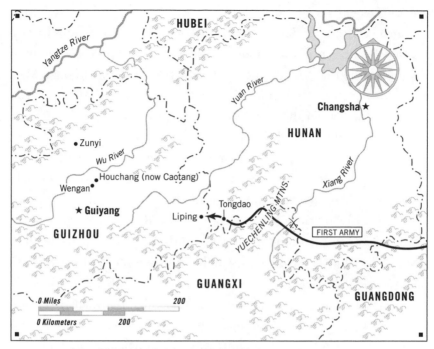

The Battered First Army Flees West to Guizhou Province

Despite all that had passed, the forces still lugged chests of silver coins and documents, artillery pieces, and large equipment as they headed northwest into Hunan. As they made their way along a muddy hillside path during a rainy, oppressive night in the densely forested Hunan mountains, Little Sparrow watched a horrific scene unfold: "Six people carried a printing press on shoulder poles," she later recounted. Carrying the heavy burden on the slippery ground quickly proved too much. "How could they walk? One by one, the porters fell off the mountain to their deaths."[13] All the while, the marchers trudged on, any tears washed away by the endless rain.

Surrounded by enemy troops, the First Army reached an obscure and destitute crossroads of wooden shacks in a Dong minority region. Here the provinces of Hunan, Guangxi, and Guizhou converged, and, as Kang Keqing put it, people from all three provinces could hear the same rooster crow. The Reds were exhausted, and desertion was increasing.

On December 11, the Military Commission—the leadership of the armed forces, under the Central Committee—met in a hastily arranged conference at a peasant house in the countryside, interrupting a wedding that happened to be taking place there. Although Mao had been forced off the commission by the Soviet-educated Party leaders two years earlier, he remained an influential voice with followers and was invited to attend the meeting.

Their situation was dire: Chiang had declared northern Hunan a "bandit suppression area."[14] As many as a quarter million Nationalist and allied troops were mustering there. Crowded into the peasant house, the air thick with solemnity, the Red leaders reluctantly abandoned their plan to join with the Sixth Army Group, which had been sent out from Jiangxi to search for a new home for the First Army. Instead, following Mao's suggestion, they decided to run west into less militarized Guizhou province. Tactically, the change in plans made sense, and Mao's role in opposing what was now perceived as a failed earlier policy and in reaching this new conclusion reestablished him as a decision-maker.

Two days later, having crossed into Guizhou, the Red Army occupied Liping, a city of about 200,000, which offered little resistance. On the night of December 18, an enlarged session of the Politburo met to officially determine their next course of action. Mao urged that they forge on to Zunyi—a wealthy coal-mining town and government seat in northern Guizhou, where Nationalist troops were sparse—to regroup, recruit, and reassess. From there, he argued, they could scout out the possibility of establishing a new base somewhere in the convergence of Guizhou, Yunnan, and Sichuan provinces. Not everyone agreed, and the discussion became heated. Some wanted to cross the Yangtze to meet up with Zhang Guotao's Fourth Army in Sichuan. Others suggested heading to the southwestern province of Yunnan to establish a new southern base.[15]

The next day, the group met again and concluded that the army should head to Zunyi, where they would rest and recruit. Once again, Mao had carried the argument.

Wireless operators transmitted the news to the Fourth Army and the Sixth and Second army groups, along with orders to engage in diversionary maneuvers to assist the First Army in its new plan. After a hasty exit from Liping, the First Army sparred with Nationalist and regional forces in the area over the next week while moving steadily northwest.

ON DECEMBER 9, the Twenty-fifth Army and its seven women nurses encamped outside the Shaanxi town of Yujiahe, on the edge of the Qinling Mountains, whose ancient forests of fir, pine, and ginkgo (one of the world's oldest tree species) provided shelter to clouded leopards and golden snub-nosed monkeys. Until now, the Twenty-fifth had maneuvered nearly continuously, a few steps — but only a few — ahead of its pursuers. Posted east of town, the youthful Red soldiers collapsed into exhausted slumber.

The next morning, as Red Army officers met with the provincial Party committee, a division of Nationalist troops attacked. Their first barrage woke the Red soldiers from their weary sleep. What followed was one of the most intense engagements of the civil war, with twenty separate Nationalist assaults, each bloodily repelled by the Red troops. Eventually, the Communists claimed a victory, but they had paid a terrible price. The Nationalists had killed more than a hundred Red soldiers, but, more ominously, they had wounded almost every senior Red officer.[16]

The medics hastily assembled a field hospital. Woefully short of supplies, the doctors and nurses washed the soldiers' wounds with saltwater, applied tincture of iodine, and then bandaged the damaged bodies with threadbare rags that had been washed and dried in the sun. Young Orchid and the other nurses did everything they could for their patients. As was always the case after a battle, they scavenged for medicine from the enemy and searched the woods for medicinal plants. They boiled grass roots and tree leaves with water to make a disinfectant.

On one stretcher, Commander Xu lay in a coma. While driving the Nationalists from a strategic position, he had been shot in the

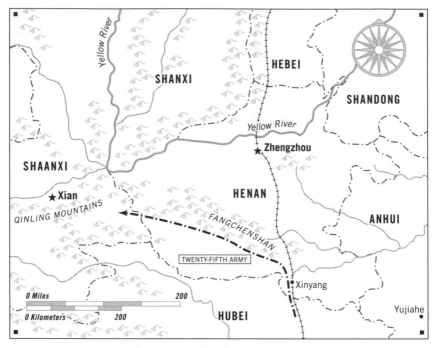

The Twenty-fifth Army Veers West

head, the bullet penetrating below his left eye and exiting his neck below his left ear. Young Orchid was assigned to attend to him. For four days and nights, Xu remained unconscious, his face partly hidden by bandages. Hour after hour, Young Orchid remained by his side. Looking at her silent patient, she studied his body — lean, muscular, and marked by decades of armed struggle. Scars were his military decorations, and there were plenty of them, on both legs and arms, on a shoulder and a hip, and on his chest. Young Orchid worried that Xu had been awarded his last medal.

However, on the fifth day after the battle, Commander Xu came to. The first thing he saw was seventeen-year-old Young Orchid, the daughter of a poor Anhui carpenter, a Youth Leaguer from age fourteen who, when she heard of the establishment of the Twenty-fifth Army in 1932, had crossed county lines for a chance to join. Deemed too small to carry a gun or even to run fast enough, Young Orchid was enlisted as a nurse only after she refused to go away.

"What time is it?" Xu demanded. "Isn't it time for the Army to leave?"

"You have finally come to!" Young Orchid gasped. "You have been in a coma for five days without saying a word. Everybody was so worried."

"I wasn't in a hurry," Xu responded, with a reassuring grin. "I did have a good sleep."[17]

"Quiet now," Young Orchid hushed him. She fetched a bowl of noodles. Careful of his wound, which creased in both directions when his jaw moved, she spoon-fed the commander. Once he had eaten, Xu revived even more and began to question Young Orchid loudly, as if he were in a quarrel. She realized that he had, not surprisingly, lost the hearing in his left ear.

For several more days, Xu slept, waking in pain and ill-tempered. Young Orchid often heard him mumble in this fitful slumber, worrying about his responsibilities. She nursed him as well as she could. The commander cooperated, eating heartily. Though weak, he soon stood and attempted steps.

But Young Orchid could only do so much. Medical resources were slim, sanitary conditions problematic at best. Before long, Xu grew sick with fever and a cough so deep and persistent that it reopened his facial wounds. The more he suffered, the harder Young Orchid struggled to help him. This was not only a personal quest for her: Xu was their battlefield commander. Without him, the Twenty-fifth had little chance of survival.[18]

chapter 9

Into Guizhou

DECEMBER 1934

Twenty-three-year-old Guangdong native Liao Siguang now waddled along with the burden of carrying a nearly full-term baby and also worrying about what to do with it once it was born.

It is difficult for most Westerners and modern Chinese to imagine any circumstances in which they would abandon a newborn baby. But to put the Long Marchers' dilemma into perspective, circumstances and cultural differences must be examined. Foremost, the women did not know whether they would survive the *dabanjia*. They did not know how far or how long they would travel. Being bombed and strafed from the air and hunted on the ground, it seemed as if death awaited them around every corner. It would also be much more difficult to keep up with the rapid pace of the army while carrying and tending to an infant. A cry in the night could lead to fatal consequences. Furthermore, in China, the raising of a child was often given over to the clan. In many villages, cousins roamed from house to house and slept wherever they fell. Those who were best suited to look after the children looked after the children. Those who were best suited to work worked. Grandparents looked after toddlers whose parents toiled in the fields all day or had moved to the city to earn money in factories. Even before coming to the Jiangxi Soviet, many of the women had already left babies in the care of others as they moved around in the name of the revolution.

But nothing had prepared the Long March women for having a child under the conditions they now faced. Although they were striving to create a better world for themselves and their families, their present circumstances mirrored the worst that past generations had seen, when mass starvation beset China, causing peasants to drown newborn babies whom they knew they could not feed. The Long March women had seen friends and comrades die and were prepared to sacrifice their own lives for their cause, but soon Liao Siguang would have the life of a newborn in her hands.

In mid-December, the reduced First Army plunged into eastern Guizhou, one of China's poorest provinces, a backward, isolated, almost-unbroken landscape of mid-level mountains rife with opium traders and sallow addicts. The marchers themselves, having already walked more than seven hundred miles (yet only a fraction of the way to their destination), were no prettier a picture, ravaged by battle, road sores, and malnutrition.

Sitting on top of China's 53 billion–ton sea of coal, Guizhou peasants were in the habit of taking what they needed from natural seams to cook and keep warm in winter. But the barren, rocky terrain yielded little in the way of clothing and food. The peasants went hungry six months out of the year and walked around semi-naked. An old adage encapsulated Guizhou's harsh conditions: "The weather never sees three days of sunshine. / There are no three *li* of level ground. / No one has three silver coins."[1]

To make matters worse, what little income the locals had was often smoked away by the men. The British had helped create a nationwide epidemic of opium use by importing high-grade opium from India to China beginning in the eighteenth century. People who lived in these poor parts indulged in the lower-quality but equally insidious crop cultivated by provincial drug barons.[2]

As the First Army trekked through the southeastern Guizhou hills, passing through villages of ten to a few dozen families, Wang Quanyuan observed that the people indeed spent most of their time smoking opium. They were so destitute that the men's pants and shirts were patched layer by layer, while the women wore only scraps of cloth.[3]

As had been the case during their previous encounter with ethnic minority tribes, word had spread that the Red hordes bearing down on the province were ruthless brigands, who would rape, steal, and murder. As a result, those who could flee had, taking or burying their food supplies and dismantling their mills. In their abandoned huts, the women in the convalescent company quartered those wounded at the Xiang River. All but six of the thirty women were now assigned to the convalescent company, helping to recruit porters and usher along the stretchers. Shorty was responsible for four stretchers, meaning she had to find, provision, and retain the porters while also feeding and caring for the patients. It was also her job to maintain the morale of the porters, many of whom were picked up locally and became despondent once they discovered what they had gotten themselves into. There was no opium for solace, no sympathy for shirkers. Insubordination could mean a bullet, or more likely the sword, since ammunition was too valuable to waste.[4]

Strapping Wang Quanyuan was particularly useful at carrying the stretchers, but when they ran short of porters, even the smallest of the women, Liu and Shorty, were forced to take up the bamboo poles, sometimes together at one end with a man stationed at the other. The sick and wounded, who were also usually hungry and thirsty, were not always appreciative of these efforts. When the ride grew bumpy, those lying on the stretchers often cursed the women to vent their frustration. Some even swatted them with their canes.[5]

Despite the women's best efforts, the seriously wounded eventually had to be left behind. This, too, became the women's task. Time was tight, since the march could not be delayed. Finding suitable homes for those being left was difficult, and "suitable" often meant simply a place with a roof, since there was no way to judge the qualifications of owners who were not there. The wounded especially dreaded being left in the bare huts of the Miao, with whom they could not even communicate. There was a lingering suspicion that quite a few soldiers left behind were robbed and murdered as soon as the Red troops were out of sight. And, in fact, this was true.

A few days after taking over the Military Commission stretchers from its ill captain, Kang Keqing met Zhou Enlai at a fork in the road. As Kang reported in her memoir, she deferentially halted her stretcher team, but Zhou, leader of the Central Committee guard, waved her on, saying, "The wounded should go first. We'll follow." With Zhou behind her, Kang felt extra pressure, and she instructed two guards to scout ahead, where some hills and a graveyard lay. A little later a volley of gunshots rang out, narrowly missing her, as the guards rushed back to report an enemy unit of twenty or thirty men. Kang ordered the stretcher-bearers to retreat to safety and sent a messenger to warn Zhou while she and some soldiers investigated. Locating the shooters on a hillside ahead, Kang watched as they moved onto the road. As they began to advance toward her, she sent a second messenger for help. Meanwhile, she and the soldiers took cover in the graveyard. "The leaders are behind us," Kang told her men. "We can't allow the enemy through, even if it means we fight to the death. The Red Army will arrive if we can hold out for a while!" She further instructed the men not to waste ammunition, to shoot only if they had a clear target, and to change positions after taking two shots. Before she could say more, the enemy soldiers charged.[6]

As the attackers hurried down the hill, Kang took aim with her Mauser and fired at the leader. Her men fired, too, and the attackers dove for cover. As hoped for, a contingent of soldiers of a Red special task team, hearing the gunfire, ran up. Kang told them to outflank the attackers and hit them from the rear. She dispatched another messenger to apprise the leaders of the plan. The enemy soldiers fired at the grave mounds where Kang and her men squatted. As bullets peppered the tombstones and the muddy hillside behind them, she ordered her men to hold their fire.

Suddenly, the enemy soldiers charged again.

Kang and her men took aim and shot several. Two made it to within fifty yards before Kang and the squad leader kneeling beside her downed them. The others fell back about a hundred yards and took cover again. While Kang considered what to do next, she heard shots and saw the special task team assaulting the enemy from behind. Her plan had worked, and after a hot exchange of gunfire, the enemy — a local militia, it turned out — fled over a hill. Only two Reds, both from the special task team, had been wounded.

THE RED ARMY'S biggest advantage was its mobility through the primitive countryside. However, two months of constant maneuvers, battles, restless sleep, and poor nutrition finally caught up with Liao Siguang. Seven months into her pregnancy, she went into labor.[7]

Hou Zheng, captain of the convalescent company, put Liao on a horse, promising her that she would reach camp soon. Her belly felt like it was exploding with each thrust of the horse's hooves. In her agony, sweat poured down her face and her back, but she willed herself to hold on. They raced up the incline and crossed a ridge, coming under heavy fire. As soon as they started the descent, the Reds returned the fire. When she could take the pain no more, Liao tumbled off the horse. By the time they reached camp, she was writhing on a stretcher of hempen rope between bamboo poles. The women moved in and took over. Finally, the thin mountain air was filled with the wails of her baby, a boy — good luck.

It was the first baby of the journey. In normal circumstances, eggs dyed lucky red would be handed out at the birth of a boy, a joyous occasion, but the circumstances were not normal. "He's a future Red Army soldier who should be carried on a stretcher to the people's area to be raised," announced Deng Yingchao. This was another way of saying that the little boy would have to be left behind.

The next morning, Liao used a towel to wrap her tiny son — under-fed and overworked before he had even left his mother's womb. She scrawled a note explaining that he had been born as the Red Army was passing through, that she hoped he would be well cared for, and that she would be back to get him. She included his birth date, thinking that whoever found him would want to know. Liao, who herself had been sold as a *tongyangxi* at age three and who had left her firstborn, a daughter, in Shanghai, placed the baby and the note in an abandoned house and prayed that the owners would come back soon and that they would be able to read her note. Then she climbed on a stretcher and was carried away.[8]

More babies would be left behind. "It was very sad," Liu Ying later commented. "But under the circumstances, we could not pay attention to feelings." The mothers, she said, "had to make a decision. Did they love the revolution better? They did, and that was their hard choice."[9]

It was not only wounded soldiers and babies who risked abandonment. When Deng Liujin, known as "the Cannon" for her booming voice, suffered from severe dysentery, she became too weak, dehydrated, and feverish to walk. She did not have the *guanxi* to command a stretcher, and it was decided that she should be given her departing funds and left with a local family. Upon hearing this, the other women rallied around her. One took over Shorty's stretchers while Shorty made a cane for the Cannon and found her water. Then Shorty heaved the Cannon's gear onto her back with her own, and the pair set off together. But soon they lagged behind. Turning to her small, overburdened savior, the Cannon cried, "Shorty, you must leave. Then only one of us will die. That's better than both of us." But Shorty would not give up on her suffering friend. At night, she slept intertwined with her to keep her warm. For four days, the pair hobbled along arm in arm until the Cannon recovered enough to keep up by herself.[10]

After more than two months on the trail, all of the women longed for an extended break to heal their feet and satiate their hunger. As they walked, they served themselves what they called "mental meals," lavishly describing favorite dishes from their hometowns, each trying to outdo the others, invariably ending in laughter as their fantasies grew more and more grandiose. In reality, they ate whatever they could get. If a pig was slaughtered, they devoured every bit except the hair and teeth. The same went for a mule, a horse, or a dog. Somehow they managed to scavenge enough food to keep going, feasting on nutritious blood puddings when available and also on mountain rats, a southern delicacy. Even a freshly killed common rat would do.[11]

As terrible as their hunger was, their feet were their chief concern. At the end of the day, the women would sooner miss their meal than skip their footbaths. First, they drained their blisters by poking them with a needle sterilized in the fire. If they did not have a needle, they used a bamboo splinter or stiff horsehair. Then they put their feet in pots of steaming water — the hotter the better to increase blood circulation and clean open sores.[12]

Lice infestation was common, and as the women walked and their bodies heated up, the insects became more active, causing them to itch all over. Such distractions could prove dangerous as they traveled over sheer and narrow trails in the dark. During breaks, the women busied themselves catching lice on one another and pinching them dead, but it was a losing battle. When they finally found a day to rest, He Zizhen insisted that they take off their clothes and boil them even though they had almost nothing to cover themselves with. Zhong Yuelin looked in the pot and was amazed: her underwear peppered the water with lice. Peng Dehuai tried to make light of the situation: "There is no army without lice," he quipped. "Those who have no lice now are not real soldiers." But there was not much laughter.[13]

The women rarely had the chance to wash their faces, let alone bathe. However, it rained continually in Guizhou — a blessing and a curse, as they could wash their hands and faces in a downpour, but the rest of their bodies ended up even dirtier due to the mud. All matters of hygiene were rudimentary. They used leaves to wipe themselves after defecating. (The Chinese invented toilet paper by the sixth century and were mass-producing it by the fourteenth, some of it even perfumed, but such luxuries were unknown on the march.)[14]

Dealing with menstruation was another challenge. The women had no special sanitary napkins, and the doctors told them that using a cloth could make them sick, suggesting instead that they use clean paper. But since clean paper was hard to come by, the women usually made do with wads of cotton, torn-off pieces of pant legs, or bandages wrapped around dried leaves or ashes from the fires. Often, according to Li Guiying, they had no protection at all.[15]

Chinese women were raised to believe that their private parts

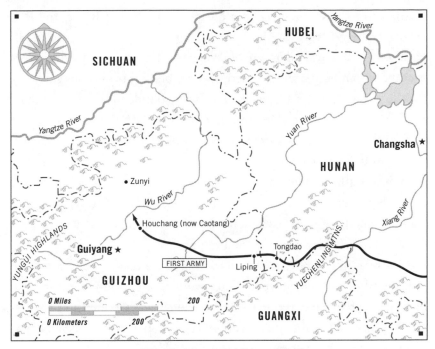

The First Army Continues West

should always be kept dry. Frequently, after fording creeks and rivers or while walking in the rain, the women had to wear wet clothes, sometimes for long stretches. Most had no extra clothes, and there was no privacy anyway, so they dried their pants while wearing them. Modest by nature and in need of protection against the elements at night, they did not even take off their clothes to sleep.

When they reached a resting place, exhaustion overwhelmed every other feeling. But rest was uneasy during daylight hours. Often they had no shelter, not even a wall for partial protection. Horses munched, snorted, caroused, and fought; donkeys brayed; dogs prowled, barking and growling. Men snored. The wounded groaned. Though the waking bugle call was gentler than all others, the women dreaded the summons to quickly fold their blankets, stow their possessions, and fall in again.[16]

FOUR WEEKS after their narrow escape at the Xiang River, the Red troops emerged from the heavy morning mist to surprise the small garrison in the walled town of Wengan. The garrison's defenders resisted for an hour and then fled, leaving behind provisions saved up for their New Year's celebration. The Reds rounded up the pork, mutton, chicken, and vegetables and shared them with the town's poor.

Guizhou's warlord triumvirate commanded about 100,000 loosely allied, relatively well-armed irregular troops. The Communists, who had outlawed opium use in their own territories, ridiculed them, however, calling them "double-gun soldiers," because many of them smoked opium — commonly known in China as *dayan,* or "big smoke" — through a pipe, or "opium gun."[17]

As they moved northwest into Guizhou's interior mountains, the fighting — mostly chance encounters and small-scale cat-and-mouse chases — ebbed, and the marchers no longer felt constantly threatened. These mountain ranges were of remarkable, ancient beauty, and Wang Quanyuan was particularly fascinated by the immense primeval fallen trees blocking their path. The trees lay where they fell, rotting and eaten by worms. Guizhou's mountains were so sparsely inhabited that no one used the wood, and Wang, like most of the women, conditioned by a lifetime of deprivation, thought it a pity that they could not make use of the fallen timber. While the trees lay in their path untouched, the forests were not empty. Every so often, the marchers met Han peasants who did not fear them, and they would pause to tell the peasants about the revolution, giving themselves an excuse to rest at the same time.[18]

As the threat of attack eased, the troops' chronic discomfort — fatigue, hunger, aches and pains — inevitably brought a variety of internal tensions to a head. Despite the Communist rhetoric of equality and unity, the women only rarely questioned the men. They were too freshly liberated from a tradition in which it was unthinkable for a woman to challenge a man outside the house. One day in these quiet hills, however, their weariness and frustration boiled over. A light but constant rain had drenched them all day. At dusk, fog enveloped the dense forest, and the convalescent company advanced methodically over a muddy path, motivated only by the thought of a campfire to dry their skin and clothes. Ahead of them, the commanders and staff had already stopped in a small village, been assigned houses, and set about soaking their feet. The guards were laying out bedding for the leaders. In a kitchen, the cooks were butchering a pig for dinner.

When the convalescent company reached the village and Liu Qunxian, the twenty-seven-year-old wife of Bo Gu, heard that they had to march several more miles to another village, she flew into a rage: "Just because the commander's unit is ahead of us, you think you can take over the nearest village with the best houses and butcher a pig? The convalescent company is already lagging. Are you asking the women and the wounded to walk eight more *li* in the dark?"

Supported by the other women, Liu demanded that they trade places with the men. She and the wives of the senior officers could not be taken lightly, and Chen Yun, the central column political commissar, finally gave in. "Alright, alright, please stop," he said. "We'll move, and you can stay in this village." The women went into the kitchen and insisted that the cooks leave the butchered pig. "You travel ahead of us and can *datuhao* whenever you want," the women asserted. "We in the back can only smell the scent of your leftovers." Fearful of these influential women, the cooks handed over the delicacies and joined the officers and their retinue in making a hasty exit.[19]

The respect Liu Qunxian enjoyed was hard-earned. The grand-daughter of a dung collector, she was working sixteen hours a day, seven days a week, in a silk factory by the age of fourteen. She started work at 4:30 in the morning, ate her meals next to her machine and rarely saw the light of day. She was scolded if she went to the toilet for more than two minutes and was searched at the end of each day to make sure she had not stolen anything.

Sent to university in Moscow after emerging as a labor leader, Liu married Bo Gu there in 1928. Back in China, she was made director of the Female Labor Department in Jiangxi, overseeing more than 10,000 women as they made sandals and clothing and took night classes to learn to read.

Toward the end of their time in Jiangxi, Liu was pregnant with her third child and run-down by stress and poor nutrition. She went to bed one night and awoke in pain: a centipede had bitten her on the head. It was a terrible omen. The Chinese consider centipedes, snakes, scorpions, spiders, and toads to be the "five poisonous creatures" and fear them for real and sometimes mythical dangers. After being bitten, Liu became feverish and ended up losing the baby.[20] Before she could fully recover, the *dabanjia* had begun.

THE LARGEST TRIBUTARY on the southern side of the Yangtze, the Wu—located in the rainiest province in China—moved a tremendous amount of water. It was broad, in some places nearly half a mile wide, and still ran swift and deep. Warlord governor Wang Jialie's troops had only recently vacated their positions on the Wu, ferrying to the north bank and taking, burning, or scuttling all the river craft. There were no bridges and no fords. Properly defended, the ferry crossings, every three miles or so, would be nearly impossible for the Communists to take.[21]

Thus stranded, on the last day of 1934 the marchers occupied several towns along the river's south bank. It was snowing, and a frigid north wind blew fiercely across the bald hills. Soldiers shivering in thin clothes sang as they removed doors from their hinges to use as beds, swept snow out of the street, and built snowmen. They spent their New Year's allowance, coins given them from the government's coffers, on food and other necessities.

The women and the central column, including most of the Military Commission, spent New Year's Day in a small village on the river's precipitous south bank. Here the Political Department orchestrated the New Year's festivities. Although the drama troupe had been forced to ditch a lot of its makeup and costumes, the performers sang, danced, and put on skits, including one particularly well-aimed production for the troops—most now wearing improvised footwear—that made light of their moldy sandals. Li Bozhao performed traditional plowing and sewing dances before offering a sexy rendition of a high-stepping Russian navy dance that brought the house down. The march had been a cascade of loss and misfortune, but their laughter was real and their cheers hearty. Though exhausted, bandaged, filthy, and hungry, the revolutionaries got up and danced. Far from splintering them, the incredible duress they were under was drawing them closer together.

Mao himself grudgingly acknowledged New Year's Eve, telling his aides they would celebrate once they were across the Wu. A more reverent celebration would be saved for the Chinese, or Lunar, New Year, still over a month away. Mao kept his officers focused on the matter at hand—figuring out how to cross the river.

The Communists conferred with the locals about building a bridge, concluding that the current was too dangerous and too fast. Indeed, the 250-yard-wide area where the marchers needed to cross presented a logistical nightmare. It sat deep in a gorge of vertical bluffs, which allowed only a few approaches and presented a perfect setting for Governor Wang's men to take target practice on them.[22]

At dusk on January 1, 1935, with temperatures below freezing—though not cold enough to freeze the flowing river and make for an easier crossing—the operation commenced. Teams of five handpicked soldiers armed with rifles, machine guns, and grenades scrambled down to the river's edge. Boarding light rafts constructed of wood and bamboo, they began to row across, fighting the swift rush of frigid water.

The plan was for the soldiers to land on the north bank, then signal with flashlights to their commander on the opposite bank. But almost instantly, Wang's troops spotted the rafts and opened fire. The boats carried on until they were out of sight. But no signal to indicate a successful landing ever came.

It looked like they would have to do it the hard way. Early the next morning, as a preamble to an all-out assault, the Communists commenced a heavy barrage of machine-gun and small artillery fire aimed at the fortifications across the river. Wang's troops responded in kind, and the air filled with smoke and the slither of bullets. Amid the chaos, the Reds managed to hit a blockhouse, which exploded. In the light of the blast, they could just make out distant figures ascending the hillside on the opposite bank. Some of the raft teams had in fact succeeded in crossing the river and had hidden overnight, waiting for the battle to begin.

As Wang's troops frantically turned their attention to the teams' assault, Communist soldiers poured across the river to join in the battle. During the three-hour fight that followed, the Red Army uprooted and drove off Wang's division and gained control of the crossing.

Red soldiers on the south bank had collected doors to use as bridge planks; others had made rope from hemp and grass. Engineers now constructed a floating bridge of bamboo poles and doors weighted with sacks of stones to keep the current from washing it away. The planks swayed under the pressure of the water, sometimes jerking downstream or snapping back upstream. After ten hours of chill and mishap, the precarious span was deemed secure enough for the crossing to begin. More than 25,000 marchers had to cross. One by one, they scurried and hopped and clung to the planks as the river yanked the doors and poles to and fro.

The plan called for the horses and mules to swim, but as the troops proceeded, the animals suddenly balked at entering the bone-chilling water. Panicking, they tried to dash onto the planks. In the heat of the moment, soldiers shot half a dozen horses to save the bridge and themselves. The icy water filled with blood as the dead horses tumbled downstream. It was a wretched sight, even for those who had witnessed the worst of war. Stunned by the sudden, violent demise of her small red roan, the tall, square-shouldered Li Jianzhen, known for her courage, wept.[23]

chapter 10

Love, Power, and Revolution in Zunyi

JANUARY 1935

On special occasions, the Chinese erect small shrines to their ancestors or the gods, an honor also bestowed on heroes or great leaders as a gesture of welcome. Now, across Zunyi, the townspeople burned lanterns overnight for the marchers and set up small shrines in front of their houses, chanting, "Open all four gates and greet the Red Army." Entering the town through the south gate — the entrance traditionally used on ceremonial occasions for those deemed important — the Communist leaders received a hero's welcome. The townspeople played drums and gongs and lit firecrackers, which snapped like gunfire. Most of the women entered the gates of Guizhou's second-largest city with the First Army's convalescent company. [1]

Zunyi was a city of only about 40,000, with the electric power of a single generator and uneven brick roads designed for horse-drawn carriages and pedestrians. The First Army had taken it so rapidly that many of its officials and wealthy merchants, along with vast stores of food and textiles, were still there. The Communists traversed the old city, mostly government buildings and residences, and then crossed a stone bridge to the new city, the business district. There they seized warlord Wang Jialie's salt business, including a small fortune in salt and great quantities of Platinum Golden Dragon cigarettes, produced by Shanghai's South Sea Tobacco Company. These they released on the market at the bargain price of eight pounds of salt or four tins of cigarettes for a silver dollar, generating goodwill with the citizens of Zunyi and hard currency for their own use.

Cold, wet, and weary, the Reds needed time to rest and recuperate before facing the grueling winter months ahead. The soldiers transformed schools, offices, churches, and temples into barracks and eagerly washed themselves and changed clothes — a rare occurrence on the march. Cai Chang and Li Bozhao billeted together in a Christian church, while Li Jianzhen, head of the Women's Department, stayed in an elementary school. Kang Keqing and Zhu De shared the mansion of an absent Nationalist Army division commander with Deng Yingchao and Zhou Enlai. But pregnant He Zizhen, nearly full-term now, did not board with her husband. Preoccupied with Party politics and increasingly distant, Mao resided by himself and focused on consolidating his control over the Party while evading the grasp of Chiang Kaishek.[2]

Many of the women bivouacked in a large school in the old part of town. In its library, the women and other cadres discovered devastating reports in newspapers and magazines about what had happened since they had left Jiangxi. Back home, Nationalist forces and armed landlords had entered the former Central Soviet, reclaiming property and wreaking gruesome revenge. As they read, some of the women wept quietly for family and friends left behind.

Across from the school, the Political Department set up shop in a Catholic church. Here a number of the women, including Li Jianzhen, Cai Chang, Little Sparrow, and Wang Quanyuan, tended to the trunks of vital documents that had survived the journey from Ruijin. The army needed to replace lost soldiers and porters, and Little Sparrow took over the recruiting efforts. The army also needed to procure food and funds, and Li Jianzhen and Kang Keqing dedicated themselves to *datuhao*. For her part, Liu Qunxian helped establish Red Worker unions for local carpenters, masons, and the employees of Zunyi's match and silk factories, groups that would form partisan teams and carry on the fight after the First Army moved on. A group largely made up of local schoolteachers and students, many of them female, formed the Friends of the Red Army Corps to assist with *xuanchuan* and *datuhao*. The female students gathered in the Political Department office across from the school and started on the first major task: staging a mass rally, which would take place the following evening on the school grounds, to help fuel the popular uprising. Such activity by Chinese women would have been shocking to most Chinese.[3]

Meanwhile, shops closed by looting reopened for business. The citizens of Zunyi filled the streets, where the Reds carried their message to them. Li Bozhao directed *xuanchuan* efforts, singing and performing along with Wang Quanyuan, Little Sparrow, Ah Jin, and Cai Chang.

The afternoon of the rally, the crowd began to gather on the school sports field for the promised speeches and festivities. A platform had been built at one end beneath three large willow trees, and a large banner hung in front of it, succinctly stating the First Army's message: "Only the Soviets can save China."[4] By sundown, the locals were still coming; Kang Keqing would put the number of attendees at "more than 10,000."

Mao and Zhu De took the stage. "The crowd was finally able to meet the two men face to face," a Red Army University instructor wrote, noting that "the peasants at Zunyi were just a bit disappointed that Mao"—depicted by Nationalist propaganda as a fanged green monster—"turned out to be an ordinary-looking person." Jaundiced Cai Xiaoqian recalled that Mao "gave the same . . . worn-out speech and hailed the same old slogan 'save the nation and defeat the Japanese.'" Zhu spoke next, reinforcing Mao's message. The Red Army's march was not a retreat, both men insisted, but the start of an offensive against the Japanese invaders in the north, whose mention raised the ire of all Chinese, whatever their political stripe.

As inspiring as the leaders were, at least to those who had not seen them before, it was an unlikely local who stole the show. Li Bozhao had recruited Li Xiaoxia, a fiery seventeen-year-old, to appeal to her fellow students. Xiaoxia was deeply motivated. Teased for being a tomboy, she despised the gender roles forced upon her. Why should she not be as free as a boy? Why was it shameful for her to talk to a male, even her own cousin? Unmarried girls could not even leave their homes or the fields without a chaperone. Women had suffered under men for too long. Indeed, Xiaoxia's own sister had been beaten to death by a cruel husband less than a year after her arranged marriage. Life as a woman in China was a constant imprisonment or worse. Revolution meant jailbreak. The Red Army's arrival was the answer to Xiaoxia's prayers.

Encouraged by her new comrades, the teenager looked out over the sea of faces in front of her, where some of the young women swayed over lilied feet. "Why should women be second-class citizens?" Xiaoxia shouted, begging the crowd to help free women, who would in turn help build a new society. "Why should women suffer the inhumanity of lily feet? Why should they always be humiliated?"[5] She could not believe the intensity and exhilaration she felt onstage. She, who had been nobody, was somebody. The multitude erupted in cheers, and Xiaoxia realized that she had found her calling.

The rally ended with a twenty-eight-year-old schoolteacher leading the crowd in chanting revolutionary slogans. Afterward, on an outdoor basketball court, a Red Army team squared off against students dressed in long-sleeved shirts with high collars. To the cheers of the crowd, the soldiers, who had often played together before the march, put on a show, hitting open men with passes and sinking long shots from all around the court.

After the game, the festivities recommenced on the playground. A stand-up comedy act got the crowd howling with laughter. Then a band of performers put on a series of skits, danced, and sang, an encore of the New Year's celebration a few days earlier. Following the performance, both the provincial revolutionary committee and the Friends of the Red Army opened up their offices at the buzzing school. Students poured in to join and to offer their services.[6]

Over the next few days, Red instructors organized them and sent the new recruits out into the streets or to nearby villages and towns to rally the people. Many of the students enlisting were female, and the school quickly became a hangout for soldiers and cadres, who milled about the offices looking for opportunities to invite girls to visit their barracks. Quite a few accepted, according to Cai Xiaoqian, and the "revolutionary resolve" of some soldiers was eroded by the "'satisfaction' they received from these curious young girls" (p. 244).

Zunyi catered to other appetites, too. Flocking to stalls and markets, the Red cadres and officers snapped up fresh blood oranges and rich sponge cakes, plus toothpaste, soap, towels, galoshes, and cigarettes. The town's three bookstores promptly sold out of pencils and ink, notebooks and novels. Sichuan Guizhou Restaurant, the largest in town, lured the newcomers with its spicy diced chicken, twice-cooked pork, vinegar fish, congealed pork-blood soup, and Sichuan pickles made from bitter melons, cabbages, radishes, and other vegetables. Before long, restaurants originally offering heaping diced chicken dishes featured pork instead, then cabbage, and finally portions shrank to the point that embarrassed waiters apologized as they set down sparsely filled plates.

While the rewards of the city were many, the common soldiers did not get to enjoy them. Instead, they were kept busy in the countryside drilling, doing sentry duty, and providing manpower for the cadres for such tasks as removing confiscated provisions from the condemned farms of the wealthy. They slept under the stars. Eager to partake of the pleasures of Zunyi, they made it known to their officers that they would like to enter the town. Their request was granted, one young recruit named Wang Daojin later reported: they were allowed to march into town, through town, and out the other side.[7]

As hard as such isolation was for Wang Daojin and his comrades, the quick passage was necessary. Many of the young rural soldiers were incredibly naive. Most had only a rudimentary knowledge of anything unrelated to the land; a considerable number had never seen an electric light. When the CCP's vice minister of education, Xu Teli, visited Wang Shishan, a famed Zunyi calligrapher, he had to stop the soldiers who had accompanied him from burning Wang's books for warmth. Discipline was easier to maintain outside of town.

WITH EFFORTS WELL UNDER WAY in Zunyi, the Communists now held mass meetings in four nearby villages. The women performed illustrative skits to dispense Red Army news. In one, willowy and seductive Wang Quanyuan strode across the platform scowling as meanly as she could. Dressed as a man in dark sunglasses and wearing a beard of black ink beneath evil eyebrows — the frowning arches that identify a bad guy in Chinese opera — she aped a ruthless, hardhearted landlord. The peasants snorted and howled with laughter. Wielding a walking stick, she next portrayed Wang Jialie as a doddering knave. (Wang's provincial army commanders were, in fact, being bribed by the Nationalists to betray him, and he would be deposed by Chiang Kaishek soon after the Communists departed the province.) More chortles and catcalls followed.[8]

The women also joined and often led work teams in raiding the area's snow-covered farms. Li Jianzhen now directed such *datuhao* efforts, helped by Kang Keqing, Li Bozhao, Deng Yingchao, and Cai Chang (the latter two both recovering from tuberculosis). Together the women burned deeds and confiscated — or, from the Nationalist perspective, looted — food, clothing, money, and other valuables.

The marchers imposed their rough justice like a cyclone, sweeping through an area with a fury energized by two millennia of oppression. To their eyes, wealth automatically meant guilt, and guilt by association — a prevalent concept in China, where, thanks to ancient codes, vendettas and punishment for crimes often extended to near and distant relatives — was widespread. Against the wealthy or those assumed to be so, the Reds initiated a reign of terror.

In scoping out a village and its surrounding farms, some leaders depended on the peasants to quickly pinpoint targets, but Li Jianzhen — whose elongated (what the Chinese call a *mu*-shaped) face indicated that she was intense, fiery, and willful, as she indeed was — found this method to be unreliable. Suspicious of the Communists, cowed by local strongmen or perversely loyal to them out of habit, the peasants, she discovered, often lied. Instead, Li would look for an elevated place to scan for large houses, especially those made of brick or tile or having painted walls. Once she found such a house — by this point abandoned by its owners — she would listen for a watchdog left behind. Those of rich masters, she had noticed, barked more and were

The popular Cai Chang in Yenan in 1937. *(Helen Foster Snow Archives, Brigham Young University)*

more aggressive than those of the poor, which often merely whined. Another telltale sign of wealth was a large and well-kept pen for cows, pigs, or horses.

When they entered the house, the women searched for correspondence addressed to "Mr." or "Honorable," indicating status and wealth. In the kitchen, they looked for large pots and eating utensils. Often the signs of prosperity were apparent: mahogany cupboards; intricately carved tables; chests with heavy brass hinges and locks; scales for weighing money and abacuses for counting; walls lacquered in red, green, or black, bordered with fancy designs and hung with ancient paintings on scrolls. If the evidence confirmed their suspicions, the home was condemned and sealed. It was only at this point that Li would question the peasants — who were more truthful when presented with hard evidence — to confirm the owner's status before confiscation began.

Her team would then pack the provisions and valuables they

discovered into baskets, boxes, and trunks, which they placed by the road. Teams of soldiers picked up the goods to be processed and distributed for use. A note listing the confiscated items and signed by the Red Army was left to prevent false accusations and retribution against the peasants. A portion of the confiscated goods—food, clothing, medicine, salt, rice, grain, and opium—was allotted to the peasants, who were especially eager to receive the salt and opium, commodities that were easy to transfer and hard to trace.[9]

After a raid, Li and her work team would call a community rally, often around a nighttime bonfire, where they would display the extravagances of the fallen lords—fancy clothes, silver candlesticks, porcelain and gilt chamber pots—and agitate the crowd with songs and declarations. Their slogan "Destroy bullies; share fields and land" was an emancipation proclamation to the impoverished, who largely embraced it. For the peasants, there was little not to like. Encouraged to join the "troops of the poor" and promised that they would be paid and could return home when they reached a certain point, 3,000 men enlisted.

*

Su NU, the Chinese goddess of sex, said that the two chief human desires are for food and sex. For four millennia, many Chinese had pursued Su Nu's pleasures with abandon. Ancient tableaux depicted outdoor trysts and orgies. Porcelain figurines and paintings on fans and teapots celebrated the nine recommended sexual positions. Su Nu taught that men must have a tranquil mind and be disciplined during lovemaking. According to Su Nu, couples in their twenties and thirties should have sex daily.

It was only in the last millennium that repression and censorship had increasingly entered China's sexual life, with modesty becoming not only a virtue but a necessity. In the nineteenth century, a woman convicted of "licentiousness" might be paraded through the streets on a donkey in a saddle with a sizable wooden phallus angled painfully forward inside her. In the early twentieth century, a bride wore crotchless pants during sex because it was shameful for her to be naked even in front of her own husband.

Now that the Reds were stationary, rested, and fed, some, at least, indulged in the pursuits extolled by Su Nu. On the trail, exhausted marchers slept on the ground, en masse, clothed, and usually with men and women segregated, making sex, which was already against the rules, unfeasible. The lack of contraception and the fear of pregnancy further cut back on desire, at least for the women. Now, despite the fact that sex could likely lead to hardship and heartbreak and that Party rules still forbade it, human nature took its course.

Wang Quanyuan's beauty made her a natural target for romance. She was a tulip among the weeds of war. Although she had initially been overwhelmed at working with the likes of the prominent and educated Li Jianzhen, Li Bozhao, and Cai Chang and, as an actor, had needed reassurance from Cai before facing the Zunyi crowds, she had come into her own here, and one could detect the slight swagger of a blossoming star. Ephemeral though the crowd's love affair with her was, there was one whose heart was deeply smitten — Wang Shoudao, the twenty-six-year-old Ninth Army Group Political Department head and her boss on the *xuanchuan* team.[10]

Although the Reds had changed the traditional rules of courtship, making it a far less formal process, a matchmaker was still expected to introduce a couple to prevent any scandal, and the influential trio of Li Jianzhen, Cai Chang, and Ah Jin played that role for the two Wangs. On the surface, it appeared to be a good pairing. Wang Quanyuan and Wang Shoudao had worked together recruiting in Jiangxi. Both had been married before, and both had known more sorrow than their years justified. Four years earlier, Wang Shoudao's first wife had been executed by the Hunanese warlord He Jian.

The traditional wedding ceremony in China took place in the groom's family home and was simple enough. The couple stood at the family altar to its ancestors, usually a wooden plaque on a table, where family members burned incense and left offerings of fruit for the dead. The couple paid homage to the ancestors, and then the ceremony director, a family friend, led them in bowing to heaven, to the groom's parents, and finally to each other. That was all that was required. The bride and groom did not need to utter a word.

On the seventh night in Zunyi, with the formality of the "official" introduction out of the way and with the tacit approval of the Party leaders, Wang Quanyuan and Wang Shoudao — unsure of where they would be the next day let alone in a year — married, simply by spending the night together. If nothing else, they had found a way to keep warm and to boost the spirits of those who celebrated their union. It was also a way for Quanyuan to buffer herself against other suitors. Indeed, affection was hardly part of her calculation. "I didn't think about things like that back then," she later recalled. "We didn't think about romantic love. . . . It's not a bad thing to think about these things, of course, but we simply did not have that luxury." There was no point to it, she felt. They could be separated at a moment's notice, forced to leave any children behind. And indeed, the couple spent only one night together before orders came to decamp. They would not see each other again for three months, and, Quanyuan later admitted, they made love only three times before fate would end their marriage.[11]

Another notable romance took root more clandestinely. Li Jianzhen, Wu Fulian, the Cannon, Shorty Wei, and the small but strong nineteen-year-old Liu Caixiang, now nicknamed "Porter Girl," bunked together in a row on the floor of a building. After one breakneck day of *datuhao,* recruiting and rallying the locals, the women, minus Porter Girl, returned to their quarters. They ate dinner, soaked their feet, and prepared for bed, still without a sign of their roommate. One of them speculated that she had deserted, while the others argued that Porter Girl was deeply committed to the cause, pointing out that though young, she had already served as a provincial women's department director. They went to bed confident that she would soon return.

In the middle of the night, however, they woke and found that Porter Girl was still gone. Some of them became convinced that the hardships had driven her to desertion and decided to search for her. But Li Jianzhen was not so easily excited. Originally from a three-family mountain hamlet in Guangdong, she had seen much in her life since being sold as a *tongyangxi* at eight months old for eight coins (one for each month) to be the future wife of a carpenter's son. Half her eleven siblings had died in their youth, and all her sisters had been sold. "Go back to bed!" Li shouted. "Where do you search for someone in the middle of the night? If she has run away, no one will find her. If she's still here, she'll return. Let's deal with this tomorrow."[12]

After breakfast the next day, Li took Shorty aside and said, "Go to the Ninth Army Group and look for staff officer Bi Zhanyun. Ask him to return Porter Girl to us."

"Did she spend the night with Bi Zhanyun?" an astonished Shorty asked. After all, had the Red Army not posted the Three Prohibitions for all to follow? Those who were single were not allowed to date, those who were dating were not allowed to marry, and those who were married were not allowed to sleep together and have children. How could Porter Girl break these rules so audaciously?

Doubting that she would find Porter Girl, Shorty reluctantly walked to the Ninth's encampment. There she discovered Porter Girl and Bi seated on the ground talking intimately. Shorty saluted.

"Commander, Li Jianzhen has ordered Porter Girl to return," she announced, eyeing him with scorn.

"All right, Shorty," Bi responded. "She's coming." Perceiving a slight to Li Jianzhen's authority and forgetting her deference, Shorty shot back, "All right or not, you don't have a choice. You've violated military discipline." Bi chuckled at Shorty's pluck and began to go with them. Shorty stopped him with an angry verbal fusillade. "How can you, a commander, possibly fall in love now? How can you hurt us women? What'll you do if she gets pregnant? Leave her behind?"

Chuckling, Bi Zhanyun retreated. More questions were aimed at Porter Girl when they returned to the women's quarters. "Where were you last night?" began the interrogation, though by now everyone knew. Her head bowed, the teenager blurted out: "I had not seen him for so long. . . . I missed him very much. Now that the troops were in town, I thought we would not go anywhere for a while, so I . . ."

"Did you sleep with him?" the other women continued. "What if you are pregnant?" Porter Girl was speechless. "Think about what you have done wrong," the women concluded. To satisfy them, she vowed not to visit Bi at night again. However, Porter Girl and Bi would marry before the journey's end.

ON JANUARY 15 and for two more days, the Politburo, military directors, political commissars, and other leaders met in an upstairs room in the house where Deng Yingchao, Zhou Enlai, Kang Keqing, and Zhu De were lodged. "The Central Committee had called for an important meeting," Kang later recalled, and she had a premonition that this gathering would mark a turning point. She insisted on special security arrangements. "We must do all we can to ensure the safety of everyone attending this conference," she said.[13]

At the meeting, a "self-examination," the leaders lay blame for the crushing losses at the Xiang River and grappled for control of the Party. Having been on the outside since 1932 in all but his lofty title—Chairman of the Jiangxi Soviet—Mao had lined up several allies, and with the recent stinging defeats suffered under the leadership of Bo Gu, Zhou Enlai, and Otto Braun, he now had the leverage to maneuver his way into power.

The meeting was still going on in the afternoon of January 17 when a Nationalist airplane buzzed Zunyi, a clear sign that Chiang Kaishek's main forces were bearing down on the city. Some Red Army troops had already headed north and for several weeks had been testing the border of Sichuan province. Though they had not broken through, the moment had come to follow them. It was time for the march to begin again.

chapter 11

Little Devils

JANUARY 1935

Back in the mountains of northwestern Hunan, young Ma Yixiang knew nothing of the events in Zunyi. Winter had arrived and slowed life down. Ma had little to do but tend to the livestock and try to avoid beatings while fending for her own share of warmth and food. All fervently prayed for the arrival of spring. In the Communists Ma's mother now recognized the hope that Ma had seen, impressed that the Red women dressed like men and held jobs. At last, in the new year, she agreed to let Ma join the Red Army. "It's time for you to find a way out," she said, "so you won't be beaten to death."[1]

Liberation was not so easy, however. If Ma ran away from her parents' home, her in-laws could insist that her parents return the money they had received for her — money that had long since been spent. So Ma had to make a plan to escape from her in-laws' house and in the meantime return there and hope that she would not be punished too severely.

That hope was in vain. Her mother-in-law dragged Ma down to the government offices to file an official complaint against her. Although the Communists had installed new officials, this one, a former traveling puppet-show singer, showed old proclivities. Either unenlightened about new rules forbidding *tongyangxi* abuse or reluctant to run afoul of the old power structure in case things changed, he lectured Ma and vowed to catch her himself if she ran away again.

Ma's in-laws chastised her for having made off with a quilt when she ran away. (Although it had originally come with Ma and was made by her mother, she, like any *tongyangxi,* owned nothing.) Ma insisted that she had not taken the quilt, that she had run away empty-handed after being beaten. The family called her a liar and beat her some more. They then brought out a Buddhist idol and made her swear in front of it. When that failed to produce the desired confession, they decided to put her to a test. They told Ma that they were going to kill a cat and make her drink its blood. If she was lying, she would vomit. If not, she would be absolved.

That night while the others slept, Ma, who often worked late to finish her chores, chopped and combined the ingredients for the pig mash in a pot, fetched water, and climbed up on a stool to simmer the concoction on the stove. The thought of cat blood on her mind, she went outside and poured the mash into the barrel where it was stored. She left the gate ajar so that when she came down later, it would not creak. Then she went up to bed.

After a short, restless nap, she made her move. With a knife in her hand and the family dog by her side — a dog that she had raised from a puppy — Ma crept away from the house for a rendezvous she had arranged with her mother's cousin. A dog was a lowly companion (and sometimes a meal) to the Chinese, not an object of affection and doting, but Ma knew this one would protect her from any wolves she might encounter.[2]

Frightened and sweating, she finally reached the meeting place — the Red Army's execution ground, of all places — in the pitch dark. She coughed, but no one answered. She knocked a rock against a large stone. There was no reply, but several dogs began to bark. Suddenly worried that she might be caught, Ma lost her nerve. She bolted back home, her heart pounding all the way. She lay awake in bed until dawn. Later, she found out that the cousin had been involved in a *datuhao* raid and could not get away.

Ma's excursion went undiscovered, but her in-laws were unrelenting and told her that the next day she would face the cat-blood test. In the evening, Ma greased the door hinges to keep them from squeaking and waited while the others slept. As soon as the sky began to lighten, she snuck out. She did not head for home, the first place her in-laws would look, but instead ran up the mountainside toward the house of her aunt Peng, about three miles away. She did not bring the dog this time but carried a knife for protection. "If I met a wolf," she later said, "I would have had to use the knife to fight it. Otherwise, it would have eaten me."[3]

Descending the mountain, she crossed a marshy field to her aunt and uncle's house. She arrived as Peng was getting up. In her aunt's embrace, Ma unleashed a torrent of tears. Peng fed her breakfast, promised to help her join the Red Army, and departed.

Peng went to see friends she knew from her work leading the women's union. Ma was young for the army, her aunt conceded, but she was mature and used to hard chores. The officials agreed to interview her. One look, though, and it was all they could do to keep from laughing. Ma had been a sickly child — her only medicine incense ashes mixed with water — and was so puny that she looked even younger than her eleven years.

Soldiers had to be at least seventeen and able to march for days on end and to fight. Furthermore, though there were women in uniform, the army was not actively seeking them. No matter how much Ma pleaded — she would tirelessly collect wood, wash clothes, do all the chores — they refused to accept her.

But Peng did not give up. She kept Ma at her house and continued searching an opportunity for her. Before dawn one morning, Peng roused her niece and led her on dark paths to the Red field hospital. On the way, she instructed her to always work hard, to address those around her as "Aunt" or "Uncle," and to make sure to please them. When they arrived at the hospital, Peng cleverly offered Ma not as a soldier or a nurse but as a laundress. (Despite the talk of equality, here, too, gender roles remained traditional.) Hoping to strike a chord with the head nurse, Peng emphasized that Ma was an abused *tongyangxi*. The Reds opposed prearranged marriages. Surely they would come to the aid of this victimized girl.

The head nurse pointed out Ma's obvious defects, but Peng and Ma refused to take no for an answer. "Auntie, you can't let them beat me to death!" Ma pleaded. As they talked, a crowd gathered and began to rally around Ma. "We are fighting to free the poor," someone declared. "She is a poor *tongyangxi*. Let's liberate her." Finally, the head nurse relented. "All right, we'll see what we can do," she said. "But we'll have to send you home when there is a battle."

Because she was illiterate, Red officials helped Ma fill out the required forms. For all her courage, she cried when it was time to cut off her braid but submitted when they told her the alternative was to go home. Next she put on a flowered cotton-print outfit and a hat with a Red Star and bolted out to the well to see her reflection.

"What are you doing, Little Devil?" a passing officer asked her, using a common nickname for children and young women.

"Er, measuring how deep the water is?" Ma answered, turning red, embarrassed by her vanity.

Ma did not have long to bask in her new image. She was too busy trying to prove herself. When not doing the patients' laundry, she was building fires or preparing vegetables for the cooks. Ma worked so diligently, leaping intently from one chore to the next, never grumbling, that some of the soldiers told her to slow down, that she could not keep it up. But just as Ma had instinctively gravitated toward the Communists for her own preservation, she understood that the hard work that she could cheerfully provide would be her ticket to a better life. On the coming march, these instincts would serve her well.

In JANUARY, the young Twenty-fifth Army made its way into southern Shaanxi province. The soldiers and nurses had traveled more than six hundred miles from their base and eluded an enemy force twenty times their size — not to mention their own allies: in the upheaval of the troop movements, radio contact among the Communist factions had been lost, and none of the other Reds knew where they were.[4]

The Twenty-fifth prided itself on being flexible and resilient, and no one better represented these qualities than the seven nurses. Led by their head nurse, Zeng Jilan, and the male hospital director, Qian Xinzhong, they worked together not only as a medical team but as a support system against the rigors of the trail. They suffered in varying degrees from their once lilied, and for some still agonizingly deformed, feet. The process of *fangzu,* or "letting feet out," was a gradual and limited matter. As one influential female Chinese reformer declared in exasperation, "No magical pill can grow a new set of bones; a severed head cannot be reattached. If you insist on bending crooked feet into straight by force, you create something that is neither a horse nor an ass."[5] The bones had taken unnatural shapes. Sores created from flesh rubbing on flesh had healed and callused into hard knots. To ease the pain, the nurses took turns riding horses lent to them by the hospital leaders.

In Shaanxi, it rained a lot, and at night the Twenty-fifth marched rapidly on pitch-dark, slippery trails. The women succeeded in keeping pace as the army gained elevation, heading into the Qinling Mountains, a massive range lying south of the ancient capital city of Xian.

Known locally as the "greatest barrier under heaven," the Qinlings rise to more than 13,000 feet, high enough to create a climate divide: cold, dry winds buckle on its northern granite, while warm, wet breezes fade amid its southern crags. To the north, the weather is temperate; to the south, it is subtropical.

Through the range's peaks, five ancient routes connecting Shaanxi to Sichuan weave along *zhandao,* paths of wooden planks attached to the sides of sheer cliffs. In January, even the southern side of the mountains was covered in snow, and the rare giant pandas that inhabit the Qinlings had headed to lower elevations to graze on bamboo. During the day, the women trudged up the frigid slopes, and at night they cut down tree branches to sweep sleeping spaces free of snow, spread out their blankets, and huddled together for warmth. The thin gruel, though hot, did not go far. "The only way not to feel starved," Young Orchid joked with her friends, "is to have been starved enough times that you don't feel hungry anymore."[6] She had worn the same clothes since she had set out two months before. When her shoes gave out, she wrapped her feet in rags. When the troops eventually confiscated shoes from the wealthy for her, they were too big, so Young Orchid poked holes in the uppers and cinched them tight with vines.

Finally, on February 2, 1935, the penultimate day of the lunar year, the Twenty-fifth Army reached Gepai, an ancient town of wooden houses and stone fences on the Rice Soup (Mitang) River, about fifty miles southeast of Xian. More than half of the army had been destroyed, according to Zhang Guotao, and they had almost no ammunition left.[7]

Gepai lay in the jade-producing county of Lantian. Although its jade contained creamy streaks and was considered of an inferior quality, the jade industry was profitable and had brought the town above-average amenities. The Twenty-fifth sent several men dressed as merchants and street performers into town to investigate. They found Gepai undefended and the streets crowded with townspeople preparing for the lunar New Year festival. The next day, the Reds surrounded Gepai and took it over.

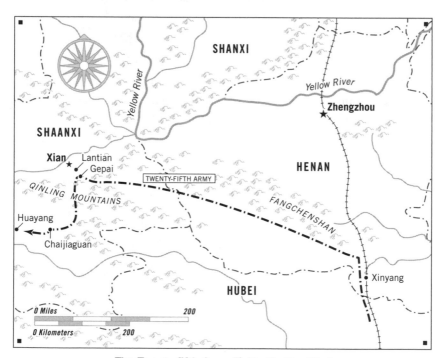

The Twenty-fifth Army Fights Its Way West

The Twenty-fifth needed shelter, time to regroup, and, ideally, a temporary new base. Young Orchid and the six other women performed skits for the locals, illustrating that they were the army of the poor and that the young villagers should join them. Many did. Young Orchid also continued to attend to Deputy Commander Xu, whose head wound still confined him to a stretcher. During a snowstorm on the morning of February 5, gunshots rang out as she was changing his bandage. Soon a messenger rushed to General Xu's side. The commissar was requesting Xu to command the battle. As soon as that messenger departed, another arrived with the same dispatch, only more urgent. Xu still could not walk well, but he told Young Orchid to bind his wound. With the support of four guards, he proceeded through the falling snow to the command post. Two battalions of Shaanxi troops were attacking them south of Gepai. Buoyed by the return of their military leader, the soldiers of the Twenty-fifth fought with new confidence, and by the afternoon they had repelled the enemy.

That night, the weather abated, and in the warm glow of victory and spent adrenaline, the Communists sat around the crackling fire in a jovial mood. Xu joked and laughed with the guards and nurses. All eyes were on him, including Young Orchid's. She was gratified by his high spirits and recalled his improbable conviction: "When I join the battle," he had said repeatedly, "I will recover from my wounds." Now she thought he was right: the fight had revived him.

Among the casualties the nurses had attended to was a light machine gunner they called "King Ironfeet," who had been wounded in the head. At one point, squad leader Zeng Jilan boiled two small pots of water to wash his feet. The nurses scrubbed away a crust of hard mud, revealing an awful sight: thick layers of calluses and dead skin covered the toes and soles of his feet, while cracks between his toes were split open, raw and oozing. King Ironfeet told the nurses that he had been barefoot the entire journey because his feet were too big for shoes. Zeng decided that the nurses should make a pair of shoes for him. She traced the outline of his feet on a piece of paper, and she and three other women stayed up all night fashioning the parts out of pig hide. The next morning, Zeng found a shoemaker in town to stitch together the largest pair of shoes any of them had ever seen. When King Ironfeet saw the shoes, he was speechless. Like so many of the marchers, he had endured a life with few instances of generosity and fellowship. There were simply no words to express the depth of his gratitude. For those at the top, the revolution was about Marx and Engels. For so many more, it was about moments like this.

After two days, King Ironfeet took his new shoes off and hung them on his back. When the women asked him why he was not wearing them, he told them he was saving them for the next battle. He would not have long to wait.

The Communists pushed on again. Eighty miles southwest of Gepai, they reached the town of Chaijiaguan, located in a heavily forested strategic pass beside 8,800-foot Bald Head Mountain (Guangtoushan). Chaijiaguan was only lightly defended, and the Twenty-fifth took it and settled in for a brief rest. Here the woes of the trail caught up with one of the seven nurses. Zeng Jilan suddenly fell seriously ill and died. The rest of the nurses were devastated. With the help of the hospital director, they bought her a fine coffin made of cypress, the scent of which repels animals while its resin slows the decay of the body. Zeng, who had helped save many lives, whose own life was one of extreme poverty and hardship, could now rest easy.

A few weeks later, they marched to Huayang, a town that lay on an ancient route through a narrow basin in the southern Qinlings. There they surprised and routed two Shaanxi regiments, and for his bravery King Ironfeet, shoes on his feet, was awarded a piece of red damask. He wasted no time in presenting it to the nurses.

chapter 12

A New Year

January–February 1935

On a cold day in mid-January, the First Army passed through the gates of Zunyi and set out for Sichuan, three days of hard marching to the north. They quickly found themselves hemmed in on three sides by rivers and enemy forces. While the Reds had been transforming Zunyi, Chiang Kaishek had been busy outside the walls, positioning troops along the Red (Chishui) River to defend crossings and to prevent the Communists from entering China's heartland. Closer to Zunyi, Chiang's soldiers and warlord militias lay in wait in every direction. Trapped, the marchers would spend the next three months—about a quarter of the entire *dabanjia*—wandering tortuously, groping blindly, and banging their heads against Chiang's ubiquitous walls.

From the start, harsh terrain and wet weather challenged the Communists as they headed north, slowing them down. By the time they reached Tongzi, about thirty miles from Zunyi, even the strapping Mao was coated in mud from slipping and falling. It would have been tempting to stop here for an extended stretch. Enriched by the opium trade, Tongzi offered Western-style houses, cars, and town comforts. But the central column had an unavoidable imperative now: to push on, to escape. The marchers paused for only a day to rest and then continued toward Tucheng, a strategic town on the east bank of the Red River, which forms the Guizhou-Sichuan border.[1]

As they made for the river, they dodged and fought not just local militia forces but also the better-trained and better-armed Sichuan Army, sent to prevent the Reds from entering their province. The two sides fought from village to village and battled for each strategic hilltop. Sometimes the Reds circled around, crossing and recrossing their own path. In the confusion, Shorty fell in with the advance troops. One day her unit collided with Ah Jin's. Enemy troops lay somewhere ahead, the locals warned. Ah Jin volunteered to act as a scout, but the commanding officers said that it was too dangerous for a woman. "Women draw little attention," Ah Jin argued. Now Shorty jumped in. "If Ah Jin's going, I am too," she said. "We can take care of each other." The commander consented, and they set out dressed as local women, with baskets on their arms.[2]

After they had gone about a mile, they stopped near a small abandoned hamlet, and Shorty scanned the hills. "There was no wind. The trees shouldn't have been moving," she later recalled, "but I saw trees moving and birds flying out of them." She suspected that enemy soldiers were hiding amid the vegetation. Shorty tugged on Ah Jin's sleeve and discreetly pointed. Ah Jin squatted down. Pretending to tie her shoes, she whispered, "We have to go back to report this at once." They nonchalantly turned around and went to relate what they had seen. Thus informed, the Red troops were able to clear the way, and Ah Jin and Shorty earned the admiration of their fellow soldiers.

The central column reached Tucheng (literally, "Mud City") in late January. Despite the Nationalists' efforts to brand the Reds as bandits who shared wives, the residents who remained in town admired the troops and did what they could to assist them, contributing their doors and bed boards for the tattered soldiers to sleep on in the frozen streets.

The marchers did not stay long. Near dawn on January 28, fighting commenced, and Guizhou and Sichuan forces quickly drove the Communists out of town. As the Reds, under the direction of Mao and Zhu De, retreated, Sichuan troops shelled them with artillery. Instead of making a clean break, Mao, eager for a morale-boosting counterpunch, reversed course, hoping to surprise and punish the two regiments in pursuit. His intelligence, however, was bad: not two but four well-trained Sichuan regiments hit his men like a battering ram.[3]

Mao radioed the First Army Group to come to the rescue, but they were twenty miles away. The Sichuan forces knifed through Mao's lines, captured an oak-topped knoll, and poured fire down on the confused Communists. Desperate, Mao and Zhu De ordered their personal guard regiment into battle, but it was too late. The Communists

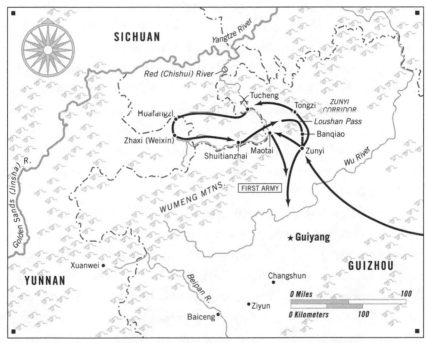

The First Army Pushes North to Sichuan Province from Zunyi and Returns

had to fall back. Rain-muddied paths added to the chaos. When hurrying and pushing turned to panic, some of the less seasoned soldiers and many of the hired stretcher-bearers abandoned their burdens and ran. The sick and wounded—as well as the women caring for them—lagged behind and were left to fend for themselves.

The women helped those on stretchers dismount amid a hail of bullets and artillery fire. The convalescents frantically lumbered away on foot, the enemy pursuing them, shooting as they advanced. Kang Keqing, among others, fired back.

Soon the women and their charges encountered a mud-walled embankment that many of them could not climb. Standing at the bottom, Porter Girl shoved the others up with her shoulders, one after another. Finally, she was the only one left. She jumped to reach the top of the embankment, but she could not make it. Above, the others had already moved on. Digging her fingers and toes into the mud, Porter Girl tried to scramble up. As she did, enemy soldiers closed within firing range and began to shoot. Bullets struck the embankment around her, one coming so near her head she could feel the percussion as it struck. Porter Girl frantically made a final leap. She grasped the top of the wall, hung there for a second, and then threw herself over. For a moment, she lay on the ground catching her breath. A dead soldier slumped nearby. Next to him was a backpack. She instinctively grabbed it as she leaped to her feet, running to catch up to her friends. When she reached the group, she discovered that she had picked up the Cannon's hastily abandoned pack.

The battle's toll was horrific, some 4,000 casualties. It was the Reds' worst defeat since setting out from Zunyi. While the engineers hurriedly constructed a floating bridge across the Red River, paving it with the doors and bed boards that the soldiers had slept on, the women, under Li Jianzhen, searched for houses for the wounded men. The bloodied soldiers often clung to them, weeping and begging not to be abandoned, even to be shot instead. Many locals had fled or hidden, so again the women were forced to deposit some of the men in unoccupied houses. Quite a few would die alone where they had been left.

Once the Reds crossed the river, they cut the ropes fastening the bridge so that the boards could be pulled back to the shore and returned to the houses they had come from. Having finally entered southern Sichuan, they faced another challenge. Local warlord Liu Xiang, allied with the Nationalists, had them pinned along the river. Short on ammunition, they had no choice but to march southwest along sheer river cliffs. All the while, they were under constant threat of ambush by the Sichuan forces.

There is no way to know for sure, since the Communists had no time to calculate the casualties, but Liu claimed that he killed more than a thousand Reds and captured hundreds of prisoners and weapons. The roads were in fact lined with Communist corpses, the victims of hunger, exhaustion, and wounds. The battered First Army slinked across the Yunnan province border into the mostly barren, destitute, malaria-infested region near Zhaxi (now Weixin). With the Reds' massive losses from disease, starvation, and battle, Liu and media sources would put the First Army's numbers at a scattered and disjointed 7,000. The losses were exaggerated, but still the mighty force that had set out from Ruijin was now starving and on the run. This was another low point of the journey. However, they managed to find light even in the wilderness: despite the freezing temperatures and snow, the soldiers reported coming across a vast orange grove belonging to a wealthy landlord and eligible for raiding. Here, on a "mountain golden with oranges," they ate until they could stomach no more.[4]

Chinese New Year's Day 1935 fell on Monday, February 4. The advance troops probably overnighted in Huafangzi, a village surrounded by ten small hills, while the others were still en route there. Normally, even the poor saved up for a New Year's feast. It was a day to court good fortune by hanging red banners with lucky sayings on doors, wearing red clothes, and giving money in red envelopes to children. It was a day to refrain from saying unlucky words, such as the number four (which in Chinese is a homonym for the word that means "death"); from cleaning the house for fear of sweeping away the wealth; and from washing one's hair and thus rinsing away good luck. It was a time to visit and wish family and friends a happy new year. But the fragmented First Army had neither the provisions nor the spirit to celebrate this most important of Chinese holidays.

For some of the marchers, feelings about New Year's were mixed, as the holiday had only ever emphasized their poverty. The Cannon's crippled father-in-law had been so poor that all the rice he harvested went to his landlord. He had also worked as an itinerant barber, and she had helped him, carrying his kit. Even though he was perpetually in debt, he always managed to save a little of the money he earned year-round to buy a New Year's meal—meat, bean curd, and a delicacy or two. The New Year's Day when the landlord's thugs had burst in and swept this meager feast off their table, chastising her father-in-law for his debts and leaving the family in tears, was a black one forever etched in the Cannon's heart.

The day after New Year's, the convalescent company, pursued by enemy forces, marched nonstop, covering more than twenty-five miles on winding mountain paths. All were exhausted by the time they stopped at Huafangzi at around six in the evening, and He Zizhen's pregnant body had absorbed all the punishment it could take. The women settled her into a mountain shack.[5]

That night, as rain pattered on the roof, He Zizhen went into labor. Nineteen-year-old Zhong Yuelin, who had never had a baby herself, was there to assist, along with a male doctor who would act as midwife. This being her fourth baby, He Zizhen did not need much help, and she delivered a baby girl before nine o'clock. Like other babies born in the year of the boar, her child was expected to possess inner strength, courage, and a passion for life. She would need them. Mao is said to have commanded his tearful wife to abandon the baby. He Zizhen could not have been surprised, though perhaps she had held out hope for an exception to be made. Such hopes were quickly dashed in the First Army. She handed the little girl over to her sister-in-law, who went out that evening with one of Mao's bodyguards to find the baby a home. The problem, as they soon discovered, was that everyone had fled, except for an elderly blind woman. The old woman objected to the idea of keeping the newborn, protesting that she was too old to nurse her. He's sister-in-law told the woman to feed the baby rice porridge and gave her ten silver dollars. Finally, the woman took the baby. He Zizhen would never see her little girl again.[6]

He Zizhen would also have to forgo her thirty days of recovery from childbirth, as the very next day, Wednesday, February 6, the Reds set out before dawn. This third day of the lunar year was traditionally "homecoming day," when daughters visited their parents with their husbands and children to eat a special meal together and catch up on each other's news. Homecoming day would always haunt Liao Siguang and He Zizhen and several others who would have to leave their babies along the trail. "After Liberation, many wanted to find their children," Liu Ying would later relate. "To no avail. Most of them were dead." Because of the war, most of the women had to wait many years before they had a chance to journey back to the remote villages where their children had been left. "Some found their children," said Liu. "They had been raised like peasants. They left them."[7]

The Reds inched on to Zhaxi the following day, where it was snowing and bitterly cold. "We were frozen and starving," Cai Xiaoqian later recalled. "We did not even have firewood for cooking." The convalescent company arrived the next day with some of the wives of the senior leaders. Cai noted that some of the wives could be "hard to deal with and full of opinion, and often quarrelsome." Still, he often found them good company. War stories, the leaders' secret spats, and even rumors about their sex lives were bandied about. "We joked around and had interesting conversations," Cai says. "The madams liked to gossip."[8]

On February 10, the Politburo reconvened. Afterward, the leadership called an assembly of the cadres. As they gathered in whispered anticipation, Little Sparrow noticed the rushed and somewhat dour setting—the absence of the fanfare, Party flags, and banners usually prominent at such assemblies. When Zhang Wentian mounted the stage, a tense hush fell over the packed benches. He cleared his throat and began his announcements. Five days earlier, he told them, he had been chosen to replace Bo Gu as general secretary. Otto Braun had also been demoted. Zhou Enlai, Wang Jiaxiang, and Mao Zedong would be taking over as the top military commanders, and Mao had been elevated to the secretariat of the Politburo. A buzz erupted from the crowd. These were big changes.

There was more. With forces arrayed to stop them from going north or west across the Yangtze, Zhang continued, they would now return to Zunyi to reestablish a base. This was good news. Their recent miles had been exacting and frustrating. The prospect of returning via the site of their recent defeat was appealing if only by comparison to staying in this cruel section of Yunnan.[9]

Although it was not immediately apparent to all, with the elevation of Zhang Wentian, Mao's former housemate and confidant, to the Party's most senior position, it was in fact Mao — the charismatic leader from Hunan, a man educated within China's borders — who had effectively slipped into the driver's seat. This was a sea change. Although Zhang was one of the Russian-influenced Twenty-eight Bolsheviks, his views were now in line with Mao's. The Twenty-eight Bolsheviks, also known as the Stalin Group, were out permanently, and the homegrown Chinese Communists were in.

Amid the reorganization, there was a change that would have an immediate impact on the women. Li Jianzhen, who had proven to be so adept at *datuhao,* had been asked to join the cadre convalescent company. It would be backbreaking work, but she felt strong and was willing to make the change, in part to be with the other women. "I'll go where the Party asks me to go," she had answered. In high spirits, she joined the convalescent company, expecting a warm welcome from Hou Zheng, its head. But Hou greeted her sourly, hissing through his nose, a Chinese expression of scorn. "Oh, you're here," he huffed.[10]

Li was taken aback. "Not everyone wants to work at the convalescent company, and this is how you treat me?" she thought but said nothing to Hou.

Hou added, "We have enough women here already." It was an inauspicious start to their partnership.

The next morning, the First Army pulled up stakes. With survival now the first priority, Mao ordered all unessential burdens to be left behind. Across rivers and up and down mountains, eight porters had lugged a wooden case that looked like a large coffin. Inside was an X-ray machine. "It's too heavy, and there's no electricity where we're going," Mao said. "If you carry such heavy things, the carriers will be tired to death." They buried it outside a peasant house in the hope of returning for it one day.[11]

They recrossed the Red River on February 18 and 19. Although they caught the Nationalists by surprise, they had to fight at the two river crossings they used, and they would not stop fighting until they retook Zunyi, further depleting their ranks. Trudging back across the Guizhou highlands, as rain poured down and paths turned into muddy streams, advance troops continued south.

Following these advance troops, the Central Committee and the convalescent company slipped and fell with regularity. Kang Keqing stationed herself at the rear to help any stragglers. She organized the weary into teams of three, with one of the three as leader, and ordered them to help one another. Backtracking even more, she eventually found herself among the stretchers and out of sight of the rest of the First Army.[12]

As night fell, the stretcher teams invited Kang to camp with them, but she preferred to catch up with the main body of the army. Although the rain had stopped, dense clouds blanketed the hills in milky gloom as the sun sank. Walking quickly, Kang moved along the narrow path, which glistened, she thought, "like a wet belt." As the shadows closed in around her, Kang felt for her gun. In a row of trees, pairs of worn-out sandals dangled hauntingly from the branches where Red soldiers had left them. As she passed, a whimper came from the shadows. Kang stopped in her tracks. Listening intently, she ducked behind a bush. Then she made out the form of a man, head bowed, sitting on the exposed roots of a tree. Kang stepped forward.

"Who are you?" she barked. "Why are you sitting here alone in the dark?" The man did not respond, did not even seem to hear her. She saw that he was a Red soldier, so she approached and shook him by the shoulders.

Finally, he looked up and said, "Director, it's me." It was Pan Kai-wen, General Zhu's bodyguard. Grasping Kang's hand, he explained that his foot had become grotesquely swollen. Using a cane, he had hobbled along in increasing pain. One of Zhou Enlai's bodyguards had helped him for a while until being called to assist Zhou. Pan had lagged farther and farther behind until he had collapsed under the tree, alone in the dark and in fear of being attacked by a tiger.

Kang slung his pack on her back and boosted him to his feet. "We'll make it to camp together," she reassured him. Pan's legs had seized up. Leaning on his cane, he stumbled forward. Arm in arm, they headed

Strategic Loushan Pass on the route between northern Guizhou and southern Sichuan.

up the path. "Director, I can walk on my own," Pan insisted, trying to shake off her grip. But Kang held on tight just the same.[13]

Warlord Wang Jialie had dispatched a division of 20,000 soldiers to meet the First Army. One of Wang's regiments stopped and secured the town of Banqiao, while the others proceeded to Loushan Pass, the choke hold of the Zunyi corridor. At the same time, the First Army approached the spectacular heights of the pass, where the road of packed earth and gravel that connected northern Guizhou and Sichuan could easily be controlled. For centuries, this narrow strategic pass between sheer forested peaks had been a battleground for warlords looking to dominate the region.

On the morning of February 26, the rivals—one to the south, the other to the north—reached the twelve-mile mark to the summit at about the same time, in the late morning. With heart-pounding strides, the trail-fit Reds powered their way to the top, arriving there first by a matter of minutes. By the time they overwhelmed a Guizhou outpost, took up positions, and prepared for a struggle, they could see Wang Jialie's forces sprinting up the southern slope. A savage battle ensued, lasting into the night. In the end, the Communists retained control of the pass, opening the way to the south.

THE COMMUNISTS WOULD tout the battle as Mao's first big victory and a watershed event. The following day, the marchers continued on to Zunyi, which advance troops were already in the process of retaking. Having recovered from childbirth, Liao Siguang joined an advance team of women who helped prepare the camp. When air-raid signals suddenly blared, the unit scurried for cover beside the road. Young officers Hu Yaobang and Luo Ming left their hiding places to help conceal the baggage, including green-and-red poster boards and oilcans, and several wounded soldiers who had been left on the roadside. Just then, the bombers roared in low to the ground and dropped their payloads. Both men were hit. Unconscious and bleeding, Luo was rushed to the medical unit. Shrapnel had ripped into eighteen-year-old Hu's right hip. Bleeding, he tried to get up and limp along. Xiao Yuehua made him get on her mule and secured him there with her blankets. He was then dispatched with all haste to Zunyi to see a surgeon. Little did Xiao know that she had just helped save the life of a future leader of China.[14]

Bivouacking in a small town seven miles north of Zunyi on February 27, the convalescent company bought food and began to prepare their evening meal around several fires. Suddenly, they got word to prepare to move out. The Third Army Group had retaken the city, and if the convalescent company hurried, they could sleep under a roof that night.[15]

They arrived in Zunyi to discover that much had changed. The reopened shops and warehouses had been looted again. The houses of merchants and landlords had been plundered. Some were boarded up, others partly destroyed. The slogans and posters that they had covered the town with were shredded or defaced. For some there was also heartbreak. Guizhou warlord You Guocai had taken revenge on those who had collaborated with the Communists, executing them and destroying property belonging to their families.

Red doctors quickly established a hospital in the Catholic church. One of the wounded regimental commanders was told by the doctors that he had to have his lower leg amputated. When he refused, Mao and Zhou Enlai sent Deng Yingchao to reason with him. She reassured him that he would not be abandoned and that he could keep his bodyguards. The commander consented to the amputation, which saved his life.[16]

The Reds wasted no time in trying to win back Zunyi's citizens. The morning after they arrived, Deng Xiaoping ordered the *xuanchuan* workers out on the streets. It was freezing, but they did not care. "We were all young and took to the streets spiritedly and happily," Little Sparrow later recalled. They repainted the damaged Red slogans and added new ones. At one point, they came upon General Secretary Zhang Wentian. He called to Little Sparrow, waved for her to cross the street, and asked her to come with him. Zhang was staying with Mao in a large house with a courtyard, but Mao had gone to the front line. While they sat in front of a wood fire burning in a basin, Zhang's guard boiled *laozao* (fermented glutinous rice) for them.

Zhang had first met Little Sparrow in Moscow, where he was her teacher. He admired her fine oval face, that of the traditional Chinese beauty, with its softly curved cheek and delicate jaw, conveying the feminine virtues of gentleness and inner strength. After an awkward silence, he proposed marriage to her.

Little Sparrow was taken aback. Though the prohibition had not been strictly adhered to—especially among the leaders—marriage was forbidden. "I respected Zhang Wentian a lot but had never thought about love," she said later, perhaps unaware that Zhang, who had been married to a Russian in Moscow, was a notorious womanizer.[17]

Little Sparrow was moved by his desire for her, but for now she resisted. "I have a plan for myself," she told him. "No marriage for five years." Marriage, she well knew, meant pregnancy and hardship on the trail, and a baby meant "abandoned flesh and blood."[18] Seeing He Zizhen and Liao Siguang suffer had convinced her to remain single and childless until the journey's end and beyond.

After a weighty pause, they talked about the fighting and the tasks at hand. Zhang dropped the subject of marriage, but he had not given up. He invited her to dinner. She responded that her superior was very strict and would not allow it.

The Communists' second stay in Zunyi was brief and precarious. The morning after the First Army recaptured the city, Nationalist troops counterattacked. The Reds held them off for several days and would later claim that they had outflanked and "annihilated" the enemy troops. In truth, the Communists were forced to abandon the city in haste shortly after they took it. On March 6, the convalescent company left Zunyi again, only a step ahead of the Nationalists.

The Reds' departure was chaotic. After tending to the wounded, some of the women had fetched a basketful of silver dollars and helped process the prisoners of war. They handed out travel allowances to released Nationalists so that they could make it back to their homes. Whenever possible, they tried to win over the prisoners, especially the wireless operators, doctors, weapons specialists, and others with technical skills. Enlisted men who changed sides were given three silver dollars each.

As Shorty busily handed out coins, she was approached by a white-bearded elder. "You and your friend must leave now," he whispered in her ear. "The enemies have entered the city."

"The Red Army is still in the city. How can the enemy come in?" Shorty replied.

"The Red Army left the city a while ago," he said. "Hurry and pack up. I'll show you the way they went."[19]

In her diligence to recruit new allies, Shorty had not noticed the absence of her comrades. She and her cohort scampered after their kind old guide, listening to the shouts and boot steps of the Nationalist soldiers as he led them through back alleys to the edge of town, where he pointed the way. They had to run more than three miles to catch up to the Red troops.[20]

chapter 13

Where the Han
Are Unwelcome

MARCH–APRIL 1935

Following their escape from Zunyi, part of the First Army ventured west again across the winding Red River, while others headed south to the Wu River. The Reds now felt a sense of desperation. They were not sure where to go, but all agreed that speed was of the essence.[1] Although the First Army was not recruiting women, eight female students, including the outspoken Li Xiaoxia, had joined the Reds. Because of her brashness, the Nationalists had killed her entire family. The Red Army would be her family now.

Still looking for a way to penetrate Sichuan province, the Communist troops that headed west occupied Maotai, a river town famous for its clear, fragrant liquor of the same name. Next to almost every house sat a large wooden vat with its own batch of fermented sorghum and river water aging inside. Some established families had vintages dating back a century, and the drink itself dated back eight hundred years. (Several decades hence, Zhou Enlai would serve it to President Richard Nixon.)[2]

Red soldiers inundated the town, sleeping on the streets and along the riverbank, bivouacking in the hastily vacated houses of the wealthy, and getting drunk on Maotai. In the well-groomed courtyard of the Yicheng Traditional Distillery, which contained a few dozen huge vats, the Reds doled out Maotai to the locals. Many of the soldiers did not know what it was. "This is excellent water for soaking feet!" one soldier declared. When Dong Biwu came to investigate, they said,

"Elder Dong, you have seen more than the rest of us. What is this magical water?" Dong furrowed his brow and shook his head: "This is no magical water, you silly kids. This is alcohol, precious Maotai!"

On the gates of the commandeered distillery Flying Fairy Maotai, they pasted posters saying:

THE RED ARMY ARRIVES AT MAOTAI
OPENS THE WAREHOUSE AND SHARES THE WEALTH.
WHILE THE TYRANTS TRY TO HIDE THEIR HEADS,
THE PEASANTS LAUGH HEARTILY.[3]

While Maotai provided some with a pleasant distraction, scouting parties determined that there was no promising route into Sichuan through the town. The First Army headed south toward remoter and safer regions, reaching the turbulent Wu River three months after having crossed it farther east on their way to Zunyi. They would attempt to cross it this time on three floating bridges made out of bamboo rafts, boards, and iron cables. Their load was made heavier by their Maotai booty: they had toted off as much of the liquor as they could carry. With medicine tightly rationed, the doctors and nurses largely controlled the supply of Maotai, using it to clean and numb wounds, to neutralize poison, and to cure colds and fevers. Indeed, "Maotai Is My Medicine" would become a popular Red Army song.

As THE REDS HAD MOVED, so too had Chiang Kaishek, personally carrying his anti-Communist and modernization crusade into the provinces. He campaigned against foot-binding, though he drew the line at women being able to choose their hairstyles. He even forbade his soldiers to marry women who bobbed, curled, or in any way "unnaturally" arranged their hair, which, he believed, "destroys a woman's health and beauty."[4]

With his fashionable wife Soong Meiling — one of the three famous daughters of the Chinese Methodist minister and Bible tycoon Charlie

Soong—by his side, Chiang had arrived in Guiyang, capital of Guizhou province, at the end of March to personally oversee the demise of the dwindling First Army. Aware of his presence there, Mao and his fellow leaders decided on a daring ploy. Instead of forging on, First Army Group commander Lin Biao, Mao's protégé, abruptly took the offensive, making straight for Guiyang and threatening Chiang's personal safety. Chiang countered by ordering the forces that were blocking the Reds' passage to redeploy in defense of Guiyang. This was as the Communist leaders hoped. While Chiang's forces moved to guard Guiyang, the First Army bypassed the city, crossed through the Wumeng Mountains, whose peaks rose up to 12,000 feet, and headed for Yunnan.[5]

The Nationalists now had major forces in Guiyang and in the Yunnan capital, Kunming. Nationalist forces that had fought the Reds at the Xiang River and pursued them ever since continued to push them from the rear. "The march increasingly resembled a retreat and eventually degenerated into outright flight," Otto Braun would

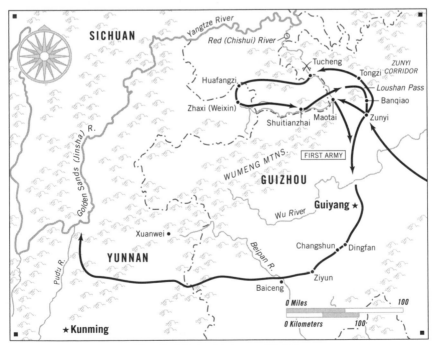

The First Army Makes an End Run

later note. They marched mostly at night because the Nationalist air force flew frequent bombing and strafing sorties during the day. "Especially insidious were the low-flying planes," Braun recalled. "Hugging the ground, they would rise up from behind an elevation without a sound, and immediately machine-gun fire would be raining down upon us."

One foggy morning, near the town of Chicheng, a bugled alarm sounded down the column, and everyone dove for cover. The convalescent company, with all the necessities of a traveling hospital — stretchers, mules, horses, medicine cases, and cooking gear hanging from shoulder poles — was one of the least nimble units. He Zizhen, Liu Qunxian, and their orderlies ran, stumbled, fell, got up, and kept running. Suddenly, a bomb exploded in the woods in front of them. Screams and curses filled the air. More bombs exploded nearby, and smoke choked the woods as cases of supplies burned. "Limbs dripping blood hung in trees," recalled Cai Xiaoqian.[6]

Though it felt like an eternity to the victims, the airplanes soon flew away, leaving an eerie silence broken by moans that sounded distant but were merely muffled by ringing eardrums. Those not hurt too badly scrambled from their shelters to triage the wounded, who writhed on the ground, some disfigured beyond recognition.

Finally, a bugle blew, assembling the troops. Gathering, the shocked convalescent company speculated on what had made them the target. "It must be because the cooking squad did not conceal their load in time," said several of the women. "No," argued others. "It was because of the old groom Huang. He was still running around with the horse when the airplane arrived." But, as Cai observed, at this point "neither assumption nor complaint was useful." They had been discovered and had paid a high price.[7]

Recovering, the First Army occupied the towns of Dingfan, Changshun (now Changzhai), and Ziyun, a small community of about three hundred houses, where the convalescent company stopped for a day. The women helped with *datuhao,* distributed clothes and food to locals, and recruited. In a tailor's shop, they found and confiscated two hundred Guizhou army uniforms, which would come in handy later.

The marchers continued on toward the Beipan River, nearing a village called Baobaoshu. Walking for hours, they saw no one. Then suddenly gunshots rang out. Whistles shrilled from the hilltops, identifying the combatants as Yi, an agrarian people found primarily in the mountains of Guizhou, Yunnan, Sichuan, and northwestern Guangxi. The Communists, ethnically Han Chinese, had hoped to avoid fighting the Yi, who were known to be fierce, slave-holding, and Han-hating. Now, forced to defend themselves, they had no choice.

The two sides exchanged fire for about an hour before the Reds secured a defensible hilltop where they could camp safely for the night. The next day, they captured a Yi sentry and gave him a conciliatory letter to deliver to his chief. After a while, an emissary came out, bowed, and apologized for the hostile reception. Others brought the marchers water as a sign of friendship.

The Reds stayed that night inside Baobaoshu's mud walls, where there was a school and a small church. The villagers, fascinated by their Han visitors, invited them into their homes, which were decorated with the women's embroidery and lacquer paintings. The Yi served *sandao* (three-taste) tea, in rounds of three — *yingbin* (for welcoming guests), *xuku* (for confiding hopeless thoughts), and *sanmen* (for dispelling boredom). The Yi also drank wine, sitting in a circle and passing it in a goblet made of an ox horn and an eagle claw.

Fifty arduous miles across two foggy mountains and through dense forests of kapok, lacquer, tea, and dragon spruce trees brought the Reds to Beipan, the realm of a Yi warlord called Commander Wang, who owed his allegiance to the Nationalists. Yet when the marchers sent envoys to meet him, Wang proved to be practical, guaranteeing the Reds safe passage through his territory and providing them with a guide and supplies of pork, mutton, and buckwheat as long as they promised to assist his army and not tax or recruit while in his domain.[10]

Similar deals were cut at the Beipan River, which the marchers crossed by boat, primarily at the town of Baiceng, known for its bustling commercial wharf, through which cotton, cloth, and kerosene moved north while opium, tung oil (a wood sealer pressed from the nuts of the tung tree), and herbal medicine went south.

Near Pig Field—a town named after the Chinese zodiac symbol corresponding to the village's annual gathering—close to the Yunnan border, the convalescents took another blow. "It was late afternoon," recalled Liao Siguang, who had narrowly dodged the attack at Loushan that had felled Hu Yaobang and Luo Ming. "We thought the enemy's fighter planes would not come, so we took off early." Three miles from camp, they stopped for a break, setting down the stretchers without taking the usual precaution of tucking them in under the cover of trees. Amid the horses, stretchers, soldiers, and orderlies, He Zizhen and Xie Fei, a twenty-one-year-old female soldier who was known for once having destroyed secret documents by eating them, dozed on the grass beside the road. Suddenly, a lone plane swooped down on them with its machine guns blazing. He Zizhen bolted for cover, while Liao Siguang dove to the ground and crawled between two rocks, badly scratching her hands and face in some briars. Slowed by her formerly bound feet, Yang Houzhen, the twenty-seven-year-old wife of the Ninth Army Group commander Luo Binghui, was hit, as were several men. The plane circled around and again bore down on the group. As He Zizhen ran to help a one-legged general named Zhong Chibing, the plane released its explosive payload. She instinctively leaped on top of Zhong to protect him. Shrapnel tore into her body.[8]

As the plane soared away, those hidden emerged to assess and assist. Seven men had been killed, and He Zizhen was unconscious and apparently mortally wounded. The shrapnel had hit her in seventeen places, gashing her right shoulder; penetrating her chest, arms, and legs; and slicing open her skull. For several days, a doctor probed her body for shards of steel. He removed what he could, dousing the wounds with iodine. Mao visited his wife and encouraged her to endure. He assigned his own litter bearers to carry her. In her waking moments, He Zizhen begged to be left behind to die.

To make matters worse for the convalescent company, its chief, Hou Zheng, now became incapacitated. The continual slog through mountainous territory had worn the skin off his feet. This was a common injury among the marchers, and Hou had paid little attention to it, continuing to walk while using his horse to carry his baggage. But his feet had become dangerously infected and were now so swollen that he was unable to walk. A Political Department official recommended that he be left behind. Li Jianzhen vehemently opposed this. Hou, a male nurse who had risen through the military ranks to become a captain before being trained as a doctor in the Red Military Medical School, had both combat experience and medical expertise. Under attack, he could lead the guard in defending the company, and once the fighting was done, he could operate on the wounded. Li was incredulous that they would even consider leaving him behind. Besides, the wound was not life-threatening.

When Li came to Hou's defense, the harsh official peppered her with questions: "Can you guarantee that he'll recover in just a few days? Can his horse take him all the way to the destination? With his injury, he can't perform his duty as the head of the company. Can you take responsibility for that?"

"I can't say when he'll recover, but we'll help him and speed it up," she responded. "If his horse dies, he can ride mine. If mine dies too, I'll carry Hou on my back." But the official remained unconvinced. Realizing that it was futile to argue any further, Li turned to Cai Chang, who had persuaded the reluctant Hou to lead the convalescent company in the first place. Cai spoke to her husband, Li Fuchun, who, as head of the Political Department, ordered that Hou not be left. Hou rode the horse for a few days, and his feet healed.[9] The women's intervention quite possibly saved his life.

IT WAS EARLY APRIL, a time of sunny weather and thus the Qingming (Clear, Bright) Festival, when villagers traditionally visited their ancestral graves to pay homage to and commune with the dead. They would sweep and weed around the family tomb and offer food, wine, tea, and prayers to their ancestors, who were believed to visit the living regularly and could protect them and bring them good fortune.

As the Red columns advanced through a variety of small towns in the toothed mountains of the Guizhou-Yunnan border, they might have been mistaken for the dead returned. The rigors of the trail punished them worse than ever now. Stony paths led them up and down barren mountains. While the mules managed to keep their footing, many horses fell and broke their legs. Running out of provisions, the soldiers carved off slices of raw meat as they passed the fallen horses, until the animals were reduced to skeletons.[11]

Hunger, fatigue, and disease were constant now, and the precipitous trail vexed many of the wounded. Before they could cross Qipan Mountain and enter Yunnan, it became apparent that Xie Xiaomei's husband, Luo Ming, tormented by his Loushan Pass wounds, could go no farther. Xie herself had fallen ill, and it was decided that she should remain with him. It was a heartbreaking decision. Having logged nearly 2,000 miles across southern China in less than six months, Xie left her friends at what would turn out to be the halfway point of the Long March. A local Communist partisan led the couple away. Two days later, the three were arrested by provincial authorities and imprisoned.[12]

The exit of Xie, the first woman of the First Army to have to leave the *dabanjia,* was a sad milestone. For the remaining twenty-nine, the experience and toughness they had gained on the trail had started to show in their confidence and even in official promotions. Around this time, Little Sparrow received a written message. Opening it with curiosity, she was stunned by what she read: Deng Xiaoping, head secretary of the Central Committee, had been reassigned. "Comrade Liu Ying," the note read, "the Central Committee has decided that you will take Deng's place." Little Sparrow mounted her horse and proceeded to the Political Department, but not without misgivings. It was known that Party leaders sometimes wooed would-be lovers through promotion.[13]

At the Political Department, a collection of tents like all the department headquarters, she found Li Fuchun, who had signed the message. "I'm only a local-affairs worker unqualified to be a secretary," she insisted. Having studied in Moscow and headed the Hunan Women's Department, Little Sparrow was, in fact, highly qualified. But even in Communist China, self-effacement remained a necessary trait, especially for women. Beyond that, Little Sparrow wanted to confirm that her skills had recommended her.

"You can do it, Little Sparrow," Li reassured her. "Someone will help you." She found out from Mao that it was he who had suggested her for the position. "The local work is too heavy and intense for you," he reasoned. "Here, you only have to take care of several of us." Still, as Little Sparrow assumed the responsibilities of the prestigious position — handling logistics for the Party leaders, supervising their guards, and recording the minutes of their meetings — Zhang Wentian, denied once, ramped up his pursuit of her, even lending her his fine calligraphy pen to record the minutes.[14]

WITH AN AVERAGE ELEVATION of 6,500 feet, Yunnan — China's southwesternmost province — was even more mountainous than Guizhou, making it harder for Nationalist planes to operate there. Having a subtropical climate, it was also China's lushest region, with dense forests and more than half of the country's 30,000 plant species and crops of rice, wheat, barley, corn, and cotton. Still, though the province provided good cover from air attacks, the First Army had difficulty provisioning here. The problem was that the locals had given over their fields to their chief cash crop, opium. "Everywhere the eye looked," Otto Braun lamented, "poppies swayed in the wind." Easily divided and durable, raw opium was the area's chief medium of exchange.[15]

Bordering on Myanmar, Laos, and Vietnam, far from the Han centers of power, Yunnan was also traditionally a place of banishment. Here two more of the thirty Long March women fell by the wayside. In order to accelerate the First Army's progress, its leaders had decided to leave behind two hundred soldiers, about half of whom were wounded. The hope was that they would unite Communist partisans operating on the Sichuan-Guizhou-Yunnan border into a guerrilla force capable of distracting the Nationalist troops pursuing the First Army. Li Guiying was ordered to stay behind with her wounded husband, Dai Yuanhuai. Han Shiying was also told to stay behind. She was from a wealthy Sichuan family, and her feet had been bound when she was younger; her movement was still somewhat hampered from the damage done.

The two women soon found themselves instrumental members of the guerrilla force, numbering about a thousand, organizing, fighting, and routinely running more than thirty miles a day to avoid clashes with stronger forces. "It was harder than the Long March," Li Guiying later judged.[16]

Hoping to find a place to cross the upper Yangtze River and to pass through the province quickly, the First Army divided into two. While a diversionary group approached Kunming, the capital of Yunnan, the main force moved along the Guizhou-Yunnan border, fending off Nationalist-allied forces along the way. The Red Army continued to lose enlisted men to disease and desertion even more than to enemy bullets, but according to Chen Yun, the Reds managed to recruit thousands of new soldiers in the Yao region.

At sunrise one late-April day, outside Kunming, the convalescent company moved out just as Nationalist attack planes dove down to strafe and bomb them. Soon ground forces also attacked. Red soldiers at the rear absorbed the offensive, but the buffer they provided grew increasingly thin.

Two women, Chen Huiqing and Liu Qunxian, were now in mid- or late-term pregnancy and struggling to keep up. In the midst of the fighting, Chen, a twenty-five-year-old originally from Guangdong, cried out in pain. Security chief Deng Fa, her husband of five years, had recently tried to get her to remain behind with a Han family, but Chen had refused. She did not speak the local dialect and did not trust the people, who she felt would betray her. Now she was going into labor. The convalescent company leaders Dong Biwu and Hou Zheng and the doctor who had helped deliver He Zizhen's baby were summoned. Porters carried Chen into a roadside hut. The doctor attended to Chen while Dong and Hou waited outside. Writhing in pain on the floor, Chen bitterly maligned her absent husband. Hearing this, Dong and Hou sent a messenger to fetch him. Deng rushed to the hut, but there was little he could do to help.

As the battle raged outside and bombers flew overhead, Chen's child refused to be born. Chen grew weak with exhaustion. The doctor paced the room fretfully, while Hou, outside the hut, anxiously asked Dong to move Chen to a safer location. "Don't panic," Dong answered. "Let's see if she can give birth now." He sent a messenger to the Fifth Army Group commander, telling him that a comrade was giving birth and that he must hold the line for her. The commander coolly responded that their comrade could take her time.

Two hours later, at almost eleven o'clock, Chen delivered a baby girl. Semiconscious, she held the baby in her arms only briefly before the porters were ordered to resume carrying her. The doctor wrapped the infant in an old shirt and placed her in the shanty along with a few silver dollars and a note. Then the men hurried on their way.[17]

Around the same time, twenty-seven-year-old Commander Lin Biao's First Army Group was threatening Kunming. As they approached the capital city, the Reds recruited impoverished villagers, many of whom had bowl-size goiters on their necks due to a lack of iodine in their diet. In one small community, the Health Department issued an urgent warning: "The water at this place contains miasma; it's poisonous." As a precaution, Red teams boiled and distributed drinking water while they were there.

This was the heart of spring in lush Yunnan, with green bananas sprouting on trees growing among the rice paddies and medicinal herbs shooting up in the forests. Among the Reds' most coveted acquisitions would be Yunnan Baiyao, or "White Medicine." Introduced in 1902 by the Yunnanese doctor Qu Huanzhang, the remedy's potency in healing sores, broken bones, and even gunshot wounds was legendary, as was its discovery. While picking herbs in the woods one day, Qu had observed a fight between two snakes. The loser slithered into a patch of weeds, where it rolled around. After a while, its wounds were miraculously healed. When the snake left, Qu examined the plants and determined that they had coagulant properties. He combined his discovery with other herbal medicines to create what he called "Powder of One Hundred Treasures," which was later renamed Yunnan Baiyao, based on its color. The medicine came in two forms, a powder for both internal and external use and a small pill, which some believed was magic.[18]

The Yunnan Baiyao given to the convalescent company was said to have been captured from a Yunnan warlord, Long Yun, who had loaded it onto a truck after a pilot got sick and had to cancel a planned airdrop. But it was more likely a gift from Long to help speed the Communists on their way. A few dozen military maps were also part of the shipment, and they provided the Communists with accurate route information, something they sorely needed to make their exit. Now they were at last ready to run north to the Golden Sands (Jinsha) River, the natural barrier between Yunnan and Sichuan.[19]

chapter 14

Dead Child

Far off in his northern Sichuan stronghold, Zhang Guotao, political commissar and overall leader of the Fourth Army, tracked the First Army's movements by two-way radio. His communications with the Central Party leadership had been tenuous for some time, and he had been surprised when the Jiangxi Soviet was abandoned six months earlier. Now, as the First Army moved west of Zunyi, he began preparations to leave his stronghold and move his 90,000 soldiers—including a regiment of 2,000 women—west to join it.

Zhang had more fully integrated women into his army than any Chinese general ever had. He had created the women's fighting force, he said, "in order to satisfy the demands of the women," whose "stamina was no less than that of the men." Zhang Qinqiu, a twenty-eight-year-old woman, had briefly been head of his political department, giving her the highest Party position held by any woman during the revolution. Although she had quickly been demoted after criticizing Zhang Guotao, she now commanded the Women's Independent Regiment. In addition to this regiment, another seven hundred women worked in the hospitals, several hundred filled the ranks of *xuanxuan* and manufacturing units, and five hundred formed the Women's Transport Battalion, which would be entrusted with much of the army's treasury. Each of these sturdy peasant women carried a pack stuffed with sacks of gold and silver coins and weighing nearly sixty pounds.[1]

For Zhang Guotao, forsaking this new stronghold, which he had sacrificed so much to attain, was a major decision. Having been driven out of Eyuwan in the summer of 1932, he had left behind the young, the old, and the infirm, either in the ranks of or protected by the Twenty-fifth Army, and they had subsequently been pummeled by the Nationalists. Zhang Qinqiu had left without her husband of seven years, Shen Zemin, a member of the Central Committee and their representative in Eyuwan, because he had been ill (and, in fact, died there shortly afterward at the age of thirty-three). She and Zhang Guotao and 16,000 soldiers had fought their way 1,600 miles across three provinces in three months. Only 9,000 survivors had reached the remote mountains of northeastern Sichuan, where they had discovered a small but potent local band of Communists. The group, known as the East Sichuan Guerrilla Force, under Wang Weizhou, controlled much of the countryside of eastern Sichuan. In October, Wang had coordinated the combined Red forces in a pincer attack that routed ten warlord regiments at Xuanhan.[2]

The day the Red Army captured the town, Wang Weizhou's ten-year-old niece, Wang Xinlan, squeezed in among the crowd of people watching and cheering the soldiers. The youngest of eight children, Wang came from a wealthy, educated family. Until recently, they had resided with her uncle on a hereditary estate with two gates in the courtyard wall, one for each family. The courtyard was full of fruit trees, and the house was surrounded by bamboo forests, fields of roses, and a large pond. But under her liberal-minded relatives, the estate had become a Communist haven, where clandestine meetings took place.[3]

According to Zhang Guotao, his soldiers looked like beggars, each wearing "filthy rags," shaggy-haired, unshaven, "dusty and deeply tanned."[4] To Wang Xinlan, they were an astonishing sight. Her eyes went especially wide when she saw women dressed as soldiers, in military uniforms with pistols hanging on their hips. They looked strong and beautiful.

Within a few days, the ranks of the East Sichuan Guerrilla Force swelled from 2,000 men to more than 10,000, many fleeing the local

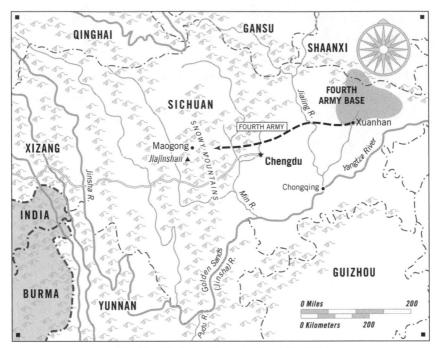

The Fourth Army Moves to Meet the First

coal mines. The Fourth Army commanders decided to incorporate the guerrilla force into the Fourth, keeping Wang Weizhou as its commander. Xinlan and her next-older sister, Xinguo, carried red flags to the rally celebrating the establishment of the new division, whose ranks included their two brothers and a brother-in-law. Fireworks and the sound of gongs and drums filled the air as the soldiers filed past flag-draped buildings, many festooned with slogans in red paint. Farmers presented clean-shaven pigs to the soldiers and chanted: "Down with landlords!" "Abandon feudalistic ways!" "Build the Red Army!" Eager to see her brothers in their Red Army uniforms, Xinlan searched the crowd, but she found neither. They were already on guard duty, east of Xuanhan.[5]

Having secured the area, the Fourth Army turned its focus to local concerns, introducing better hygiene and herbal medicine to a populace "used to relying on deities, fortune tellers, and opium," according to Zhang Guotao. Cases of dysentery, malaria, cholera, flu, venereal disease, and eye disease packed Red Army hospitals as quickly as they could be established. Recruiters made the most rapid strides among the local women, who did not use opium and were anxious to improve their lot. A thousand handpicked women helped the hospital take care of the army's sick and wounded. A newly formed chapter of the Women's Federation sewed clothing, delivered food, and did defensive military work, standing guard, digging trenches, and building breastworks. When the Communists decided to establish an independent women's force — the first of its kind in the Red Army — recruits poured in.[6]

A few days after cheering on the Red troops in Xuanhan, Xinguo enlisted and donned an octagonal cap with a red star. Xinlan followed her older sister and her comrades around all day, learning how to sing army songs and write slogans. Finally, Xinlan prevailed upon Xinguo to help her enlist, and Xinguo took Xinlan to the Political Department, where the director looked her over. Little more than four feet tall, with rosy cheeks and a short, boyish haircut, Xinlan wore a long dress with a mandarin collar, looking the schoolgirl that she was. Nonetheless, she came from a notable revolutionary family, and she had attended school and studied dancing from the age of five. The director assigned her to a *xuanchuan* team. Xinlan giddily donned her own red-star cap.

Xinlan's elders on the *xuanchuan* team taught her how to read music and play the *xiao* (a vertical bamboo flute) and the drums. Since she was the only one who had studied dance, Xinlan instructed the others in it. Full of charisma and a favorite of her comrades, who chose her to be the announcer at performances, her star quickly rose. Soon everyone knew Xinlan.[7]

One day, after a morning spent rehearsing a new dance, she returned to the dorm room she shared with her sister. Xinlan found a note on her bed. "Little sister," it said, in Xinguo's beautiful handwriting, "I have been transferred to the provincial committee. I do not have time to say goodbye, but take good care of yourself from now on." Xinlan had never been separated from her sister before. Holding the note in her hand, she cried.[8]

Xinguo had no idea how careful her sister would need to be. A Party purge was soon launched, and although the Wang family were stalwart Communists, they were also wealthy intellectuals and a potential challenge to other Red leaders. Xinlan and her uncle, Wang Weizhou, would escape harm, but the rest of her family would be persecuted. In fact, unbeknownst to Xinlan, her teenage brothers, Xinmin and Xinzheng, had already been executed in the brutal purge, their chief offense being that they were the sons of a wealthy man.

At around the same time, Xinguo, who had been transferred from the Fourth Army to the provincial committee of Sichuan and Shaanxi, was secretly accused of belonging to the Anti-Bolshevik (AB) League, a group started by the Nationalists in Jiangxi in 1926 that quickly fizzled but lived on as a Communist bugaboo. Fearful that AB spies had infiltrated their ranks, the Reds purged anyone who came from a wealthy family or had any Nationalist relations. Shortly thereafter, Xinguo vanished.[9]

In February 1935, Wang Xinlan set out westward with the Fourth Army to rendezvous with the First Army.[10]

While waiting to cross the Jialing River, she stood on the riverbank carefully watching the soldiers stream by, hoping to catch a glimpse of her brothers or her sister Xinguo. Xinlan was nearly — or perhaps even already — an orphan. Her father was dead, and her ailing mother, to whom she had recently said farewell, lay dying in a house near their family home in a nearby village. Xinlan had seen much death in her short turbulent life. A major cause had been a dysentery epidemic that had swept through her region, filling the hospitals and, on the worst day, killing 170 patients. Two hundred herbalists had died while treating the afflicted.[11]

When a soldier who looked just like Xinlan's brother Xinmin, whom she had not seen in more than a year, walked by, Xinlan anxiously jogged up behind him and called his name. The soldier and several others turned and stared at her. When Xinlan realized it was not her brother, she stood staring blankly and almost started to cry. The soldiers walked on, laughing.

In a late March downpour, the Fourth Army crossed the wide

Jialing River in seventy-five small boats. When a soldier punting one of the nine-person boats was shot and killed, a nineteen-year-old female soldier named Shi Moyu grabbed the pole and continued to guide the boat. As they neared the shore, Shi was also shot. The bullet hit her in the stomach. She managed to secure the wound with her belt and navigate the boat to shore before collapsing dead.

Now, as Xinlan sat in a boat crossing the Jialing, with guns and artillery booming in the distance, her trademark perkiness faded. The members of the *xuanchuan* team did their best to comfort her.[12]

East of the Jialing, the Fourth Army took the steep mountain pillars of the Gate of Swords Pass (Jianmenguan), a vital landmark on the ancient route linking Sichuan and Shaanxi. (It was said that one man in the pass could hold off 10,000 men trying to take it.) Although performing had come easily to Wang Xinlan, keeping up with the Red column's scorching pace on the march did not. To avoid lagging behind, she sometimes joined other soldiers roped together at their shoulders. If one fell, the others would pull him or her up, and together they would continue.

About two weeks after leaving home, Xinlan grew weak and feverish. She could not walk without a stick. She knew she must not flag, or the others would have no choice but to abandon her. Nevertheless, her energy continued to wane, and her stomach ached. Soon she had diarrhea and headaches.

Little Xinlan had contracted typhoid fever. A bacterial disease spread by poor sanitary conditions and bad hygiene, which were givens on the trail, typhoid was potentially deadly, known to sometimes kill even the sturdiest of people in just three weeks.

Xinlan lost her appetite and grew weaker by the day. One morning she struggled for about three miles and then collapsed. There were no extra stretchers, but she was small and had many friends. Constructing a makeshift litter out of tree branches and rags, they took turns carrying her. But day after day, Xinlan did not improve. She was feverish and barely able to eat; her already tiny body grew thinner and thinner. By the time the Reds reached western Sichuan, she was in the third week of the disease and had entered the "typhoid state," lying motionless, eyes half-closed, her body fighting off death, and sometimes sinking into delirium. A ghost of the vibrant child she had been, Xinlan lost her hair and eyebrows and did not respond when spoken to.

One day the cook brought her food, felt her head with his hand, and said softly, "I'm afraid this girl can't live."[13] Desperate, one of her friends chewed the food for her and slowly fed it to her.

United in their determination to save Xinlan, her friends managed to keep her alive. A month and a day after she was stricken, as if by magic, she opened her eyes. Her fever had waned. The disease had lost its grip.

Xinlan was not, however, out of danger. While she was recovering from her illness, she became the target of an investigation. Some security officers, on a campaign to eliminate counterrevolutionaries and perhaps knowing her background, suggested that the sick girl be left behind. She was, they claimed, a burden that the busy *xuanchuan* team did not need. When the director of the Political Department of the Fourth Army heard this, he hurried over. "The girl is a talented performer," he said. "A good performance plays a great role in inspiring soldiers' spirits. No matter what the difficulties, do not abandon her, or you'll be punished."[14] The director, who would later marry one of Xinlan's friends and go on to become one of China's top generals, had saved her.

For more than a month, Xinlan rode in a litter, over the most rugged terrain any of them had ever seen — a jagged land of rocky, overgrown slopes. The rivers here were "rapid torrents," according to Zhang Guotao, and as they approached Sichuan's Lifan County, just east of the Snowy Mountains, they faced a "vast primeval forest where timber felled by the lumber companies that were run by the Sichuan warlords . . . lay crisscross on the ground, waiting to be plunged into the rivers" (p. 374). Obstructions and flooded roads made the going very slow. It was hard to be carried on the stretcher. The path was tortuous and uneven, and the stretcher-bearers, thin and weak as they were, often stumbled. Xinlan understood that she was a burden and hated it. Again and again, she begged to be left behind.[15] Her fellow *xuanchuan* team members only laughed and told her that they could not leave her because they wanted to see her dance again. That would be their reward.

Despite its remoteness, a number of Western missionaries had reached the region. The market towns all had Christian churches. A Western priest was in charge of Lifan's large stone chapel, which had an apiary, fields under cultivation, a barn full of corn, and imported apples, wine, liquor, and even Sunkist oranges from California. The priest, however, had fled.[16]

Gradually, Xinlan began to eat, and the color returned to her face. By the time they reached Lifan, she could sit up.

The Fourth Army hoped that it would soon join ranks with the First Army and the Party leaders. Both armies were staking a lot on this rendezvous. Morale was deeply invested in the belief that the sum of their parts was not merely greater than the whole but would be their mutual salvation.

*

WHILE WANG XINLAN found herself cared for beyond her expectations in the Fourth Army, back in He Long's Second Army Group, still in Hunan, eleven-year-old Ma Yixiang struggled for acceptance. Her experience had started off relatively well. Two months earlier, when her harsh mother-in-law had stormed into the hospital to find her, Ma had been so terrified that she had hidden under a bed. The hospital director finally had to insist that she come out and defend herself or be sent home. In front of the Red officers, Ma's mother-in-law castigated her as insolent, stubborn, and rebellious. Ma told the officers that the family beat her, fed her only scraps, and called her "Miserable Devil." "I would rather die than go back with you," she shouted. "You'll only beat me to death anyway!" The officials sent the mother-in-law off with a scolding.[17]

Ma had quickly bonded with her new "aunts" and "uncles" at the hospital and felt secure with them. She ignored their warning that they would send her home as soon as the fighting started, even though her first experience with the wounded frightened her terribly: a soldier who had been shot in the mouth was swaddled in so many bandages that he looked like a mummy, his eyes and the hole for his mouth all that she could see. Indeed, when Ma first glimpsed him, she bolted in horror. The next time, she started to dash away, but he grabbed her arm. "How can you be a revolutionary," he croaked, "if you're afraid of a wounded soldier?"

Ma had been part of the Second Army Group for two months now. They were on the move, and the eleven-year-old was determined to prove to her coworkers that they should keep her. Her first indication that the Second Army Group was preparing for battle came when the hospital started transferring the severely wounded into village homes. Then an order came for Ma to go home herself. She refused. Instructed to report to the official who had ordered her departure, she instead slipped away in the confusion of battle preparations.

Ma's plan was bold. She made her way to the headquarters of the provincial revolutionary committee in a nearby village. She knew that the leaders and their wives, like He Long's wife, Jian Xianren, would accompany the army. She lied that the hospital had sent her and set about making herself busy building fires and doing laundry, even brazenly demanding the grungy shirts off people's backs. Life was so hectic that no one sent her away, and when the group pulled out, Ma went with them. When they caught up with the hospital, Ma did not hide. Instead, she threw herself into the mix, assuming correctly that the busy nurses could not worry about her now.

To further prove herself, Ma went to the front where the fighting was. At first, she had no idea what she was doing and angered some of the wounded by pulling them up in an attempt to force them to walk or by handling them too roughly. The soldiers cursed her and called her "Dead Child" and other names, but she ran about fearlessly and eventually earned their admiration. Ma began delivering medicine to the wounded, fetching them water, and washing their faces. There were many patients and few nurses to tend to them. Ma worked long hours, frequently to exhaustion. When she was not caring for wounded soldiers directly, she was washing their clothes.

Surrounded by Nationalist troops and moving often for two days straight before stopping to sleep, the Second Army Group forged its way along the Hunan-Hubei border onto the eastern edge of the Yunnan-Guizhou Plateau, which they would cross in seeking out the First Army. The leaders considered what lay ahead — fiercer mountains and harsher weather, even more primitive living conditions and hostility from the Tibetans — and told Ma and some other women to return home. Soldiers escorted them out of camp and beyond the battle zone and left them to find their own way. None did. There was no place to go. The Nationalists now controlled the areas they had left. To return meant death. Instead, Ma ended up in the camp of some wounded soldiers, who fed her and allowed her to lie low.

When the soldiers finally sent her away, Ma sought work at the office of a local government group, hiding for a time from Red Army officials and doing the things that others were glad to have her do — building fires, chopping vegetables, and washing clothes. Ma's friends in the hospital knew she was there, and when the hospital finally grew severely shorthanded, they called her back. It was a happy day for Ma, who assumed that now that they had readmitted her, they would never send her away again. Then things started to go terribly wrong.

Like the Fourth Army, He Long's forces had purged hundreds of suspected counterrevolutionaries and continued to do so. No one, no matter how battle-proven, who did not have a pristine background was safe. Former landlords, landowners, employers of laborers, and rich peasants suffered expulsion or death at the hands of Party inquisitors. By any stretch of the imagination, Ma would seem to have been an unlikely target of such a campaign. However, inquisitions sweep broadly. A Chinese folk saying states, "One would rather wrongly execute one thousand men than allow one guilty man to escape." There was always the possibility, amid the tensions and shifting loyalties of war, of saying the wrong thing and being taken for a counterrevolutionary.

Ma's difficulty started with some teasing. "Little Devil," one of the wounded men addressed her, "there were lots of landlords' bandits in your hometown."[18] Talking a bit about himself — how he had been forced to hide as they had searched for him in Xuanhan — the soldier then returned to Ma, who had unusually fair skin for a peasant. "You don't look like a child from a poor family," he teased her. "Children from poor families have dark, coarse skin, but yours is like that of a landlord's child."

For a while, the Ma family had lived in a straw lean-to built by her father. "My family was so poor we didn't even have a house," she shot back. "How could I have been from a landlord's family?" The soldier and the youth bantered back and forth, passing the time until the soldier returned to his unit. Ma promptly forgot about the encounter, but it would soon come back to haunt her.

PART THREE

NORTH THROUGH SICHUAN

chapter 15

Two Raging Rivers

MAY 1935

And so on went the mobile First Army.

Otto Braun marveled at the marchers' speed. "The soldiers did not, strictly speaking, run," he observed, "but jogged in their light cloth shoes and straw sandals, slowly and reserving their strength, at a pace which allowed them to cover great distances without serious symptoms of fatigue." He called the technique "endurance run" and noted that they were truly a "mobile army." The marchers covered between twenty-five and thirty miles a day. In Yunnan, he had seen the command column cover more than forty miles in a day.[1]

Now as the First Army barreled toward the Golden Sands River, some were said to have covered an astounding fifty-eight miles in one day. The convalescent company did its best to keep up, marching through the night to the light of the stars. When they reached a Yi village and an elder informed them that they were less than twenty miles from the river, they let out a weary cheer. About an hour past midnight, after leaving several more hills behind, they suddenly heard the distant roar of the Golden Sands. All they wanted to do was lie down and rest their aching bodies, but the leaders rallied them on. A pause might be welcome but a Nationalist attack was not.

As the convalescent company made its way toward the river, the trail offered new challenges. Debris from the powerful mountain torrent blocked their way, stones sheared by the river's violence jabbing at their sandaled or bare feet. Many twisted their ankles on the jagged,

On a remote bend of the Golden Sands River, the Jiaopingdu crossing had been used since ancient times by caravan traders carrying grain, hides, silver, and Tibetan herbal medicine south and gold and opium north.

undulating path. Finally, after two hours of crabbing their way across what seemed like a vast lumpy carpet of shark teeth, they dropped their blankets and collapsed on warm silt.

Their rest was brief. Before dawn, they rose, rubbing their tired, gritty eyes. They ate breakfast on the riverbank and set out again, bypassing a small village at dawn and skirting a mountain. As the sun rose in the sky, they trudged, sweating profusely, on the deep silt, which moved under their feet. They covered fifteen hard miles in the morning. Word came that they needed to reach the wharf that day, the sooner the better, and they slogged on. At around two o'clock in the afternoon, they reached the river port of Jiaopingdu.[2] The river, about two hundred yards wide, was swift and turbulent and swept by a fierce wind. Its banks, rising to hundreds of feet, teemed with Red soldiers waiting to be ferried across.

As soon as they arrived, the women heard about the action that had started two nights before. Local forces occupying the river wharfs had pulled the ferryboats across to the opposite bank. The advance First Army troops had reached Jiaopingdu at eleven o'clock at night, surprising a lone Sichuan Army tax clerk on patrol. Seizing him and his boat, they slipped across the river to the tollhouse on the north bank, where they captured thirty soldiers. A Red platoon then drove off a Sichuan garrison stationed on the heights above the crossing. The original plan had been to traverse the river at three places, but the powerful current made surface bridges impossible to build, especially with Nationalist bombers targeting them. The marchers would somehow have to produce their own boats.[3]

On a ten-foot-high riverside boulder, First Army Chief of Staff Liu Bocheng, the bespectacled "One-Eyed General," set up crossing headquarters, and with the help of Chen Yun, commissar of the operation, directed the action. Red troops found and repaired six boats and recruited several dozen local boatmen to help ferry the troops across the river. For nine days and nights, they rowed the boats back and forth, hauling at least thirty and up to sixty passengers at a time, with horses and mules tied to the back, treading water as they went.

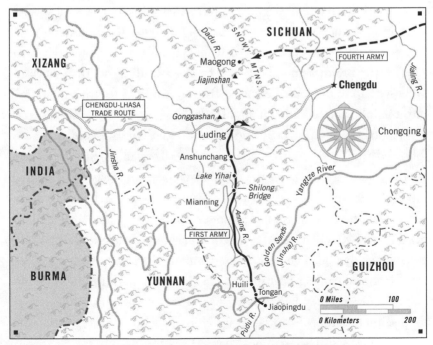

**The First Army Crosses the Golden Sands River
and Moves Up the Tibetan Plateau**

When the women arrived, Liu moved them to the front of the line. After waiting on the banks only a few hours, they crossed the swift and mighty Golden Sands.

On May 9, the rear guard crossed the river. The Red soldiers then destroyed the boats to prevent them from being used by Nationalist troops. (Communist treasurers compensated the rivermen with silver dollars and a feast of rice and pork.) A few days later, the Nationalists reached the river's south bank. They beat and imprisoned the rivermen and seized their livestock and money. By then, the Red Army had vanished.

CROSSING THE GOLDEN SANDS marked another turning point for the First Army. They had now reached Sichuan province. Here, according to Chen Yun, the epic journey entered its fourth stage, the 250-mile stretch north to the far side of the Dadu River. There was a general sense of relief; with the Golden Sands behind them, the strategic situation had improved. Though they were marching into a land of lush river valleys, they were intent on passing through southwestern Sichuan as rapidly as possible. "We had shaken off Chiang Kaishek's pursuit," Otto Braun remembered. "The road leading north was clear. Now we had to prevent the enemy from pushing us further westward into the inhospitable Tibetan highlands."[4]

The morning after crossing the river, the convalescent company followed the Third Army Group north to Tongan, a diminutive but bustling gateway town on the Yunnan-Sichuan border. The trail led immediately up a bald, rocky mountain on cruel switchbacks. Without cover, the marchers broiled under a relentless sun. "It felt like a desert," Cai Xiaoqian later recalled. Carrying sufficient water was a constant challenge. The Red Army would not be able to issue standard manufactured canteens until the 1950s, and most of the limited number of canteens they had—oval-shaped metal containers with ring-topped metal stoppers in laced-up cloth covers—were taken from the Nationalists. The marchers paused on the mountainside to buy water from a peasant woman carrying buckets of it on shoulder poles, paying two copper coins for a bowl. After they drained the buckets, she fetched more, making, in Cai's estimation, "a fortune that day." Still it was not enough.[5]

Later, while marching at night, Shorty Wei saw the glimmer of moonlight on a small puddle. She jumped at the chance to quench her thirst. She skimmed the puddle with her ceramic cup and drank. It felt good on her parched throat. Then she filled her canteen and caught up with her friends. At daybreak, Shorty shared her canteen with a thirsty male comrade. On his second cup, the soldier asked with a grimace, "Why does this water taste like piss?" The water had seemed fine in the night, but now it tasted bitter to Shorty, too. They looked in the cup and saw that the water was yellowish and contained flecks of cow manure. Shorty explained how she had gotten it. As they laughed, she apologized but reassured him: "We have a saying in Jiangxi, 'Eating dirt or manure has never killed a man.'" Agreeing, the soldier gulped down the rest of the cow urine.[6]

The line of marchers snaked down the mountain and came to Tongan, which had several dozen stores. Before the famished convalescent company arrived, however, those in front had picked the shops clean of peanuts, tea, sugar, salt, and cigarettes. Little but forbidden opium remained for sale.

By the time the women reached Tongan, the Third Army Group was fighting in the town of Huili, in a broad valley thirty-five miles to the north. Huili lay on the ancient Southern Silk Road, which stretched from China's old capital of Changan (now Xian) to Persia. The Red soldiers had stormed Huili's walls, but Sichuan troops had fended them off, pouring down cauldrons of boiling rice porridge (which, unlike water, stuck to the skin), flooding tunnels under the walls to keep them out, and torching houses outside the walls to prevent the Red soldiers from using them for cover. The convalescent company bypassed the roiling town and at a safe distance stopped and encamped, proselytizing and recruiting while waiting for its warring comrades.

Five days later, clouds of smoke still billowed from Huili as the battle continued to rage. Meanwhile, the Politburo met and reaffirmed the course decided on by the newly installed leadership: they would keep moving north to join up with the Fourth Army.[7] Along the way, they were to find villages where the women could recruit 5,000 new soldiers. There was an urgent need behind the effort: the Politburo predicted a serious fight along the western edge of the Sichuan basin, where they were to join up with the Fourth Army. Without more troops, they would be in real trouble.

The First Army's next step was to trek 150 miles along the Anning River to the city of Mianning. Local guides estimated it would take eight days, but the Red commanders, in a rush, accelerated the pace, sending a diversionary force down the main road and the bulk of the army on less conspicuous side paths. They marched rapidly every night, camping at daybreak in the lush valley beneath 12,000-foot peaks. Although they bypassed the many small towns along the way, they raided outlying houses, executing or kidnapping the wealthy landowners they took by surprise and confiscating stores of food, money, and other valuables.[8]

From Shilong Bridge, they marched the final twenty miles to Mianning, which lay in a wide, flat part of the valley. As they neared the town, its company of Nationalists fled, and the local militia did not resist. In the town of squatty one-floor shops, the marchers found little in the way of food or supplies and a populace deeply divided between Han and Yi. (The Communists promptly angered the Han by releasing more than a hundred chained Yi from jail, perhaps a strategic gesture as they were heading into Yi territory.) It was here in the town of Mianning that the term "Long March" first appeared in writing: "The Red Army's unstoppable Long March has now arrived in western Sichuan," Zhu De proclaimed in a message to the troops.[9]

From Mianning, the First Army climbed over a low pass into Yi territory, entering a land of bewitching hills covered with ancient pepper tree forests and evening mists rising from cerulean lakes. On the horizon, seventy miles to the north, loomed the massive 24,600-foot Gonggashan, Sichuan's tallest mountain and the world's eleventh-highest peak, ice-capped and almost perpetually veiled in clouds. Locals worshipped the holy behemoth, which stood supreme amid

more than a hundred minions surpassing 16,000 feet and as many glaciers. Nearby, the labyrinth of gnarled pepper trees grew so dense
that it blocked out the sun. Kang Keqing later recalled a story that circulated about a Han official and his family who were attacked as they
traveled here with a small company of soldiers. The Yi had robbed
them of everything: the mortified official and his wife and children
had run all the way back to the city stark naked. The women laughed
at the story, but it also sent shivers down their spines. Surely the Yi
bandits would not be so audacious as to assault the Red Army?

As they walked, sharp turns revealed sheer rock cliffs, creating endless bends in the route through the increasingly eerie woods. In front
of the women, engineers hewed a path with axes and saws, felling trees
and building bridges over rivers and streams. But still there were count-
less detours. The women carried the stretchers as best they could.[10]

Deep in the forest, the terrible story proved prophetic. The women
were shocked to come across a group of naked scouts and road builders
from one of the engineering units. A band of Yi had ambushed them
from a thicket and, shrieking wildly, jabbed them with long poles.
The soldiers, forbidden to fight back, had tried to parley with them,
but the Yi had ignored their peaceful gestures, shoved the soldiers to
the ground, and robbed them of their weapons, tools, personal possessions, and clothes.

The women tried to dispel these images as they went out in small
groups to find the Yi and trade with them for food. Li Jianzhen found
a handful of them roasting an animal, some forest rodent, on a spit and
attempted to communicate her mission. The Yi could not understand
her but handed her a hunk of the meat they were eating. Li took the
sizzling meat in her hands and bit into it. It was nearly raw, but she ate
it anyway. Nodding thanks, she hurried away and began to wretch.
In camp that night, she lay awake in pain. The next day, her stomach
ached, and she felt weak. As the Reds moved out again, she stopped
often to relieve her bowels and fell behind. Hearing of her woes, the
young captain of the division in charge of collecting stragglers found
her and gave her an opium pill to stop the diarrhea. He then helped
her catch up to the convalescent company.[11]

Soon afterward, Xie Fei and some others went to find food. Most Yi had abandoned their villages ahead of the Red invaders, so Xie and her comrades combed the dense hillsides in search of trading partners. At the top of one hill, they encountered a group of Yi, squatting, filthy, and primitively dressed. The Red women approached them cautiously, but as Xie began to speak, an arrow winged past her head. The women retreated hastily, but with the wounded in camp waiting to eat, they could not go back empty-handed. Xie now approached the small band alone. Moving slowly, she spoke in even tones, trying to explain that they had come only to find provisions. Eventually, a man who understood some Mandarin descended toward her. After Xie gave him some money, he explained to his tribesmen what the women wanted. Xie was able to buy enough food, probably buckwheat and potatoes, to feed the wounded for one night.

The Reds' next encounter with the Yi came when they crested the top of a mountain and ran into a few dozen of them, barefoot or wearing hemp sandals and dressed in stolen clothes and sleeveless wool coats. An interpreter explained their demand for passage money. The Reds tried to proselytize to them, but the Yi insisted on the tribute. Finally, the Reds handed over several hundred silver coins.

Later, the marchers heard gunfire (one marcher described the sound as *pi li pa la*). They now discovered that they had entered the land of the rival Yi tribe, whose heads were shaved, except for a forehead tuft two inches long and an inch wide. Red agate and coral earrings adorned their left ears. News had already spread that the Communists had paid off their cousins, and now these rivals demanded their own gift and, more cleverly, a pact. On the calcium-encrusted west bank of Lake Yihai, whose water was so clear that individual rocks could be seen on the bottom dozens of feet down, Chief of Staff Liu Bocheng and the Yi leader, Xiao Yedan, agreed on terms and sealed their alliance ritually. Each held a bowl of lake water in his hands. A rooster's neck was cut and bled into the bowls. The two knelt down shoulder to shoulder and held their bowls in the air while declaring their allegiance to each other. Then they drank the contents of their bowls and, according to one witness, smeared blood on their mouths to confirm their oath of friendship.

Xiao Yedan's wife holding the flag given to the Yi by the Red Army. The inscription says: "The Guji Yi Citizens Branch Army of the Red Army."

The next morning, Xiao Yedan sent thirty warriors to observe the Red military. Xiao received money, opium (which the Communists had confiscated and used for trade or as gifts when it suited their purposes), thirty rifles, and a Mauser pistol as a gift, as well as a Red flag. In return, Kang Keqing recalled, the Yi promised the Communists safe passage; gave them horses, oxen, and sheep; and invited them to stay in their huts. Yi mothers were distinguished by black hats, while other women wore headbands of blue cloth. At night, both slept with their skirts as blankets. Some had Han slaves, a fact that made the Communists somewhat ill at ease.

"Afterwards, most Yi tribes were friendly to us," Chen Yun noted. "Some were neutral, and a few followed us, trying to attack us. We fought back." At the foot of a mountain, they encountered a naked Yi girl in the middle of the route. Kang Keqing guessed she was about fourteen years old. With large dark eyes, she surveyed the strangers coming toward her. The column stopped. Kang wanted to ask her why she was standing in the road. Instead, she took off her coat and wrapped it around the girl. Pan Kaiwen gave Kang a pair of pants and a cloth belt to put on the girl. Pleased, she beamed at Kang, chatting excitedly in Yi. Kang took these as words of thanks and posed with the girl for a photograph. Then she watched her disappear into the woods. At that point, a guard indicated the Yi warriors armed with swords and guns hiding in the trees ahead. They had observed the exchange with the girl. Moving on rapidly, the Reds concluded that they had just been tested by the initial group of Yi, who resented their alliance with their rivals.[12]

LEAVING THE REGION, the Reds aimed for Anshunchang, one of the few places where the Dadu River broadened and slowed enough to be crossed. There they hoped to ferry troops across rapidly and give the slip to the Nationalists. But this would not be easy. Even at Anshunchang, the Dadu was torrential. Not only would ferrying the troops present a major logistical challenge, just as it had at the Golden Sands, but it was a perfect place to be trapped by Chiang Kaishek. He had shown that he knew the strategic use that could be made of a river, and the Dadu was already infamous as the site of a military disaster.

Every Red leader knew the story of Shi Dakai, a principal in the Taiping Rebellion, who became disillusioned with the movement's infighting and struck off on his own with 10,000 men.[13] Pursued by a Qing dynasty army, Shi eventually reached the Dadu. His soldiers began to ford the river, and then, as the story goes, his favorite concubine gave birth to a boy. Shi called a halt to the crossing, even recalling troops that had to pass back through the swelling waters for a celebration. The delay allowed the royal army to catch up and pin Shi's troops against the increasingly raging river. Shi was killed and dismembered; his army was annihilated, the captives buried alive. Chiang Kaishek hoped that Shi's debacle would soon find its modern corollary, going so far as to have his airplanes bombard the Red troops with leaflets branding Zhou De and Mao Zedong the "new Shi Dakai" and warning them of a similar fate.

Anyone in the vicinity of the Dadu in the spring could understand why it was said to be the haunt of 40,000 water devils. Draining the towering mountains surrounding the Sichuan basin, the Dadu roared with ferocity, its rapids gnashing like chattering fangs. Intelligence from locals indicated that a battalion of Sichuan troops defended the ferry crossing at Anshunchang, where four boats plied the tumultuous current. A crack Red regiment descended to investigate, and again timing and luck were on the Communists' side: they captured the garrison commander and, more importantly, his boat. With the advantage of surprise, they decided to strike, despite some serious drawbacks. The boat held just seventeen men, who would be exposed to the enemy garrison during the half-hour passage. After landing, they would be on their own for an hour before reinforcements could arrive.[14]

The leaders armed the boat with six heavy machine guns for raking shore positions. "We also set up machine guns, mortars, and snipers on our bank to cover them," Chen Yun recalled. Seventeen volunteers, carrying light machine guns, rifles, and daggers, set out, six of them pulling oars through the frightening current. They landed several hundred yards downstream. Immediately, the enemy opened fire, but according to a witness who lived in the town and joined others in watching them, the Nationalists simply fled. The Reds had taken the garrison before they even stormed the beach.[15]

That proved to be the easy part. Now they had to start transporting troops across the Dadu. It soon became apparent that this was futile: they had secured only two more boats on the other side, and the river was too swift and wide for them to build a bridge. Chiang's bombers showed up the next day, and with Nationalist forces closing in fast and no more boats available, the marchers were too pressed for time to transport 30,000 troops and their gear across the river. The operation was called off with only the vanguard having crossed. The women were told that they must continue north a hundred miles along the west side of the river to Luding and that they must do it in three days.[16] They and the central column would then cross the river on a bridge that had been built in 1701 as part of the trade route between Chengdu, a center of agriculture and Chinese traditional medicine, and Lhasa, the capital of Tibet. The lead First Army Group would travel north on the east bank of the Dadu and meet them there.

With all the preparations that were needed to transport so many soldiers and support personnel, no large movement remained secret for long. Inevitably, spies or informants carried word to the enemy. The following day, troops belonging to the Sichuan Thirty-eighth Regiment rushed to Luding to reinforce a garrison at the bridge. The central column had not gone ten miles before it was attacked, forcing it to detour off the riverbank. For long intervals, often at double speed, they hurried forward, breaking only for quick meals and a few hours of rest. After dark, they traveled by torchlight. To Kang Keqing, they looked like a dragon gliding along the winding riverbank.

The first night, they reached Ferocious Tiger Mountain (Menghugangshan), one of the last passes before Luding. No detour was possible here. Silently, they climbed undetected, then lobbed grenades into the warlord outposts, subduing Ferocious Tiger. They had marched forty miles.

The next day, after about fifteen miles, they met another Sichuan force entrenched on a mountainside. After several assaults and some hand-to-hand fighting, the Reds were able to drive the Sichuan troops off. Weary yet determined, they passed through or by numerous small river towns without stopping. New obstacles continually beset them in the form of cliffs, narrow paths, roiling white water, rushing creeks, and pouring rain. When necessary, they chopped down small trees and built temporary bridges and roads. At times, they walked gingerly beside sheer faces, concentrating on not stumbling. Hungry and drenched in the driving rain, they passed through one riverside village but continued on.

On the third day, the Nationalist air force found the Reds again. As Li Jianzhen and the young soldier who had served as her horse tender since Ruijin made their way along a remote stretch of trail, bombs suddenly rained down. Shrapnel riddled the chest and legs of the groom, and he began to bleed badly. Li could not find a stretcher, but she was determined not to abandon him in the wilderness. She hoisted him onto her back. "You're carrying a wounded soldier?" a passing officer coldly rebuked her. "How can you keep up? Put him down." But she refused, struggling on and falling behind.

The soldier grew weaker, and soon he could not hold on to her shoulders. At last, he passed out. Li bent forward to keep him on her back. They came to a small temple surrounded by several houses, all empty. Exhausted, Li knew that she could not carry the groom any farther. She took him into the abandoned temple. He deliriously murmured a word over and over. It seemed he was asking for water, but she had none to give him. Helpless, she left a little food, salt, and a few silver coins, hoping that someone would soon return and consider the gift worthy of caring for the dying young man. Then she walked out through the gate, suppressing her emotions, telling herself that she had no choice, and focusing on catching up with the others.[17]

By the time Li reached Luding that evening, the vanguard had already taken and begun crossing the bridge, joining those who had crossed the river at Anshunchang in Sichuan. The battle for the bridge would later be spun into a national legend. The Sichuan forces, as the story goes, had removed most of the wooden planks that created the bridge's floor. All that remained were the thirteen massive iron chains that formed the structure. The chains, nearly four hundred feet long, were bolted to the cliffs on either side of the gorge. In preparation for storming the bridge, the Communists had set up heavy machine guns and fired on the artillery-supported garrison on the east side of the chasm. The Sichuan troops had returned their fire. Under the cover of darkness, a team of twenty-two young Red soldiers, armed with grenades, pistols, and sabers and led by an officer and a political instructor, shimmied forward on the chains. A misstep meant plummeting into the river and near-certain death. Engineering troops followed behind them, laying down wooden planks on the chains to replace those taken by the Sichuan troops.[18]

As the young soldiers neared the east end of the bridge, the Sichuan guards set their hut on fire, sending a wall of flames onto the sporadic remaining planks of the bridge. "Comrades, this is it," the cadres shouted to the volunteers. "Show no fear." Lofting grenades, the soldiers charged into the flames. Their uniforms ignited, and the acrid smell of their burning hair filled the air, but they reached the garrison and engaged it at close range. As they did so, the troops of the First Army Group that had crossed at Anshunchang arrived on the scene. The Sichuan force, realizing it was outflanked and about to be overrun, fled.

Later, several locals added a twist to the Reds' orthodox version of the story. According to a woman who grew up near the bridge and watched the crossing, Red soldiers stripped her family's house of its wood siding to use in replacing the missing floorboards on the bridge, but it was the locals who actually led the assault on the bridge. They alone, she claimed, could cross the chains, though under the withering fire they were all killed.[19] Some other local eyewitnesses are reported to have said that only five soldiers made it across in the initial assault, while the rest were either shot and killed or fell to their deaths in the white water thirty feet below. In any event, it seems that the battle for the bridge may have cost more than the three or four deaths usually attributed to it.[20]

GIVEN THE CONDITIONS under which the Red engineers had been forced to work, they had pulled off a logistical marvel. Following the assault, Nationalist airplanes "opened an unremitting bombing attack" on the bridge, according to Otto Braun, and still it withstood the beating. Yet it was also horribly unstable; when walked upon, it swayed perilously above the churning water—an experience so frightening that some of the hired stretcher-bearers deserted rather than attempt a crossing.[21]

When morning broke, the convalescent company was bogged down at the west end of the bridge, their stretchers and the medicine cases strewn on the ground. As director of the unit, Li Jianzhen was trying to get the situation under control when Mao arrived.[22]

"What is the matter? Why are you still here?" he asked her.

"Chairman Mao, we can't keep walking. No one will carry the stretchers," she told him. Mao called the leader of his guard team and told him to have the guards help move the convalescent company across the river. The women bound medicine cases to their backs and then inched across the swaying bridge, which creaked and groaned

The 370-foot iron-chain Luding Bridge crossing the Dadu River was a part of an ancient Chinese-Tibetan trade route. Treasure caravans from as far away as Nepal once passed over the plank-covered nine-chain bridge floor carrying tribute to Beijing.

underfoot. The immense volume and power of the snarling river made them feel tiny. "Look straight ahead," the officers instructed them. "Don't look down, and don't look to the side." Crossing and recrossing many times, they finally reassembled on the far shore.[23]

Afterward, Li Jianzhen celebrated, singing, "Ai ya lai! The Red Army crossed Luding Bridge! / The women soldiers carried all the stuff over the bridge!"

At the end of the day, the cadres bivouacked in a large temple in a secluded high valley. The cooks waited impatiently for the provisions to arrive so that they could prepare the evening meal. Others, anxious to get their gear from the porters so that they could rest a little, began to grumble among themselves. Kang Keqing managed to quiet everyone down before she and Pan Kaiwen left to patrol the temple grounds. Even with guards stationed at the front gate, Kang felt the need to check the perimeter herself. As they walked, a fine mist began to fall. Kang noticed the lantern light glistening on a fresh-looking grassy plant protruding from the cracks of the town walls. Thinking it might provide fodder for the horses and donkeys, she pulled a stalk out and bit it. It tasted like wild chives, a luxury she had not had for half a year. Raising her lantern, she saw chives growing everywhere.

Pan's eyes lit up. They went back to the temple, roused some soldiers, and told them to bring knives and follow them.

Soon they returned with bundles of fresh chives, some twenty pounds' worth, and presented the crop to the cooks, who were delighted. The supply team had by now arrived with their provisions, but there was no firewood. It was past midnight, so dinner was canceled, and all were ordered to turn in immediately. In the morning, the rain stopped, and the troops moved out, with no time for a hot breakfast. The cooks packed up the chives and carried them along.

By noon, they reached the village of Shuizidi, or "Land of Millet," in a dammed river valley, where farmers grew abundant fields of the grain. Finally, the Reds rested and ate. According to Kang, the good food, seasoned with flavorful chives, revived their spirits even more than their bodies.[24]

The First Army was now on the cusp of what would prove to be the two hardest legs of the journey. As the trail threatened to break the women, they would have to monitor and encourage one another in order to survive.

chapter 16

Hitting the Roof

JUNE 1935

As they moved farther onto the Tibetan Plateau, the First Army gained altitude. They had now reached the most treacherous of terrain. To head west meant to veer deeper into hostile Tibetan remotes, while to head east meant confronting Sichuan and Nationalist forces. As a result, the Reds chose what they believed to be the least of three evils: to go up and over the mountains to the north, partly to evade the Nationalist air force, which continued to harry them. They had to traverse an unknown number of high mountain ranges separated by narrow twisting valleys to reach the potential safe haven of remote Gansu province. Jiajinshan (Great Snow Mountain) was the first and would prove to be the most daunting. Those who survived its breathtaking heights would then face Mengbishan, Changbanshan (also known as Yakexiashan), and Dagushan.[1]

From Luding, it was 160 miles to the base of Jiajinshan. The Sichuan Army had heavy garrisons on the open road, so the First Army used remote trails instead. First, they headed for Erlangshan, the highest mountain yet, its looming bulk dominating a tea-producing region on the divide of the Sichuan and Tibetan plateaus. The stiff climb from 4,000 to nearly 10,000 feet gave the marchers a taste of things to come. Most of them had never seen such heights or felt the effects of high altitude. Jinggangshan, their Jiangxi mountain redoubt of earlier days, lay at a mere 2,200 feet.

Still dogged regularly by the Nationalist air force even while winding through the precipitous mountains, the Reds sought cover under the forest canopy during the day and traveled on after dark. Once they had crossed Erlangshan, they carved their way through a dense, ancient hardwood forest toward 7,500-foot Baoxianggang, often traveling on a wild boar path covered in a sludge of rotten leaves. This channel through the dense woods finally vanished in a massive bamboo thicket. The Red column, now a ragged 8,000 strong, waited while engineers cut through it. This was not just ordinary bamboo, but a species known as "sting bamboo," which had rings of thorns that lacerated the workers' arms and faces as they removed it.

The column resumed marching in the dark, past the heaps of downed bamboo, until a local guide informed them that they could not possibly cover the remaining ten miles that night. Orders came down the line to halt and make camp. The trail was so narrow that there was barely room to set down their packs. Many soldiers, unable to lie down, slept standing up, Cai Xiaoqian said, "like cranes" (p. 288). Others lit piles of bamboo in the hopes of fending off the cold and sat on their packs to keep off the wet ground. They had no water to boil, so they could not make dinner. Instead, they distracted themselves with conversation, until a heavy downpour forced them to hunker down. Those who had them put up oilcloth or oil paper umbrellas or donned bush raincoats, some made of sewn-together chaff. Then they drifted off to the thrum of rainwater filling their pots.

At daylight, the cooks used the water they had collected to make corn gruel and passed it around. The night's deluge had turned the path into a mud slick. On an incline, it was as slippery as a water slide; where it was flat, the marchers sometimes sank in up to their knees.

Getting the horses through the mud required much strenuous pushing and pulling. "On this peak," Mao later told Edgar Snow, "one army corps lost two-thirds of its transport animals. Hundreds fell down and never got up" (p. 200). In some places, footholds were so tenuous that the marchers had to cling desperately to grass or trees beside the trail in order to stay standing. When they came to a stream, they preferred walking on the rocks in the water rather than on the miserable path.

At last, they reached a small river at the base of Baoxianggang, and the sun appeared through the mountain mist. The soldiers broke ranks and rested, taking turns washing their feet and clothes in the stream and then counting the number of leeches on their legs.

Soon basins of water were boiling over fires. "Luo Ziming and his little devil were cooking something in their washbasin," Cai Xiaoqian later recalled. "'Water, porridge, whatever it is, give me a bowl!' I called. They handed me a large mug, and I took a sip. It tasted funny. Luo smiled and told me it was mule soup." His helper earnestly pointed out that it was one of the pack animals that had fallen to its death the night before.[2]

The isolated villagers of Xiaojiaba, half a dozen families of the Xiao clan living on the north side of the mountain, were shocked when the Red soldiers walked into their midst. Their ancestors had talked about a path that led over the mountain, but that had long since vanished. No one had attempted to go over the top for as long as anyone could remember. Some of the villagers thought that these strangers had descended from heaven.

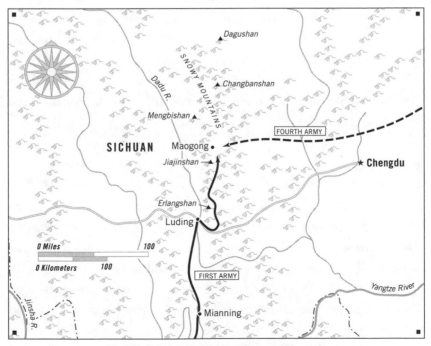

The First Army Enters the Snowy Mountains

As the First Army forged on, however, things became less quaint. About a hundred miles southwest of Chengdu, the Sichuan capital, in a strategic pass through the mountains lay blockhouses manned by the Sichuan Army. Red troops attempted to storm these fortresses, but after a day of intense fighting, they were unable to rout the tenacious defenders. The Red leaders decided to attempt to outflank them by climbing another difficult mountain. The maneuver quickly turned disastrous. Three regiments of Zhu De's troops were cut off and surrounded by enemy soldiers. After a day and a night of fighting, a thousand Red soldiers were taken alive, and more than twice that many leaped into a frigid river in an effort to escape. Only a few survived.

As usual, the marchers had no time to dwell on this devastating defeat. The Fourth Army was pushing west and south to meet them, and it was critical that the union be made with all speed. Now more than ever, the women, who had resumed the grinding work of carrying litters, needed to keep up, since irregular Tibetan forces loomed in the recesses of the mountains waiting to pick off stragglers.[3]

In anticipation of the rendezvous, the First Army's commanders ordered the soldiers to make gifts for their comrades in the Fourth Army and to prepare skits, dances, and songs. They were instructed to cut their hair, shave, and otherwise make themselves presentable. After eight months of marching, this was a relative matter. Although they washed and mended, their uniforms still had holes in them and many lacked shirtsleeves and pant legs.

THROUGH THESE HILLS, one woman carried a greater burden than the others. Technically, Zeng Yu, who had been pregnant since they had set out from Ruijin, was not enlisted in the Red Army. Making matters worse, her husband, Zhou Zikun, had commanded and lost an entire division at the Xiang River battle and had been disgraced for not perishing with them. But while Zeng had not been issued the First Army's standard gear and provisions at the outset of the *dabanjia* and had lost any hope of official recognition because of her husband, several of the women had looked out for her, especially as her pregnancy had advanced. Now, while climbing a hill with the Cannon, Zeng suddenly felt the intense stabs of labor. The Cannon and Porter Girl supported her on either side and helped her to keep walking. After they crossed the peak, Zeng was barely able to proceed. The Cannon tried to hoist her onto her back but could not support her. She and Porter Girl continued to tug Zeng along. There was no time to stop, even as the contractions grew stronger and the risk of something going wrong increased.

According to one account, convalescent company cohead Hou Zheng called for a stretcher, but an ill-timed advance by the enemy frightened away the porters. The women shouldered Zeng onto a horse. She rode until her water broke and it was too painful for her to stay on. Even in labor, she was not allowed to stop doing what she had been doing since October — putting one foot in front of the other. With the help of the Cannon and Porter Girl, she staggered along in the protection of the troops.[4]

As they neared night camp, Zeng begged Qian Xijun to go ahead to the campsite, an abandoned village, and find some grass paper (the coarse straw, bamboo pulp, or tree bark paper the Chinese used as toilet paper) for cleaning up after the birth. Qian hurried ahead to search for some, but she could not find any in the village. Instead, she gathered dry grass and rice straw and made a bed on the floor of the empty stone house she and some other women were assigned to. Somehow Zeng managed to reach the house. That night, she gave birth to a baby girl on the straw bed. The Cannon and Qian were by her side. They cut the umbilical cord with a knife, but the sweaty, trail-dusty women had no way to clean the newborn. Indeed, they had no way to clean up at all.

For three days, the women stayed at the desolate site, which had no apparent source of water or food. They ate the sour leaves of pea plants. Cai Chang gave them flour, which they mixed with canteen water to make a kind of soup. At last, although Zeng was still bleeding, they had to move on. The baby could not go with them. The little girl was left alone on the straw bed. Perhaps someone would discover her and care for her, but the women, including her mother, knew that was unlikely. Zeng took one last look at her child and did what she knew she had to do. She and her friends left the village.[5]

Later that day, they reached a bridgeless river. This presented a particular problem for Zeng Yu. It was traditionally held that for health reasons, a woman should not allow her vaginal area to get wet for a month following childbirth. But Zeng, to the dismay of her female companions, had no choice. Many of the women crossed the swift river, which reached to their waists and pushed forcefully against their legs, holding hands or grasping the tails of the fording horses to keep from being swept away. Weak though she was, and bereft, Zeng carried on.

In a long line of semidetached parties, the marchers trudged over the mounting foothills toward the stunning snowcapped peaks that separated the Tibetan highland from China proper, at least geographically. Politically, China had long had an uncertain relationship with Tibet, ever since a kingdom had been established there in the early seventh century. Kublai Khan's Yuan dynasty later swallowed both China and Tibet whole. But by the time Dalai Lama rule was established in Tibet in the mid-seventeenth century, the Qing dynasty, Nepal, and even Western nations were disputing its borders and autonomy. As recently as 1909, a lamasery-sacking Chinese commander known as "the Butcher of Monks" had cut a bloody swath to Lhasa to subdue the place and recommended partitioning off eastern Tibet. In 1927, this eastern region became Xikang province of China.[6]

The outbreak of World War I and the internal struggles in China had brought Tibet a relatively tranquil period of isolation. That had ended with the death of the thirteenth Dalai Lama in 1933, when Tibet accepted a "condolence mission" from Chiang Kaishek and then permitted him to open a diplomatic office in Lhasa.

The Red troops now passed through dense virgin forests and over boggy moors. They forded many more rivers gushing with snowmelt. They were run-down, malnourished, and susceptible to many ailments. Otto Braun recalled, "Bleeding dysentery was rampant; the first cases of typhus appeared."[7] Many wore only thin cotton uniforms and either worn-out sandals or rags on their feet. In this decrepit state, they approached the area aptly known as the "roof of the world."

"All of us were unbelievably lice-ridden," said Braun. While most species carry only one type of lice, humans can carry three. The Long

Marchers had all of them, each uniquely adapted to a different environment: head lice thrive in fine hair, pubic lice in coarse hair, and body lice in clothes. Body lice were the chief carriers of typhus, a bacterial disease whose telltale dark red rash and burning fever often resulted in delirium and death. The marchers also had fleas, another carrier of typhus.[8] The infestation was no surprise, given that everyone had been sleeping on straw and grass and had been busy tending and riding the beasts, as well as sharing coats and huddling together at night to keep warm. In addition, most of the time there had been no way to wash. During the entire trek, Little Sparrow would later boast, she never removed all of her clothes at the same time. At every rest break, the women loosened their clothing and pulled lice and fleas off one another, crushing them between their fingers. Xu Teli would later lampoon the lice picking with a dance. Inverting his sheepskin coat so that the wool faced out and tilting his ragged fur hat, he danced about scratching the fleece. Catching pretend lice, he held them up quizzically and said, "Lice?" then popped them into his mouth. "Mmm!"[9]

The Cannon knew how to get rid of head lice. By the age of six, she had begun carrying her adoptive father's barbering gear, learning his trade. The barber had taught her how to shave heads with the only tool he had, a broken knife blade, and now she put her skills to use, shearing her friends' soiled bobs, ridding them of one last vestige of traditional beauty — and the vermin it harbored.

Ashamed to be bald, the women fashioned caps for their heads. Shortly afterward, a party of mischievous young soldiers burst into a cadre assembly and pulled the women's caps off, chanting, "Nuns! Nuns! We welcome the nuns to the revolution!" The crowd roared with laughter. The epithet *Nigu*, or "Buddhist nun," soon applied to all the women. They had chopped their braids to join. Now they had shaved their heads. In the mountain cold, this new mark of their suffering was but one more source of discomfort.[10]

AS IF THESE HARDSHIPS and the mountains themselves were not enough, the marchers were routinely chastened by sniper gunfire from

Tibetans and Sichuan patrols. While the rugged terrain forced them to keep their eyes on the trail, terror also rained from the sky. When two fighter planes caught them exposed on a hilltop with few trees for cover, Kang Keqing shouted for the soldiers and cooks around her to hit the ground. As the planes swooped in low, strafing and dropping bombs, Zhu De and Zhou Enlai ran into a cemetery and dove into a ditch. Though Zhu was unharmed, the force of an explosion blew one leg off his pants. Mao and his entourage were walking with the convalescent company at the time. A blast killed one of his bodyguards and nearly got Mao.[11]

The farther they went, the narrower and more tilted the paths grew. Daytime temperatures hovered in the forties, which was not uncomfortable, even in thin clothing, as long as they kept moving. The chill on sweaty, starving, exhausted bodies at rest, however, was not only agonizing but dangerous. Many would succumb to hypothermia at higher elevations.

One long day merged into the next as the army led their beasts and hauled provisions, gear, the sick and wounded, and even their leaders, who often sat in litters modified with long poles to smooth the gradients. While the exact chronology of days and the organization of the column remain blurred, the patchwork of individual experiences paints a grim picture. The weak staggered along, many falling by the wayside and remaining behind to freeze or starve to death. Those who fell to the rear of the long column grew used to seeing corpses scattered and piled like fallen trees in the forest. Certain sections of the climb were so harsh that the stretchers could not be employed and the wounded had to be piggybacked. He Zizhen, who had been on the brink of death for two weeks from her shrapnel wounds, clung doggedly to the back of her porter. All day long, political leaders implored exhausted soldiers to keep moving.

The lack of food and shelter made it impossible to take a day off to recuperate. The marchers mounted and descended one peak only to climb another at midnight. Nature was not their only adversary in this region. They also feared the Tibetans. These *manzi* (barbarians), as

the Reds called them, "lay in wait to ambush small groups and stragglers," Otto Braun recalled bitterly. "More and more, our route was
lined with the bodies of the slain."[12]

THEN CAME A MOMENT to pause. The mountain trails the marchers
had thus far traversed had been brutal, but they had not yet reached
the true monsters of the Tibetan Plateau. According to the American
journalist Agnes Smedley, the Reds now halted and spent ten days preparing to cross the forbidding ranges known collectively as the Snowy
Mountains, or the Snowies. They surprised a regiment of Tibetan cavalrymen on its way to join forces with the Sichuan Army and captured
wool coats and fur-lined uniforms, and a number of white fur coats
from the Tibetans' concubines. The Reds also nabbed several boxes of
silver pieces and a number of horses. These horses were short, sturdy,
and well suited to the terrain, unlike their own, and were especially
admired by the Communist women, who joked that they were more
valuable than husbands, because husbands were easier to replace.[13]

Around June 16, the First Army found its path blocked by the
14,000-foot snowcapped Jiajinshan. They had no choice but to go over
it. Many of the rank and file would die on Jiajinshan, while others
would simply collapse from exhaustion, unable to go on. But as the
marchers began the climb, they were amply motivated. The Fourth
Army awaited them somewhere on the other side. This was their
grail: the hope of joining allies, of being reinforced, of arriving somewhere at last.

At Jiajinshan's base, some of the marchers rested in Highland
(Yaoji), a village of several hundred houses—large for this remote
region—nestled in a boulder-strewn forest and surrounded by cultivated fields. The people of Highland ate yak, air-cured pork, roasted
yams and corn, steamed buns, boiled soup of pickled vegetable leaves,
and jellied bean curd. They drank yak-butter tea sprinkled with
ground walnuts and white wine simmered with honey to stave off
the cold. The village, with fewer than a thousand people, had little to

share with the Red Army, however, except for a warning: "Before you cross Jiajinshan, first erect your own tombstone." Gods inhabiting the mountain, some said, killed intruders by suffocating them when they opened their mouths. The only beings who could successfully traverse the peaks, other locals declared, were flying fairies.[14]

Gazing up from 6,900 feet, Kang Keqing would later report that the mountain, enveloped in clouds, resembled a giant wrapped in a white shawl and that when the clouds parted, it peered down benignly through the mist. But Kang was not seeing Jiajinshan's peak, which is not visible from Highland. Her youthful assessment would prove to be remarkably naive in other ways, too. The upcoming heights were quite the opposite of the "tame and harmless" rises she imagined.[15] In fact, the vanguard that had gone ahead to scale Jiajinshan had already sent back ominous warnings.

Already at this altitude, Kang felt ill and breathed with difficulty. As she went about her efforts mobilizing the troops, she asked others how they were doing and discovered that most felt as poorly as she did. Even sleeping and eating were a challenge. The doctors warned them to be especially careful crossing the mountain because they were suffering from altitude sickness. The Long Marchers may not have used that term (which was coined in the West around 1920 and does not appear in early Long March accounts) or fully understood the malady, but they would record its effects in horrific detail.[16]

As they prepared to ascend, Kang listened carefully to the Central Committee's climbing instructions: Wrap your feet in cloth. Put on your straw sandals, but do not make the knot too tight or too loose. Do not run, but climb with steady steps. To conserve energy, do not talk loudly. When you reach the top, do not stop to rest. Everyone should strive to descend the mountain by noon to avoid the afternoon storms.

The plan was to set out early to make the noon descent deadline. They ate breakfast in the dark, huddling around crackling brush fires for warmth. Kang found that she had no appetite, but at the urging of her friends, she forced down half a bowl of gruel. Wang Quanyuan awoke with bad menstrual cramps. She and her husband, along with a small group of cadres, had spent the past month politically organizing the locals. Though their work had been hard and dangerous, this respite from life in the ever-watchful army had served as a sort of honeymoon for the recently married couple. They had only just returned to the fold. Although Wang was relieved not to be pregnant, these pains were unusually strong and troubling on a day when she would need all her strength. She pulled her tattered cotton shirt around her and cinched her straw sandals, though not too tightly; her feet, she understood, would swell with the pounding and the altitude. As she prepared to depart, her pelvis felt as if it were weighted with sharp stones. For her part, Kang, setting off as soon as the last of the gear was stowed, already felt light-headed and weak.[17]

As the marchers headed straight up the mountain, aiming for a pass near the summit, Kang witnessed all four seasons in less than an hour. The green vegetation of spring thinned and coarsened to that of late summer. Soon even the grass blanched and withered. Finally, it vanished in slopes of snow-covered boulders. In the morning light, she had to squint to protect her eyes from the blinding glare of the snow.

Within a few hours of setting out, they climbed above 8,000 feet, the point at which air contains about half the oxygen it does at sea level. Above this elevation, blood oxygen levels can drop dangerously. At sea level, almost all blood carries oxygen, but the level drops to 95 percent at 9,000 feet. Even this small decrease can be problematic, yet in about a third of people, blood oxygen levels drop even lower. Recognizing the need to feed the body oxygen, plasmatic fluid with oxygen-carrying hemoglobin leaves the blood and enters the tissue. Thus, the blood thickens, causing dehydration, which in turn further impedes the distribution of nutrients and oxygen and the elimination of toxins. In the flu-like state known as acute mountain sickness that results, victims suffer headaches, labored breathing, fatigue, nausea, and extreme thirst.

Halfway up the mountain, the wind whipped the marchers' faces, and the air became too thin for some. "My heart felt an incredible pressure," cavalryman Lin Wei recalled, "and breathing was very difficult" (pp. 204–5). Placing one foot in front of the other took great effort, but he forced himself to do it.

As the climbers' bodies became increasingly starved for oxygen, the snow became deeper, until it was more than two feet in places. The marchers' straw sandals were quickly saturated; their feet froze and turned numb. Those who fell compounded their problems, adding soaked clothes and wet hands to their collection of woes. As they climbed, the wind gusted even stronger. Dark clouds rolled in from the southwest, obscuring the sun. Although the clouds cut the glare from the snow, they did not bode well. Soon they engulfed the peak. It began to rain and then hail. The hail became heavy snow, and the marchers' wet uniforms froze. Many wrapped themselves in their blankets.

Soon, according to Dong Biwu, the marchers could not talk, their breath froze, and their hands and lips turned blue.[18] At between 8,000 and 14,500 feet, acute mountain sickness can lead to a buildup of fluid in the heart and lungs. Sufferers feel sluggish, congested, and short of breath, and they have coughing spasms. Their heads throb, and they are beset by flashes of blinding pain. They stumble and hallucinate. At 13,000 feet and above, during a rapid ascent, the small blood vessels in the retina can burst, causing maddening splotches in the victim's field of vision. Derangement and paralysis set in, and the condition grows lethal. Many of the marchers became so spent that they simply sat down. There was little anyone could do to help them.

Everyone could see that Kang was suffering badly. She had been given a stick to walk with, but clearly it was not enough. Still strong, Li Bozhao, one of only two female marchers native to Sichuan, came to Kang's side. "You're really suffering. Why don't you ride your horse?" she asked. "You might not be able to cross Jiajin on foot." Such a solution was against regulations—to keep the circulation flowing and prevent frostbite of toes and feet, no one was allowed to ride over the mountains—and Kang objected. Li took Kang's grain sack and linked arms with her to help her walk. Kang tried to shake her off, leaning on her stick. Nevertheless, Li stayed by her side, propping her up and boosting her over rocks and up inclines.[19]

With each step, Wang Quanyuan's pelvic cramps grew worse. Struggling to lift her legs, she staggered into the wind and snow. In a haze of pain, she heard a friend's concerned voice: "Quanyuan, are you all right? Why don't you rest?" Pressing her hands against the cramps, she shrugged off the idea. The day's marching instructions flowed through her mind: "You must get over the mountain before midday to beat the afternoon snowstorms. . . . Don't talk on the trail. . . . Move forward slowly but steadily. . . . Do not sit down." Her eyes focused on the ground and each ensuing step. She would not let the nauseating pain stop her.

Soldiers crossing Jiajinshan.

Some of the other women had begun to experience amenorrhea—the cessation of their menstrual periods. Although extreme exercise does not necessarily disrupt menstruation, if too few calories are consumed and a woman's body fat falls to below 25 percent, oligomenorrhea (occasional rather than regular periods) is likely to occur. When body fat drops below 20 percent for more than three months, especially at times of high mental stress and fatigue, menstruation often ceases altogether. For a number of the other women, the Snowies seemed to trigger a sort of premature menopause, and several would end up infertile for life. Wang, for one, would end up never having children, and she would always blame it on the Snowy Mountains.

Kang, meanwhile, could barely catch her breath. The higher they went, the worse it got, and by the time they had reached the snow line, all of her senses told her to lie down and sleep. She knew she had to fight this impulse. Li Bozhao tugged her forward. "Do anything but sit," Li implored. "Once you sit, you'll never get up." Evidence of this risk was soon forthcoming: a bit farther along, two soldiers who had ascended the mountain the day before sat together on the ground, back-to-back, looking like a tree stump covered in snow. In disbelief, Kang stumbled over to shake their shoulders, but they were dead. As she drew back from the corpses, she felt a trickle of sweat run down her back.

The two women kept moving. Finally, Kang, who was normally full of bravado, routinely strapping several rifles onto her body while walking, whispered, "I don't think I can make it across the mountain. You'd better go on by yourself." Li paid no attention. Kang's eyelids slowly closed. She sagged, wheezing heavily, her legs buckling. Li grabbed her under the arm and held her up. She motioned to a mule tender.

Zhu De's groom immediately recognized Kang. "Director," he croaked, "what happened?" His familiar voice jarred Kang into consciousness. She saw Zhu's mule, which hauled baggage. The groom led the mule in front of her and said, "Director, hold on to its tail, and make sure you hold on tight. Don't let go, and you'll be okay." His assuredness buoyed Kang, who grabbed hold of the beast's tail, wrapping it around her arm. She motioned for Li to also get a grip on the tail, but Li stepped aside and indicated that she was okay on her own.

The mule did not object to its new burden and in fact, Kang thought, seemed to understand its role, walking with a steady cadence. At hills and ditches, it paused for her to steady herself before towing her effortlessly along. Kang still felt drained and breathless. Her hands clenched the tail, and her arms throbbed with pain. With each step, she imagined letting go, and with each she gritted her teeth and held on. When she looked up, she saw the mule's long tail, its large haunches, the pack on its back, and its long floppy ears. Looking down at the snow, she lost track of time and distance as she slogged forever upward. Finally, the intensity of the glare increased. First she sensed and then saw light and sky. She was above the clouds.

The sun shone in Kang's eyes like a revelation as the gusting wind hit her face. "We're finally at the top!" Li Bozhao croaked hoarsely to Kang.[20] Kang felt a wash of relief.

As always seemed to be the case, there was no time to rest. On the summit, the weaker marchers "breathed so fast they were panting," Lin Wei recalled. "Shaking all over, their teeth chattered and their faces turned black." They had to keep moving. Like Kang Keqing had done, Little Sparrow, Liu Qunxian, and Cai Chang had reached the top by holding on to the tails of mules. As they began to head down, Cai's assistant, a pale young girl wearing a red sweater given to her by Cai, collapsed. She heaved for air. Her lips turned purple. Then her breathing stopped, and she died. She was left where she had fallen.[21]

As many as 3,000 Reds would perish on Jiajinshan that day — and this was only the first of the great peaks they would have to conquer.

Looking down from the summit, the women saw an icy path made slick by the straw-sandaled marchers who had preceded them. In the distance, past the blanket of snow, green foliage dotted the mountain-side. The groom told Kang to let go; she would not need the mule anymore, and he must lead it on switchbacks down the mountain. She released the tail and rubbed her numb hands together furiously to restore their circulation. Wind whipped across the exposed ridge as if it had a race to win.[22]

Many of the men were sitting and sliding down snow chutes formed by those who had already descended on their rear ends. Li told Kang to follow. Like the others, Kang pushed off, finding a groove in the snow that catapulted her forward at what quickly became a frightening pace. The wind whistled in her ears as she shot past snowy boulders. Soon she was completely out of control. The incline and the terrain determined her speed and direction. Finally, she slid off the trail at the snow line, where she breathed deeply for the oxygen her body craved. She climbed to her feet and staggered down the mountain. Turning her head to look up at the summit, she saw many others behind her, tiny dots careening down the trails.

chapter 17

A Meeting of Armies

MID-JUNE 1935

Even before crossing Jiajinshan, the First Army had begun preparing to meet up with Zhang Guotao's Fourth Army. This would be a momentous and joyous occasion but also a delicate one. Coming from two different geographic regions — Jiangxi and Eyuwan, respectively — the two armies had cultural, structural, and philosophical differences, as well as a gross imbalance of power. While the First Army contained nearly the entire Party leadership, its troop strength had been devastated. The Fourth Army vastly outnumbered the First, with better-armed and better-equipped troops, but its leadership was essentially provincial.

The Fourth Army had left its Sichuan-Shaanxi base in February and had traveled across central Sichuan. In April, the Fourth had crossed the Pei and Min rivers, fighting Nationalist and Sichuan troops as it moved west. By the end of the month, it controlled a vast territory that stretched north to the Sichuan-Gansu border, including the lands of more than twenty ethnic groups — primarily Tibetans, Muslims, and Hui — and the pine and fir forests near Pingwu, one of the last redoubts of the wild panda. But it had lost 10,000 soldiers in the process and would lose more if it stayed. In mid-June, the Fourth entered the Snowy Mountains in search of the First Army.

Wang Xinlan had mostly recovered from her bout of typhoid fever, though she leaned on a stick as she struggled to keep up with the troops. They walked day and night. "My strongest impression was that the road was endless," she later told her son and biographer, Xiao Yun.[1]

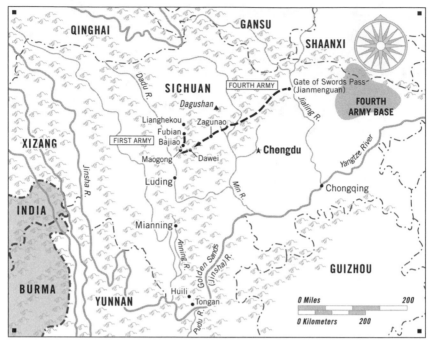

The First and Fourth Armies Meet

Now Wang stood at the foot of a 13,000-foot snowcapped mountain. The night before they were to begin their ascent, Commander Xu Shiyou sought out the *xuanchuan* team to discuss the rules for climbing it. "When you feel cold on the mountain, do not cry," Xu teased Wang. "Your tears will become icicles that can never be torn off."

"Who will cry?!" she responded defiantly. Everybody laughed at her fearlessness. Xu instructed the group in their job of boosting the morale of the soldiers, who would be severely tested by the cold, the altitude, and the crystalline winds in these mountains.

At 3:00 a.m., Wang's comrades awoke her. The troops would set out in two hours, and the *xuanchuan* team was to precede them and establish posts where they could encourage the marchers as they passed. She was told to wear all the clothes she had. Rags were passed around so that they could wrap their feet. The cooks served vats of fiery pepper soup. The spices, the marchers were told, would keep them warm as they climbed.

By the time the *xuanchuan* team reached the middle of the mountain, the predawn wind gusted snow and ice in their faces, easily penetrating their thin clothes and pricking them like needles. As they climbed, breathing became more difficult. A swift advance group passed them, but one exhausted soldier fell out, sat down, and was still there when the team set out again. As they continued to climb, the sun rose, glaring brightly off the snow. Finally, the command came to stop. The team set up its post and waited. When they saw the troops approaching, they banged bamboo clappers, and Wang sang out:

> *Comrades, keep on moving.*
> *Hurry up and cross this windy place.*
> *Don't stop, don't rest.*
> *Always remember the Three Don'ts:*
> *Don't sit down, even if you're tired.*
> *Don't drink the water in the pools on the ground.*
> *Don't run or horse around.*
> *Help each other to move on.*
> *Red soldiers are real men and heroes.*
> *You will conquer the Snowy Mountains.*

The soldiers filed past in a long line. As they did, a division commissar caught sight of Wang Xinlan. He stroked her red face. "The wind is too strong here," he said. "You must go." He conferred with the *xuanchuan* team leader, who ordered the team's youngest members to move out. Wang was reluctant to leave the team but obeyed the command. When she reached the summit, she looked back and saw the chain of troops dividing the snow-white mountainside in two, stretching all the way to the lower horizon. The sight was so breathtaking that she began to sing.

✳

BY THE TIME most of the women of the First Army descended to the alpine meadows and pine forests of the lower rises of Jiajinshan, vanguard troops had already reached the valley beyond. On June 14,

left: The Fourth Army officer Xu Shiyou, just twenty-nine, was a father figure to Wang Xinlan. Xu, who had studied martial arts at the famous Shaolin Temple for eight years, would go on to become a general in the People's Liberation Army. *right:* Wang Xinlan. Picture taken at Tonghua City, Jilin province, in the spring of 1948. *(Courtesy of Xiao Yun)*

twelve miles north of the mountain, as they approached the town of Dawei, their feeling of relief at being back on relatively level ground was suddenly shattered. An army lay in wait. Shots rang out and bugles sounded, calling units to arms but also identifying them. Both sides now realized that this was not to be a day for fighting: the soldiers facing the First Army vanguard were part of the Fourth Army, which had been sent out to find them.[2]

Some eight months into the *dabanjia,* the women of the First Army—Shorty, the Cannon, Wang Quanyuan, Little Sparrow, Kang Keqing, and the leader, Li Jianzhen—arrived at Dawei, wearing ragged uniforms, many now without sleeves and pant legs. They suffered from a multiplicity of wounds and ailments, and their legs were blood-streaked and sore-ridden. The Fourth Army troops were comparatively well fed and neatly dressed, and quite a few had fresh caps with red stars. "Even with all our effort to look presentable, we looked pitiful," Kang said. "But they were gracious and seemed equally excited to be united with their southern comrades and the Party leaders. Luckily, none of the soldiers of the Fourth seemed to notice our shabby attire. They welcomed us like family" (p. 161).

Located in a deep valley and inhabited by a few hundred Tibetan families living in wooden houses with bark or stone-shingle roofs, Dawei was a large community for the area, but it had few amenities to offer. Around a square in front of a grand Tibetan monastery, a number of stores sold only salt, beans, and black tea. In one café, opium smokers, heedless of the Communist occupation, lounged on mattresses on the floor in a haze of smoke. The Fourth Army did its best to welcome the new arrivals, vacating its quarters for the exhausted members of the First Army and feeding them corn-flour congee mixed with potatoes and pea leaves. While it was not the rice they craved, the congee was hot and filling and better than nothing, which was what they had.

The following day, the First and Fourth armies set out through a land of abrupt mountains and valleys. Reaching the town of Maogong, the leadership and many of the cadres settled in for four days to recuperate. With its highland climate of cold winters and cool summers, Maogong was dry year-round. The Red soldiers drank water from snow runoff, but dysentery swept through the ranks and prevented the medical workers from getting any rest. The only thing to eat was the corn that the Tibetans had stored for seeding. The women, like the others, eagerly gnawed on the cobs, swallowing the waxy kernels whole. Only Cai Chang sat in a corner and patiently chewed, crushing each kernel slowly between her teeth. "Do not swallow the kernels whole," she urged the others. "Chew slowly and taste its sweetness."[3]

Later, the women made a fire and cooked some of the corn. When it came time to eat it, they craved salt, which they had lacked since Nationalist blockades of the Jiangxi Soviet had cut off supplies. Salt and the trace minerals it contains are so essential to life — aiding nerve and muscle function and making it possible to digest protein — that the tongue has a special sensor for them. The lack of salt in the Reds' diet had caused headaches, leg and stomach cramps, and lethargy. When

Ancient bridge near Maogong crossed by the First Army on the Long March. *(Andy Smith)*

the body lacks salt, it tries to get rid of water to maintain its salt-fluid equilibrium, which leads to dehydration and its ramifications — dizziness, loss of coordination, spasms, heart arrhythmia, and, in severe cases, death.

Earlier in the march, Kang Keqing had stopped some soldiers carrying what she thought was a large rock. "Don't you have enough to carry?" she asked them. "Why are you carrying a rock?" They told her that it was actually a cake of salt. Kang's friends would retell the story frequently, but the memory was all that was left of the essential seasoning.[4]

Now Liu Qunxian hurried into their midst. "Hey, sisters, salt!" she called out. "I have some salt!" They gathered around her. She held a cigarette tin in her hand.

"Qunxian, do you have cigarettes or salt?" someone asked.

Liu opened the lid to reveal ocher-colored crystals. "It's cooking salt. Ah Xian hid this tin of salt from me," she told them, referring to her husband, Bo Gu, the former general secretary. "I found his stash and raided it." The women sprinkled some of the precious commodity into the pot of corn, all the while praising Liu.[5] They ate the corn, and then they gulped down the brine.

Despite these hardships, the leaders called for a torchlight rally on the church grounds to celebrate the meeting of the two armies and invited more than 1,000 high-level cadres to attend. The senior commander of the Fourth Army formally welcomed the First, Kang Keqing later recalled, and thunderous applause frequently interrupted speeches by Bo Gu, Zhu De, and Mao. Afterward, the First Army soldiers presented precious gifts of Chinese Soviet banknotes, Red Army textbooks, postcards, handkerchiefs, and small knives to the Fourths. A feast followed, with eight people around each table sharing hot dishes of food and grain alcohol — manna from the Fourth Army — and harrowing stories of the paths they had taken to this place.[6]

After dinner, the First's drama team performed, starting with "Song of the Meeting of the Two Major Armies," which Li Bozhao had helped compose weeks earlier. The First team belted it out, riding the emotion. As they sang the second line, "Welcome to the Fourth Army," the soldiers of the Fourth clapped to the tune and nodded their heads in approval. Many on both sides had tears in their eyes. After the song, the women performed folk dances and skits. Li Bozhao dazzled the men with "Yablochka" ("Little Angel"), the Russian sailors' dance she had learned in Moscow. Enchanted, the men would not stop cheering after the number — made famous by ballerina Ekaterina Vasilevna Gelcer in the revolutionary ballet *The Red Poppy* — until Li returned for an encore.

The drama team then performed a comedy penned for the occasion called *A Tattered Straw Sandal,* which poked fun at the Nationalists' failure to destroy the Red Army on the banks of the Golden Sands. When the stage Nationalists arrived to find only a single tattered straw sandal left behind, the audience roared its approval.

The celebration was a great success, and for Kang Keqing, the only disappointment was that the Fourth Army was represented by its division commanders instead of its leaders, Zhang Guotao and Chen Changhao. When she mentioned this to Zhu De, he smiled reassuringly and said, "The leaders are still at Zagunao, about a hundred *li* from here."

"Do they not know that we are here?" she persisted.

"They are just delayed," Zhu replied. After a while, he added, "The situation is complex."[7]

As the First and Fourth soldiers continued to get to know one another, telling tales, singing together, and exchanging gifts, Wang Xinlan, who was about to turn eleven on June 26, wanted to participate. She would not expect anything on her birthday, as the Chinese only celebrate birthdays of infants on their hundredth day (with food, clothing, and, for the wealthy, a locket to mark the end of the risky first months) and those over forty. At best, older children might receive the rare treat of a boiled egg. Thus the soldiers' gift giving was quite exciting. Wang searched her small pack. The only thing she had of any worth was a new shirt. She showed it to her instructor, who unfolded it and asked, laughing, "Who can wear a small girl's shirt?"[8]

"Don't they have girls in the First Army?" inquired Wang. "This is all I have." The instructor told her that none were as young as she.

Seeing her disappointment, he told her to perform for the soldiers. Wang obeyed. She recited *kuaiban* (rhyming lyrics) while clacking bamboo castanets, danced, played the harmonica, and sang "The Meeting of the Two Major Armies," modifying the line "Welcome to the Fourth Army" to "Welcome to the First Army."[9] Adorable in her diminutive uniform, she won the hearts of the First Army soldiers the way she had those of the Fourth. They cheered her on and begged for encores.

THE TWO ARMIES set out north along the Xiaojinchuan River. Several days later, in the villages of Lianghekou, known for its lamasery, and Fubian, fifty miles north of Maogong, the First Army met up with more of the Fourth Army, which brought food, clothes, and supplies. The Party leaders received new wool uniforms. Little Sparrow and the women reveled in the festive mood, giving oil paper umbrellas to their Fourth Army counterparts, who presented the First Army troops with tung-oiled bamboo hats inscribed with the words "Death to Liu Xiang" (the Sichuan general who had defeated them at Tucheng).[10]

The wounded He Zizhen, bereft of her newborn daughter, badly in need of rest, and often separated from Mao while on the trail, moved into a house with him in Fubian, a village of thirty fieldstone houses near Lianghekou. The busy Wang Quanyuan, however, did not find herself in her husband Wang Shoudao's bed until a number of her First Army sisters coaxed him into inviting all of them to his quarters. Intoxicated by a feast of duck, they convinced her to stay the night. Wang giggled and blushed like a schoolgirl.

The next day, Wang Quanyuan and Wu Fulian were sent to a small town about twenty miles from Lianghekou to look after wounded soldiers in a hospital there and to teach villagers about Communism and the evils of landlordism. Knowing only a few words of Tibetan, Wang taught through an interpreter while gradually picking up the language.[11]

On June 24, Fourth Army commander Zhang Guotao and a cavalry guard of a dozen rumbled into Fubian. Mao, the Politburo, and a select crowd were waiting outside in a torrential downpour to greet them. In anticipation of the moment, First Army engineers had cut down trees, rolled away boulders, leveled sloping ground, and built a platform beside a nearby stream. Red banners hanging from trees and above the stage cheerfully greeted the commander: "Welcome, Leader of the Fourth Army, Comrade Zhang Guotao!" The crowd cheered: "Welcome, Leader of the Fourth! Welcome Vice Chairman Zhang!"[12]

Mao and Zhang, four years his junior, were not close and had not seen each other in eight years. Mao's show of deference was perhaps meant to disarm his rival. Zhang was militarily far more powerful than he. The Fourth Army outnumbered the First ten to one. Zhang, though stately, powerfully built, and holding a better hand, was no match for Mao when it came to politics and manipulation, however. (Few were.)

On June 26, the leaders met in the Lianghekou lamasery. They wrangled over the reins of power and the consolidation of their armies. Over the course of four days, Zhou Enlai, Mao's ally, refereed. Though Zhang was militarily the superior, Mao had the support of the Politburo and in the end was able to push through his agenda: they would move north to fight the Nationalist forces and occupy the town of Songpan. They planned to take over southern Gansu and create a Sichuan-Shaanxi-Gansu revolutionary base. All agreed that the armies needed to be brought under one leader, but the issue of who that would be was another matter. For now, Zhang and Zhu De took joint command of the armies.

Later, Zhang would talk about the appalling state of discipline in the First Army. Although the cadres and ranking officers had survived largely intact, the lower echelons had been replaced over and again during the march. Zhang watched from a distance, he later reported, as inept First Army soldiers shot a Tibetan cow, not only wasting ammunition but also violating the army's strict rules for dealing with minorities in order to win them over. Looking on, the Tibetans, who measured their wealth in their herds, seethed.

The First Army cadres, however, linked to the main leadership faction, felt superior to their counterparts in the Fourth, despite their tattered condition. And even though Mao gave a speech calling for unifying the cadres, Wu Lanying, a female battalion instructor in the Fourth, noted that the First cadres were reluctant to accept them and looked down on them as uneducated and uncivilized. The Fourth cadres, she said, were perfectly willing to unite. Furthermore, Wu noted that the Fourths had something that the Firsts did not have: the Women's Independent Regiment, whose commander, Zhang Qinqiu, was arguably the most accomplished woman in the Red Army. Educated in Moscow and a former deputy political commissar of the Political Department, Zhang now commanded 2,000 armed women. Wu was also quick to point out that Zhang Qinqiu was beautiful, which to her mind added to her status (and proves that women's equality was a developing notion).

In any event, Wu did not let the attitudes of some of the First Army cadres stymie her own sociability. She joined a Fourth Army propaganda team that visited the First Army's Fifth Army Group hospital

One of the most accomplished of the women, Zhang Qinqiu commanded the Fourth Army's Women's Independent Regiment and was later a captive of the Ma.

to comfort the sick and wounded. There, as platoon leader, Wu was greeted by a handsome head nurse named Zhen Zongxian, wearing a Lenin coat beneath medical overalls. Wu, who was nicknamed Cotton Bale, due to her fair skin and soft curves, caught Zhen's eye. The two would not only reach across the two armies to marry, they would manage to get a dispensation and do it during the Long March.[13]

Meanwhile, as the First Army women interacted with the villagers, one of them, a nineteen-year-old girl, came to Li Bozhao asking to join the First Army. Jiu Xiang told Li that her Han mother had died and that she had not seen her Tibetan father, a merchant of needles and thread, for years. Li could, perhaps, see herself in the beautiful and gregarious girl, but First Army orders currently forbade the recruiting of women. Those who had joined en route earlier had not fared well, some perishing from the rigors of the trail, others having to be left behind.

But Jiu persisted, sleeping in the *xuanchuan* office, volunteering for chores, and calling Li "Big Sister." Finally, Li used her *guanxi* to request an exception to the rules. She went to Cai Chang's husband, Li Fuchun, who obtained permission for Jiu to join. When Li told her the news, Jiu was overwhelmed with joy. The other women were pleased, too. Even though they had endured so much, their belief that they would eventually find a good home and a better life persisted.[14]

chapter 18

Through the Tibetan Snowies

JULY–AUGUST 1935

O n the morning of June 30, the First Army set out to the north, again through the Snowies. Anyone who saw them might have thought that they were ghosts from some faraway hell. Ragged in dress, withered in body, their eye sockets sunken and bruised, their hair either clumped and matted or missing altogether—these remaining marchers looked less like an army than a spectral mob staggering forward in their own funeral procession.

Ghosts were very much on the mind at this time of year. According to Chinese tradition, each July the gatekeepers of the netherworld throw open their doors so that the spirits of the dead can visit their relatives on earth. During the month, rural Chinese worship their ancestors at family shrines, re-dress mannequin surrogates of dead parents, and offer papier-mâché houses, servants, and animals to the departed. They serve them food and burn candles and incense in their presumed presence. And because the dead have descended to hell to be judged by an underworld court—run by hideous half-human clerks and guards with the heads of horses and cows—the villagers also burn paper coins, or *mingqian* (money of the netherworld), to bribe the court, which, mirroring its earthly counterparts, is naturally rife with corruption.

July is a time not only for reverence but also for caution. Some of the furloughed ghosts have no living relatives, making visitations impossible. These lonely spirits, especially those who died violently or young, have been known to attack the living, sometimes even killing them in order to trade places with them on earth. It is common to avoid dark places at this time and to leave servings of rice and meat on street corners to pacify these ghosts, yet even with these precautions, July is considered an unlucky month to move or to marry.

It was only forty miles from Lianghekou to Zhuokeji, the marchers' destination, but another behemoth lay in the way: 13,500-foot Mengbishan.[1] They traveled only ten miles the first day, stopping early near the base of the massif to prepare themselves for the ascent. Learning from their experience on Jiajinshan, they carried water infused with hot chilies to warm their insides as they crossed over the mountain — a total of twenty-eight miles up one side and down the other, Kang Keqing recalled. Kang followed Zhu De's mule closely up the steep pitch. When she weakened, she latched onto its tail. With the help of the groom, she kept pace with the others and safely crossed the second Snowy.[2]

When they reached the other side, the marchers discovered to their dismay that the locals had once again abandoned their homes ahead of the approaching army, taking or hiding their stores of food. Armed bands of Tibetans harassed the Red scouts and vanguard and picked off anyone who left the safety of the columns. In a few days, twenty soldiers were killed, including one high-ranking officer, who was shot by a sniper.

Hostilities came to a head at Zhuokeji, a village of several hundred stone houses on narrow, winding cobblestone streets. Rich from the opium trade, Zhuokeji was the stronghold of the *tusi* (chief) Suo Guan Ying. On a hillside on the eastern edge of town, a fortress with cannon embrasures overlooked the Red Army's route. The Reds' goal was still to make allies and avoid fighting whenever possible. Hoping to impress these Tibetans — a band they could defeat, but not without a price — with their military advantage, they fired their guns into the air. The Tibetans, supported by their Buddhist lamas, who, it was said, proclaimed that killing Red soldiers was as good as reciting Buddhist verses for accruing merit, stood their ground. Red Army leaders now dispatched a soldier with a letter hanging from the end of his gun explaining their intention to pass through peacefully. The Tibetans, according to Kang Keqing, murdered him.

The Reds waited for the sun to go down. They had one last gambit to avoid bloodshed, and they tried it once darkness had arrived: firing two signal rockets into the sky. The red and green flashes did what the earlier display of firepower could not; they frightened the Tibetans, who had never seen anything like these dragon's eyes that pierced the night sky. "In extreme fright, they darted back and forth," Kang wrote, "and disappeared into the mountains leaving behind their supplies and ammunition." It was not a victory without a shot, but it was close, and the marchers breathed a sigh of relief. They could not afford to be bogged down in a protracted and draining battle for the pass.[3]

The Reds quickly occupied Zhuokeji and the *tusi's* mid-nineteenth-century fortress, composed of nine buildings, the tallest of which was seven stories high. Dozens of giant iron pots filled the ground-floor kitchens. Stables and servants' quarters occupied the side rooms on the ground level. Guardrooms and storerooms filled the second floor. Another floor was devoted to worship, with Buddhist murals painted on the walls and huge copper drums and gongs for prayer. A staircase of inclined planks with chiseled footholds led from level to level and was quite precarious, Kang recalled. The Reds were stunned by the *tusi's* opulent living quarters, with their massive carved wooden doors, Han paintings, antique furniture, and marble and jade Buddha figures.[4] They confiscated everything useful that the *tusi* and his men had left behind, though most of the antiques were too cumbersome to carry.[5]

A staple of the local diet was *zhanba,* or *tsampa,* a mixture of Tibetan barley (often with its husks, ground with a hand mill), tea, yak curds, and yak butter. Yet the Reds found its ingredients in short supply. Moreover, the Tibetans had cleverly dismantled and hidden key parts of their mills, leaving the marchers unable to grind what little barley they could assemble. In a frank confession to Guo Chen in 1986, Deng Yingchao acknowledged the depths to which they had fallen at this point. Their food rations were all but gone. The troops in front were sometimes able to forage leftover barley kernels in harvested fields.

Tusi fortress at Zhuokeji. *(Lawrence Gray)*

They roasted the barley, rubbed off the burnt shells, and swallowed the kernels, which were practically indigestible and often passed right through them. Those who followed behind sometimes found these very same kernels, which they roasted a second time and ate.[6]

The women were particularly withered at this stage. Gaunt-faced and bony, they suffered from various ailments, including chronic exhaustion and amenorrhea. Their starved bodies behaved as if they were two to three decades older than they were. Worried about their health, Liu Qunxian's husband, Bo Gu, brought them maotai and *donggui* (Chinese angelica root), an herbal medicine for women, which they believed fortified the blood and promoted regular menstrual flow. Bo also gave them the head of a goat and told them how to make goat-head soup. The women felt somewhat better after eating the soup.[7]

Billeted in the town's two- and three-story stone houses, whose top floors were used for Buddhist prayer and roofs for drying grain, the Reds remained in Zhuokeji for several days, extracting what provisions they could. Slowly, the villagers returned. They were rough-

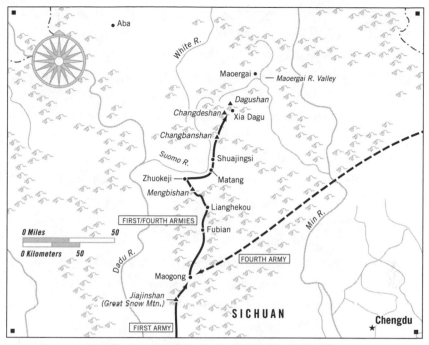

The First and Fourth Armies Move North Together

hewn men and women dressed in tall boots and dark-red belted overcoats, worn with their right arms free for working. The men wore felt or fur hats and silver earrings and carried knives. The women had long braids piled on their heads. Using translators, the Red women helped ease relations by explaining that they fought for the common people and against oppressors. They were able to establish some trust and to do a little trading, gathering enough provisions to leave, which they promptly did.[8]

Dong Biwu assigned Porter Girl, Wu Fulian, and the Cannon to lead a struggling Fourth Army family unit, consisting of several hundred women—some with deformed feet—and their children. Assigned to three women without *guanxi,* this was a virtually hopeless task that was bound to end badly. In the pouring rain, without raincoats or umbrellas, the group moved like a turtle. The children fell in the mud and got soaked in puddles. Wet and cold, the unit finally collapsed in a freezing, crying huddle. Porter Girl, Wu, and the Cannon tried to rally them, but the hobbled women could go no farther.

Finally, Porter Girl, Wu, and the Cannon decided to leave them behind. After an emotional parting, the three sped off. Following arrows discreetly left by the Red troops, they rushed to catch up, but it was not long before they saw Nationalist cavalrymen approaching in the distance. They ducked off the path and debated going back to try to warn the women and children. Since there was virtually no hope of helping them and they themselves were soldiers and believed they would be raped, tortured, and executed if seized, they determined that it was too risky. They hid until the cavalrymen had passed and then stole ahead, not looking back.

As they traveled along a footpath on the south bank of the Suomo River, they passed boulders and cliff faces, where the *xuanchuan* units had inscribed insults to Hu Zongnan, one of Chiang Kaishek's most trusted generals. It was probably near Matang, a disappointing village of only a few houses and shops, where Porter Girl, Wu Fulian, and the Cannon finally caught up with their First Army comrades. Dong Biwu was waiting for them at the campsite outside town. He rushed up and grasped their hands tightly in his, saying, "You've finally returned! We were worried that you'd never catch up." Anxiously, they told Dong what had happened. "You did the right thing," he reassured them. "You'd have been killed if the enemy caught you."[9] He had a tent erected for them and made arrangements for their rest. Both exhaustion and relief washed over them, but the matter of their conduct would not end here.

After Shuajingsi, a village at 11,000 feet — more than two miles above sea level — the Reds crossed the third Snowy Mountain in their path, Changbanshan (known locally as Yakexiashan or Yakoushan), at 14,000 feet a steep and unforgiving climb. They reached the town of Luhua just as they ran out of food. The Tibetans here were wary and inimical, hiding themselves and their food stores in the mountains and attacking when the odds were in their favor. They communicated with each other by blowing horns, howling, and whistling, sounds that came to haunt the marchers. According to Little Sparrow, they sometimes shot at the Red soldiers when they tried to approach them and laid ambushes in the hills for hunting parties pursuing yaks and wild boars.[10]

Luhua was an agricultural center with plentiful barley and wheat fields, though the crops would not be ready to harvest for at least two more weeks. The First Army did not have two weeks to spare. They negotiated with landowners to buy the premature crops in the field. Those farmers who had fled had to settle for the rates negotiated by the others and payments entrusted to their neighbors until their return. Despite rules against it, the marchers coerced many farmers, though no one would speak of such things later.[11]

The Reds harvested the grain themselves, meeting in the fields after a breakfast of watery porridge. Soldiers, officers, and cadres were each required to collect and mill at least fifteen pounds of grain, which amounted to ten days' provisions for themselves plus extra for the wounded and those exempted from active duty.

Most of the cadres had not worked as field hands for years, but they readily fell into the rhythm of harvesting by hand. Spirits were high in anticipation of plenty to eat. "Many people started singing while working," Kang Keqing later recalled. "Zhu De was almost fifty at the time, and he joined us. He was fast and efficient with the sickle and went ahead of everyone. After the harvest, he was the first to hoist the load on his shoulders. The two bundles of wheat he carried were enormous and heavy." Shorty, the Cannon, Porter Girl, and five others toiled with Zhu, and when they were finished, they built a fire right in the field, roasted some barley, and began devouring it. Suddenly, Zhu pointed at Shorty and said, "Shorty, your face is filthy. You have a mustache!" Everyone looked around. All of their faces were smeared with ash from the fire. Without pausing to wipe their mouths, they fell back on the barley, snorting with laughter as they ate.[12]

Some troops busied themselves collecting furs, wool, and cloth to make garments for the grasslands, while others focused on *xuanchuan* and harvesting crops. In the hope of finding more food, they began to spread out farther along the Heishui River, culling small parcels of unripe grain.

They got luckier when one contingent ventured south to the fertile village of Wabuliangzi, where several hundred Tibetan families — all of whom had fled — grew millet, wheat, buckwheat, taros, and radishes and raised pigs, cows, and sheep. They also possessed reserves of salt. The Reds quickly attempted to spread the word through the few locals they could find that they had come in peace and that they would pay for provisions with silver. Within a few days, they managed to lure many of the villagers back and negotiated to buy crops from their fields and salt from their mines. The Reds then helped harvest and mine their purchases. Red political teams orchestrated mass meetings and formed local governments in six villages, which banded together to form a collective People's Revolutionary Government. In an effort to establish further goodwill, they opened up an old government building where grain was stored and dispersed it to the poor.[13]

When they set out again, some of the First Army climbed Changdeshan, the highest and technically most difficult Snowy so far. Departing at dawn, they covered twenty miles to reach its shoulders at three in the afternoon. It was a sunny day, and the climbing was good. The day was not without its misfortune, though: several soldiers died after being mauled by a wild animal. (Locals would later speak of finding the corpses of Red Army soldiers mauled by bears.) Accustomed to the altitude now, Kang Keqing climbed without trouble. Those in the rear avoided having to ascend Changdeshan after receiving word from the top that there was a path around the mountain.

Given the rigors of the trail and the need to make up for longstanding nutritional deficits, the Reds' food haul from this region did not last long. When they soon ran low again, the troops killed wild goats and dogs to eat. In the fields surrounding the three villages beneath Dagushan, the next mountain, they expected to find golden fields ready for harvest. They were struck instead by colder weather and fields of grain still green and inedible, rippling in the wind like river waves.

THE CONVALESCENT COMPANY bivouacked in the village of Xia (Lower) Dagu beneath the towering mountain, where they searched for provisions. Three of the women also searched for absolution. At a cadres meeting, a soldier condemned Wu Fulian, Porter Girl, and the Cannon for abandoning the family unit outside Zhuokeji. The accuser moved that the Cannon, who had led the trio, be expelled from the Party, an act that would strip her of her rights and responsibilities.

"I was returning to the troops, not running to join the enemy!" the Cannon replied, incredulously.[14]

"You left so many people behind," the soldier remonstrated. "What good are you?"

"They refused to move," the Cannon said, "and we couldn't very well carry each one of them on our backs!"

A hand vote was taken on the motion to strip the Cannon of her Party membership. Only the accuser voted in favor. "Personally, I also disagree with this motion," Dong Biwu said, but he insisted that they report the situation to the Political Department.

When Dong reported the incident to Cai Chang's husband, Li Fuchun, Li erupted: "Who dares to try to expel Deng Liujin from the Party? The women soldiers were already exhausted. How could they be expected to tend to the whole family unit? Without weapons, they couldn't even protect themselves. From now on, the army will take better care of the women soldiers and reduce their burdens."

It was a breakthrough of sorts for the women: Li declared that they would no longer tend to the stretchers. Instead, they would be dispatched to field combat units and government offices. This was recognition not only that the women had been forced to do grueling, dangerous work — carrying heavy stretchers, which often made them lag behind, vulnerable to attack — that no male cadres would consider doing (and that even the porters and soldiers scorned), but also that they were too important to be squandered. The Cannon and Qiu Yihan, a twenty-eight-year-old from Hunan whose glasses had been

Dagushan from Xia Dagu. At 14,700 feet, the pass on Dagushan was the highest crossed by the First Army. *(Andy Smith)*

smashed early on in the *dabanjia* and who had difficulty seeing, were assigned to *xuanchuan* work for the Third Army Group. The Political Department absorbed some women. Liao Siguang was reassigned to the Supply Department, in charge of collecting food among other things, headed by her husband, Kai Feng.[15]

For the time being, their joy at being freed from the stretchers was tempered by the continued lack of food. Though expected to gather rations for ten days, they had a hard time finding their next meal, and they resorted to foraging. Zhu De collected edible wild plants, sorted them into piles, and then explained to the troops what to look for and how to cook them.

Xie Fei, Qian Xijun, and Zhong Yuelin, who were staying together in a two-story Tibetan house, found wild celery and, having no cooking oil, built a fire on the second floor of the house to boil the green stalks. Even so, the celery was stringy and bitter, and they spat the fibers out and went to bed hungry. Lying there, Xie looked through a crack in the floorboards at the animal stalls on the ground floor. What she saw jolted her: there appeared to be a small pile of grain on the manure. Calling out to Qian and Zhong, she announced her discovery.

Hearing the word "grain," the two jumped up and came over to peer through the crack in the floor. "Yuck, it's foul," one said. "There are maggots on it!" Looking at the larvae squirming on the dung, they shook their heads and sighed in disappointment. Perhaps the grain had fallen from the second floor onto the manure or had passed through a cow; either way, they decided not to retrieve it.[16]

At this point, Wu Lie, a Political Department guard, appeared. When they told him of their discovery, he peeked through a crack and then ran downstairs, rolling up his sleeves. Soon they could see that he had a small pile of grain in his hand.

The sight was enough for their stomachs to override their concern for hygiene. "We need to get some before he takes it all!" the women urged each other. They rushed down the stairs. Discarding their shoes, they walked barefoot into the pen. After collecting the grain on top of the manure, they broke apart the dried dung and picked out the undigested grain inside. Working through the night, they each collected several pounds of grain. They wrapped their precious cargo in handkerchiefs and went to the river to wash it. Having thoroughly rinsed the kernels, they roasted them and packed them in their ration bags — and considered themselves lucky.

After five cold days beneath Dagushan, the women departed at dawn to climb the towering last Snowy. Someone had posted a sign by the route warning troops not to proceed after nine in the morning; to be caught on the mountain at night would be dire. Xie, Qian, and Zhong carried handfuls of roasted barley in their pockets, snacking on the kernels for energy, but this drew jealous stares. One cadre from Shanghai offered Xie half a bar of soap for some. Soap was a highly sought-after item, and Xie felt that she could not trade her lowly manna for so precious a commodity. She gave the man a handful of the grain for nothing in return and continued upward. Worn-out and starving, the Communists could hardly wait to reach the Maoergai River valley, the region beyond and so unlike the Snowies, said to be fertile enough to produce sufficient food in a year to last for three.

But before they got there, another mountain would exact its toll. "The higher we climbed, the thinner the air became and the colder we felt," Mo Wenhua, a twenty-four-year-old *xuanchuan* officer, recalled. "A few of our comrades who were not as strong started to feel faint and became dizzy." Some turned pale, their lips blue, and passed out. The others tried to help them walk, but those affected moved like drunks, staggering and falling over. "We had no choice but to leave them in the snow," said Mo.[17]

SINCE DEPARTING THEIR HENAN STRONGHOLD more than eight months earlier, Young Orchid and the five remaining nurses of the Twenty-fifth Army had climbed many mountains and crossed many

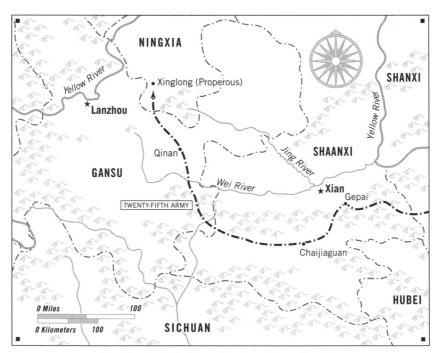

The Twenty-fifth Army Reaches Gansu Province

rivers, trekking west, north, and then west again, keeping up with the army for more than eight hundred miles. Having taken Gepai, in Shaanxi, fifty miles southeast of Xian, the provincial capital, in January and then having moved on to Chaijiaguan in February, where they had lost Zeng Jilan to illness, the Twenty-fifth had managed to provision and recruit more than seven hundred new soldiers in southern Shaanxi.[18]

It was in Gepai that General Xu Haidong had risen from his cot to lead his forces, but he had borrowed from the future to win the day. His sudden, almost miraculous recovery and his euphoria after the victory had given way to an even deeper plunge. His wounds grew infected and burned feverishly. His head throbbed until he gritted his teeth audibly. For the first time, Young Orchid saw tears of pain on his face.

Gradually, however, Xu's wounds began to improve. During the days and nights that Young Orchid nursed him, she listened to his every word. His determination to regain his health and to lead his men again moved her.[19]

During the month of March, as General Xu recovered steadily and his troops maneuvered to elude their pursuers, he and Young Orchid became fast companions. In mid-April, the Twenty-fifth reoccupied Gepai. Spring was in the air, and the orchids and peach trees were in blossom. One night, Xu and Young Orchid took a walk together alone. Returning late to camp, Xu did not want the soldiers to see them together, so he hid her inside his coat.

The next day, one of General Xu's fellow officers patted him on the shoulder. "Old Xu," he said, with a mischievous gleam, "someone was saying something about you behind your back."

"What did he say?" Xu asked warily.

"He said you have four legs," the friend replied.

"Damn it! Is someone calling me an animal?" said Xu.

"Last night when you returned from the river, you had a coat on, right?"

"Of course," said Xu.

"And someone saw four legs sticking out under your coat," the friend said, laughing. "It appears that Tiger Xu is a real tiger, complete with four legs."[20]

In July, the Twenty-fifth set out once more, heading west into Gansu province, where tragedy struck the nurses yet again. Sources are cryptic on the death of Cao Zongkai, which occurred in the vicinity of Qinan, a dry, mountainous area traversed by the ancient Silk Road and home of the Chinese goddess Nuwa, creator of animals and humans. One leading historian states that both Cao Zongkai and Zeng Jilan died as a result of the "frequent fighting and tiring propaganda duties." Another account claims that after a river crossing, Cao died on a stretcher after — and here the Chinese is ambiguous — either "being wronged" or "being unjustly accused of wrongdoing." A third source says that she "committed suicide because of a certain incident."[21]

The lack of solid information about Cao's death leads one to suspect that for appearance's sake as little as possible was said about the matter. In an army where the ratio of men to women was nearly five hundred to one, it is likely that the troubling incident was of a sexual nature. Reading between the lines, it would appear that Cao Zongkai was wronged by someone, perhaps raped by a superior, and then killed herself out of shame or anger. The women — who quite likely knew the brutal truth — were devastated, but as with so many tragedies of the Long March, there was no time to cry. There was only a relentless urgency to keep moving.

In early August, the Twenty-fifth rapidly passed through the cradle of Chinese civilization in southeastern Gansu, where the Yangtze and Yellow rivers run through remote forests. One skirmish and forced march followed another as they headed north. General Xu employed swift but furious counterpunches to keep the pursuing enemy in check.

When they got to the fast-flowing Wei, a major tributary of the Yellow River, the Twenty-fifth ferried the nurses and the wounded across in a small boat and then forded the river on foot. When they reached the Jing River and found no bridges or boats, the soldiers strung two ropes across the rushing water and helped the women make their way across. Young Orchid and the nurses took heart from the feeling that the soldiers were rooting for them.

On August 15, they arrived at Prosperous (Xinglong), a Muslim town on Gansu's eastern plateau (now part of Ningxia province), where they stayed for three days. Islam had long been established in China, arriving both via trade on the Silk Road and by delegation, the earliest a celebrated visit in AD 650 by the Prophet Mohammed's maternal uncle less than two decades after the Prophet's death. Over the centuries, Muslims had integrated thoroughly. Men who had married Han women often took the wife's surname. Others converted from "Mohammed" to "Mo" or from "Hussein" to "Hu." While successive generations of Chinese Muslims increasingly resembled the local population physically and culturally, the Muslims strictly maintained their religious practices.

Here, in an effort to show unity with the Muslim minority, or at least to avoid fighting with them, the Red Army issued Three Forbiddens and Four Attentions. It was forbidden to use mosques for any reason, to raid Muslim landlords, and to serve pork to Muslim families. In addition, the Reds must pay attention to recognizing Muslim habits and customs, using only Muslim buckets to get water from wells, trading fairly, and, for men, avoiding contact with Muslim women. The locals received the Reds warmly. The Muslim women especially welcomed the five nurses, marveling at their uniforms and appearance and inviting them into their homes. In turn, the nurses made a point to help the local women do housework and tend to their sick.[22]

ILLNESS ON THE MARCH was a rite of passage. It was not if but when, what, and who—if anyone—would help you. Tuberculosis, typhoid fever, dysentery, and a host of other diseases, often undiagnosed, compounded by exposure, exhaustion, malnutrition, and food poisoning, took more lives and caused more agony than bullets and bombs. In that sense, the women were as much on the front line as the men.

Wang Xinlan had been near death. Deng Yingchao had been carried the whole way. Now Cai Chang was battling tuberculosis.

While the First Army had traveled far from its southern base and the Fourth had moved decisively to join it — the Twenty-fifth was on a long trajectory to converge with them both — the Second and Sixth army groups were still operating on their home turf in western Hunan.

Young Ma Yixiang, in the Second Army Group, was nothing if not precocious. Even before setting out, she became desperately sick. All her life, Ma, skinny and frail, had struggled with illness, contracting pneumonia, meningitis, enteritis, and a host of other unnamed illnesses. In the army, she lived on bare rations of gruel and mush, and as a medical worker, she was exposed to every affliction the troops knew. Now, as her comrades in the mobile hospital tried to stay a step ahead of enemy forces, a high fever consumed her, and she could not keep up with the stretchers and walking wounded of the medical unit. Finally, the sweepers — those who, like Kang Keqing, corralled the stragglers and dealt with suspected deserters — put her on a mule and took her to a stationary medical unit in a village. The medics could not identify her illness, and while the nurses attended to the wounded, Ma passed her time in fever dreams. One night, she was lucid enough to know that the woman beside her had died but was too delirious to tell anyone. She slept all night next to the corpse.

It was now, when Ma was at her weakest, that fate played another dirty trick on her. For all its idealism, the revolution had a recurring dark side of paranoia, recriminations, and oppression that could manifest itself at any time. Resembling witch hunts, Party purges had already cost the Communists many loyal lives and begun to create a culture of suspicion among Red cadres, which would ultimately give rise to the brutal Cultural Revolution in 1966.[23]

The seemingly harmless banter between Ma and the wounded soldier who had recovered for a time in Yongshui, her home village, had now been threshed in the rumor mill and half-baked in the oven of the Red security bureaucracy. As Ma lay in a cold sweat, her temperature skyrocketing, Party inquisitors branded her an "alien class element." Her friends and workmates were helpless to defend her from the security officers; protest was almost unthinkable. Still, a woman known as Lao (Old) Wang rose to Ma's defense, verifying that Ma was indeed an abused *tongyangxi* before joining the army. For this effrontery, Old Wang was accused of being unworthy and herself promptly expelled from the army along with Ma.

Deathly ill and barely able to walk, Ma found herself lost and clinging to the walls of houses in a small village, moving hand over hand down the street. A local woman who had just given birth took pity on her. For the next week, Ma lay on her bed during the day and at night slept on straw on the floor. The woman's kindness more than made up for the mosquitoes and the mice that also made her house their home. By week's end, Ma had recovered enough to work in the village. She was paid in rice, which she shared with her host.

As circumstances necessitated, Ma kept a low profile. However, word of her whereabouts spread. A cousin who was a Red Army messenger came to check on her. Thinking it safer, he sent her to stay with some relatives who lived nearby. But when the relatives dispatched her to a hospital outpost to get a share of the rice expropriated from a local landlord, the wife of the head medical administrator saw her and reported her. Soon a political commissar had Ma in his sights. He expelled her from the village, threatening to shoot her if he saw her again.

While Ma considered her options, she hid outside the village by day and snuck back to the house at night to sleep. Finally, she fell in with a company of men whose task it was to guard boats of confiscated rice being transported back to the town of Sangzhi, in the area where Ma and the others had set out from. Unaware that Ma was an outcast, these soldiers took her in, sharing their rations with her as they walked along the shore shadowing the heavily laden boats. In Sangzhi, Ma found the courageous Lao Wang, who had stood up for her and suffered the consequences, hiding with a family. Wang, who had made arrangements to eat at a local Red Army school, took Ma in and treated her like a daughter. She shared her food with her, made her a padded jacket to wear against the coming cold, and arranged for her to wash clothes for the school staff.

Unbound

Few secrets lasted long in the Chinese soviets. When Lao Wang left to visit her mother in a nearby town, Communist officials seized Ma and impounded her with a group of other "little devils," mothers with children, and women hobbled by bound feet. Together they slept at night on the office floor, waiting for the officials to decide their fate.

chapter 19

Beyond the Snowies

AUGUST 1935

By the time the women set out with the First Army leaders for the Maoergai River valley about thirty miles north of Xia Dagu, vanguard troops had already secured the area. Pushed back, the Nationalist general positioned his troops defensively to prevent the First Army from moving east into central Sichuan. Pursued from the south and barricaded to the east, the Reds had two choices: they could turn west into even fiercer and more desolate mountain ranges, or they could continue north and attempt to cross the Caodi — a hellish expanse of high-elevation hills and marshes.

In either event, Mao's army had preparations to make. While Sun Tzu's classic treatise *The Art of War* emphasizes deception ("When capable, feign incapacity") and cunning ("The best battle is the battle that is won without being fought"), the military master also urges commanders to carry enough supplies with them to be self-sustaining. In this case, it would take a herculean effort to find enough provisions to feed the troops on either route, but the fertile Maoergai Valley at least offered a chance.

The Communists arrived to eerie villages, where the Tibetan spirit guards carved of stone watched over empty lanes and vacant grain bins. The soldiers billeted in the valley's four hundred recently abandoned wooden houses, spread out over about ten miles from the small village of Wodeng in the south to the largest village, Shanbazhai, in the north. White prayer flags hanging from poles on all sides of the houses snapped in the howling wind, as if they were the admonishing voices of the homeowners, who had fled with their possessions, food, and livestock into the hills.

The surrounding fields were golden-green with ripening barley. The Communists, without much success, tried to send emissaries out to persuade the locals to return. As elsewhere, they paid the few farmers who had stayed behind and left money for those who had not, then began to cut the barley.[1]

Still, rations remained extremely tight. In Wodeng, where many of the leaders and women stayed, some hungry soldiers stole and slaughtered the mule Liao Siguang had been assigned after she gave birth. Her angry groom wanted to confront the soldiers, but Liao stopped him. It was only natural, she knew, that hunger would drive them to prey on the beasts. Instead, the groom reclaimed the mule's hide and used it to make soup.

For a week, the women subsisted largely on wild plants. Mushrooms were both a blessing and a curse. Of China's 37,000 species, only one in a hundred is considered edible. About half that many are valued for medicinal purposes, from the *pom pon,* or "monkey head," which tastes like seafood, promotes nerve cell growth, and enhances the immune system, to the silver ear, a jelly-like fungus said to be beneficial to the lungs. But in the wild, even experts have difficulty discerning edible species from the inedible, some of which are poisonous. While rounding up straggling soldiers on a Wodeng hillside, Liao Siguang, Porter Girl, and the Cannon picked mushrooms. Back at camp, they made soup and invited a Fourth Army colonel, a commissar, and some staff officers to eat with them.[2]

Meanwhile, Shorty spent the day going from village to hamlet searching for locals, hoping to trade for grain, vegetables, or livestock. Finally, around dusk, she came across an elderly man and a teenage boy. The man could not understand Mandarin, but the boy spoke a little. Shorty explained that the Reds were different from the other Hans, that they respected the Tibetans and followed strict rules of conduct. Through the boy, she won over the old man. Soon the boy was leading the villagers and their animals into town. The man invited Shorty to his yak-dung house.

In the family quarters on the second floor, he heated up jerked meat and potatoes in an oven. Although Shorty was famished, Long March rules forbidding her to take food for herself were so ingrained that she refused the food. The man growled, and the boy translated: "You think it's not good enough for you?" Flustered, Shorty pretended to be ill and, holding her stomach, rushed down the stairs and out of the house.

She arrived back at camp after dark, deflated. The Cannon, Liao Siguang, Porter Girl, and some men lay sleeping haphazardly around a silent room. Shorty lit a candle and found a bowl of dark soup. Faint with hunger, she took a few gulps. She recognized it as mushroom soup, though it tasted bitter. She set the bowl down and made her way to the bed, where Porter Girl was sprawled. She nudged Porter Girl with her foot. "Porter Girl, move over a bit," she whispered, to no avail. "Porter Girl," she said louder, "make room." But Porter Girl did not stir.

Shorty scanned the room, suddenly feeling the silence. No one stirred, and she did not hear the usual nighttime snores and snuffling. It dawned on her that something was wrong. She jumped up. Inspecting her friends, she saw vomit on their clothes and foam around their lips. She grabbed a bowl of water and poured some into Liu's mouth. Porter Girl's eyes opened. "Xiuying," she moaned, "we ate bad mushrooms." Shorty ran to the river for more water and mixed in some vinegar and potassium permanganate to make an emetic. She revived her friends and gave them some of the hastily made concoction. Then she attended to the soldiers. All survived.[3]

The First Army regrouped along the remote Maoergai River for more than a month, and with the extended pause, the leaders relaxed the rules prohibiting marriage. By now, according to Cai Xiaoqian, Little Sparrow had succumbed to Zhang Wentian's pursuit. Mao often made fun of the two by quoting from classical love poems to insinuate their affection. In one billet, when a row of four rooms was available, he had placed them in the two in the middle, while he and Chen Yun took the outer ones. "You be the guard tonight," Mao joked with Chen. "Be sure you have them under surveillance."[4]

Porter Girl and her sweetheart in the Ninth Army Group took

advantage of this opportunity to wed. They had few resources for a celebration, but that did not stop her friends from following the tradition of *nao dongfang,* revelry in the honeymooners' bedroom. It was traditionally believed that ghosts and evil spirits envious of earthly happiness would attempt to ruin the celebration by sneaking into the newlyweds' bedroom and causing trouble. But these spirits could be repulsed by the energy of the living, especially in crowds. Thus, "on your wedding night," one saying went, "you're either disturbed by the living or the dead." Since many couples did not know each other before they married, friends and family would gather and try to ease the awkwardness, especially for the bride, who had usually been sheltered from men. Revelers often told the couple risqué jokes to break the ice, made the groom fish for candy in the bride's shirt, or had the couple try to bite an apple on a string, which was yanked away at the right moment to make them kiss.[5]

When several of Porter Girl's friends rushed into the couple's room shouting, the newlyweds met them with surprise. They had no candy, the traditional inducement to get wedding night revelers to leave, and despite all that had passed, Porter Girl bowed her head shyly. "We don't have candy," said Bi Zhanyun, her new husband. "All we have is bullets." Giggling and wishing the couple well, the women departed, so that Porter Girl and Bi could finally be alone.[6]

OVER SEVERAL DAYS during the first week of August, the Central Committee and other leaders, including Fourth Army commander Zhang Guotao, held a crucial meeting in the heavily guarded village of Wodeng. While he would later reside lower in the valley at the commodious Maoergai Lamasery, Mao perhaps planned the historic Shawo "Sand House" Meeting—so called because the two-story village house where it took place looked out on a sandbar in the Maoergai River—in the narrow, remote upper reaches of the valley in order to intimidate Zhang, whose Fourth Army was hundreds of miles away in the town of Aba.[7] During the meeting, the leaders reaffirmed the plan—despite Zhang's lack of enthusiasm for it—to march north to cross the Caodi,

Shawo House, where Mao Zedong and Zhang Guotao met to reorganize the First and Fourth armies. *(Andy Smith)*

to fight the Nationalists in the north, and then ultimately to drive out the Japanese occupiers in the east. Their more immediate goal was the formation of a new revolutionary base in the borderlands where Sichuan, Gansu, and Shaanxi provinces converged.[8]

The leaders also wrangled over how to unite the two forces and share power. Since they could not reach a consensus on who should lead and in what capacity, they finally reorganized the troops into two columns, mixing army divisions. The Left Column would be led by First Army chief of staff Liu Bocheng. It would also include Zhu De, now commander in chief of the entire Red Army, and Zhang Guotao, overall military commissar. Mao, other Party leaders, the Military Commission, and most of the women joined the Right Column, under Fourth Army commander Xu Xiangqian and political commissar Chen Changhao.[9]

Of the thirty women who had set out with the First Army, this would be the first significant dispersal. The few who had dropped out along the route had struggled to survive.

Xie Xiaomei had stayed in Guizhou, and Li Guiyang and Han Shiying in Yunnan. Li and Han had soon found themselves on the run with the guerrilla force. "We ran and fought," Li later said. "We would run more than one hundred or two hundred *li*. You couldn't keep your eyes open." In the spring, her husband, Dai Yuanhuai, had been gunned down in front of her. She had tried to recover his leather bag and gun but was stopped by her comrades and whisked away to safety.[10]

Xie and her husband, Wang Ming, had been imprisoned for ten days and then had hidden out in Guiyang. Destitute and ill, Wang got a job as a street cleaner but was fired when his supervisors saw him spitting blood. While Xie worked as a live-in housemaid, Wang stayed at a Catholic church that gave shelter to indigents at night, until they too turned him out because of his illness. Finally, Xie and Wang had given up on the idea of establishing a partisan force in Guiyang and set out on foot toward Wang's home in Guangdong, which they would reach in February.[11]

Of the twenty-seven remaining women who had set out from Ruijin, five were assigned to the Left Column. Wu Fulian would work in the convalescent company. Zhou Yuehua would accompany her husband, He Cheng, the doctor who would run the General Medical Corps. Kang Keqing would stay by the side of her husband, General Zhu De, whose telegrapher also brought along his assistant and wife, Li Jianhua. Also placed in the Left Column was Kang's close friend and fellow military instructor, Wu Zhonglian, recently married to Political Department staffer Zeng Risan. Li and Wu were both pregnant, and Wu would march with musk tied around her waist, a folk method for aborting a pregnancy.

The women had no choice in these assignments and no way of predicting that fate had dealt their small clique a blow. Their trek would be longer and more demanding than that of the women who remained with Mao, and for some the suffering would be beyond compare.[12]

While the marchers were waiting to set out in the newly formed columns, Deng Yingchao struggled to keep ailing Zhou Enlai— devastated by the stress of the trail, battle, and long hours of work— alive. Suffering from what was said to be an attack of the liver (acute hepatitis, Harrison Salisbury later surmised), Zhou's temperature soared to 105 degrees. Soldiers relayed snow from the mountains to cool him. Deng fed him sips of a white-fungus broth to nourish him.

Finally, they could wait no longer. Soldiers of the Third Army Group hoisted the failing Zhou on a stretcher and set out.[13]

For Wang Xinlan, the interval in Maoergai was also a trying time. She longed to start the new life they were all struggling for. But here they were stuck in limbo, struggling not against the imperialists but only to feed themselves. As the weather turned colder, they had to forage even farther afield to supplement their thin rations. Sickness raged all around them, and Xinlan attended the funeral of one Red Army big brother or sister after another.

Now, at long last, it was time to move on. Both columns, the women were told, would soon set out north across the treacherous Caodi, and while they would take different routes, they would join up again later.

As Wang Xinlan's team went about their tasks, chilling tales about the high-elevation steppes, with their capricious weather, raced through the ranks. The Tibetans told them that the marshes they would traverse were a vast wintry trap. Indeed, the Caodi was so wild, shifty, and indecipherable that it had never even been mapped by Chinese cartographers.

A week after the Shawo meeting, both columns set out. The Left Column headed west over a mountain range and then turned north into a chaotic sea of ridges and valleys. They soon entered a "vast, limitless steppe," according to Zhang Guotao, unlike anything they had seen before.[14] Here they picked their way through dangerous marshes along flooded rivers that lapped against sheep trails.

The drudgery of marching was occasionally relieved by sublime swaths of bright green grass and meadows of wildflowers as vivid as berry-dyed silk. Every three or four days, the Reds encountered a Lamaist temple and its complementary collection of houses and shops. At each outpost, the local market was surrounded by the tents and pens of the region's seminomadic herders. There was plenty of wool and grain to be had, but soon the marchers began to dread these way stations: the rigors of the trail were taking their toll, and more and more sick soldiers had to be left behind at each stop amid tearful farewells and a swelling sense of resentment among those marching on.

Meanwhile, Mao and the Right Column marched north on a more easterly route over rough, barren terrain toward the town of Banyou at the northern edge of the swamps. The idea was that the columns would move separately but in unison. The reality was that, even apart, Mao and Zhang continued to scheme. Although Zhang had agreed to go north, he remained convinced that they should actually be heading west, deeper into Tibetan territory, to regroup and rebuild farther from the reaches of Chiang Kaishek's troops and bombers.[15]

Everyone would be reduced by the schism — now geographical as well as philosophical — but Wang Quanyuan heartbreakingly so. In the turmoil and the rush to move out, she and several comrades on assignment in a remote village were left behind. After discovering that the armies had decamped, they scrambled to catch up on their own. In the heat of the moment, they ended up joining the Left Column. Wang's husband, Wang Shoudao, had moved out with the Right. She would never see him again.[17]

chapter 20

The Caodi

AUGUST 1935

Not once in the literature of the Long March do any of the women mention the flowers. In summer, the Snowy Mountains and the Caodi—at elevations of between 9,000 and 15,000 feet—burst to life in fireworks of alpine meadow flowers, many of which were once collected and cataloged by the famous American botanist Joseph Rock in 1928. As the women trudged along, golden geraniums, bright purple irises, fuchsia orchids, and pink and mauve rhododendrons stood like a testimony to perseverance and optimism in a harsh world. The Himalayan blue poppy radiated a brilliant indigo unseen elsewhere in nature. With its delicate beauty and its hispid stem glistening with dew in the morning sunlight, it invited and repelled—with the promise of fine bristly pain—the women passing by. The pendulous Tibetan red poppy, on the other hand, with its four-petal flower drooping like crinkled silk, would be an apt symbol of the oppressed women the marchers were trying to liberate. In 1918 the English botanist Reginald Farrer, who traveled extensively in China and Tibet, described the "royal crimson" flower in militaristic terms, saying its bulb was "so floppy and tired in texture that each blossom hangs on its stem like a bloodstained flag hoisted to its pole on a windless . . . day in autumn."

On August 21, the Fourth Regiment of the First Army Group, leading the Right Column, forged onto the Caodi. No continuous path crossed the inhospitable plateau, some four hundred square miles of barren ridges, grassy meadows, swamps, and sinkholes. The

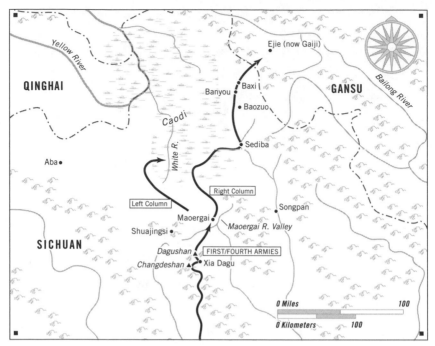

Turmoil on the Caodi (Grasslands)

regimental commander had hired Tibetan guides, the main one being an old man carried on a litter. Despite the warnings they had been given and the stories the Tibetans had told them, from a distance the misty steppes appeared relatively benign. No looming snow-covered peak confronted them, no cliff face or roaring river.

Wang Xinlan had been assigned to the Right Column. On her back, she carried a blanket, a pair of straw sandals, and a bamboo flute. Little Xinlan was glad to be moving again but apprehensive about the spooky place where they had been told mules and people could suddenly sink and never be seen again. "I took a stick and walked in the footprints of the comrades in front of me," she later said. "I moved step by step and followed them closely."[1]

Even on these grim steppes, the troops looked a motley horde. Many wore pants and shorts that had shredded and rotted on the trail, these rags exposing their bruised, lacerated legs to the cold, wet, and wind. Those more fortunate wore coarse Tibetan serge—though scratchy, it was water-resistant—with buttons made of cloth wrapped around coins. Coats fashioned of tiger, camel, and dog pelts could be found here and there. Zhong Yuelin wore a padded wool vest that He Zizhen had stitched together for her out of pieces of sheepskin and rose-colored silk smudged from the Mausers they had once wrapped. Zhong's junior status served her well among the First Army women, who pampered their "little sister." Others less lucky simply stuffed raw wool under their threadbare clothes, puffing them up like blowfish, or wrapped themselves in their blankets. To cover their heads, some wore large, round hats of plaited bamboo; others carried battered umbrellas.[2]

On the first day in the Caodi, as Chen Huiqing rested with the convalescent company during a break in the nearly constant rain, the sprawl of marchers parted, and Deng Fa walked up, wearing a tattered cloth on his head. Chen had not seen much of her husband in recent days. Grinning, he handed her a threadbare raincoat. Chen took it and then examined her husband tenderly. Like the rest of them, he had been living on starvation rations. He was so gaunt that he looked wide-eyed and, ironically, almost spry, but she knew that the stress of the past ten months had taken a toll. "Old Deng, have you been very busy?" she asked. "Have you been eating?" He nodded. She knew he would not be honest. "Hunger has made your eyes bigger," she said.

"We survived the Great Guangzhou–Hong Kong Strike," he nonchalantly replied, referring to the general strike in 1925 protesting the May 30 killings of dozens of demonstrators in Shanghai by British and French troops. The violent strike had spread nationwide and lasted for almost two years. He looked beyond the sprawl of tired bodies. "The Caodi does not compare to that," he said.

Nodding, Chen placed a cloth bag on the ground for Deng to sit on and set to work preparing some food. Her husband was a powerful man, and her friends silently assented to her taking flour from their mutual stores. Chen said nothing as she worked. A pot of water boiled over the open fire. After a while, she handed Deng a steaming mug of porridge. He looked inside, scowled, and refused to take it.

"Even though you won't admit it, I know you're eating grass,"

Chen said. "Eat it while it's hot." She held it out to him. Deng refused it again, declaring that Chen was carrying his baby and needed the strength. "While the others are eating grass, how can I eat porridge?" he said, pulling a dark grass cake from his pocket.[3]

As the army entered the Caodi, some soldiers killed a feral yak. Mao told the guards to take care of the convalescent company, and the meat was doled out over several days. Little Sparrow, among others, relished the much-needed protein. But when Mao discovered that He Zizhen and the women had been given more than their share, he grew angry. Mao knew the importance of appearances in the midst of his political struggle. "How could this happen?" he rebuked his guard, insisting that his wife could not be treated differently. Of course, Mao himself had been granted extra food supplies—mostly dried beef, flour, and yak butter—earlier in the march. Though it was against Communist ideals, the distribution of provisions inevitably varied in quantity and quality through the ranks. Access to the leaders could make all the difference.[4]

At dusk, the temperature plummeted. The marchers stopped, built fires, and had scarcely finished drinking the hot barley water that many of them prepared when a wet wind swept across the flat plain, bringing loud, slapping waves of rain, destroying oilpaper umbrellas, and dousing their smoldering fires. Hail followed and pelted them throughout the night.

On the second day, the marchers trudged deeper into the morass. A bitter rain poured down, cold and relentless, and the earth seemed to belch up water. They were now surrounded by a great series of interlinked ponds, lakes, and bogs, cut through with bloated streams and rivers. Wang Quanyuan and her comrades called the nearly liquid sky *mafengyu*—*ma* meaning "pock," *feng* "wind," and *yu* "rain." *Ma,* the first character, is often used as a colorful if derogatory term for a person having a pockmarked face. The wind-driven rain, often mixed with sleet or hail, vexed the marchers, like the scars on a face ravaged by smallpox.[5] Periodically, the women stripped off their saturated clothes, wrung them out, and put them back on.

Yet they forged on, picking their way through the maze of fetid

Dark pool on the Caodi. *(Andy Smith)*

pools by sticking to the solid clumps of wild grasses, even though these scrubby islets and tenuous walkways wrenched their ankles, sucked off their sandals, and coated their feet with putrid black mud. The sodden ground squelched *pu-chi, pu-chi* with each step. Fortunately, they had long since shed most of their heavy burdens, but those with stretchers, sacks of wheat, or bundles of firewood for cooking teetered awkwardly beneath their loads, on the brink of disaster should they misstep.[6]

In some places, "the grass was thicker and people wouldn't sink into it, but it varied greatly," Liao Siguang later explained. "Some grass was thin. People sank in fast. The water was dark with aged rotten grass and reeked so badly it couldn't even be used to wash." One soldier described the water as stinking like horse urine.[7]

Some men carried poles and used them to try to rescue comrades who had stepped in the wrong place and were being sucked into the mire. But many were too weak or heavily burdened to be saved.

"We went very slowly," the Cannon said, "little by little each day because it was such hard going."[8] The elements here reduced the women so much that the last remaining status barriers among them melted away. Although some held positions of authority or had access to the leaders and better resources, the suffering was almost universal now. This was the trial that they would look back on as their defining moment.

At night, the they sat leaning back-to-back or huddled beneath lean-tos of blankets, brush, and umbrellas. Cai Chang and Little Sparrow made a tent out of a piece of oilcloth propped up with a branch. Using one of their two blankets as a ground cloth, they curled up together beneath the other. He Zizhen, Qian Xijun, and Zhong Yuelin crowded under a tarp supported by the litter Mao had given He when she was wounded.

As hard as it was to endure the long, miserable, saturated nights, the marchers dreaded the predawn bugle that called them to shoulder their burdens, form up, and set their aching legs in motion again. Yet there was no other option.

On the third day, they reached the rising Hou River. Despite being only a hundred feet wide and in most places no more than chest-deep, it was still a significant impediment to so large and downtrodden a group. The river floor had depressions of up to a dozen feet, and its icy current could easily sweep the exhausted and underfed downstream. As the troops piled up by the river's edge, Deng Yingchao arrived on her stretcher. Uncertain how to cross, a number of officers stood on the bank. An authoritative figure by nature as well as by dint of being Zhou Enlai's wife, she did not hesitate. "How deep is the river?" she asked, wheezing. When told, she suggested that the soldiers link arms and form a chain. Like a concerned mother, she chided them to keep together as they crossed.[9]

Standing nearby with a pistol strapped to her waist, Cai Chang looked on. Despite her delicate build, she had a *guo*-shaped face (similar to the square character for *guo,* or "nation"), which the Chinese consider masculine and indicative of strength, and looked as tough as the men around her. As the men tentatively prepared to enter the river, she began to sing the French revolutionary anthem, the "Marseillaise." Catching the spirit, the soldiers broke into song too, and some even danced down toward the water.

The marchers used many methods to cross the Hou. Some made a chain out of their ragged puttees and crossed hand over hand. Others clung to the tails of the mules and horses. Many of the officers crossed in the saddle, though the very ill, like Deng Yingchao and Zhou Enlai, had to be carried across on their stretchers. Some of the weaker men were swept away in the current. Kicking furiously to stay afloat, most but not all managed to drag themselves ashore at a bend forty yards downstream.

On the far side, the bank was fairly solid, and the marchers built grass fires that billowed with smoke. Their eyes watered as they crowded around to dry off. Others found wood and added it to the fires. The usual makeshift shelters of blankets and tree branches and thatch sprang up, forming what the marchers jokingly nicknamed a "Maoville." While some collapsed into exhausted sleep, others clustered around the fires, chewing raw wheat and brewing bitter tea, telling stories, playing their harmonicas, and singing plaintively. They were not quite halfway across the Caodi.

The fourth and fifth days were the hardest. Although they crossed a road — a merchant's route between Sichuan and Qinghai provinces — and even walked on firm ground for several miles, they quickly found themselves bogged down again. While various provisions were still squirreled away in small parcels among the troops and officers — fried noodles, rice, dry biscuits, and roasted wheat — the larger grain bags were empty. The yak meat was long gone. "The food ran out, and we had no salt. People felt weak all the time," Little Sparrow recalled. "The swamp was dangerous, and many people sank in and never came back."[10] She saw corpses every day — and these were the ones who had not been sucked into the muck, their lungs flooded with mud. Many marchers later confessed that at times they helplessly watched friends sink, making no effort to save them for fear of suffering the same fate.

Almost all of the soldiers and women were now harvesting grass, which they discovered was most tender after it had flowered. They ground the shoots, mixed them with the little remaining flour they carried, and roasted the resulting cakes over coals. These cakes were of only marginal benefit, since grass is made up of cellulose, which humans cannot effectively digest. (Cows have five specialized

Horse skeleton on the Caodi. *(Andy Smith)*

stomachs that allow them to break down cellulose, in part by fermenting it in bacteria, which converts it into absorbable sugars.) Starving people forced to eat grass at length suffer not only from malnutrition but also from bleeding bowels.

By the fourth day on the Caodi, some began to report the deaths of their comrades from starvation. Dysentery became so common and insistent that men and women alike frequently dropped on the spot to relieve themselves.

Whenever they could build a fire, the women boiled their drinking water, now drawn from the Caodi. Mixing in a few flakes of barley made it go down better. To reduce the organisms in her water, Little Sparrow filled her mug, let it settle, and then poured it into another mug, leaving behind the dregs. Still, on the sixth day, she came down with diarrhea. "There was no time to be shy," she recalled. "I squatted down anytime I had to."[11]

Until this point, the horses had been considered almost sacred. One officer later lamented the death of one of his grooms, who had lost a mount through accidental negligence and was summarily executed for it. Now the officers who had so strictly guarded the horses ordered some to be slaughtered. But with so many mouths to feed and so few bites to go around, the smell of cooking meat only served to make most feel even hungrier. Sheepskins and leather shoes, belts, and harnesses went into pots of boiling swamp water.

Wang Xinlan was so weak that when she moved, she saw stars. In the morning, she was reluctant to rise. She sometimes carried her pack on her head to protect her from the rapid succession of rain, snow, and hailstones as big as walnuts. Her shoulders and body took the pounding instead. At night, she and some of the other young marchers found a patch of dry grass, where they lit a fire and sang songs to pass the hours. "When dawn came, we found some people sitting motionless," Wang recalled. "We went to help them but only found them cold. They had died."[12]

For several weeks, Li Bozhao had taken comfort in the company of her new "little sister," the pretty Han-Tibetan nineteen-year-old Jiu Xiang, who had joined the march in Fubian. Jiu had shown Li and the other women how to use the local flour to bake cakes. When the flour had grown scarce, she had found food where others could not. Li loved her as much for her cheerfulness as for these tangible gifts. In the Caodi, however, even Jiu was out of her element, and she began to waste away. In the confusion of the crossing, one day she disappeared.[13]

PART FOUR

HOME STRETCH

chapter 21

Life After Death

SEPTEMBER 1935

On August 25, Fourth Army troops in the Right Column routed Nationalist regulars and locals at an important crossroads on the north edge of the Caodi, in the Axi Valley near the village of Yalong. This opened up exit routes from the Caodi near the villages of Banyou and Baxi and allowed these Right Column troops to continue on to Baozuo, where a victory over Nationalist troops would lay open the main route to the north.

Also at the front of the Right Column, the First Army Group reached the northeastern edge of the Caodi on August 27. The sight of large, solid hillocks encouraged the soldiers as they emerged from the liquid desolation. They had marched with such single-mindedness, blazing the route, that they had to radio back to the Third Army Group to look for their stragglers and to bury their dead. They estimated that in their haste, they had lost at least a hundred soldiers in the mire behind them. But when Zhou Enlai, who was with the Third, caught up with them, he informed them that they had found and buried 400 men, not to mention those who had vanished beneath their burdens in the opaque pools.[1] Although no exact count is available, in all perhaps more than 1,000 marchers died on these northwestern Sichuan steppes.

The first village the advance troops had come to was Sediba, on the route from Songpan to Banyou. On the banks of the Songpan River, they had cut trees for firewood and tent poles. The soldiers who arrived later would find these tented shelters, one still occupied by a

Red soldier so sick he could not speak. Nearby, next to a dung heap, they would discover a stack of corpses. They buried their comrades and fed the sick man. Some picked through the human feces for undigested grain.[2]

On August 30 and 31, in the hills and woods around the village of Upper Baozuo, six miles from Banyou, Red Thirtieth Army troops under Captain Li Xiannian (future president of the People's Republic of China) fought the Nationalist Forty-ninth Regiment supported by a band of Hui Muslim cavalry. These Fourth Army troops, which had previously defeated the Nationalists in the Axi Valley, now drove them in a fierce eight-hour battle from the Buddhist lamasery, where they were based, seriously wounding the Hui commander. According to reports, the Red Army killed or wounded more than 4,000 enemy troops and captured 800 soldiers, 1,500 rifles and handguns, and more than a dozen machine guns, as well as 700 yaks and other provisions.[3] *Xuanchuan* units posted signs reporting the victory to encourage other Right Column soldiers as they spilled off the Caodi.

It took several more days for all of the marchers to reach the small Tibetan settlements that marked the end of the wilderness. The herdsmen who lived here had fled hastily with their livestock, leaving behind a few strays, which the famished soldiers slaughtered and roasted. A guide showed them how to cook the hide, first singeing off the hair, then slicing and boiling it, and finally gnawing it before it cooled and turned to leather again. Still, there was never enough food. The soldiers captured and ate the rats living in the villages and even discovered that some painted figurines at family altars were made of wheat and butter. They scraped the paint off and made porridge.[4]

Banyou was a village of ten huts, two of which had been burned, probably by a careless smoker among the vanguard or by a cooking fire left smoldering by some of the soldiers. No furniture or food of any sort remained in or around the huts, only heaps of dried dung, the area's all-in-one fertilizer, fuel, and building material. With great relief and extreme exhaustion, the marchers straggled into the village and billeted inside and outside the vacant huts, where beside cow-dung fires they dried themselves and their wet, mildewed clothing.

At Banyou, Little Sparrow felt as if she had reentered the world after spending a week in hell. In the nearby village of Axi, Liu Qunxian ate beef and mutton. Later she would say that this was her "happiest memory of the Long March."[5]

After the wilderness crossing, Banyou and Axi may have initially looked like paradise, but that notion dissipated overnight. Even yak dung had its limitations, and without food or adequate shelter, Banyou's novelty quickly faded. Those who arrived late were urged on to Baxi, a town of more than a hundred wooden houses, an ancient lamasery, a number of abandoned blockhouses, and a thousand or so Tibetans. As the marchers passed through Banyou, they read a sign painted on boards by a Red Army *xuanchuan* team: "Baxi is only 50 *li*. It has houses to stay in and food to eat. Comrades, don't delay!"[6]

The Tibetans, not surprisingly, had fled Baxi with all their stores. But some of the women were delighted to find fields of carrots, beans, and wheat and a groundcover of edible radish leaves. While the Right Column leaders stayed in Banyou, the Central Committee and the Military Commission ensconced themselves above Baxi in a Buddhist lamasery established in 1679 by the permissive Sakya Sect, which allowed its monks to marry. Inside its erotic hillside temple, statues of couples in coital rapture surrounded a gleaming Buddha. The

Storm over the Caodi. (*Andy Smith*)

Reds compared the temple's gilt and red-lacquer splendor to that of a Shanghai movie house.[7]

While the statues might have excited the minds of both men and women, grave matters were at hand. Zhang Wentian, Bo Gu, and Mao, all staying here, led high-level meetings to discuss, among other things, the desperate need for supplies, the makeup of the standing committee of the Central Committee, and the future of the combined armies.[8]

The women at least focused on practical matters. Cai Chang, for example, decided that something must be done about Little Sparrow's footwear. Her sandals were in shreds. Cai asked her husband, Li Fuchun, head of the Political Department, for permission to search the stockpile of confiscated goods. Using her hands to measure, she found a cloth pair just right for Little Sparrow. Holding them behind her back, she said, "Little Sparrow, I have something for you!"[9]

"What is it, Older Sister?" Little Sparrow asked. When Cai revealed her surprise, Little Sparrow's face lit up. To have such shoes would make marching so much easier. But then she remembered that "all raided items must be turned in." Sensing her hesitation, Cai assured her that Comrade Li Fuchun had given his permission. Cai shot her husband an expectant look, and he agreed.

After a few days' rest, Wang Xinlan could see no good reason to remain in the area. "Shall we continue our march?" she asked her team leader, as she had in Maoergai. Yes, and soon, he replied: "North to fight against the Japanese invaders." It was getting cold, he added, and they wanted to move while they could. Now that they had crossed the Snowy Mountains and the Caodi, they had good roads ahead of them.[10]

Even with winter coming, Wang looked forward to going north. However, no command to pull out came. Day after day, as the clouds scudded across the plains and the geese flew south in formation, she watched forlornly, unaware of the unfolding political struggle in the Party leadership.

As the right column paused, the Left Column struggled. Before setting out to cross the Caodi, Zhang Guotao's troops rested for three days, grilling the locals on the passage through the wilderness and filling in their blank maps. As they moved out, it began to pour. That night the Left Column troops slept miserably on the wet ground beneath tents made of their blankets. On the afternoon of the third day, they reached the White (Gaqu) River, which according to legend had been formed when a goddess shook raindrops off a wool blanket she was knitting. Unable to drain efficiently, the stream created by these celestial drops backed up in still tributaries that veined and then mired the steppes.[11]

In the midst of the deluge, the White River had swollen. "It had been just a small stream, less than knee-deep," Zhang later wrote. "Now the water had risen until it was more than ten feet deep and 300 meters wide."[12] As the Fifth Army Group commander prepared his 3,000 men to ford the river, Zhang stopped him, insisting that it was too dangerous. "There didn't seem to be any chance that the river would recede in a few days," he later said, justifying his decision not to cross and not to wait it out. But according to Kang Keqing, Zhu De conferred with their Tibetan guide, who said that they should be able to cross the river as long as it didn't rise any more. "I looked at the river," Kang later said. "The water flowed calmly and didn't look swollen. However, Zhang insisted that the river was rising and we could not pass" (p. 169). Pan Kaiwen volunteered to explore it. Riding Zhu's horse and carrying a sounding pole, he and another mounted soldier made for the crossing place that the guide had indicated. In the middle of the river, Pan plunged the pole in. Hitting a firm bottom, he proceeded across. "The water isn't deep," he bellowed. "The deepest part only reaches the stomach of the horse. It's safe!"

"No one may cross!" Zhang Guotao insisted. "Call those two back." He then turned to Zhu. "It's clear the water is rising," he said. "I won't endanger the lives of tens of thousands of men."

Eager to keep the Left Column on track with the Right, First Army chief of staff Liu Bocheng approached Zhu De. "Commander," he said, "the front guards would like to cross first!"

Before Zhu could respond, Zhang flew into a rage: "No! No one may pass! I'll decide what to do when the water stops rising." To the dismayed First Army marchers, Zhang's reaction could only be explained as a renunciation of the agreed-upon plan.

On September 2, Zhang learned from a wireless telegram of the Right Column's victory at Baozuo. The following day, he responded, saying that the flooded White River had prevented him from advancing farther north. He had decided to take the Left Column back to Aba — a Lamaist stronghold with a grand temple flanked by smaller ones, home to a thousand monks — where he would find shelter and amenities. Zhang urged the Right Column to turn south and take Songpan.[13]

Zhang maintained that after collecting more food, the Left Column would join the Right in Songpan. But his prevaricating, along with Mao's intransigence on the issue, threatened the fragile harmony between the two Red armies and thus placed the fate of all the marchers in peril.

Mao and the Central Committee responded by urging Zhang to continue north, even offering to send troops to assist him in crossing the White River, but Zhang was unyielding. Feeling matters coming to a head, Mao weighed his choices. His contingent at the monastery above Baxi pulled up stakes and departed. Immediately after they left, the temple began to burn, due to improperly extinguished fires, it is believed. They noticed when they were a mile away and watched forlornly as the smoke blotted out the horizon. The symbolism cannot be ignored: the bridges were burning behind them. On September 6 and 7, Mao and the other national leaders met in the mud-walled temple of Yalong, where Zhou Enlai stayed in a nearby house. On September 8, an emergency session of the Politburo determined to disregard Zhang and continue north with or without him.[14]

REPORTS OF WHAT TRANSPIRED NEXT VARY. According to the official Communist Party history, on September 9 Zhang sent a secret telegram ordering Chen Changhao, commissar of the Right Column, to reverse direction and head south. Mao was tipped off and, after meeting with Chen to confirm his suspicions, called an emergency session with the Central Party leaders. The forces loyal to Mao were grossly outnumbered by Zhang's Fourth Army troops. Fearing that the Fourth Army troops among them might side with Zhang, Mao and the other leaders decided to slip away that night. They sent a message to Chen claiming that in order to turn back and recross the Caodi, they needed more provisions and so would mobilize at dawn to harvest barley.[15]

After midnight, word circulated among the First Army troops to prepare to depart. Even Little Sparrow, who had friends in high places, was caught by surprise at what happened in the early-morning hours of September 10. Roused from her sleep, she opened her eyes to see Liao Siguang's husband, Kai Feng, head of the Communist Youth League, standing beside her. "Get up, get up," he commanded with hushed urgency. "Get going right now!"[16]

"What's the matter?" groggy voices inquired. "Where are we going?"

"Don't ask, just go!" Kai responded. "Keep silent, and no torches!"

Stealthily, the First Army contingent of the Right Column mobilized. It was not a simple matter for several thousand soldiers to disappear into the night. In a furious whisper, they jostled along more than three miles to a small valley before stopping to rest and regroup. Horsemen galloped up in the dark. But it was only Zhang Wentian and his guard. "Zhang Guotao is separating from the Central Committee," he informed them, according to Little Sparrow. "That's why we have to get away from his troops."[17]

Back in camp, sudden noises awakened Wang Xinlan from her sleep. Looking around, she saw her fellow Fourth Army sisters astir. "What's wrong?" she asked, still bleary.

"Hurry up," a woman in the dark urged her, hastening to the door with the others. "Something important's happened." Wang had not heard any bugles call them to muster. She followed the others outside in the early-morning chill and found many soldiers moving about. Shouts, curses, whistles, and footfalls filled the frantic camp. She tried to figure out what was going on. "We're all Red Army," she overheard someone say. "If they didn't want to be with us, why didn't they tell us they were leaving?"[18]

Scowling and wielding a pistol, Commander Xu Shiyou, who usually joked with Wang, stalked by her several times without noticing her.

Now frightened, Wang listened as her team leader finally confirmed the rumors: "The First Army has fled with Mao Zedong," he said. "Everyone should stay calm. Commander Xu and Commissar Chen are still with us. We're waiting for instructions from Chairman Zhang." Wang was stunned. After all the celebration of the joining of the two armies, the gifts exchanged, and the hopeful talk, how could this be? What did it mean? Had she heard correctly? For so long, they had marched to unite with their comrades and together defeat both Chiang and the Japanese occupiers. Their journey had been a nightmare in search of a dream, but now that dream seemed to be unraveling.

In Banyou, Right Column commander Xu Xiangqian and Commissar Chen received urgent messages. "The First Army has pulled out," Chen said. "Shall we send troops after them?"

"Have you ever seen the Red Army attacking the Red Army?" Xu responded.[19]

Instead of sending soldiers to fight, they dispatched a group of students and Fourth Army representatives. These emissaries found Mao, who had not yet departed, and tried to convince him to stay.

Mao countered: Those who wanted to go north could join him. Those who didn't could go back to Banyou.

In the morning, Mao's sister-in-law Qian Xijun urged He Zizhen to find Mao and ask him what was happening. The women were concerned not only for themselves but also for their six female comrades, including Kang Keqing and Wang Quanyuan, who were with the Left Column, and Li Bozhao, who had spent the night in Banyou. Again, they were merely told that the Fourth Army was separating from them. There was no elaboration, no mention of a schism between Mao and Zhang.

Without pause or appeal, Li Bozhao and her husband, Yang Shangkun, were thus split, one to follow Mao, the other Zhang. They were not the only couple sundered. Yang Houzhen's husband was with the Left Column, while she marched with Mao, never to see her husband again.

Two days later, on September 12, Zhang Guotao's response to the recent events was relayed to the Fourth Army cadres left behind by Mao. Zhang accused the Central Committee of wrongly splitting the Red Army. He predicted that the faction heading north would be decimated by fatigue and exposure.

That same day, the Central Committee met in the Tibetan village of Ejie (now Gaoji), where they had rejoined the First Army Group, which had been sent ahead to scout. They denounced Zhang and rechristened their troops the Shaanxi-Gansu Branch of the Anti-Japanese Vanguard Force of the Red Army, claiming the moral high ground. Mao was named commissar and Peng Dehuai commander. The original First Army women now with Mao numbered just twenty-one.

Now even Wang Xinlan realized that a calamity had occurred. The departure of the First Army and the actions of the leaders felt to Wang and her friends like a punch in the gut.

The next blow was even worse: Zhang ordered the remainder of the Right Column to return south. With no spare food or clothes, Wang and her friends, along with Li Bozhao and the other six First Army women, walked in stunned disbelief back into the Caodi.

Leaning on walking sticks, like old women, Wang and her young friends followed the troops and whispered among themselves, "Why aren't we following the Central Committee north?"[20] As they struggled forward, more and more lagged and vanished into the muck. In camp, Wang watched ill and wasted marchers succumb, and most mornings she awoke to the sounds of soldiers digging burial pits. She rushed to pick wildflowers to lay on the graves before setting out in the mornings.

It would take the women seven exhausting days to reach the

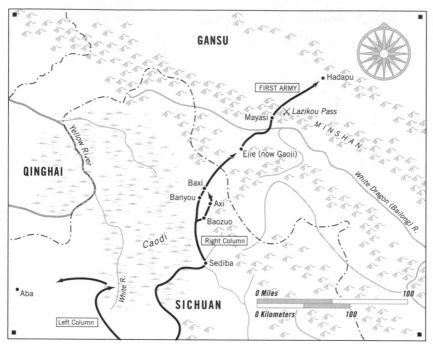

The First Army Contingent of the Right Column Moves North

southern edge of the marshes. Years later, Wang's son would say that she had left her smiles in the Caodi.

IN THE DAYS THAT FOLLOWED the rupture, Kang Keqing observed the fallout in the Left Column. Zhang stripped Zhu De and Liu Bocheng, both of whom continued to favor the plan to go north, of power and isolated them. Zhu was deprived of his security detail and humiliated by having his horse slaughtered for food. After Zhang learned that Kang had been gathering intelligence for her husband, he prevented Zhu from seeing her. Zhang posted Kang out in the field rounding up laggards.[21]

After three days of marching, the Left Column reached Aba. At an elevation of 10,500 feet, the town was perched on a river amid large fields of barley. Forewarned of the Communists' arrival, the lamas had abandoned Aba, but in such haste that they had left behind enough food to feed the Red column for several months. On September 15, Zhang held a meeting at Aba's spectacular Buddhist temple and denounced the Central Party leaders and their dash to the north, which he reiterated would lead to their demise. He and his loyalists decided to move southeast about a hundred miles. According to Kang Keqing, Zhu remained critical of Zhang, a position that led to his house arrest. Kang was harassed for being "Zhu's spy" and finally transferred—effectively exiled—to the Women's Independent Regiment, the unit of more than 2,000 female soldiers commanded by Zhang Qinqiu.[22]

Once there, Kang stayed busy marching, doing *xuanchuan,* and bonding with the women cadres, including her assigned "companion," Xiao Zhaoying. They all lived together, eating, sleeping, and working as a unit and confiding in one another. Kang and Xiao became friends, and finally Xiao told Kang that she had been ordered to watch her and, if necessary, to use force against her. Xiao, who now knew that Kang was armed, asked her what she would have done if she'd tried to take her weapon. "The gun was given to me by my superior for self-defense and to fight the enemy," Kang responded. "It's as important as my life, and unless ordered by my superior, I'd never allow anyone to take it from me."

"What if I'd insisted?"

Kang patted the gun at her waist. "Then I'd have had no choice but to shoot you," she replied.[23]

Now that Kang had made allies of her keepers, she was even better positioned to help Zhu. With their complicity, Kang snuck away once a week early in the morning to bring him news and check on him.

Meanwhile, the part of the Right Column that Mao had left behind, including Wang Xinlan, rejoined the Left Column at Aba and was now part of the Fourth Army again.

★

DEPARTING THE ANCIENT FORESTS of Ejie, Mao's contingent marched north along the Big (Da) River and then continued east on the precipitous edge of the White Dragon (Bailong) River, making for the strategic Lazikou Pass, a key route through the mountains between

Sichuan and Gansu. On the White Dragon's sheer banks, they crawled along a dizzying path of wooden planks built out from the face of the cliff. Opposition forces had removed some of the boards to slow the marchers down and at strategic locations sniped at them or pushed boulders down on them. Below, the roiling White Dragon thundered. Warned not to look down, the women stared straight ahead, making their way along this nerve-racking stretch. On September 14, they reached Maya, a town of Lamaist temples and clean well-built dormitories, where chrysanthemums, morning glories, and grapes grew by the entrances. Some of the forces, including the headquarters unit and the women, stayed here several days in dormitories that could sleep five hundred lamas — or thousands of Red soldiers, who needed less room. The locals branded the voracious Red Army the "Eat Everything Army."

Mao stayed in a private residence in the attached village of Cirina, where he conceived a battle plan to wrest control of Lazikou, a pass on 10,000-foot Minshan critical to advancing through Gansu province, from the warlord Lu Dazhang.[24]

Two days later, the Red Army stormed Lu's formidable positions in a narrow, steep-walled pass, most of which was consumed by a tumultuous mountain river. Spurred on by the dread of returning to the Caodi if they failed, they repeatedly attacked bunkers and crow's nests clinging to the cliffs defended by machine guns and stocked with grenades. Time and again, they failed to rout the entrenched Gansu fighters. Finally, a handpicked team of volunteers was sent to scale the heights behind the bunkers. Forty men, some of them Miao mountain men — each armed with a dozen grenades, a pistol, and a sword with its hilt wrapped in red cloth for identification — outflanked the enemy positions, climbed the cliff faces, and hurled grenades down onto the warlord fighters, forcing them to flee.[25]

The troops and cadres to the rear now eagerly marched to the pass, which marked an exit from Tibetan regions and a return to Han, as well as a route to lower elevations and level terrain. But storms turned the sky dark and drenched them on the mountainsides, hindering their progress, and they were finally ordered to stop and camp. Many propped themselves up against trees and waited for dawn. When they reached the pass, they saw the battle carnage—trees demolished by explosives, blasted boulders, and corpses. Using wood stored in the bunkers, they made fires to boil water for drinking and to dry their sodden clothes. However, a midnight storm soaked them yet again.

In the morning, urged on by their leaders, the marchers, including the women and the wounded, hurried through the pass. They now reentered territory protected by Nationalist airplanes, which promptly found them and, circling overhead like buzzards, forced them to hide in the woods during daylight hours.

Looking like a barbarian horde in their rags, skins, and hand-spun wool, the marchers descended into a broad valley of rounded, terraced hills, where potatoes grew and chaff dried in the fields for the animals. They relished the comforting stench of coal fires wafting up to them while they made their way down to civilization as they knew it. Over centuries, the wooden wheels of ox-drawn carts had deeply grooved earthen paths. The landscape was a stingy brown, but Han resided here, scraping out a living, and the southerners touched their mud homes and the ground in disbelief. Overjoyed to have escaped the Tibetan region—to leave behind the Tibetan mountains, with their haunting prayer flags and mountain horns and their hostile villagers—they cried, hugged one another and the locals who had not run off, and danced and sang.[26]

Although they claimed to be liberators, the Reds hardly looked up to the task. We were "as gaunt as skeletons, and thousands . . . were sick," one marcher later told Agnes Smedley. "The nights echoed with our coughing." Despite their initial relief at having reached Han territory, they soon discovered that this, too, was a land suffering from decades of drought, famine, war, and crippling rents and taxes. Syphilis had ravaged the villages, leaving many women sterile and many places devoid of children. Naked peasant women hid in their huts for lack of clothes.[27] The marchers ate dogs, cats, and even rats to survive, then quickly pushed on.

On the morning of September 21, they reached Hadapu—a town of several thousand people, half of them Hui Muslims—known for

Along the White Dragon (Bailong) River, the marchers sometimes had to walk on roads carved into the cliff side and exposed to snipers.

The Lazikou Pass was the last major choke hold through which the First Army had to move to reach northern China.

Wang Zhen, who led the successful efforts of the First Army to intercept and decipher Nationalist radio field communications, with ethnic Miao soldiers, February 1936.

its production of the medicinal herb *donggui*. It was harvesttime, and there was food to be bought. Each marcher was issued one Mexican dollar from the coffers the porters had carried so far.[28] Even after the local merchants tripled their prices, the Reds could buy a dozen eggs for ten cents or a chicken for twenty. A pair of marchers could roast a goat or a sheep for two dollars, while friends supplied vegetables and bread. The troops also confiscated heaps of wheat, rice, and millet, six tons of flour, and a ton of salt.

Like a trapper coming in from the wilderness, Li Jianzhen was elated to shed her gear. At five feet nine, she was the tallest woman in the First Army. She looked like a man, she thought. Beneath her short-cropped hair and army cap, her face was rough from the weather. Her improvised sheepskin shoes were better than most—the wool turned inside on her feet, slipper-like, and the leather tops lashed to the soles—but she was ready to eat rice and to feel clean clothes again. She would remember this two-day rest as one of the happiest moments of the trek.

The women of Hadapu were fascinated by the female march-ers, with their shaved heads, uniforms, and pistols. They had never seen women with no fat on their bodies. They took them inside their homes and felt their small breasts. Still unconvinced that they were in fact women, they watched as the Reds urinated. Satisfied at last, they embraced these warrior women.[29]

The local women soon made new clothes for their visiting sisters, replacing their shredded, filthy, and stinking outfits, and gave them cloth shoes, a welcome improvement over the disintegrating straw or makeshift hide pairs they had.

In the Hadapu post office, the news-starved leaders discovered August and September issues of the newspaper *Dagongbao* (the *Independent*). Combing the pages for intelligence, for any clues to the whereabouts and status of friends and foes, they found reports of the burgeoning soviet base in the remotes of northern Shaanxi province, led by Liu Zhidan. It was a base that they almost certainly knew existed, but not one that they could have confidence *still* existed. "At long last . . ." Harrison Salisbury later reported, "that exact goal, that specific place, took real shape. . . . The rumors they had heard as far back as the meeting with Zhang Guotao in Lianghekou were true! There was a Communist force in being in northern Shaanxi and a soviet base area."[30]

The wandering First Army's heretofore unknown destination had manifested itself to the First Army leaders as suddenly and as unceremoniously as that — in an old newspaper article. It was a mere five hundred miles away. "Naturally," Little Sparrow wrote, "they decided to go there."[31]

chapter 22

A Five-Hundred-Mile Sprint

SEPTEMBER–OCTOBER 1935

A little over a week before the First Army pinpointed its destiny, Xu Haidong's Twenty-fifth Army had reached the town of Yongping, forty miles northeast of Yanan in northern Shaanxi, where it united with Liu Zhidan's forces. Before arriving, they had no contact with this remote nascent North Shaanxi (or Shaanbei) Soviet.[1] Such was the vastness of China and the isolation of the marchers.

Xu and his youngster army had barely made it. On the buff-colored plateaus of the Gansu-Shaanxi border, where drifts of loess — rock ground by glaciers into fine mineral crystals — shifted in the wind like desert dunes, they had run low on provisions. By butchering the officers' horses and buying enough fodder — potatoes and black beans not meant for human consumption, but good enough in this case — from the scarce locals, they managed to hang on. They boiled the beans in nearly dry kettles, drinking the runoff; the nurses then gnawed on the tough beans as they walked. The Twenty-fifth was finally saved when it crossed paths with a wealthy sheep owner and Xu bought the man's entire flock of several hundred head.[2]

When Xu arrived in Yongping, a bustling market town, he found it occupied by a local Red force of 7,000 troops. Liu Zhidan, the Communist rebel and North Shaanxi peasant hero who commanded them, accepted Xu's seniority. As the ranking officer, Xu, who had arrived with a force less than half the size of Liu's, suddenly found himself in a relatively stable position, with his power magnified several times over.

Five of the seven nurses in the Twenty-fifth Army had survived the 3,000-mile trek.[3] The joy of finishing the journey was short-lived, however, dampened by an atmosphere of mistrust among the united forces. As the armies merged, rumors spread that Liu Zhidan's ranks were full of Nationalist spies. As so often happened in the Red Army when its leaders felt vulnerable, the result was a purge of supposed counterrevolutionaries. Liu himself, who had so openly welcomed Xu and his marchers, would come under suspicion.[4]

In October, the Twenty-fifth Army held a wedding for a couple who had met at dawn on the first morning of the journey, when a feisty young woman refused to be sent home just because she was female. The groom was thirty-five-year-old Xu Haidong and the bride eighteen-year-old Young Orchid, his nurse. Xu had recognized and admired her tough breed: uneducated but smart and resourceful. It was his own.

Young Orchid now took the new name Dongping, combining the "Dong" from Xu Haidong's name, with "ping," meaning "shield." She had protected him when he was wounded and vulnerable, with his face torn apart, and now they would protect one another. Their new home was a loess cave with hay for a bed and an army blanket for cover.[5]

BEFORE LEAVING HADAPU on September 23, Mao spread rumors that the First Army was heading east to Tianshui, a strategic southeastern Gansu town. The marchers set out to the north instead. Despite their rapid pace, the Nationalist air force managed to find and harass them.[6] In the evening, orders came to keep moving to the town of Xinsi, no matter how long it took. A thick fog blocked out the moon and stars. The women in the convalescent company stumbled along with their sick and wounded charges, many on stretchers, through the night. The vanguard reached Xinsi at dawn; the women ushered in the last convalescents in the late morning. The late arrivals ate only a cold meal. They had another fifteen miles to go before they would reach Yuanyangzhen (Town of Mandarin Ducks), on the Wei River, about two hundred miles west of the ancient capital city of Xian. Once

Long March route in the Minshan Range. *(Lawrence Gray)*

they arrived, Shorty, the Cannon, and the rest of the women fed and tended to the sick and wounded and then collapsed in weary slumber. They had marched for thirty-six hours with only short breaks.

They were roused early the next morning to cross the Wei, the swift-flowing Yellow River tributary that the Twenty-fifth Army had crossed back in August. Though shallow, the river was wide, making the marchers vulnerable to bombers and shore fire in midstream. But while machine guns and cannons opened up on them as they began to cross, no bombers came, and their assailants quickly fled when the Reds returned fire.[7]

The following day, as the First Army crowded into the small town of Bangluo (Tibetan for "basin"), Nationalist bombers attacked them, dropping their payloads during five passes. The bombs did little damage, but the community of several hundred could not support the army for long.

Early the next morning, the Red cadres rose and assembled at the entrance to the primary school. They were directed to a mud-walled wheat-threshing ground. Mao, Zhang Wentian, Peng Dehuai, and Lin Biao all took the stage. Mao announced that they were heading to the North Shaanxi Soviet. The others reiterated the troops' marching orders and warnings and exhorted them to march on to their destiny. Their failed reunion with the Fourth Army was in the past now; it was time to look to the future. Not far away, just on the other side of the Nationalist lines at Guyuan and Pingliang, the Red Twenty-fifth, Twenty-sixth, and Twenty-seventh armies awaited them in the North Shaanxi Soviet. Never mind that this soviet and these units were recently virtually unknown—indeed, beneath the notice of the Party leaders. Now they represented the First Army's salvation.[8]

Before dawn the next morning, the First Army set out for Tong-wei, a former stop on the Silk Road, in arid central Gansu, where the average altitude is 6,500 feet. Once marking the limits of Chinese civilization, Tongwei's nearby stretch of Qin-period Great Wall, built of rammed-earth blocks, was now no more than five feet high. Its square watchtowers, which previously housed border guards, had long since reverted to dust beneath the barrage of gusting loess. Indeed, it was no longer the wall but the yellow loess that defined the region: the ancient town's crumbling loess walls provided little protection to its loess-coated citizens, who lived in loess caves.

Advance troops drove off a regiment of Nationalists and a local force, and the Reds occupied the town. The townspeople were amazed to find Mao himself in their midst.

The First Army officers bivouacked in the caves around town, which were warmer and more bombproof than the houses and were thus laughingly nicknamed "the people's life insurance company." Troops erected a dais with red flags and bunting in the town square and called for a celebration of Communist liberation. They gave speeches, sang a rousing rendition of the "Marseillaise," and feasted on chicken, pork, and duck. More singing and skits carried them into the night.

But Tongwei was not their final destination. The Red Army pulled out the next morning before dawn to try to evade Nationalist forces based in "the Two Nings"—the ancient stronghold towns of Jing-ning and Huining. The vanguard moved on rapidly, heading for the Xian–Lanzhou Highway, a two-day march through many small villages. They traveled with such speed that they secured the highway and ambushed a Nationalist convoy of ten vehicles carrying provisions

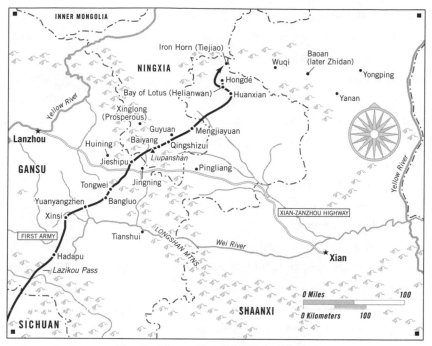

The First Army Heads to North Shaanxi

for the troops. The slower-moving elements, including the convalescent company, arrived to find fresh supplies and new clothing.

The Communists divided into multiple units taking different routes to make faster time over tight trails and to forage more efficiently. Still, Nationalist forces, aided by air reconnaissance, soon had a bead on them again. In the town of Jieshipu, Mao's white horse is said to have suddenly bucked and neighed in the direction of the rising sun to warn his master of danger. Mao ordered the troops to depart an hour earlier than planned, just minutes ahead of Nationalist troops that stormed the town from the east. (Today a statue of the horse stands in Jieshipu to commemorate the event.)[9]

That night, the First Army camped near the city of Hongfa, while the Nationalists bedded down about five miles away, so close that their outposts could hear each other's commands. With no desire to fight, the weary Red Army set out stealthily after midnight, but the Nationalists were not deceived by this now familiar tactic and tailed them. At the foot of a mountain, the Red rear guard turned to stall the pursuers while the rest of the First Army carried on. Before long, Red scouts spied Nationalist cavalry ahead. The First Army came to a sudden halt.

At noon the next day, the Nationalist cavalry, apparently unaware that the First Army was so near, entered the town of Qingshizui for a meal. As smoke rose from the chimneys of the houses where the cavalrymen were eating, Communist troops surrounded them. Without a fight, the Reds took many prisoners and more than two hundred horses, which allowed them to mobilize the convalescents and to give many officers mounts.

Turning east, the marchers entered the Longshan Mountains, the last serious elevation they would face. In the pouring rain, they climbed 9,000-foot Liupanshan, pulling themselves up a slick face one stunted tree at a time. Above the timberline, they grasped at rock and clumps of grass to hoist themselves up.

They reached the far side in the early evening and set up camp, but at 3:30 the next morning, they set off for the town of Baiyang. En route, they ran into a cavalry regiment under a Hui commander sent by Chiang Kaishek to protect eastern Gansu. The Red Army troops killed many of the Hui horsemen and took eighty prisoners, plus rifles and ammunition. The quality of the arms was so bad that the Reds ended up smashing many of them on boulders so that they could not be used later to intimidate the peasants. Of far more value in these northern winds were the uniforms and coats that they confiscated from the enemy soldiers.[10]

On a riverbank near Baiyang, the Nationalist air force found the Reds again, targeting their recently acquired white horses, which could be seen from afar, and wounding a number of horses and men. With only twenty-five houses, Baiyang itself had little to offer the Reds. They quickly bought out the two shops of their tea, oil, sugar, and *mantou*—steamed buns made from wheat flour—a Chinese staple. Still flush with provisions from Hadapu, they even left behind some salt and beans on their way out of town.

In the early afternoon of the next day, the marchers reached

Mengjiayuan, a town whose name is derived from a legendary event. In the Qin dynasty, there lived a virtuous woman named Meng Jiang. On her wedding night, a Qin officer seized her husband, invoking the emperor's command that one man from every family must be sent to work on the Great Wall. Years passed, and Meng Jiang's husband did not return. Unable to bear it any longer, Meng made herself a coat and set out to find him. Reaching the wall, she heard that he had died of exhaustion and a broken heart. Meng began to wail. Her sorrow was so great that her tears are said to have cracked the wall, revealing the skeletons of many who had died while working on it and been cast into the foundation. Meng bit her fingers and dripped her blood on the skeletons, praying that, as a sign, her husband's skeleton would be the only one to absorb it. In this way, she found him, and then she, too, died of a broken heart.[11]

Cai Chang perhaps felt a kindred spirit in the suffering Meng Jiang. Cai still grew emotional when she thought about her brother and sister-in-law, both of whom had been executed by the Nationalists. Her brother, Hesen, had been an inaugural Party member and a friend of Mao's and Zhou Enlai's. His wife, Xiang Jingyu, a classmate and close friend of Cai's, had been a leader in the fight for women's rights and was considered a "mother of the revolution." Their bones had joined those of the many other Red corpses hastily buried in the struggle to establish a new sort of nation.[12]

Mengjiayuan, however, brought a temporary end to one kind of suffering. When the Communists raided a landlord's estate, they confiscated a hundred sheep, half as many chickens, and loads of rice, millet, and flour. After feasting on a portion of this booty, they traveled ten miles, driving their newfound flock, to a campsite near Huanxian, a town of twenty shops and a church. They rested for a day, bathing and washing their clothes.

But this was all the time they could spare. Already the sound of gunfire rang in the gorges outside town, where Red guards fended off Nationalist forces. The next morning, the marchers set off again.

After storming the guardhouses at Bay of Lotus (Helianwan), the Reds split up to make quicker time. Some headed for the town of

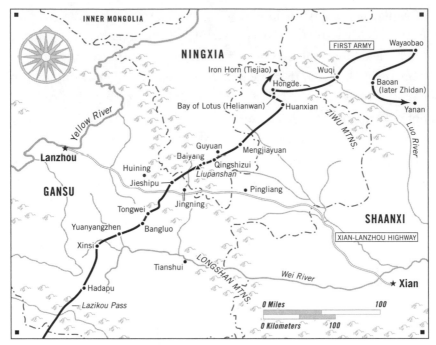

The First Army Reaches Its New Home

Hongde, about twenty miles to the north, and others for Iron Horn (Tiejiao), a mountain village on the Gansu-Shaanxi border and a common way station for traveling merchants.[13]

Those marching to Hongde were pinned down en route by Nationalist bombers, giving Nationalist cavalry in Huanxian time to stage a ground assault. Hundreds of Communists were picked off and killed in the field, and the Nationalists took two hundred prisoners. Those headed to Tiejiao—including Mao, the political leaders, and most of the women—reached it without mishap the following morning, but scouts informed them that Nationalist cavalry troops were gaining on them. The marchers hit the trail again and were crossing a mountain when, according to Mao's bodyguard Chen Changfeng, five turbaned horsemen carrying Mausers came galloping up.

The riders demanded to speak to Mao. "What's your business?" the Red guards asked.

"We've been sent by Old Liu," they responded, "with a message for Chairman Mao." It was from his old friend Liu Zhidan, who had sent these roughriders as guides to lead them to the North Shaanxi Soviet.[14]

As the First Army pushed north, the Fourth entrenched in western Sichuan. On October 5, Zhang Guotao announced at a meeting near Maogong that he was establishing a new and rightful Chinese Communist Party, disenfranchising Mao and his supporters.[15] But Zhang was politically isolated and not in a position of power. Even worse, he was headed back into the teeth of the enemy. When the Nationalist-aligned Sichuan militia learned that the Fourth Army was marching south alone, its leaders positioned more than fifty regiments in defenses at Baoxing, Tianquan, and Lushan, important farming centers in the rich alluvial soil beneath the Snowies. Then they lay in wait to destroy Zhang's army.

WITH THE HORSEMEN to guide them, the First Army proceeded to Laoye Mountain, where they bivouacked in and around three ancient stone-and-brick temples. Due to their recent luck in provisioning, sufficient rations were doled out. However, they were still short of water, and each soldier received only a dusty teacup full.

Crossing the Ziwu Range and then a broad plain, they reached Shaanxi. Though the territory was regularly traversed by the North Shaanxi Communists, it was still a place of danger — open and thus providing enemy cavalry a distinct advantage. The First Army units that had split off at Bay of Lotus now reunited with Mao's group, just in time to face the cavalry of Hui warlord Ma Hongkui. By lurking in the shadows, Ma's troops had already managed to kill a Red officer, eighteen soldiers, and thirty invalids. Now his emboldened army charged head-on. The Reds, commanded by Zhou Enlai, waited until the thundering turbaned attackers were unmissable in their gun sights. The volley of rifle and machine-gun fire they unleashed at close range blasted the Hui riders out of their saddles and felled dozens of horses. Other horses reared and fled, some dragging bloody warriors over the rock-strewn terrain.[16]

On the evening of October 19, the First Army reached the town of Wuqi (or Wuqizhen), a bandit-plagued dust bowl alongside the Luo River on the western edge of the North Shaanxi Soviet. The town's heyday had come in antiquity, during the Warring States period, when a Chinese commander had stationed his army there. Now another army arrived in Wuqi: some 4,000 Communist troops, battered and bony, loess in every pore of their bodies, streamed in over the next day. From Hadapu they had trudged some five hundred miles in less than a month, an astounding pace for any army, let alone one that had suffered the deprivation and hardships that they had in the previous year.[17]

Some historians consider this the end of the Long March. Others regard the arrival of the First Army in the town of Wayaobao (later Zichang) in November as the end of the trail. More recently, historians have preferred to include the ordeals of the other Red Army factions in their journeys to the north as part of the greater Long March story, and since the Fourth Army contained a number of the thirty women who had set out with the First Army, it is an essential part of this account, too.

In any event, Chiang Kaishek had hoped to eliminate the First Army and had failed. Only a fraction of those who had set out remained, but from these stalwart fighters and elements of the other Red armies, who also endured perilous marches, the modern Chinese nation would rise.

At first, as elsewhere, the inhabitants of Wuqi, fearing that the invaders were the "White bandits," fled with their sheep and oxen. Only eleven households stayed put. The newcomers had such different dialects that the locals could barely understand what they said. The first day, the Reds set about cleaning the streets of Wuqi and scrawling anti-Japanese and Red-unity slogans on walls. By the next morning, the villagers had returned en masse. The marchers could now buy pigs, sheep, and other provisions to feed their famished bodies. With assurance from the villagers that there were no enemy forces within twenty miles, the Communist leaders declared a weeklong period to rest, feast, scrub up, mend or replace clothes, and drill fresh recruits.

On the third morning, however, four regiments of Nationalist-allied cavalry, each with about a thousand riders, suddenly materialized, ready to attack. The battle- and trail-hardened Communists had not let down their guard. They fired accurately into the first wave of horsemen, knocking many riders off their mounts. Confused and scared, the horses in front reared about and shattered the next wave of riders. Two chaotic, bloody hours later, the attackers fled.[18]

That afternoon, two local leaders informed Mao of the unfolding purge in the combined Twenty-fifth and Twenty-sixth armies. Mao dispatched troops to Wayaobao to save his friend Liu Zhidan, who had been placed in chains, condemned to die. About eighty-five miles east and north of Wuqi, Wayaobao was a dusty backwater and regional Red stronghold sitting on hills of coal. Its narrow dirt roads quickly turned to mud in the rain. It was here and at Wuqi and in a cluster of nearby communities — including Yanan, forty miles to the south, and Baoan (later Zhidan) — that the Central Soviet would put down new roots.

Mao's embracing of local leaders, including Liu, who was revered by his men and would command large forces before being killed in battle in the spring of 1936, helped smooth the transformation of this unlikely region into the national Red headquarters.[19]

For the better part of a year, the marchers had dreamed of nothing but stopping — relief from the bugle song that forced them to rise from exhaustion and set out yet again. Although they had merely traded one untenable base for another, even remoter and less civilized, they could now turn to rebuilding their lives as they reshaped the world around them.

Three of the original First Army women, however, having been left behind, were still fending for themselves. Seven were still on the trail with the Fourth Army. Their prospects were far different from those who had reached Shaanxi. For some of them, as tough as the going had been so far, it was about to get worse.

chapter 23

The Fourth Army
Hunkers Down

In late October, the Fourth Army attacked Sichuan military positions. During ten days of fighting, the Reds took three cities—Baoxing, Tianquan, and Lushan—inflicted 5,000 casualties on Sichuan forces, and shot down an airplane. With the victory, they now held large areas of the western Qionglai Mountains, which lie east of the Dadu River. From here, they had easy access to the provincial capital of Chengdu, the economic and transportation hub of the breadbasket of China. On November 11, fifteen of the army's regiments occupied the town of Baizhang, which was less than sixty miles from Chengdu. The notion that Sichuan's capital was in danger of falling to the Communists shocked the nation. Sichuan governor Liu Xiang ordered his forces to repel the Communists at any cost.[1]

Baizhang was surrounded by fields of alluvial soil separated by gentle hills. As the fighting commenced, Red Army and Sichuan forces maneuvered through the patchwork of rice paddies, dry at this time of year, savagely contesting each hilltop. During three days and nights of bloody fighting, the Sichuan forces suffered tremendous casualties but refused to give up, heedlessly pushing forward to retake Baizhang.

Waves of warplanes bombed and strafed the Red lines. On the fourth day, Liu Xiang's troops penetrated the town walls. Now the two armies clawed at each other. As houses on every street burned, spewing acrid waves of smoke into the streets, Communist and

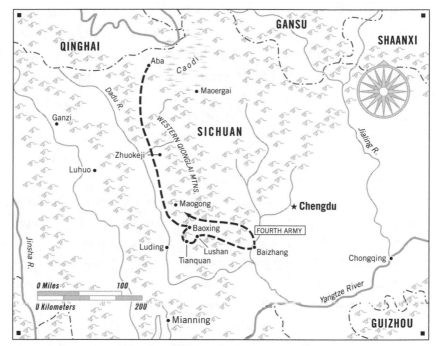

The Fourth Army Struggles in Sichuan

Sichuan soldiers grappled with one another, shooting, stabbing, gouging, and biting.

Wang Xinlan had never seen such fierce fighting. She and her frightened comrades ran through the streets, dodging the fires, looking for wounded soldiers to triage and evacuate. Mangled bodies from both sides lay intertwined, blood and viscera everywhere, the air thick with the smell of death.

When Xinlan found the soldier Wang Youfa, who had often carried her stretcher when she was sick, he was wounded in the head and chest and dying. His face was twisted in pain, his eyes clenched, his breath labored and rasping. She talked to him and put water on his lips. He opened his eyes and tried to smile at her. Such a personal moment with a friend who was dying terrified Xinlan. She began to cry and begged him to hang on. Youfa opened his mouth and moved his lips. Drowned out by the gunfire around them, his voice was nothing more than a croak. She leaned close and listened. "Sing 'Down with Liu Xiang,'" he whispered. It was the song denouncing Sichuan's governor. Xinlan held up his head. "Brother, I'll sing for you," she said, but before she could get through the song, he lost consciousness. She shouted at him to stay alive, but he was gone.[2]

It cost the Sichuan forces a staggering 15,000 men to drive the Communists out of Baizhang. The Fourth Army's casualties were almost as bad: nearly 10,000 dead. Battered and bloody, the Reds abandoned the burning city and retreated to the north.

Amid the chaos, Wang Xinlan, having endured so much on the trail and the battlefield, was finally asked to join the Communist Youth League. At the age of eleven, she became the youngest member of its *xuanchuan* team and joined a group of thirty trainees studying under the famous performer and troupe leader, Li Bozhao, who had originally set out with the First Army.

Soon word arrived that crack Nationalist troops had arrived from the south. Meanwhile, Sichuan forces were amassing to the east. Urgent orders sent Wang back to her unit.

The Fourth Army decamped and marched west back into the Snowy Mountains, a defensive maneuver that had to be accomplished before winter snows prevented it. The tide had turned for Zhang Guotao in Sichuan. He was no longer on the prowl; he was now the quarry.

WHILE THE WANDERINGS of the Fourth Army were still far from over, Mao began mythologizing the First Army's yearlong march. In a December written discourse, he denounced Japanese imperialism, bashed Zhang Guotao, and recast the trek—in reality, a strategic retreat—as the epic journey of a heroic underdog. He called it the "Long March" seventeen times, effectively christening the odyssey:

> For twelve months we were under daily recon-
> naissance and bombing from the skies by scores of
> planes, while on land we were encircled and pursued,

obstructed and intercepted by a huge force of several hundred thousand men, and we encountered untold difficulties and dangers on the way; yet by using our two legs we swept across a distance of more than twenty thousand *li* through the length and breadth of eleven provinces. Let us ask, has history ever known a long march to equal ours? No, never.[3]

The length of the Long March has been discussed by historians ever since. In the tradition of classical Chinese literature, Mao chose a large round number to characterize the difficulty and epic nature of the journey rather than put an empirical number on it. At the end of 1935, he variously used "20,000 *li*" (6,200 miles) and "25,000 *li*" (7,750 miles) in conversations and speeches. In *Red Star over China,* Edgar Snow reduced those estimates to a more plausible 5,000 miles. Agnes Smedley in 1943 topped even Mao, giving the distance as 12,000 miles. Jonathan D. Spence got it right in *The Gate of Heavenly Peace* when he said it was almost 4,000 miles. Ed Jocelyn and Andy McEwen, the only Westerners on record to walk the entire Long March, pegged the distance at 3,750 miles.[4]

The Long March, Mao argued, had exposed the futility of the imperialists' and Chiang Kaishek's attempt to destroy the Communists, and it had actually helped spread the "great message of the Red Army," seeding revolution among the 200 million people living in the eleven provinces through which it had passed. "We will harvest its reward in the future," he predicted.

In January 1936, Comintern representative Lin Yuying arrived in the North Shaanxi Soviet from Moscow. By telegram, Zhang Guotao blamed Mao for the separation of the armies and claimed to represent the legitimate Chinese Communist Party. Lin telegrammed back endorsing Mao, the First Army, and the Party leadership it supported. With Lin's decision, Zhang was effectively ordered to return to the fold. But first he moved farther west into still remoter territory.[5]

While Mao was busy staking his claim to the moral high ground, the women set about the practical work of transforming the backward region into which they had been delivered, where health, hygiene, and poverty levels were as grim as anything they had seen.

A limited feminist revolution resulted, as the Long March women campaigned against arranged marriages, where, according to Li Jianzhen, girls were "treated like donkeys" until it was time to produce and rear children. She declared that the "yoke" that had suppressed women for so long was "broken" and that women now had a "voice in the government of the family and society."[6]

The Communists redistributed land, giving both women and men equal shares, and taught the women agricultural techniques. In one area, Li Jianzhen noted, there were soon 15,000 women cultivating their own land. This in turn freed up 20,000 men to serve in the army. According to Li, the women encouraged their husbands to enlist, and any "who don't send their husbands to the front are despised by the others."

At the same time, the First Army women helped organize the region's women in cooperatives and factories, collecting homespun wool and turning it into blankets, uniforms, and socks. Between October 1935 and October 1936, these young factory workers (their average age was nineteen) would make 600,000 uniforms.[7]

IN FEBRUARY, THE FOURTH ARMY — its numbers reduced by half to 40,000 due to fighting, disease, and attrition — began its third ascent of the Snowies. To prevent a typhoid epidemic from sweeping through its ranks, Dr. Nelson Fu, a former senior physician at a British missionary hospital in Fujian province, implemented strict sanitary practices. He ordered the use of bellows in the thin air of the high plateau to raise the heat of the fires and bring water to a boil faster in order to kill germs. An adherent of Western medicine, which at this point was essentially unavailable, he adapted to the use of Chinese herbs to help his patients, of whom Kang Keqing was now one.[8]

Under such brutal living conditions, the weary marchers were primed for collapse and infection. Kang had developed a virulent fever and other symptoms of typhoid. Since Zhang Guotao had strictly

Cheery Yanan factory workers. *(Helen Foster Snow Archives, Brigham Young University)*

Women workers in Yanan. *(Helen Foster Snow Archives, Brigham Young University)*

limited Kang's contact with Zhu De, he was not allowed to come to her, and only her friend Xiao Zhaoying was permitted to tend to her. Kang fell into a coma with a temperature of 104 degrees and looked to be near death.

When a high-ranking Fourth Army official suggested that Kang be left behind, Xiao realized the extreme danger her friend was in. At great risk to herself, she took a horse and dashed off to alert Zhu De. Under virtual house arrest, Zhu promptly summoned his doctor and guards, brushed aside his restrictions, and rushed to see her. In a last-ditch effort, the doctor injected Kang with what she later described as "the last remaining fever-reducing medicine."[9]

Furious about the intention to leave Kang behind, Zhu found the official and poured out his anger: "She's worked so hard for so long. And now you'd abandon her when she's sick?" he shouted. "You also tried to hide it from me, the commander. Is this how you treat your comrades?" Zhu continued, "Kang Keqing is extremely sick. Is there anyone who doesn't get sick? We will not leave her with the locals — ever."

"The women comrades will carry her," Xiao Zhaoying volunteered, and she went to find women cadres to carry Kang's stretcher.

Two days later, Kang's fever broke, but only temporarily. After riding a horse on a winding road and crossing icy mountain streams, it returned, and she began shivering again. The women camped near Jiajinshan, the formidable mountain in the Snowies where so many First Army soldiers had lost their lives, and Xiao and others watched Kang through the night, rubbing her body with cool wet rags.

Nationalist airplanes found them the next day. As the fighters zeroed in on the line of marching troops, Kang's stretcher-bearers looked for a place to hide her, but the stretcher was too big to fit in the roadside gully. Zhu's bodyguard Pan Kaiwen tried to help her off the stretcher, but Kang said, "I won't be able to get back up again if I go down there. Leave me. They won't see me if I lie here alone. Lead the horse away before the plane sees it."

Pan quickly led the horse away. Kang lay shivering on the stretcher, watching the plane dive down to release its bombs. The resulting blast shook the ground beneath her but left her unscathed. When the planes departed, Kang's female comrades retrieved her and once again started their trudge forward.

When they reached the snow line, however, it became too difficult to carry her. Instead, as before, she grasped the tail of a horse. Pan Kaiwen lashed her hands to the animal with a puttee. "The horse dragged me along as I followed with uneven steps," she later recalled. "My body was weak, and my head felt heavier than my feet." Her friends propped her up and supported her from behind. Although they moved slowly and fell behind, they finally crested the mountain.[10]

Back in the town of Maogong, where the First and Fourth armies had joined up so long ago, it now seemed, Li Bozhao visited Kang. Her friend—who weighed 120 pounds when healthy, had big strong hands, and spoke in a virile, throaty voice—had wasted away. Li, who was now the director of cultural recreation and whose performances were much prized by Zhang Guotao, was stunned at the degree to which typhoid had ravaged her.

The two women had very different personalities—dramatic Li, the actress and artist, and serious Kang, the consummate soldier. But such distinctions mattered little now, after so much suffering and with such uncertainty ahead. Cold, tired, and hungry, in the hands of a leader they feared and mistrusted, Li and Kang simply embraced each other and wept.

chapter 24

A Union of Forces

While Mao and the First Army rested and Zhang and the Fourth Army fled, the Second and Sixth army groups found themselves within a noose. They had been holding territory in Hunan province, in the understanding that the region was the Central Party leaders' first choice for establishing the new Central Soviet. But the First Army had long since passed them by, and now it was their turn to evacuate a failing stronghold and to go in search of a new one.

With Hunan strongman He Jian mobilized and Nationalist troops on the offensive, it was determined that the Second and Sixth army groups must immediately cross the Li River, thirty miles to the southeast of their current position, before Nationalist air and ground forces could destroy the river crossings and pin them down.

The night before they were to set out, the officials met with the band of misfits that Ma Yixiang had been grouped with. The officials told them to return to their homes and gave them a small amount of money. Ma was devastated. On the sly, though, the same officials then told them that the army was moving out the next day. If they chose to follow along, they should not get too close — they were only tagalongs — but they had better not fall too far behind either, or the Nationalists would grab them.[1]

ON THE MORNING of November 19, 1935, Rudolf Bosshardt, a Swiss-English missionary captured by the Red Army thirteen months earlier, was awakened before dawn: they were moving out again. The previous March, the *New York Times* had erroneously reported that he and his fellow captive and clergyman, Arnolis Hayman, a New Zealander, had been executed by the Communists. That mistake had been cleared up, but since then, negotiations for his ransom had stalled. Middlemen had made many dangerous trips on foot into and out of the Northwest Hunan Soviet to relay ransom demands to Bosshardt's benefactors. Then the Chinese had played him a mean trick.

As citizens of Western nations allied with the Nationalists and thus enemies of the Communists, Bosshardt and Hayman had been beaten and abused. They had witnessed disturbing military executions of prisoners of war and had suffered through hunger and privations and a host of illnesses. Finally, as a result of the tedious negotiations, the two were supposed to have been released on November 18. But the Communist negotiator, a fierce man Bosshardt knew as Judge Wu, claimed that only half the $10,000 ransom had come in. "We shall be able to release only one of you," he declared, choosing Hayman. "And don't you try to run away again," he warned Bosshardt. "If you do, I'll shoot you myself."[2]

Now Bosshardt was alone. After breakfast, he warmed himself beside the blaze that consumed the prisoners' remaining wood. Still stunned by the sudden absence of his companion, he staggered out of town, clutching a small bundle of possessions, including the periodicals he had collected and reread, keeping pace with the crowded column of men as it alternately shuffled along and surged ahead at a trot.

Also in the escaping throng was a small group of women, several dozen of them, including the two beautiful Jian sisters, who were married to the two leaders. Jian Xianfo, General Xiao Ke's wife, who had joined his Western Hunan Red Army in 1929 and had been the only woman among a thousand men, was newly pregnant. Her sister Jian Xianren, General He Long's wife, had given birth to a baby girl less than three weeks before and was riding on a stretcher clutching her daughter, Jiesheng (Victorious), to her chest. She had hoped to leave the optimistically named baby with He's relatives, but first the relatives had put her off, saying they were trying to find a wet nurse, and then they had secretly fled the town, fearful of possessing He's child once the Red Army pulled out.

Half a *li* back, Ma and her group of misfit women and children tailed along, carrying a bag of recently harvested rice. The villagers watched from behind closed doors as the Communists vanished from their streets, like a dream at dawn.

Before the sun had been long in the sky, Nationalist airplanes discovered the crowded columns and flew in low to drop their bombs.

In the afternoon, Bosshardt, who suffered from bouts of malaria and rheumatism, among other maladies, was overwhelmed. He took quinine, and one of his guards gave him smelling salts. Another, nick-named "the Chinese Alien" because unlike most Chinese men, he had a full beard, allowed the prisoner to rest. When the pair resumed marching but fell behind, a section leader and the Chinese Alien carried Bosshardt's haversack and umbrella.

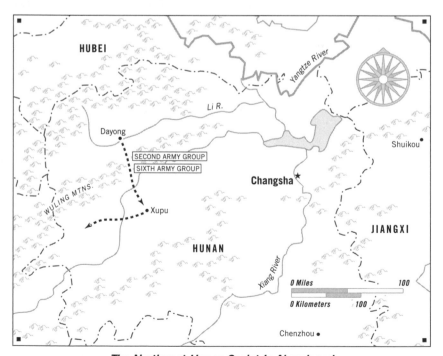

The Northwest Hunan Soviet Is Abandoned

Ma Yixiang arrived in Dayong, the town along the Li River where the marchers hoped to cross, well before Bosshardt. Though not officially attached to the army now, she and another girl were ordered to keep watch on a grove of ripe oranges, which the soldiers were forbidden to pick (most likely because they belonged to small farms, not landlords). Instead, the road-weary duo crawled inside a barrel used for rice husking and fell asleep.

In the morning, Ma and her friend awoke to the sounds of footsteps and hammering and had just enough time to scurry across the nearby bridge and join the fleeing ranks before the soldiers finished dismantling it to slow the pursuit of the Hunanese. After crossing the river, the soldiers fanned out to avoid providing an easy target from the air. Ma and her friend ran after them, keeping far enough behind but not falling so far back as to be adrift for good.

Assigned to the convalescent company, Jian Xianren had been unable to get used to being a burden. At the same time, she resented the halting pace of the invalids. No matter how hard they marched, they could not keep up. At around noon that day, the convalescents finally reached Dayong, only to discover that the bridges had already been destroyed. The grooms drove the mules and horses upriver to ford the Li in a shallower place, while at a landing the soldiers ferried the invalids across in small boats. As Jian and her baby boarded one, she heard a buzz in the sky. "Airplane coming!" she shouted. The passengers on board scrambled ashore and ran for cover. Jian could not run, so she stayed in the boat. "I'm not getting out," she said.[3]

A Health Department official joined her. "Let's just go," he said. "If we're bombed, then we were meant to die! If we're not bombed, then we're across." Jian agreed.

The official shoved the boat off the bank. As he poled them into the current, the plane circled above but then found other targets. Still, they were not safe. The official was no boatman and could not handle the current. Out of control, the craft careened downstream, missing the ferry landing. Only after a frantic and exhausting struggle was he able to wrestle the boat ashore. Jian's stretcher-bearers carried her across a wide, soft-sand beach. Another carried baby Jiesheng, who would not stop crying. "Little girl, what are you crying about?" the official cooed. "You're full of piss and shit! Twenty years from now, when you're pretty and vain, we'll remind you of this! We'll see if you think it's funny then."

Jian had a mount prepared and a *beilou,* a baby-carrying basket, strapped to the back. She caught up with the headquarters unit and announced that she would no longer ride on a stretcher. The slow convalescent group had been bombed six times; traveling with them was too risky. He Long ordered a bowl of rice and a cup of water for her. In two days, Jian, a nursing mother, had traveled more than thirty miles without eating.

Ma Yixiang continued to shadow the soldiers as they crossed the Wuling Range. In the remote river valleys between the mountains, locals proposed that Ma and her friends abandon the Reds and stay there and work for them. They would be safe and well fed, the locals promised. But these places were profoundly foreign to Ma, and she kept on, never entertaining the notion.

Finally, the marchers reached Xupu, the hometown of the feminist paragon Xiang Jingyu, who in 1916, when she was just twenty, had revived a girls' school here, urging families to unbind their daughters' feet and seeking out even the poorest of the poor in the mountain hollows. Before she could carry out all of her plans for the school, she was driven out because of her progressive brand of education. Xiang later headed the Communist Party's Women's Department, bringing women of all ilks — not just the Christian elite and upper classes — into politics, education, and revolution. She helped found the China Women's Federation, a watershed in the advancement of women's status in China, but in 1928 was captured and executed.[4]

In Xupu, the Red Army stopped to regroup and gather supplies. Ma and four of her misfit friends holed up in a house abandoned by a landlord who had left an old manservant in charge. She hid when some workers from the Red Army school came to deliver bushels of unhusked rice confiscated from wealthy landowners. Then she and her friends husked the rice, kept some to eat, and bartered the rest for oil, salt, and vegetables.

After several days, officials in the Political Department discovered Ma, summoned her, and deliberated on her fate. "This child may be from a landlord's family, but she's not afraid of hardship," a section head finally declared. "Since she herself hasn't exploited anyone, we'll let her stay." Ma was readmitted to the Red Army and put to work doing laundry for the revolutionary committee's busy cooks. Thankful to be reinstated, she worked hard and became a favorite of the cooks.[5]

Like Ma, the resourceful Bosshardt found a way to be useful. Having fashioned crochet hooks from chopsticks, he made sweaters for Party officials, who kept him supplied with yarn. Bosshardt and four other special prisoners were also put to work making sandals, which led him to suspect that his journey had just begun.[6]

Nevertheless, the order to evacuate Xupu came with shocking urgency. One late afternoon about a week after they had arrived, the command came to break camp immediately. Ma was washing clothes by the river when the alarm went out. Other than her padded coat, she had few possessions. She quickly took to the road with the others. Soldiers, prisoners, and guards dashed about, grabbing bed gear, clothes, and other essentials. Bosshardt despaired, as he had time to snag only his haversack, abandoning his spare clothes, bedding, and some treasured reading. His rheumatic joints throbbed as he hobbled up a hillside, supported by his Spanish-speaking guard, a tall muscular man whom the others called "the Romanist." They joined the throng of men and beasts stampeding out of town — a far cry from the usual orderly column. Gunshots rang out nearby as they hustled away.

*

HAVING FAILED TO CONNECT with the First Army, the Second and Sixth army groups now hoped to connect with the Fourth Army, still hundreds of miles to the north of them.

From Maogong, Zhang Guotao moved west to the town of Danba. In late February, the Fourth Army approached the 17,950-foot Danglingshan, whose glacial peak was visible against the blue sky from miles away. Dangling was the tallest mountain any of the Red Army factions would attempt to cross during their collective Long March and as fierce as the warlike tribe of the Tang dynasty for which it was named.

Zhang's army had to cross over the behemoth by midday or risk getting caught in the storms that often made the mountaintop a death zone after noon. To do so, the troops ascended its gradients, dotted with mountain tarns and hot springs, over two days, spending the night above the snow line in animal-hide tents crammed with people.

In one, Kang Keqing, now recovered from her illness, shared the body warmth of Zhu De and several of his bodyguards and orderlies. That night, the sky turned pitch-black, and snow fell in wild arctic gusts, encasing every exposed surface in ice. The Fourth Army soldiers took turns emerging from the tents to reinforce them against the wind and the weight of the ice and snow. Praying that she would not get blown off the mountain, Kang held a lantern aloft while several men from her tent tightened the lines, hammered down stakes, and scraped the frost off the sagging leather. By the time they finished, they were freezing and sheathed in crackling ice. "Crawling back into the low but warm tent," Kang said, "was like entering into heaven."[7]

In the morning, they continued the climb. The sky had cleared, and they squinted against the glare of the snow. The leaders sank in past their knees in places, their footsteps carving out a trench that eased the way for those who followed. Still, the thin air made breathing difficult. "Fortunately, the path on Dangling was winding, unlike the vertical climb of Jiajin," Kang recalled. "At this point I was mostly recovered from my previous illness, and walking while holding on to the tail of the horse was not as difficult as before."

On the far side of Dangling, the Reds reached the town of Luhuo, on the Sichuan–Tibet Highway. Surrounded by a vast area of snow-covered slopes, Luhuo was bitterly cold in April. The temperature rose above freezing during the day but sank drastically at night, when frigid winds made even squatting outside to relieve oneself potentially deadly. Spitfire rivers blasted through it, carrying away glacier runoff and snowmelt.

They had reached the Tibetan heartland. Locals kept warm in oily goatskin coats weighing thirty pounds. Lamas in crimson robes filled the towns and ruled all aspects of life with religious zeal. "Iron-bar" lamas enforced the laws with metal rods, so terrifying that even their fellow lamas dispersed at their sight. Although the local women wore veils, they avoided the lamas while walking down the street for fear of arousing their desire and being sent to convents to become nuns as punishment.

Because of the centuries of enmity between China and Tibet, relations between the Communists and the Tibetans were tenuous at best. "To them we were just a hateful tribe that came to rob them of their food, but at the same time we treated them kindly and peacefully," said Zhang Guotao. "This surprised them, and they could not understand it." According to Zhang, women were particularly degraded here. Polyandry was customary, with several brothers marrying the same woman, who was responsible for all of their needs and for maintaining their brotherly spirit. "Any case of jealousy, regardless of the reason," Zhang learned, "is the responsibility of the wife." Because women who caused lust or jealousy were considered immoral, many cut their faces and rubbed charcoal into the open wounds to create ugly black scars.[8]

Wang Quanyuan, who had become familiar with Tibetan customs while doing political work with the First Army, recruited and organized the locals. One *tusi,* however, was angered by Wang's success and branded her a witch. He predicted that disasters would befall the locals if they did not kill her. But Wang would not be intimidated. With the help of a bilingual half-Han, half-Tibetan boy, she spread the Communist message and gained the trust of families by treating their sick.

Still determined to kill Wang, the *tusi* prepared an ambush along her path, but a Tibetan peasant rushed to find her and warn her of the plot. Moved by the peasant's courage, Wang asked him, "Aren't you afraid that the *tusi* will cut your head off? Why did you come to warn me?"

"You're a good person," the man replied. "You can't die!"[9]

After establishing a number of village youth organizations and adding many new members to the Communist Youth League, Wang was made the Youth League's Party secretary. It was an honor and showed her vital role in the organization.

The women of the Fourth Army began to prepare for the arrival of the Second and Sixth army groups. As welcoming gifts for them, Zhu De and the women decided to knit warm sweaters and pants for the march north. The women bought raw wool from the Tibetans, but it was matted with mud, sheep droppings, and grass, and they choked on the foul dust that rose as they struggled to unknot its tangles. Kang went in search of help. Walking by Zhu's campsite, she saw Pan Kaiwen hanging clean wool on a line to dry in the sun and stopped to talk to him.

Following his instructions, the women boiled their wool to rid it of its natural sticky residue, then washed it in a solution of hay ashes and water to remove the dirt, debris, and odor. In two days, they too had transformed the gamy bundles into mounds of snowy floss.

Using a stick and a sheep-bone spindle, a Tibetan woman showed them how to spin, first coiling the wool around the stick and then twisting one end into a strand of yarn and tying it to the spindle, which she twirled. The women had spun cotton the same way back home, but the wool was thicker. They each made a spindle out of wood or bone, but unused to the wool's thickness, they had trouble producing even strands. Often they had to stop, cut the yarn, and start over, creating a heap of wasted wool.

They were growing discouraged when Zhu came to check on their progress. Taking up a spindle, he produced a fine, even yarn. When he held it up, a cry of surprise rippled over the women. "Look at his yarn," someone exclaimed. "It doesn't look handmade but machine-made." Zhu, it turned out, had spun yarn since he was a little boy.

Within two weeks, the knitters in camp had taught the others how to knit, and men and women alike carried balls of white yarn around with them, filling the camp with the soft clatter of needles at meetings and late into the night.[10]

BY THE END OF JUNE 1936, the Second and Sixth army groups had marched some 3,000 miles to the west and north from their Hunan base and were approaching the Tibetan city of Ganzi, to which the Fourth Army had moved in May. Here Wang Quanyuan and Kang Keqing lived and worked together. Among her many duties, Kang encouraged crowds of townspeople to join rallies. Wang performed, mimicking local tyrants and convincing the villagers that the Red Army had come to free them from their cultural shackles. She had grown proficient enough at speaking Tibetan that when the troops needed a place to sleep, she could bang on the door of a house and ask the residents for lodging.[11]

Situated at an altitude of more than 11,000 feet, Ganzi (Tibetan for "white and beautiful") is known for its long cold winters—the average annual temperature is only 42 degrees—but also for its plentiful sun-light. Ganzi is a sacred city to the Tibetans. In 1662, as lore had it, the fifth Dalai Lama traveled to the region to find a site on which to build a temple. As he crossed a river in a cowhide boat, an eagle swooped down from the sky and plucked a string of Buddhist beads from the bow, where the Dalai Lama had hung them, and flew off. The Dalai Lama followed the eagle, which left the beads on a beautiful white rock that resembled a sheep. Taking this as a sign from above, he ordered the new temple to be built upon this rock, and the town grew up around it.

Relations between the Red Army and the Tibetans remained tense. With so many soldiers in the area, food was in short supply. The Living Buddha of Ganzi, the revered spiritual leader of the region, told the Fourth Army that because it was in "a state of poverty, its action in searching for food and other supplies is worse than that of Liu Wenhui." Liu was the commander of the Sichuan Army forces that opposed the Fourth Army. Zhang Guotao later admitted that the Living Buddha had been right. "We were trapped in a remote corner, there was no food to eat, and the resistance of the Tibetans made us feel ashamed," he said.[12]

As the Fourth Army's morale sagged, the arrival of the troops from the south was all the more anticipated. Three different groups of scouts sent out to help guide the Second and Sixth army groups to Ganzi had been ambushed and killed. Finally, Zhang Qinqiu dispatched Wang Quanyuan, telling her to do her best to buy food to help the incoming troops but also imploring her to be careful.

Wang Quanyuan explained the situation to her interpreter, emphasizing that the troops were coming to protect the Tibetans and to let them rule themselves. He listened and then guaranteed her that she would be safe.

They set out together with a horse and a young Han boy to tend it. When they reached the foot of a mountain, the interpreter shouted the news of their approach three times to the Tibetans hidden above. At two houses on the mountainside, Wang explained the situation and the need for food to feed the incoming troops the next day. Wang, the interpreter, and the boy spent the night with the Tibetans but in the morning woke to find their hosts gone.

Wang did not know whether they had gone to get reinforcements to seize her or to line up the food supplies she needed. She stationed the interpreter outside as a lookout and waited. Soon, the Tibetans returned. To Wang's great relief, they led a caravan carrying baskets of food.

Next Wang asked the Tibetans if they would prepare a reception for the newcomers. They agreed. When the Red troops from Hunan arrived the next day, locals waved triangular red paper flags on bamboo shafts in greeting. This warm welcome was much appreciated by the exhausted travelers. North of the Golden Sands River, they had shed the Nationalists pursuing them, but like the First Army, they had faced nature in extremis.

To make traversing the narrow trails easier, the Second and Sixth army groups had taken separate routes, agreeing to converge again near Luhuo, in the midst of the Snowy Mountains, where they planned to meet up with the Fourth Army. "The more mountains we crossed, the fewer people we had," Ma Yixiang later observed. "Our health went from bad to worse. We didn't have much to eat. When we ran out of barley, we began to eat wild herbs. At first we picked the ones we knew, such as fennel and wild rape. Later we had to eat others that we were unfamiliar with."[13] They were also often thirsty. Before fleeing, the Tibetans had disconnected and hidden aqueduct pipes that channeled drinking water to their villages from hidden sources. According to Zhang Guotao, during their journey the two army groups had been reduced from 20,000 to a mere 5,000.

The Fourth Army presented the soldiers of the Second and Sixth army groups with wool socks, gloves, sweaters, and pants. The newcomers tried them on, called for their comrades to admire them, and then took them off to keep them pristine. The Second and Sixth army groups had little to give in return, but Kang Keqing reassured them that they need not reciprocate for these welcoming gifts.

Reduced as the two army groups were in number, their leaders soon announced the consolidation of the two units into one, the newly christened Second Army, to be led by Political Commissar Ren Bishi, Commander He Long, and Deputy Commander Xiao Ke. This was only the smallest ripple in the sea of change that was to come. Earlier in the year, Lin Yuying, the Chinese Communist representative to the International Labor Union, had returned to China, to the North Shaanxi Soviet, with instructions from Moscow. Because of the growing menace of Hitler and his fascist allies, including Japan, all Chinese forces were asked to unite against the fascists in the Anti-Japanese National United Front. Unwilling to join ranks with the hated and mistrusted Chiang Kaishek, who had already turned on them once, the Central Red Army leaders had secretly formed an alliance with the Manchurian warlord Zhang Xueliang. Better known as "the Young Marshal," Zhang was a former ally of Chiang's. His father had been executed by the Japanese, who now occupied his homeland.[14] The new campaign would be captured in a slogan: "Unite with Zhang, oppose Chiang, and resist Japan."

The renewed emphasis on fighting Japan provided an impetus to resolve the Communist Party infighting. Everyone agreed that securing northwestern China would strengthen the Young Marshal–Communist Party coalition, protecting their back door. They could then turn their attention to fighting the Japanese invaders in eastern China. Thus, Zhang Guotao was instructed to move the Fourth Army and the Second Army north to take the Hexi Corridor, part

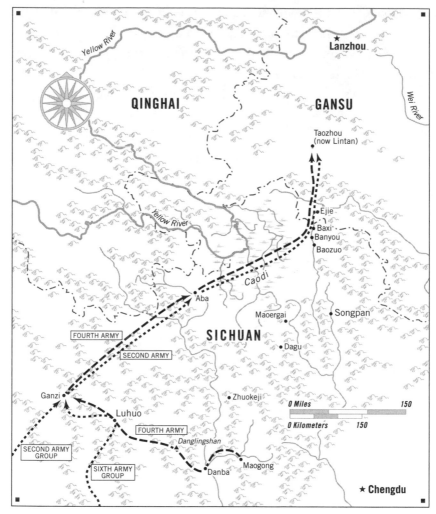

The Second and Sixth Army Groups Meet Up with the Fourth Army

of the ancient Silk Road connecting China to the West and known as the "throat" because of its shape and strategic location. The corridor snaked northwest from the Yellow River along the edge of the Gobi Desert to the western terminus of the Great Wall, linking five main cities (Lanzhou, Wuwei, Zhangye, Jiayuguan, and Dunhuang) on its way to Central Asia and, more importantly, the Soviet Union. Zhang embraced this mission.

The Second Army would go north via a more easterly route and the Fourth via a more westerly one, before reuniting to cross the Yellow River. "After a year of twists and turns," Kang Keqing noted, "we were finally on our way to the north."[15]

In his memoir, Zhang Guotao makes the march north sound like easy traveling: "We had no difficulty in climbing the Snowy mountains and crossing the steppe land," he wrote. "No one lagged behind. The river that blocked our way the year before could now be forded, as the water was below our knees."[16]

Kang Keqing also found the first days of the march placid. They had food rations, each carrying six pounds of millet flour, which would last for two weeks. "The soldiers were cheerful and lively," she said, despite the fact that they would soon be crossing the Caodi again. "Dressed in clean clothes, we sang while we marched on energetically: 'The Second and Fourth Armies are brave and true. / With determination we march north to fight the Japanese. / We march forth, awaiting victory.' "[17]

Not all was song and solidarity, however. Seen as coddled because they still had long pants as well as a horse to carry their things, Ma and her young Second Army friends, who were now attached to the Fourth Army, were bullied by some of the women in the Fourth. These women's rotting pants had been reduced to shorts, and they carried everything on their backs. As they berated and kicked one listless girl who was sick from malaria and refused to get up, Ma and her cowed friends clung to one another and cried.

Such petty tyranny, not unusual in an army, was, relatively speaking, only a nuisance compared to some of the other threats they faced. As the column approached Zhuokeji and Maoergai, the Tibetans increasingly pressed the Reds. "These Tibetan men were heavily armed and fanatical," Kang remembered. "We called them the 'barbarian cavalries.' While we were trying to cross a hill, three hundred of them rushed toward us, screaming and yelling, hacking at everyone in their path." Reinforcements arrived just in time to fend off the assault and prevent severe losses. Among the battle's casualties were two dozen Tibetan horses. The Red Army cooks butchered and roasted most of them, and after a feast, they prepared the rest for transport.

On the way to the Caodi, Ma witnessed a tragic scene involving her friend Qing Jinmei. Qing had already left an infant behind after her first husband, a gun repair specialist, was killed in battle. Two weeks before her second child was born, her new husband died on the trail. Suffering from early labor pains, she rode on a supply department horse. After a while, she went into full labor and dismounted. In traditional China, it was considered unseemly to make a lot of noise during childbirth. If a laboring woman yelled or cried, her mother-in-law and the midwife would scold her. If she carried on, they would send for her mother and shame them both.

Several of the women, including Ma, ushered Qing to the roadside. Overwhelmed by the death of her husband, the future of her child, and the powerful contractions, Qing screamed in pain as she pushed the baby out.

The women cut the cord. They had no time to look for a home where they could leave the baby, so they set the infant in a clump of grass and walked on.[18]

THIS WAS MA'S FIRST TIME crossing the Caodi, but it was Wang Xinlan's third, and it would be the worst.

Wang and her comrades had little food left by the time they reached the Caodi. As their calorie intake diminished, they traveled more sluggishly. Senior officers told them to tighten their belts and orchestrated a marching competition. Winners received a knotted-cloth model airplane; losers had to carry around a knotted-cloth turtle. "Fast troops will take a plane," they sang as they went. "Those who lag behind will carry turtles." But such inducements could only do so much.[19]

"Sometimes we marched day and night," said Wang Dingguo, who had been placed in charge of the costumes of the New Theatrical Company under Li Bozhao. The women suffered especially. "When we had our periods, blood streamed down our legs, as we had nothing in the way of sanitary napkins. Our blistered feet got soaked in the dirty, stinking water. Running sores broke out on our feet. When we unwrapped our caked bandages, they stuck to our skin — a grisly experience." A painful blister on the little toe of her right foot festered. "There just wasn't any medicine to be had."[20]

Li Bozhao herself fell seriously ill. Although starving, she lost her appetite. She became delirious and was made a ward of the hospital.

Icy winds swept across the plain, bringing snow, freezing rain, and hailstones so massive that they pummeled some marchers to death. Even when the precipitation stopped, the cold made sleep difficult. Little Xinlan and three other children put their blankets together and crawled underneath, haunted by the sight of death all around them.

One night, yet another storm socked them with snow and freezing rain. "The wind blew open the oilcloth and overturned our cowhide tents," Kang Keqing said. "Everyone was soaked to the bones, and we shivered in the cold."[21] By dawn, the tempest had passed. The marchers made a fire with hay and kindling that had been kept dry, changed out of their wet clothes, and moved on. Kang, feeling light-headed, worried that her body might fail her again. She also discovered that her young assistant, Zhao Ke, was gone. No one had seen him, but someone said that he had been feeling ill and might have strayed.

Kang asked two strong soldiers to go with her to search for him. They backtracked for nearly a mile and found Zhao facedown on the grass not far from their campsite. His forehead was burning hot, and he was delirious. They tended to him and fed him some wheat flour gruel. Then they took turns carrying him on their backs as they hurried to catch up.

They could hardly wait to leave the harrowing Caodi, but there was one more impediment in the way. The crossing of the "deep, swift" Banyou River would haunt Wang Dingguo the rest of her life. "There was no bridge. Several of us particularly short young women were apprehensive," she later related. "Li Bozhao, our commander, came along with a horse in tow. We linked ourselves arm in arm, latched onto the horse's tail, and made our way through the chest-deep water, stumbling as we went on the slippery stones." When the horse suddenly shied and bolted, they all lost their balance and were swept away by the current. Not one could swim. "I flailed at the water but couldn't make any headway," said Wang. Finally, as they were about to drown, a bunch of male soldiers jumped into the water and pulled them to safety.[22]

It had taken two eventful weeks to make the crossing. Widowed since just after setting out from Eyuwan, Zhang Qinqiu had married Fourth Army Political Commissar Chen Changhao on this brooding landscape. She and her first husband, Shen Zemin, had had a daughter, Maya, in Moscow in 1926. When hastily recalled to China in 1930, they had reluctantly left their daughter behind at the International Children's Hospital. Now Zhang Qinqiu was pregnant again.

AFTER ARRIVING AT Taozhou (now Lintan), a town on the edge of the Tibetan Plateau in southern Gansu, Kang Keqing rushed to see Li Bozhao, who had been carried off the Caodi on a litter. Kang was eager to repay the kindness of the friend who had comforted her during her crisis back in Maogong. In ancient times, Taozhou was one of the four trading posts where Western merchants swapped horses for tea from Sichuan and Shaanxi. Farmers and herders, Tibetan and Han, all mixed in the town, which for six hundred years had held a "10,000-man tug-of-war" in its square to celebrate the Lantern Festival on the last day of the New Year's celebrations.

Feverish and vomiting blood, Li found herself in her own tug-of-war between life and death. She had fallen sick on the Caodi, losing her ability to stand, and had not eaten for several days. Her eyes were sunken. Weeping, Li clutched Kang's hands and whispered, "Keqing! While alive, I belong to the Communists. When I die, my ghost still belongs to the Party. If I don't make it, please take my body to Shaanbei and give it to the Central Committee."[23]

Tears streamed down Kang's face as they held each other. She would never forget how Li had treated her like a sister on their long journey, assisting her over icy Jiajinshan.

Kang went off to find Dr. Fu, whose efforts to fight typhoid fever among the Fourth Army had prevented many deaths and drew praise and thanks from its commanders. He gave Li a shot to reduce her fever. Kang waited for Li to fall asleep and then, gently letting go of her bony hand, returned to her campsite. A couple of hours later, the doctor found Kang. "Li Bozhao's fever has gone down," he exclaimed. "She's going to be all right."

chapter 25

In the Throat

In July 1936, Edgar Snow, a correspondent for the *Saturday Evening Post,* and a young American doctor named George Hatem had found their way to Baoan, in the North Shaanxi Soviet. Snow had driven with Hatem in a Dodge truck north from Xian, past fields of swaying opium poppies nearly ready for harvest. Hatem, who was affectionately dubbed "Doc Ma" by the Communists, did emergency medical work and was already becoming a leading public health official. But Snow had something else in mind.

Operating in the remoteness of the vast Chinese hinterland and trapped behind the Nationalists' blackout curtain, the Chinese Communists were a virtual secret without a compelling story line — until now. They had been viewed only in rare secondhand glimpses in the world media. Rumor and legend far outweighed the body of facts known about the Red leaders, their ethos, and their actual practices. Snow wanted to take home news of the epic journey they had just completed and to reveal the personalities behind it. Mao welcomed him and gave him broad access to the town and to himself and the other Communist leaders.[1]

In their short time there, the Reds had transformed the Song dynasty town. When they arrived, according to Kang Keqing, Baoan was a backward place of eighty homes belonging to shepherds and buckwheat farmers. The running joke was that temples to various deities — the gods of wealth, medicine, and the earth — and Buddha images outnumbered

Dr. Nelson Fu and his Red Army nurses. *(Helen Foster Snow Archives, Brigham Young University)*

people. The Red Army soldiers bivouacked in the temples and within a few months transformed the place into their revolutionary capital, scrubbing it clean, repairing and building shelters, and plastering the streets with bright posters hailing the upcoming reunion of the First, Second, and Fourth armies and the success of the "anti-Japanese" Long March.[2]

Snow discovered that forty-three-year-old Chairman Mao, as he was now known, had a sharp mind, deep feelings, and peasant habits and that he lived as he preached—austerely. He and his wife, He Zizhen, occupied a humble two-room cave dwelling with a few maps covering the bare walls. Their chief luxury was a mosquito net for sleeping. Mao had only two uniforms, without decorations, worked fourteen hours a day, and ate what everyone else ate—except, in the Hunanese tradition, he added hot peppers.

Night after night, Snow sat with Mao and a translator. The chairman, Snow discovered, rarely commented on himself or his role in any event. He recounted their adventures from a group perspective.

The Third Division of the Red Army, at Dianzi, Gansu, guarding the perimeter of the North Shaanxi Soviet. *(Helen Foster Snow Archives, Brigham Young University)*

This was not contrived. Snow interviewed many of his compatriots as well. They simply did not tend to see or remember events from a personal perspective. Using their accounts, Snow emerged with a detailed story of the Long March and the years leading up to it. Mao proclaimed that those who had survived the journey were heroes and the following May granted all Long March veterans automatic Party membership.[3]

Snow came to know all the military and political leaders on many levels. He found them to be both fascinating and down-to-earth. He played tennis on the town's courts — one grass, one clay — with three faculty members of the newly reestablished Red Army University for Communist cadres, including a one-armed veteran who played a mean game of doubles. At night, Snow organized gin rummy and poker games on his candlelit *kang,* where the First Army officers often gathered, including a number of prominent female veterans of the Long March—Deng Yingchao, He Zizhen, Liao Siguang, Chen Huiqing, and Liu Qunxian.

Outnumbered as they were, nearly all the single female marchers of the First Army married in rapid succession. Little Sparrow and Zhang Wentian finally made their relationship official, and Xie Fei married Politburo member Liu Shaoqi (who would serve as chairman of the People's Republic of China from 1959 to 1968). Zhong Yuelin married Song Renqiong, a political commissar who would later be considered one of the Eight Elders of China, and Li Jianzhen married Deng Zhenxun (aka Zhongming), a leader of revolutionary activity in Xingguo, Jiangxi, best known for saying, "It is often necessary and right to sacrifice one's small family for the greater good of the big family."[4]

Most of them had, none more so than Li Guiying and Han Shiying, who had been left behind in Yunnan.

After her husband had been killed in a battle at Dashipan, in Sichuan, Li had married Yu Zehong, the political commissar of her guerrilla group. Pregnant in the heat of summer in 1935, she and Han had hidden out with Yu's family in Sichuan, squatting in the cellar as Nationalists ransacked the place, overturning the urine bucket, which dripped through the floor onto their heads. Later, as Li was about to deliver, her new husband was killed. Within ten days, she had left her newborn baby with her parents-in-law, and she and Han had returned to the field to re-form their scattered guerrilla force.

Their return was enough to reunite three hundred partisans, but the vastly stronger Nationalists hunted them down mercilessly. One day while being chased in Yunnan, Li stepped on a sharp piece of bamboo. The shaft penetrated her straw sandal and went through her foot. She removed it but had to keep running another forty miles before they could stop. She boiled water with salt and bathed her swollen foot. As she did, however, shots rang out. She tried to run again but was slowed by the wound. She and Han were captured.

The Nationalists marched them to prison in Zhaotaong, Yunnan, where they were beaten and interrogated, and a Nationalist officer raped Han.[5]

On OCTOBER 9, representatives of the First and Fourth armies finally reunited, at Huining, Gansu, south of the Yellow River (though the Second Army bypassed the town). It was a festive time, and so many were gathered that the walled town was too small to accommodate all of them. Eleven-year-old Wang Xinlan slept with her *xuanchuan* comrades on the floor of a peasant house in an outlying village, where they practiced their songs and dances for a big celebration performance on a threshing ground. At the performance, on a stage built of peasants' doors set up in a field, Wang, dressed in a white shirt and a gray uniform with a red tie, was the lead dancer. Soldiers showered her with gifts of candy, eggs, tinned meat, and even a small portion of lard to be mixed with rice for taste and calories.[6]

"Celebrations and rejoicing were held in Pao An [Baoan] and throughout the soviet districts," Snow noted after the radio transmission from Huining announced the union. "The long period of suspense during the fighting in south Kansu [Gansu] was ended. Everyone now felt a new confidence in the future."[7]

Before leaving Red territory, Snow interviewed Mao one last time and was impressed by his sincerity in wanting to make peace with the Nationalists to fight the Japanese. Afterward, Snow made his way out of the Communist-controlled region with a sack of evidence that he would use to tell the story of the Red Army's Long March in his book *Red Star over China*.

But even as Snow rushed to get that story into print, for some the final stage of the Long March was still unfolding. Two years after the First Army had set out from Jiangxi and a year after its Long March was declared over, ten First Army women were still on the trail, seven having been, through no choosing of their own, diverted into the Fourth Army. They had reached another critical juncture. Zhang Guotao had agreed to send a major force across the Yellow River to seize control of and establish a base in the Hexi Corridor, thus in theory securing a route to Moscow some two thousand miles to the west, by which aid and armaments could flow in from the Comintern. Mao, who had staked his career on defensive guerrilla warfare, now, as the supreme leader of the Communists, was going on the offensive. On the other side of the river, hostile Muslim clans—expert cavalrymen—stood ready to defend their ground against any Han army. It would prove to be an ill-begotten scheme, leading to a debacle of Xiang River proportions. (Some would later theorize that Mao had dispatched Zhang's troops to their death on purpose to neutralize his rival.)

Just who would be included among the cadres in the invasion force was still being sorted out during the celebrations at Huining. There seems to have been some foresight among the cadres that this might not be a plum assignment. "Sister Kang Keqing advised me not to go," Zhang Huaibi would say later. "My husband was not prepared to go." But Zhang Qinqiu, who was now the director of a branch of the Fourth Army's Political Department, appointed her to a position in the Women's Regiment, and the Women's Regiment was going.

"Before departure, Sister Kang said to me, 'We will meet again after the Liberation of the Country!'" Zhang Huaibi later recalled of this fateful crossroads, "I was sure that the Revolution would triumph, and we would meet again."[8]

Four of the seven First Army women who were now with the Fourth Army—Li Jianhua, Wang Quanyuan, Wu Fulian, and Wu Zhonglian—were chosen to join the force crossing the Yellow River. Wu Zhonglian, who was traveling with her husband, Zeng Risan, would be carrying her infant son with her.[9]

The three others, Kang Keqing, Li Bozhao, and Zhou Yuehua—the lucky ones—would continue on to North Shaanxi, where they would reunite with their First Army sisters. The young girls Wang Xinlan and Ma Yixiang would find their way to the new soviet, too.

Before crossing the Yellow River, the Fourth Army rechristened its Women's Independent Regiment the Women's Vanguard Anti-Japanese Regiment. Wu Fulian and Wang Quanyuan had steadily risen in prominence in the Women's Regiment, under Zhang. Despite Kang Keqing's long desire to lead troops into battle and her influential husband (or perhaps because of him), it was not she but Wang who was appointed commander of the 1,300 women, arranged in three battalions, each with three companies. Her First Army comrade Wu was named commissar.[10]

Waiting in the insular, spectacular Hexi Corridor—a borderland of intertwining deserts, grasslands, and glacier-covered mountains, dotted with vast grottoes and Buddhist and Confucian temples—was the Ma clan of Mandarin-speaking Hui. The Ma had evolved in this distant edge of China as a result of the Silk Road trade beginning in the Tang dynasty. Through intermarriage with Arab traders, these converts to Islam had become physically powerful, adept on horseback, and known for their fearlessness in defending and expanding their sprawling territory—now part of Gansu, Ningxia, Qinghai, and Xinjiang provinces—against Tibetan, Mongolian, and Han challengers. Less than a decade earlier, an American botanist named Joseph Rock had come upon the walls of the great Buddhist monastery at Labrang—founded in 1709 and capable of housing 2,000 monks—adorned with the severed heads of Tibetan warriors. Skeletons were strewn across the plain, recalling the carnage of Genghis Khan centuries earlier. It was the work of the Ma.

In his then definitive 1985 account, *The Long March,* Harrison Salisbury describes the plight of the women who crossed the Yellow River in two sweeping sentences: "The Moslems wiped out the women's regiment. The two thousand women were killed, tortured, raped, sold in the local slave markets." The truth of the matter is that fifty years after they had suffered some of the worst brutality experienced on the Long March, the story of these women remained virtually unknown.[11]

ONCE AGAIN, a river would play a fateful role in determining Chinese history, in dooming an army.

On October 24, the Fourth Army began crossing the Yellow River on rafts covered with sheepskins, entering the loess-covered realm of the warlord brothers Ma Bufang and Ma Buqing, the sons of Ma Qi. An ambitious thirty-one-year-old division commander, Ma Bufang had recently usurped control of Qinghai province from his uncle Ma

The meeting place of the First and Fourth armies at Huining in Gansu province.

Lin while Lin was away on a pilgrimage. Though seven years older than Bufang, the more retiring Buqing served as second in command to his charismatic brother.

Bufang commanded 30,000 Muslim soldiers, most of them mounted. These warriors fought beneath a yellow standard trimmed in white and embroidered with the large character "Ma" that had been awarded to them by the Qing government to signify the family's noble heritage.[12]

As elements of the Fourth Army made it across the river, four Nationalist divisions reached the town of Jingyuan, on the east bank. With superior firepower, they soon shut down the crossing and drove back the Reds who had not yet crossed.[13]

Before the remaining Fourth Army soldiers and the First and Second army contingents could figure out a way to join up with their comrades, the Central Committee abruptly ordered them to cease their efforts to cross the Yellow River and instead to continue on to North Shaanxi. Deemed sufficient to accomplish their mission, the 20,000 troops that had already made it to the opposite bank were renamed the West Route Army. Under Commander Chen Changhao and political commissar Xu Xiangqian, the former leaders of the Right Column, they were told to move west into the Hexi Corridor and to establish their base.

The Women's Regiment soon saw action. At the Silk Road gateway town of Yitiaoshan, local forces tried to prevent them from passing. The women fought them, breached the town walls, and captured thirty camels. As her comrades made off with the beasts, one badly wounded Red soldier inside the earthen walls, preferring death to capture, continued to fire at her assailants until they killed her.

At the town of Tumen, on the southern edge of the Tenggeli Desert, 120 miles into the corridor, a battalion of the Women's Regiment encountered a much more menacing threat. Ma Bufang's notorious Black Horse Team, a battle-hardened unit on powerful black mounts, assaulted them, driving right through their rifle volleys and engaging them in ferocious hand-to-hand fighting. The women swung their single-edged, yard-long swords and larger two-handed swords in a desperate attempt to drive the attackers off. The battle looked hopeless until the First and Second battalions of the Women's Regiment, which had already passed by the town, realized that something was amiss and dashed back to help. Now greatly outnumbered, the Black Horse Team rode away. But they had decimated an entire company, killing or dragging off about 150 women.

IN MID-NOVEMBER, the West Route Army settled briefly in a small Han village near the inaptly named town of Forever Prosperous (Yongchang) on the edge of the desert, another hundred miles deeper into the corridor. Since there would be no further reinforcements, they needed converts to fill out their ranks. The Red Army women did their best to mobilize the peasants, indoctrinating new recruits and training the women to sew uniforms and care for the wounded. From the locals, the women learned to wrap their feet in felt to keep from getting frostbite.

By early December, the West Route Army began losing ground on the battlefront. At the town of Gulang, alongside the road linking the Hexi Corridor to Xinjiang province (home of the Uyghurs), Ma troops pummeled the Ninth Army Group, killing or capturing half its men and seriously wounding its twenty-six-year-old commander.[14]

Early on the morning of December 5, a cavalry guard from the

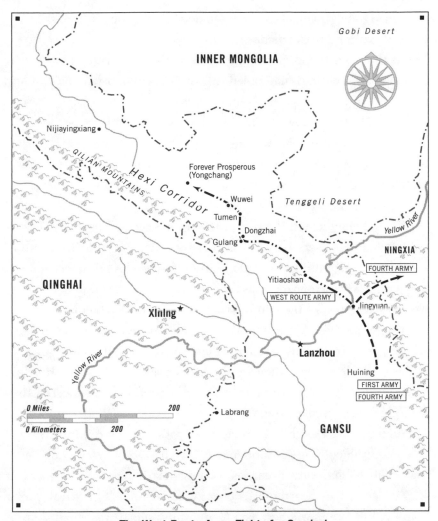

The West Route Army Fights for Survival

surviving members of the Ninth set out to find and escort in the Women's Performing Troupe, which was on its way to meet the Ninth, to boost morale. The troupe had set out under the cover of darkness, carrying costumes and props for their shows. Their organ was strapped to the back of a camel. One of the troupe members, twenty-two-year-old Wang Dingguo, was toting an array of pigments used for the performers' makeup. A nineteen-year-old performer named Chen happened to be pregnant by the wounded commander, whom she had slept with after a performance in Huining.

As the women approached the gates of the walled town of Dong-zhai, where the Ninth had holed up, they heard and felt the distant pounding of horse hooves. "Quick, quick!" the Ninth's commissar shouted. "Into the town! They're coming!" The din grew louder, shaking the ground. Through a cloud of dust, like battle smoke, the Ma cavalry appeared — brutish men wearing skins and heavy fur hats, clutching broadswords, and issuing a cacophony of hoots and war cries as their mighty horses charged.

Wang Dingguo and the rest of the troupe rushed inside the town wall. Several soldiers barred the massive gate, and the Ma cavalry reined in their frothing mounts. Although the stoves in the houses were still warm, Dongzhai was empty. Warned of the approach of the Ma force, the rest of the Ninth Army had abandoned the place.

While the Ma infantry followed the cavalry into position outside, the desperate troupe prepared to defend the town walls. They quickly realized, however, that they would only be able to do so with help. They made a rope by tying puttees together and quietly lowered the leader of their escort over the tree-covered thirty-foot south wall. "Comrades, we must be calm and wait patiently for reinforcements to come," the commissar announced. "We have only a few guns, not many bullets, and some grenades. Use them sparingly."

Suddenly, they heard more hooves approaching. "Our cavalry are coming!" shouted a soldier. The Communist squad was small, but it dashed boldly into the middle of the Ma force, scattering it. Reaching the town, the Red riders, most on captured mounts, hailed those inside and called for them to come out. "Men, go on out," the commissar ordered. "Women, you stay inside."

The Ma cavalry regrouped and, seeing the meager band of defenders, charged. The Red horsemen formed up and faced the oncoming Ma, but they were outmanned. The force emerging from the town was pathetically small. Those still on the walls could see a disaster in the making. The commissar shouted to the newly arrived Red cavalry, "You can't do it! Get away, now!" His voice carried, and the cavalrymen fled to seek reinforcements. Meanwhile, the soldiers who had come from the town retreated back inside.

Now the attackers attempted to run ladders up the thick rammed-earth walls. On a blind corner, they were able to scale the walls and climb onto the two-story tower roof, but Red soldiers picked them off. Ma snipers then climbed some trees to shoot into the tower windows. Inside the tower, the women, lacking any other weapons, hurled sticks and stones down on the assailants.

After what seemed like several hours of fighting, the smoke of battle blocked out the sun. Dozens of Communist soldiers lay dead or dying, and only about ten remained to defend the town. When the survivors heard banging on the outside of the tower, "Pockmarked" Wang (actually a handsome actor who had played a disfigured character) dashed out onto the wall to investigate. Standing on ladders, Ma's men were knocking a hole in the tower. Wang grabbed their ladder and shoved it hard, but the soldiers at the top clutched his arms. From the tower windows, the women watched in horror as he fell to the ground and was stabbed to death by the Ma.

By late afternoon, the defenders were running out of ammunition and grenades. The Ma doused the barred gate with kerosene and ignited it. Flames roared through the dry wood. The fire grew so hot that the dirt walls began to combust. "Surrender now," a Ma officer shouted, "or you'll burn to death!"

As heat and smoke rose through the tower floorboards, pandemonium broke out inside. "Here they come," the commissar declared, tears from the smoke now staining his face. "Don't be afraid," he tried to reassure the women. "We must defend the tower." As the women began to wail in fear, he took a pistol and advanced through the door.

Hearing the retort of the pistol, Wang Dingguo rushed outside. When she rounded the corner, she saw the commissar slumped against the wall. He had shot himself.

IN THE DEAD OF NIGHT—anguished, confused, and scared—Wang Dingguo and twenty other exhausted women, including a thirteen-year-old wisp named He Zhifang, trudged through the dark. The winter of 1936 was so glacial in the corridor beneath the snow-covered Qilian Mountains that Wang later recalled watching birds fall from the sky, frozen in flight. Menstrual blood froze on their thighs, and the jagged crystals abraded their skin as they marched.[15]

Finally, the women saw pricks of light on the far side of a deep valley. Eventually, they made out steps and an ominous gate lit by kerosene lanterns. Fur-clad Ma guards eyed the women as they entered through the gate under the eaves of an ancient temple. "Red Devils, you're lucky to be alive today," a bearded officer sneered. "We could've killed all of you with one cannonball. Because you aren't the real Army, we didn't."

Ma soldiers selected several of the women and took them to the officers, who raped them, including the pregnant Chen, who the day before had fantasized about telling her wounded lover that she was carrying his baby. The rest were locked up in a hall, where they huddled around a fire made from a splintered board.

The next day, they were taken to Ma Buqing's headquarters at Wuwei. The town had a martial flavor, down to its name. When the nomadic Xiongnu were ousted in 121 BC, the Han dynasty rulers changed its name from Liangzhou to Wuwei — "Military Prowess."

The women were locked up in a freezing, sunless hut. At night, wind and wolves howled outside. The women clustered together, trying to stay warm and to protect each other from the Ma, but they were helpless when their captors dragged off their comrades to be raped. Ma Buqing personally kept two of them as concubines.

ON DECEMBER 12, 1936, a shocking event occurred in Xian, the capital of Shaanxi province. Chiang Kaishek had flown to Xian — one of the four great ancient capitals of China, the home of the Qin dynasty terra-cotta army, and the most significant Silk Road terminus — to oversee his offensive against the Communists. The troops of the Young Marshal, the former warlord of Manchuria now secretly allied with the Communists, stormed Chiang's quarters and killed his guards. Dressed in his nightshirt, Chiang fled out a back window, leaving his false teeth behind. He injured his leg jumping over a wall and took refuge in a cave. Finally, he surrendered but remained defiant. The Young Marshal, a warlord without a province or ally, lacked the authority and perhaps the nerve to kill Chiang. Zhou Enlai and Soong Meiling rushed to the scene to negotiate.

Both the Young Marshal and the Comintern—if not Mao and Chiang—saw the Japanese, who were increasingly entrenched and expansive in northeast China, as the nation's greatest threat. The Young Marshal and the Comintern, despite their allegiances, also saw Chiang Kaishek as the man to oppose the invaders. Thus, instead of executing the Nationalist general, they made him commit to a truce and an alliance against the Japanese.[16]

The whole ordeal lasted a little less than two weeks. Zhou Enlai released Chiang on Christmas Day.

In a Nationalist prison cell in Zhaotong, Yunnan, Li Guiying and Han Shiying heard fireworks going off in the streets. But it was not the time of Spring Festival or any other festival when fireworks would be customary. Soon they heard the news that Chiang Kaishek had been freed and that national reconciliation had been reached in the form of the United Front. Han, who hailed from a wealthy family in Sichuan, was consequently soon released, only to be locked away by her father. Li was marched under guard 250 miles to Chongqing, the Nationalist provisional capital during the Second Sino-Japanese War, from 1937 to 1945, and the clearinghouse for prisoners under the United Front.

There she was locked away again, in a one-story house crowded not only with political prisoners but arsonists, thieves, opium traffickers, and even runaway wives. As peace between the Communists and the Nationalists raged, she rotted away in a cell with eight others for nine more months.[17]

chapter 26

The Destruction of
the West Route Army

JANUARY–MARCH 1937

Following the astonishing events at Xian, the Red Army was technically at peace with the Nationalists for the first time in a decade. At the beginning of the new year, the Communists transferred their principal organizations, including the Central Committee and the Military Academy, to Yanan. A frontier city at a crossroads known as the "throat of the five main roads," Yanan lay on the Yan River, a tributary of the Yellow. The tomb of the legendary Yellow Emperor, considered the root ancestor of the Han Chinese, was believed to be in the area. It was a better developed and more commanding place than Baoan. They were able to travel to Yanan on the open roads in broad daylight in high spirits, unthreatened by Nationalist bombers.[1]

The ancient walled town lay on an arid loess-covered plain, surrounded by mountains studded with fortresses. The muddy Yan passed outside the town's walls, like an old moat. Muslims, Christians, Mongols, and successive dynasties had made their mark on the place. A white, screwlike Song dynasty pagoda rose above one hill that was a warren of cave dwellings. On another bulged a mound from the ritual burials of an ancient, primitive matriarchal sect. In the streets, arabesque designs and Moorish arches flourished among Buddhist, Taoist, and animist carved stone monuments.

The place was both a melting pot—of cultures and centuries— and a study in contrasts, never more so than when the Communists arrived, bringing experimental politics and modern ways. The local men — mostly farmers and herdsmen with dark leathery skin — still wore their hair in long queues, but they also wore sunglasses to protect their eyes from the relentless glare and dust of the loess hills. Some had hooked noses and curly hair, indicative of the region's ethnic mélange. The women moved about on severely bound feet and carried on the practice of foot-binding with their daughters.

Yanan stretched from north to south along Phoenix Mountain (Fenghuangshan). On the north end, the town wall extended its protection over rolling hills dotted with hundreds of fine houses and farms. Many, belonging to wealthy landowners, merchants, and officials, had been abandoned before the Red Army arrived, allowing officers to move right in, yet some 3,000 people had stayed behind.

Though water in this dry land was at a premium, upon reaching the place, Kang Keqing and her comrades bathed in steamy tubs — their first thorough soak in what seemed like a lifetime. As Otto Braun put it, to the Long Marchers Yanan "reflected nothing less than peace and normalcy." The Red government would operate here for the next decade.[2]

The Long Marchers had little money to spend at the bustling open-air market proffering meat, vegetables, clothing, and supplies, but the Red Army provided them with several square servings of millet each day, garnished with a smattering of vegetables, and meat once a week.

On the first of January, a thirty-four-year-old American journalist named Agnes Smedley reached Yanan on foot. Although she later said that she was treated like a visiting sovereign, Smedley, who was also a part-time spy for the Soviet Union, lived in a stone house filled with rats. They scurried around her *kang* and in the rafters above her at night. In her spare time, she began an antivermin campaign but conceded that it "aroused only mild interest," as the Reds "regarded rats as an inevitable part of nature."[3]

The standards of hygiene in Yanan were appalling. Even if rats were considered natural, other pests, including flies, mosquitoes, and fleas, carried an assortment of diseases, not the least of which was bubonic plague, which had long ago been eradicated in most parts of the world. For the women of the First Army, now a tight-knit force,

Yanan presented a new opportunity to help a marginalized enclave of Chinese. The women set about improving the sanitation and living conditions of the inhabitants of Yanan.[4]

The Red Army applied strict discipline. At night, lamps were snuffed out by 9:30. At dawn, the cadres assembled for exercise and self-criticism, aimed at improving their performance. Later they joined their various teams, establishing government ministries, schools, and factories, organizing workers, and improving working conditions. The women took on multiple tasks, maintaining their role as purveyors of news and instruction and recruiting workers and soldiers. The men and women who had come to Yanan had begun a profound transformation.

WHILE LIVING CONDITIONS and morale soared in North Shaanxi, the West Route Army struggled for equilibrium in hostile territory. The Women's Regiment had proceeded with the battered Ninth Army Group deeper into the Hexi Corridor. Ma forces corralled and besieged them in the walled town of Hongshayazi. The women helped defend the walls, carried ammunition, dug trenches, and tended to the wounded. For twenty days, they held off the attackers. Finally, they abandoned the town and fled to the northwest. Inflamed by the chance to capture women, the Ma shadowed them, attacking whenever it was to their advantage.[5]

In early January, the West Route Army's various surviving divisions occupied the towns of Linze, Gaotai, and Nijiayingxiang in the corridor. The Central Committee telegraphed them with orders to make a stand and establish a base, but all such plans evaporated on January 12, when more than 10,000 Ma soldiers, commanded by Ma Yuanhai, poured into the area. At Gaotai, on a bend in the Black (Hei) River and its wetlands teeming with waterfowl, 3,000 Red soldiers under Dong Zhentang fortified trenches outside the town walls and tried to rally a panicky local militia to the Communist cause. But Dong himself was shocked when he saw the Ma skirt the Reds' rear guard and descend on Gaotai. They somehow seemed to know that it had the fewest defenders, and as Dong watched, the Ma force grew by the hour. Soon he witnessed an awesome and dispiriting sight: thousands of horses grouped in teams by color — ebony, blond, and roan — paraded outside Gaotai while Ma infantry surrounded the town. Dong ordered his troops entrenched outside the walls to make a preemptive strike. The Ma repulsed the attack and drove the small force back inside.[6]

The fighting that ensued was nearly medieval in its tactics and savagery. For the next week, the Communists shot and heaved sticks, stones, and bricks at the Ma warriors. The women in Dong's forces poured cauldrons of boiling water on the attackers as they repeatedly tried to scale the wall with ladders. Finally, on January 20, the Ma wheeled several cannons to within forty yards of Gaotai's walls. The cannon blasts crumbled the rammed-earth walls, creating giant breaches. Ma forces poured in, climbing over the rubble and hurling themselves at the defenders. The Red soldiers were marooned on the walls, and as the Ma climbed up, the Reds grabbed on to them and leaped, pulling them down to a mutual death.

In the midst of all this, a battalion of five hundred Red cavalry appeared, but their mounts were inferior — many being packhorses untrained for battle — and the Ma decimated them before they reached the town.

Commander Dong fought at the east gate, as Ma soldiers — motivated by Ma Yuanhai's promised reward of 20,000 silver dollars for anyone who delivered Dong alive — shouted to one another, "Take Dong alive!" The Red commander fought to his last bullet, which he saved for himself. Finally, he placed his Mauser to his head and pulled the trigger. Incensed by the loss of their prize, the Ma soldiers lopped off what remained of his head and preserved it in alcohol as a trophy.[7]

WITH GAOTAI TAKEN, the Ma turned their attention to Linze, where the Women's Regiment was stationed, along with much of the West Route Army's support personnel — the porters, ammunition team, medical workers, and provisioners. Linze was small, but it was protected by a sturdy wall and surrounded by open fields that gave defenders a clear field of fire. The Red forces inside the town formed into combat teams, combining men and women. The men guarded the walls, while the women acted in support, delivering food, tending to the wounded, and collecting rocks for ammunition.

Learning from their lesson at Gaotai and now equipped with artillery, the Ma wheeled two cannons into place about thirty yards from the south wall and blasted away, creating a huge rupture. They charged in and climbed up onto the walls, where the Communists hurled sticks, stones, and cannonball fragments at them. As rapacious Ma soldiers shouted, "Every man gets a girl!" Wang Quanyuan's female troops fought back desperately, sometimes hand to hand against the burly men. Scores of women were cut down, while others were dragged screaming into the swarm of Ma invaders and taken prisoner. In the frenzy, four hundred women were lost.

At dusk, the Reds got a break. A small band of Fifth Army Group survivors, fleeing from Gaotai, arrived. Unsure of the strength of this new force, the Ma retreated to avoid the possibility of being surrounded and trapped in a cross fire. In the town, the Red soldiers, including the women, worked that night and for the next three days without rest to repair the breaches in the walls.

During the reprieve, the Ma grew stronger. They now leveled six cannons, in three groups of two, at the town walls and began to hammer away. The Red Army had learned the discouraging news of the fall of Gaotai and the death of Dong Zhentang. At a meeting in a temple, their commander addressed the Women's Regiment and the women in the other units. "We're going to break out tonight," he told them. "You must move quietly. Don't talk, don't smoke, and if you have to cough, cover your mouth." It would be freezing after dark. He instructed the women to eat anything they could find before departing and to wear all the clothes they had. That afternoon, those who could find shards of glass made goggles to prevent their eyes from freezing and to protect them from the desert sandblast. They also bid a final farewell to those too severely wounded to travel. Wu Zhonglian, who had already endured malaria and a pregnancy on the Long March, was

The Destruction of the West Route Army

forced to say farewell to her young son, whom she left with a couple in the town.[8]

That evening, a windy night with no moonlight, decoy guards stood watch on the town's walls while the troops slipped out through the south gate. Some of the wounded rode on mules whose hooves had been wrapped in cotton to keep them quiet. Looking like bubble-eyed insects in their homemade goggles, the women set out around one o'clock in the morning. As they marched, gunshots suddenly broke the silence. In front of them, from both sides of the road, bullets cut through the brittle air. The machine guns' *tatta-tatta-tatta* was soon joined by shrieks and groans. Marchers crumpled to the ground, writhing in pain.[9]

Nine hundred women dashed through the siege lines that night. Many fell, and dozens at the rear turned back. Back in the town, cannon shot rained down on the remaining Communists. Many of the crude cannonballs splintered after being fired, but some hit home, while bullets and shrapnel whopped the earthen walls. As the walls collapsed, the Ma troops stormed the town, shouting "Kill! Kill!"

Several dozen men and women hid in a house but were soon discovered. "Don't fire!" the men yelled. "We have no guns."

"Come out!" the Ma soldiers demanded. "Come out, now! Men first." The Ma swung their sabers inches above the men's heads as they emerged. The Ma had a cheap, bloodless, and nearly foolproof way of executing the men: they stripped them naked, tied them up, and left them outside to freeze to death overnight. The women were shown only slightly more mercy, if it could be called that. "Bitch, don't go anywhere!" a soldier shouted at one of them. "Anyone who tries to run away will be shot!" The Ma separated the women and drove them into the woods, where they made them take off their clothes so that they could search them. Then they marched them into a field and ordered them to squat. Later, they were herded to makeshift prisons.[10]

Ma Bufang intended to start funneling the Communist prisoners, including some of the women, southwest from Gansu to Qinghai, an even remoter, more arid high-altitude province. There, in Xining, his hub and the provincial capital, he planned to put them to work in the textile mills, weapons and match factories, and publishing houses used to supply and fund his operations.

Before she could be dispatched to Xining, Wang Yuchun, a native of Sichuan, was approached by a Han textile dealer. Motivated by either ethnic kinship or the scarcity of eligible brides, he showed her a back door and told her to run to a straw house where two Sichuan women, consorts of Ma officials, lived.

Wang took the gamble and entered a shadowy Han network. From the women's house, a tall man in his twenties led her to a place where she met up with another runaway Communist woman who went by the nickname "Yak Leg." From there, Wang was passed to a third house, where she stayed for three days, until it was raided. Ever alert, she fled before Ma security guards could enter, dashing to yet another house, where two old grannies lived and where the tall man soon joined her. Wang would stay holed up in this house for two years. She was one of the lucky ones.[11]

On the march to Xining, the seriously wounded rode in carts drawn by mules until Ma Bufang telephoned the commander of the unit and told him to kill anyone who could not walk. The next night, an officer called "Tooth" (Yachi), because he had an ill-fitting denture, took those who could go no farther and buried them alive.

When the surviving prisoners arrived in Xining, they were paraded through the streets and then out the south gate. Li Guizhen, a twenty-eight-year-old female deputy company commander, marched with several hundred others to the God of Fire (Huoshen) Temple prison. There Ma guards interrogated them, poking bamboo needles under their fingernails and choking them with ropes until their eyes bulged. Each day, they received only a small grain cake to eat and a bowl of filthy water.

One night, Li was part of a group marched out of the city to the foot of a nearby mountain. Suddenly, the guards produced shovels and clubs and began to beat the women on the head, knocking them unconscious and shoving them into an enormous pit. Li, her foot badly injured in the assault, tumbled into the thirty-foot-deep abyss. As the Ma shoveled dirt over the writhing mound, semiconscious prisoners shouted curses and insults. "In a few years we'll be back as heroes!" they yelled, using an old saying of the condemned and reflecting the general belief in reincarnation. Li, still alive and lucid, inched toward the rim of the pit, where she shook off the falling earth and remained partially exposed while many of her comrades were smothered.

After the Ma guards fell asleep, Li clawed her way out. Fearing most of all that she would attract the attention of the packs of snarling dogs that fed on the corpses, she managed to crawl away. She staggered to a cave and collapsed inside, thus escaping the fate of the 1,800 Communists buried alive in what became known as the "10,000-person pit." Making her way to a farmhouse, Li found mercy and was taken in. After two weeks, her foot healed, and she took to the road again, begging as she went.[12]

IN MID-JANUARY, some 10,000 West Route Army soldiers, including more than 800 women who had escaped from Linze, made their way south to try to join the Red contingent occupying the town of Nijia-yingxiang. Ma cavalry had managed to divide them into several parts. As they traveled, Zhang Qinqiu went into labor. After her unit broke through enemy lines, she gave birth on the edge of the snow- and ice-covered Gobi Desert. A woman assisting her took off her own shirt, wrapped Zhang's baby in it, and handed the infant back to Zhang. Together they continued on, until Zhang, having lost a great deal of blood during the birth, passed out and had to be carried. At dawn, they broke through another Ma line, but Zhang discovered that her baby had died of exposure during the night. The baby was hastily buried. In the chaos no one had bothered to check whether it was a boy or a girl, and Zhang, who would be unable to bear children afterward, never knew.

Reaching Nijiayingxiang, the troops found enough food to last several days. About a mile wide and five miles long, the town was carved up by yellow mud walls like a Chinese checkerboard, each enclosure farmed by up to four families. The sturdiest and tallest walls, those of the wealthy, often had watchtowers, though rich and poor alike shared a few communal wells.

As Ma troops surrounded the town, the Women's Regiment supported the men stationed on the walls. They dug trenches, carried ammunition to guard posts, and stood watch. They cooked and cared for the wounded. Still, each morning, they mustered in the freezing wind for exercises, training with pikes and broadswords should they be called into combat again.

As the day began on January 23, Ma Yuanhai unleashed a cannon barrage and then sent in a wave of local militia ahead of his men to drain the Red Army's dwindling ammunition on his least valued troops. Not fooled by this strategy, the Reds held their fire. Instead, they drew the militia in and cut them down with pikes and swords. Ma Yuanhai then personally led in his regulars in a furious charge.

Though prepared to fight, the women primarily aided the fallen Red male soldiers and retrieved weapons and ammunition from the dead, but they were often in the thick of the action. "As I was rescuing a wounded soldier," the female soldier Zhang Huaibi later recounted, "the enemy cut me on the head with a cavalry sword."[13] Blood streamed down her face, but Zhang still managed to help collect seven rifles and six belts of bullets.

In this instance, the Reds were able to repel the Ma. But with each clash and each day, the West Route Army's prospects faded. The troops' clothes were tattered. Dust and mud coated their faces. Their ammunition continued to dwindle, the number of the wounded increased, and the Ma seemed only more resolute.

On February 9, General Chen Changhao and Commissar Xu Xiangqian telegraphed the Central Committee to beg for the rest of the troops that were originally supposed to have been part of the offensive. For eight days, an eternity in the West Route Army's dire situation, no reply came. Then the Central Committee responded: No reinforcements could be sent. The West Route Army must hold its ground or move farther west, deeper into the Hexi Corridor. They should not move east under any circumstances.[14]

Increasingly desperate, Chen and Xu knew that they could not stay where they were much longer, but they knew that heading west was not a viable option either. They argued about what to do: go east or head south to the mountains. Reluctantly, they decided to ignore the Central Committee and head east.

On February 21, the remainder of the West Route Army set out, but General Chen soon reversed his decision. Despite what he knew was best for his soldiers, he ultimately could not bring himself to defy the Central Committee. The army returned to Nijiayingxiang the following day.

In their brief absence, Ma soldiers had burned numerous houses, buried wells, and taken the remaining grain. They had also hunted down wounded Red soldiers, stripped them, and left them outside to die of exposure. A few had survived by huddling together in a sheep pen. As the Red Army entered the town, they captured a Ma officer hiding in a dry riverbed. They held a public trial and executed him the next day.[15]

At night, the women soldiers went to a frozen stream to fetch chunks of ice to melt for water. As they chipped at the ice, Ma snipers on the opposite bank shot and killed some of them. Later, the Ma stripped the corpses and mutilated their breasts to intimidate the other women.

Ma Yuanhai's forces, determined to destroy the starving Reds once and for all, surrounded Nijiayingxiang. The next day, they attacked the north and south ends of the town simultaneously, driving toward the Red command center in the middle. Bugles blared and ragged red flags flapped in the wind. The Reds mustered every able body, including women, porters, and cooks, and repelled the attackers once more. Yet the cost was high: after a week of fighting virtually around the clock, the West Route Army numbered fewer than 8,000, and many of those were wounded.[16]

Now Chen realized that the end was approaching. Like shipwrecked sailors, they would have to abandon their sinking vessel. They had no choice but to flee into the mountains and hope for the best.

On March 5, the Reds broke out of Nijiayingxiang again. The next day, the tenacious Ma tracked them down and surrounded them. For five days, the Communists fought their way south to the edge of the Qilian Mountains, which rise to 18,200 feet at Gansu's highest peak, Qilianshan. There, beside the Tibetan Buddhist sanctuary Kanlong, the Ma pounded the Reds and everything around them, destroying the Qing dynasty temple. The leaders came to the conclusion that the 3,000 remaining Red troops had only one hope, and a desperate one at that: to abandon all heavy burdens and disperse. They could hole up in bands on the slopes of the Qilian Mountains or try to run to Inner Mongolia.[17]

The next day, Ma Yuanhai's army drove the Reds onto several desolate snow-covered hilltops about fifteen miles from the ruins of Kanlong. The Communists stockpiled rocks, and for three days they hid among the crags and boulders, defending themselves by pitching stones at the Ma troops.

Positioned on one of the hilltops was Zheng Yizai, the supply department chief responsible for the army's coffers. He was determined not to let the treasury fall into Ma hands. On the night of March 13, he and the rest of his band huddled around a dim fire, shivering on the frozen ground and sipping cups of watery millet gruel. As the soldiers dozed fitfully, Zheng formulated a plan and comforted his wife, Zheng Yang, who was eight months pregnant with their second child. She had left their first, a boy, on the trail with strangers. Still, they considered themselves lucky, having been together since their marriage nearly two years earlier. Now they sat, mostly silent, in the fading glow of the coals.

Early the next morning, Zheng Yizai and an escort of a dozen men galloped off with the gold and silver. Before they had gone very far, Ma cavalry intercepted them crossing an exposed hillside. A bullet knocked Zheng from his horse. One of his guards grabbed the horse's reins, and Zheng managed to remount. Handing over the treasury bags, he ordered the guard to make a break for it. Zheng and the rest of his escort held off the Ma long enough for the guard to escape, but in the end the Ma killed or captured everyone else. Zheng, as their leader, was beheaded.

The money reached General Chen and Commissar Xu. The two used the funds to buy local assistance and departed secretly for North Shaanxi with a mobile and well-armed elite guard — and news of the demise of the West Route Army. Chen left behind Zhang Qinqiu, his wife of nine months; she had been captured.

As the Ma continued to gather for the kill, what remained of the West Route Army command called an emergency meeting. The battalion and company leaders assembled the troops and collected most of the remaining rifles and ammunition. They divided the soldiers into three detachments. Those who were still strong were assigned to two of them. The wounded, the young, and all the women went into the third. Rifles and bullets were distributed only to the first two. The leaders told the third to hide in the mountains and look for an opportunity to escape. "We'll meet again in three or five years," separating friends promised one another, avoiding the unlucky number four.

Around a fire built from the stocks of broken rifles, the women divvied up the opium and silver that had been allotted to them. As the fire popped and sputtered, their hope dissipating like the dark whorls of smoke, they attempted to buoy one another's spirits and informally began to divide up into smaller groups. Wu Fulian took charge of the largest, a contingent of about a hundred, while the most unlikely lot fell to Wang Quanyuan: a dozen women, children of some of the Fourth Army women soldiers, including a girl of eight and five boys, and two packhorses. Their only chance lay in crossing back over the Yellow River and making their way to North Shaanxi.

With nothing more than the experience—and luck—of having survived so many treacherous miles to give her courage, Wang and her charges set out into the pitch-black night.

chapter 27

Prisoners of the Ma

APRIL–NOVEMBER 1937

At the end of April, 430 soldiers and officers of the West Route Army, once a mighty force of 30,000, reached the North Shaanxi Soviet. Many historians consider the arrival of this remnant to mark the end of the West Route Army's abject plight.

Around the same time, however, dozens of women and children were still hiding out in the frigid mountains of Gansu. Finally, on the verge of death, they began to descend into the valleys, seeking food and shelter while keeping an ever-vigilant eye out for the Ma patrols searching the paths and roads for them.[1]

The members of Wang Quanyuan's group fumbled their way east by starlight, walking numbly, falling asleep on their feet, and toppling into snowbanks. Their frostbitten hands and feet swelled and turned purple-black. Even their horses started to stagger from exhaustion. Desperate for shelter for the night, the women and children took refuge in an empty cave dwelling. They awoke at dawn with Ma bayonets in their faces.[2]

Another contingent of about thirty women, under a female officer named He Fuxiang, was taken by a Ma cavalry guard, which abused them, forcing them to squat overnight on an ice-covered river. One woman who was too stiff to walk in the morning was cut in half with a single sword stroke. Later, on the road to Xining, when He and two others were sent to fetch ice from a river, they decided to try to escape. They crawled away on the frozen river, then walked on the ice all night. One of He's accomplices died after being mauled by a shepherd dog; the other was raped by a militia patrol and released. Eventually, she and He were captured by a Ma cavalry detachment and taken to the town of Wuwei, where they joined more than a hundred women, including Wang Quanyuan and Wu Fulian, in the hovels of Ma Buqing's walled prison. To humiliate the women, the guards paraded them in rags through the streets to a bathhouse, calling to the locals, "Come out and see what happens to Red Devils!" While the women bathed in frigid water, the guards set a pack of street dogs on them.

Though battered, the women were not broken in spirit. Hoping for more cooperation from them, the Ma changed tactics, becoming solicitous, providing them with clothes, saluting them, and organizing excursions outside the prison walls. As the senior officer, Wang Quanyuan was locked up separately and offered luxuries — hot baths, more nutritious food, better clothes. Wang, aware that it was only an attempt to manipulate her, kept silent and bided her time.[3]

Soon Wu Fulian joined her in the cell. Wu had contracted tuberculosis and, at the age of twenty-five, was dying. Wang begged the Ma for vitamin A to treat her cellmate, but by the time she convinced them, it was too late.

In Xining, Ma Bufang created a brothel prison. Captive Red Army women lived in houses on the grounds of a former primary school. Guarded by armed soldiers, the houses had heated adobe *kangs,* where the helpless women were forced to service Ma officers.[4]

Both Ma Bufang and Ma Buqing made the women form new performing troupes. Each had more than thirty members, who now sang their Communist songs with altered lyrics and danced to entertain the Ma officers. In exchange, they avoided factory work and were allowed to cook their own meals of corn and mutton, a vast improvement over prison gruel. Bufang housed his "New Troupe" in a place of worship, the God of Fortune Temple, and furnished the performers with quilts to sleep on. The New Troupe was supervised by Bufang's chief of staff, who horsewhipped the entire group when the troupe leaders refused his sexual advances.[5]

Ma Bufang himself was said to have kept a harem of twenty women and to have stuffed their vaginas with dates for days at a time. He then ate the dates, believing they brought him virility and longevity.

Despite being subjected to such perversity, the women reaped certain advantages from cooperating with their captors. When the troupe asked to have a Communist cook, "Gou Xiuying," transferred to work for them, Bufang granted the request. The woman using that alias was actually Zhang Qinqiu, who had been captured not long after giving birth to and losing her baby on the edge of the Gobi and assigned to work in a felt factory. Although Zhang was considered a beauty and the Ma had put a price on her head, she went unrecognized as the highest-ranking woman in the Fourth Army. The women of the troupe were able to protect her until the spring, when she escaped with Wu Zhonglian. The two made it out of Ma territory, only to be captured by the Nationalists and imprisoned at Xian. They were transported to Nanjing to be re-educated in a Nationalist prison camp but were rescued by Zhou Enlai at the outset of the United Front period. Both would reach Yanan in August 1937 and join in the Anti-Japanese campaign.[6]

YANAN QUICKLY BECAME A MAGNET for Chinese intellectuals and radical youths. With them, another American, Helen Foster Snow, the wife of Edgar Snow and herself a veteran reporter on China, arrived at the end of April. Snow said, only partly tongue in cheek, that she "found the Red Army engaged in the quaint occupation of defending itself against a dictatorship of thirty women":

> Not only were they veteran revolutionaries in their own right, but as the well-beloved wives and long-time comrades of the highest leaders of the Soviets, they held also the traditional power behind the throne — or the Politburo, to be exact. These Communist women, moreover, multiplied their power by working not individually but collectively, thereby presenting a solid phalanx on every issue, small or great. It was a brave Red warrior indeed who dared oppose the phalanx on any major or minor question.[7]

The Red women had made great progress in enhancing the quality of life of the local women, from improving their hygiene and living conditions to helping them achieve a degree of economic independence. At the same time, however, an influx of attractive young women arriving daily in Yanan to take up the revolutionary banner was creating havoc in the Reds' marriages.[8]

Among the newcomers was a beautiful young Shanghai film actress named Jiang Qing, who went by the stage name Lan Ping (Blue Apple). She was accompanied by her actress friend Li Lilian. Jiang began acting in traditional and modern theater in Yanan and soon started an affair with Mao. Mao divorced He Zizhen, who was sent to Moscow, ostensibly for medical treatment, not to return to China until 1948. In November 1938, he married Jiang (the infamous "Madame Mao"). Similarly, Otto Braun divorced Xiao Yuehua, who had recently borne him a son, and married Li Lilian.

The marriages of Ah Jin, who worked for the Central Committee, and Liu Qunxian, who served as a director of mines and factories, also collapsed when their husbands left them for younger women. They, too, would be dispatched to convalesce in Russia, where they are believed to have died in a German air raid in 1941.[9]

IN JULY, the Chinese and Japanese armies clashed at the Marco Polo Bridge, on a main route into Beijing from the southwest, igniting the Second Sino-Japanese War. As the radio in Yanan blared Chiang Kai-shek's call to arms, Agnes Smedley later recalled, "bugles sounded and gongs clanged and the streets filled with people." The Communists and Nationalists now joined together to form what was called the Second United Front, under the leadership of Chiang (in theory, anyway). The North Shaanxi soviet was officially dissolved, although the Reds retained control of their military forces and of large swaths of northwestern China. To fight the Japanese, the Red Army was restructured into two armies, the New Fourth Army and the larger Eighth Route Army. As they headed east to fight, Smedley stood beneath the town

left: Professors at Yanan Women's University, wearing the latest in fashion in Yanan in 1937. *right:* Women workers in neat aprons.

left: Helen Snow and Kang Keqing, Yanan, 1937. *right:* Ting Ling, China's most famous living woman author, with Helen Foster Snow in Yanan in 1937. *(All four photos are from the Helen Foster Snow Archives, Brigham Young University)*

gate and watched the gray-blue columns of men and women disappear on the horizon. She would soon join them.[10]

FOR MANY OF the West Route Army captives, the truce between the Communists and the Nationalists only made matters worse. The Ma, no longer able to legally imprison Communist soldiers, decided that it was better to kill them than to release them, if only to prevent them from reporting their brutal treatment. By one account, more than 2,500 prisoners were buried alive at various sites, some with their tongues cut out. A Communist official sent to urge the discharge of the prisoners made little progress. The Ma let a few of the old and wounded go but in August decided on a different fate for the Communist women.

At first, Ma Buqing told the more than one hundred women prisoners under his control that they were being released. "You are all heroines," he said, "but you're women. You must obey tradition and be good wives." When his aide-de-camp announced that they had been allocated to Ma officers, the women responded with curses, throat

Uniformed men and women in Yanan. (*Helen Foster Snow Archives, Brigham Young University*)

clearing, and foot stomping. "For anyone who makes trouble," the aide-de-camp bellowed, "I will rip the tendons out of your ankles and let the soldiers rape you before hanging you."

"Go with them now," Wang Quanyuan counseled the women. "But look for a chance to escape. Keep your dignity, and don't ever forget that you are Red Army soldiers."[11]

The soldiers dragged the women off, but He Fuxiang resisted and soon returned to prison severely beaten and with a broken leg. Wang was taken to the house of a regiment commander to whom she had been allocated. When she protested, he beat her with a club and whipped her. Wang succumbed at last and for the next two years was imprisoned as a concubine.

In the summer of 1937, the political prisoners incarcerated in Chongqing went on a hunger strike. For eight days, they created havoc, overturning tables and chairs, throwing their bowls in the latrines and starving themselves. The press reported on the situation, and finally the authorities agreed to release the prisoners in stages. Li Guiying was in the last group to be let go, in September. She left her cell traumatized and penniless, but she had not been forgotten by the Chongqing Communist underground, which scooped her up. She was put to work in a restaurant. She had been there for several days, when a man came to see her.

"You came from Jiangxi," he said. "You had a physical checkup."

"Yes, I did," answered Li.

"Don't you recognize me?" he asked. "I'm the doctor who gave you your exam. You were very healthy."

The doctor, having confirmed Li's identity, gave her bus money to Chengdu, where she was received by Luo Suwen, the head of the Party in Sichuan's capital. They planned to travel together to Yanan but discovered that the roads had been blocked by the Japanese.

Li went back to Chongqing, where Luo's wife helped her make arrangements to travel on alone to Wuhan. She got off the train early in the morning in Wuhan, carrying the address of her destination on a piece of paper rolled up in her pant leg since she could not read or write. She handed the paper to a young boy, who took her to the house. A rickshaw driver answered the door. His master was still asleep. Li waited for him to awake. Finally, he came down and saw Li. "This Little Devil is still alive!" he exclaimed.[12]

It was Dong Biwu. Li Jianzhen and Shorty Wei were also in town. They had a joyful reunion, recounting their separate journeys. Li and Shorty knew all the news of the others too. He Zizhen had gone to the Soviet Union. Wang Quanyuan and Wu Fulian had crossed the Yellow River into Gansu, but then they had disappeared. Xiao Yuehua was divorced from the dour German.

Li Jianzhen and Shorty were on their way back to Jiangxi to be cadres in the New Fourth Army, which was assembling there and preparing to battle the Japanese. They encouraged Li Guiying to join them.

The fight was still in her. She agreed.

Epilogue

The Second Sino-Japanese War, the deadliest Asian war of the twentieth century, merged with World War II and ended when the United States bombed Hiroshima and Nagasaki in 1945. More than 20 million Chinese soldiers and citizens were killed in the war, and nearly 100 million citizens were displaced. (The Japanese lost between 1 and 2 million soldiers.)

Having served on the CCP Central Committee in 1928, Cai Chang, whom Helen Foster Snow deemed "the most important Woman Communist in Revolutionary China," was reelected to it in 1945.[1] She was the only woman member. Deng Yingchao, Zhou Enlai's wife, was named an alternate. Li Jianzhen, the former Women's Department head, became a county Party secretary in Fujian.

At the close of World War II, a full-scale civil war broke out in China. Thanks to the Long March, the Communists already controlled large swaths of rural northern and central China, and for the next four years, as the experienced and well-disciplined Red Army defeated the Nationalists and took over more and more territory, Party membership swelled. After the Nationalists fled the mainland to Taiwan in 1949, the Communists established the People's Republic of China (PRC). Cai Chang was made the first president of the All-China Women's Federation (ACWF), a mass organization that, under her leadership for the next thirty years, became the nation's most influential voice for women's rights. Deng Yingchao was elected a full

At the dais in October 1950, Li Jianzhen encourages locals to participate in the land reform in Xingning County, Guangdong.

member of the Central Committee and placed, along with Cai, on the committee to plan the new republic. Li Jianzhen and Kang Keqing were elected to the executive committee of the ACWF.

The Communists revolutionized the legal standing of women and children in the Marriage Law of 1950, which banned arranged marriage, child betrothal, concubinage, and infanticide. The law mandated freedom of choice of partners, monogamy, and the protection of the interests of women, widows, and children. This was a key step in institutionalizing the change in the role of women in China from passive domestics to public leaders.

Meanwhile, Li Bozhao began her rise as a writer, director, and national leader in the arts. Her celebratory musical *The Long March* debuted in 1951 in Beijing, where she served as director of the People's Theater.

Despite their small numbers, the women who participated in the Long March had a huge symbolic influence on the emerging modern China. Assigned to the New Fourth Army with her husband, Liu Shaoqi, Xie Fei had become a regimental commander and one of the few women to lead troops into battle against the Japanese. She would go on to a career in education, rising to the position of deputy director of the Central People's Security College.

Shorty returned home to Jiangxi in 1937 and joined Communist guerrilla forces fighting in the mountains. She would serve in a variety of Party positions in Jiangxi, rising to deputy director of the rural workers office of the ACWF.[2]

Steered by the Party into a marriage with Zeng Shan, the chairman of the Jiangxi Soviet, the Cannon moved south with him and became the first lady of Jiangxi, a mother, and eventually an authority on children's welfare and a deputy director in the state department in charge of creating nurseries and kindergartens.

Wang Xinlan graduated from college and wireless communications school and went to work for the International (Xinhua) News Agency, the official press agency of the government of the PRC. At the age of fourteen, she married twenty-one-year-old division political commissar Xiao Hua. The two remained together until Xiao's death five decades later.[3]

Ma Yixiang went on to write a novel based on her childhood experiences called *Sunflower,* published in 1962.[4]

From 1951 to 1954, Liu Ying, or Little Sparrow, served as head of Party affairs in Moscow, where her husband, Zhang Wentian,

Wang Xinlan and her husband, Xiao Hua, in 1954. *(Courtesy of Xiao Yun)*

Xie Fei in the 1950s.

served as ambassador. Back in Beijing, she later worked for First Foreign Minister and Premier Zhou Enlai in the Foreign Ministry of the PRC.

In 1953, Wu Zhonglian, who with Wang Quanyuan had led the women across the Yellow River to fight the Ma, retrieved her adult son, "Long March" Wu. He had been raised by the family she had left him with in Linze. Wu Zhonglian held various regional military posts and eventually settled in Hangzhou, the capital of Zhejiang province, with a third husband and her son. She served as president of the Zhejiang People's High Court, responsible for judicial rulings on a provincial level, and on the executive committee of the ACWF.

DURING THE UPHEAVAL of the Cultural Revolution, a violent retrenchment that lasted from 1966 to 1976 and was presided over by the infamous Gang of Four, Mao turned on and devoured the establishment that he had helped create. Many of the women of the Long March were "struggled"—accused of disloyalty to the Party, degraded, and abused, some to the point of death—by the radical youth gangs

Many Long March women attended the First National Women's Congress in Beijing in 1949. Among them in this group are some of the most prominent women in China. Liu "Little Sparrow" Ying stands in the lower left corner, followed by Chen Zongying, who had unbound her own feet as a child and had her seventh baby on the Long March trail; Qi Yunde; Zhou Yuehua; and "Shorty" Wei Xiuying, with cap in hand. In the middle row, Deng "the Cannon" Liujin stands behind Little Sparrow; Wu Zhonglian is sandwiched between two unidentified women; and Li Bozhao and Cai Chang are on the right. In the back, standing tallest, is Wu Chaoxiang. She is next to the former Women's Independent head Zhang Qinqiu, who is partly obscured, and is followed by Kang Keqing; Li Jianzhen; laughing Li Zhen (who often encouraged Ma Yixiang on the Fourth Army's Long March and went on to become the highest-ranking female general in China); and Liao Siguang, who is partly blocked by Li Bozhao.

that had been empowered by the movement. In a perverse way, this showed how far the women had come. From their start as poor peasants, beneath notice, many of the Long Marchers had risen to positions of such power and prominence in China that they had become the focus of Mao's paranoia.

As a member of the Fourth Army, which had opposed Mao during the Long March, and a former longtime prisoner of the Ma and the Nationalists, the Women's Independent Regiment Commander Zhang Qinqiu was a prime target of the mass hysteria. Zhang, who had gone on to serve as a top Party official in the Chinese textile industry, was mercilessly persecuted, until, in 1968 at the age of sixty-four, she leaped to her death from a tall building. Eight years later, her daughter Zhang Maya, the child once left behind in Moscow but later reunited with her mother, was also persecuted to death. She died of a forced overdose of pills.[5]

Xie Fei was persecuted for her brief marriage to Liu Shaoqi, a Politburo member and another chief target of the Cultural Revolution. The two had been separated by the war in 1939 and divorced. Even so, Xie was sent to work on a pig farm, savagely beaten by mobs, and imprisoned for five years.[6]

After her husband, Yang Shangkun, was branded a traitor and imprisoned for twelve years, Li Bozhao was made a janitor of a six-story building, work that left her physically impaired for the rest of her life.

Ordered to stay behind in Yunnan during the Long March, Han Shiying, from an educated Sichuan merchant family, eventually reached Yanan, attended the Marx-Lenin College and the Party University there for a total of six years, and then went on to become the deputy director of the Sichuan People's High Court. During the Cultural Revolution, she was publicly humiliated and beaten. Her own daughter stoned her with gravel. Han was sent to a labor camp and died in 1971 after being refused medical treatment for respiratory ailments.[7]

Exiled to Hubei without proper medical care, Wei Gongzhi died in 1973, but not before being visited and comforted by her fellow Long Marcher Qian Xijun.

Wu Zhonglian, who battled malaria during the Long March, gave birth on the trail, and survived the horrors of the West Route Army, was finally brought down by the Cultural Revolution. Her imprisonment by the Nationalists was used against her as she was persecuted to death.

Mao Zedong died in the fall of 1976. A month later, the Gang of Four (led by Madame Mao), which was blamed for the worst excesses of this dark period, also fell, finally ending the Cultural Revolution. In the decade that followed "the ten-year catastrophe," as it became known, most of the persecuted women were rehabilitated, some posthumously. Despite suffering injustice and brutality—and, for several, the loss of their husbands—the survivors remained devoted to one another and to the Party, bound to it by the great, bitter Long March, when so much had been sacrificed for a shining future.[8]

Li Bozhao wrote another play, titled *Northward,* celebrating the Long March. After 1978, Deng Yingchao became a full member of the Politburo, chosen by the Central Committee, and was considered one of the Eight Elders consulted by Party leaders on matters of great import.

Xiao Yuehua, after her divorce from Otto Braun, remarried and served in a variety of regional posts, rising to deputy director of road maintenance for Hunan. In 1983, after she was diagnosed with cancer, Hu Yaobang—the wounded soldier to whom Xiao had given her mule and blankets at Loushan—now general secretary of the Communist Party (the Party's highest-ranking position after 1982, when the post of chairman was abolished), secured treatment for her in Beijing. When she died, her coffin was draped with the flags of China and the Party.[9]

★

TALKATIVE AND LONG-LIVED, Wang Quanyuan emerged as the principal voice of the Long March women in the post-Mao era.[10] In May 2006, I traveled to Taihe County, Jiangxi, to meet her. With the help of an interpreter, I interviewed her over the course of two days at her home. Wang, age ninety-three and missing all her teeth, lay in bed propped up by pillows, covered with blankets, and wearing a knit hat. She talked steadily for hours on end about her experiences on the Long March.

In March 1939, after Wang had lived as a concubine to a Ma officer for two years, her opportunity to escape finally arrived. She was left at home temporarily with the household staff and some guards, and a sympathetic member of the staff gave her a travel pass to Lanzhou. She fled at night, walking ninety *li* to the Yellow River and reaching the town before daybreak.

At Lanzhou's Eighth Route Army office, Wang told an official her story, but he had bad news for her. She was too late. Soldiers of the West Route Army had been taken back without question in the first year. In the second year, they had been accepted after a period of probation. Now no one else was being accepted. Wang Quanyuan, who only a few years earlier had been a respected Communist officer, was given five silver coins and cast out to fend for herself.[11]

A few days later, a Women's Regiment veteran married to a local peddler found Wang living on the streets. She took her in and soon introduced her to a man named Wan Ling. With no better prospects, Wang married the man and moved with him to Yunnan.

In 1941, when Wan left for India as a mechanic in an anti-Japanese *xuanchuan* force, Wang rolled cigarettes in a tobacco factory in Guizhou, where the unit's family members were housed. The following summer, Wang discovered that her mother was ill and set out walking the hundreds of miles back to her home village in Jiangxi, begging for food as she went. Once there, she stayed.

Wang never saw Wan again. In 1948, she married a peasant farmer. Resuming the agrarian life, she came full circle. But the following year, she emerged again from the anonymity of the countryside when the Red Army returned to Jiangxi. Wang went and found them and led them into her village to "liberate" it. She became the regional director of the Women's Department and her husband the head of the village. The couple would adopt and raise seven orphans. However, her husband was soon ousted from power in a scandal, and they had to return to subsistence farming.[12]

In 1962, Zhu De, then in his third of seventeen years as chairman of the National People's Congress, and Kang Keqing planned to visit Jinggangshan, the revolutionary mountain redoubt and national monument in Jiangxi province. Despite her passion for military life and her lack of children, Kang had become a leader in women's affairs and children's welfare and served as a member of the Central Committee.[13]

When Wang Quanyuan found out about their visit, she wrote to Kang. After receiving the letter, Kang arranged to see Wang. The former comrades embraced warmly. Hearing of Wang's plight, Kang interceded with local officials on her behalf, telling them that she could testify that Wang was a good comrade, asking them to reconsider the accusations against her husband, and sending Wang, who was thin and pale, to a hospital for treatment. The reprieve was short-lived, however. During the Cultural Revolution, Wang was branded a traitor and horribly abused.[14]

In 1981, Shorty contacted Wang, who was then running the village nursing home, to attend a meeting for elder cadres at Nanchang. At the meeting, Wang told of her plight and was eventually allotted the status and monthly stipend of a retired Red Army soldier.

Wang Quanyuan was the last remaining voice of the First Army women who walked the Long March with Mao. She died in 2009.

ACKNOWLEDGMENTS

Many people contributed mightily to the writing of this book. I am most grateful to the Long March veterans who sat for interviews and enriched this account of the journey with their first-hand observations. They include five women, Wang Quanyuan, Xie Fei, Wang Dingguo, Ma Yixiang, and Wang Xinlan, and two men, Chen Chixuan and Wang Daojin.

All studies of the Long March are built on the backs of the American journalists who pioneered the Long March research. Helen Foster Snow and Agnes Smedley courageously made their way across China in 1936–37 to engage the Communists, including many of the First Army women, in conversation. They followed in the footsteps of Snow's husband, Edgar Snow, whose reporting is seminal to the history of the Long March. Karen Gernant incorporated many Chinese sources into her detailed 1980 Ph.D. dissertation, "The Long March," and Harrison Salisbury (*The Long March,* 1985) traveled through China, interviewing several of the First Army women, among many others, and continuing America's deep interest in the Long March. Gernant, professor emerita of Chinese history at Southern Oregon University and a translator of Chinese poetry and novels, kindly reviewed this manuscript, adding greatly to its accuracy.

Helen Praeger Young made sure that the women participants in the Long March were not left out of the narrative and generously encouraged my work. Her book, *Choosing Revolution* (2001), and her interviews with two dozen women Long Marchers were invaluable. The Chinese scholar Guo Chen also significantly carried the torch for the women in his own country in his book *The Biographies of the Heroines* (1986, Chinese language only), while Lily Xiao Hong Lee and Sue Wiles (*Women of the Long March,* 1999) contributed to it from Australia. Guo Chen and Helen Young both graciously took the time to meet with me and to answer questions.

Fei Kanru, director of the Zunyi Long March Museum, was also welcoming and generous with his knowledge and resources. The Singapore-based documentary maker Ng Khee Jin, director of the film *Feet Unbound* (2008), likewise shared his resources and insights with me.

ED JOCELYN, a Beijing-based British expat who runs the Chinese outfitter Red Rock Trek and has logged more Long March miles (including the routes of both the First and Second armies) than any other Westerner, guided my research journey through the Snowy Mountains and the Caodi. Having the chance to feel the trail under my feet, to taste yak, tsampa, and Maotai, and to visit the monasteries and battlefields on the route allowed me to better understand the Long March experience. Having the opportunity to do it with Ed, a scholar and a friend to the locals on the route, was a rare privilege. Working with his fellow guide Yang Xiao, we were able to make several not insignificant discoveries about the Long March, which are recorded in these pages. Ed, who knows more about the Long March trail and events than anyone else who did not participate in it, was able to shed light on some of the nagging questions that have remained unresolved since 1934.

Joining me on my trek with Ed were three friends who also served as photographers and convivial companions, Andy Smith, Lawrence Gray, and Gordon Wallace, cameraman Stephen Lyons, and adventure photographer Philipp Englehorn. In addition to Ed and Yang Xiao, Mike Tan and Jaucua, a Tibetan horseman, took care of camp.

Acknowledgments

Guides Yang Xiao, Mike Tan, and Ed Jocelyn with the author, Dean King, on the Continental Divide in the Caodi of northwestern Sichuan. *(Andy Smith)*

Producer-director Lucas Krost orchestrated the filming of our trek. Ed Jocelyn's partner on his First Army trek and coauthor *(The Long March,* 2006), Andy McEwen, met with me on my first trip to China in 2006 and provided insights from their retracing of the Long March.

My friends and fellow authors James Campbell *(The Ghost Mountain Boys,* 2007), Charles Slack *(Hetty,* 2004), and Logan Ward *(See You in a Hundred Years,* 2007) read the manuscript at various stages and as always contributed their useful suggestions and encouragement, which renewed my efforts to harness and hone the story. Another friend, the Bancroft Prize–winning historian and University of Richmond President Ed Ayers *(In the Presence of Mine Enemies,* 2003), also read the manuscript and pointed out a number of ways to improve it, some of which I hope I accomplished.

BEIJING-BASED JOURNALIST and researcher Zhen Ying (Elly) found and translated numerous works for me, tracked down Long March veterans and conducted interviews, and served as my guide and interpreter in 2006. Zhu Jian (Jenny) found and translated documents. In the United States, Bruce Coffey helped me kick off the massive research that went into writing this book, and Taiwan-born American Sharon Meng researched, tracked down loose ends, provided native wisdom, translated on call, and even tried to teach me to speak some basic Chinese. Also thanks to Elizabeth Robeson, Enhua Zhang, and Hong Wu for their research assistance.

I would like to thank Russell Taylor, supervisor of reference services at the Harold B. Lee Library of Brigham Young University in Provo, Utah, and his staff for their help in reproducing photos from the Helen Foster Snow archives, found in the L. Tom Perry Special Collections.

This book would not have been possible without the diligent work of the crew at Little, Brown. Editor in chief Geoff Shandler not only suggested the subject but read several versions of the manuscript and helped shape the book in many ways. Liese Mayer cheerfully handled both me and the manuscript through all the editorial stages. Peggy Freudenthal oversaw the copyediting process, and Jayne Yaffe Kemp handled production. My agent, Jody Rein, is much more than an agent; she keeps me focused and on track and always provides wisdom.

My wife, Jessica Cobb King, is my inspiration, first- through last-pass reader, tea master, and unvarying reminder that although women and men are different from each other, working together they make each other stronger and better. Our daughters—Hazel, Grace, Willa, and Nora—provide daily inspiration.

NOTES

These notes include discussions of some finer points, digressions, and references to the sources. In an effort not to overwhelm the reader with notes, these references are by no means exhaustive and, in some instances, apply to information from multiple sources in the general vicinity of the note. Much of the information about the Long March women was originally recorded by Helen Foster Snow, Agnes Smedley, Guo Chen, and Helen Praeger Young. Xiao Yun contributed significantly in his account of his mother, Wang Xinlan. Lily Xiao Hong Lee and Sue Wiles did quite a bit to organize and analyze this material. Much of the chronology of the Long March comes from Edgar Snow, Harrison Salisbury, Cai Xiaoqian, Chen Yun, Karen Gernant, and Ed Jocelyn and Andy McEwen. I am indebted to all of these historians and chroniclers as well as to a host of others, whose works can be found in the bibliography. If a Chinese title is listed, then the book has not been translated into English. All original translations of Chinese material for this book were done by Zhen Ying (Elly), Sharon Meng, and Zhu Jian (Jenny). Elly and Sharon did additional reporting, including serving as interpreter or envoy for the interviews listed on page 375. In some quotations, I have updated Wade-Giles spellings of Chinese places to Pinyin spellings so as to maintain consistency throughout the book.

Principal Women of This Account of the Long March

1. The biographies in this section come primarily from the following sources: Lily Xiao Hong Lee and Sue Wiles, *Women of the Long March*, pp. 24, 51, 249–50, 258–59, 266–68, 272; Guo Chen, *The Biographies of the Heroines*, pp. 28–34, 174–78; Helen Praeger Young, *Choosing Revolution*, pp. 138–39, 143, 163, 166; and Harrison Salisbury, *The Long March*, pp. 89–90.

Author's Note

1. Helen Foster Snow, *Inside Red China,* 181. Fifteen *jin* is 16½ pounds.

Chapter 1: A Flowering

1. Major Chinese dynasties referred to in this book are: Shang, c. 1600–c. 1100 BC; Zhou, c. 1100–256 BC; Han, 206 BC–AD 220; Tang, 618–907; Song, 960–1279; Yuan, 1279–1368; Ming, 1368–1644; and Qing, 1644–1912. Bamber Gascoigne, *The Dynasties of China.*

2. If a woman only flowered (gave birth to a girl) but did not bear fruit (a boy), she was considered a "bad tree."

3. In Buddhism, a bodhisattva is a benevolent enlightened being who refrains from entering nirvana in order to save others.

4. A nursing mother sometimes sold her own daughter and acquired an infant *tongyangxi,* who nursed on the departed daughter's milk. One advantage of having a *tongyangxi* over a daughter was that the former was raised to serve. If never treated as a daughter, it was believed, she would not resent doing the hardest chores and eating leftovers.

5. Philip Short, *Mao: A Life,* 93–94.

6. I have chosen to use "Chiang Kaishek," the Cantonese romanization of the Nationalist leader's name and the transliteration best known in the West, as opposed to "Jiang Jieshi," the Mandarin Pinyin spelling of his name. In keeping with recent practice, I have eliminated the hyphen between the two syllables of his and Sun Yatsen's names.

7. Helen Foster Snow, *Red Dust,* pp. 212–13. Snow wrote this book under the pen name Nym Wales.

8. From Elizabeth Childs-Johnson's entry "Fu Zi, the Shang Woman Warrior," *Biographical Dictionary of Chinese Women: Antiquity Through Sui.*

9. Peter Fleming, *One's Company,* 184.

Chapter 2: The Struggle

1. Edgar Snow, *Red Star over China,* 298. The name "Eyuwan" derives from the combined ancient names of the provinces in which it lay: Hubei, Henan, and Anhui.

2. The Hakka, Han Chinese who had long ago migrated from northern to southeastern China, were inclined toward political and military service and produced many significant revolutionary and political leaders, such as Charlie Soong (the father of the three renowned Soong sisters), Deng Xiaoping, and Zhang Guotao.

3. Lee and Wiles, 43–45; Young, 178–80.

4. Jonathan Spence, *The Gate of Heavenly Peace,* 249.

5. The name Zhang Wentian was a poetic allusion meaning "the call of the crane heard around the world." In 1925, while enrolled in university in Moscow, Zhang had adopted the Russian name "Ismanlov." When he returned to China in 1931, he took the name Luo Fu (phonetically similar to "lov"). After 1945, he reverted to Zhang Wentian, and later, persecuted in the Cultural Revolution and exiled to the countryside, he changed his name again. He died in 1976 as Zhang Pu (*pu* means "ordinary man"). I have used Zhang Wentian, the name by which he is most commonly known, throughout this book.

6. Edgar Snow, 122; Guo Chen, 120–23.

7. Xu Guangqiu, *War Wings,* 40–46.

8. Alone in a damaged Chinese Boeing fighter, Robert Short attacked a Japanese squadron of three bombers and three fighters and was shot down near the city of Suzhou. A hero in China, Short was buried at Hongqiao Airport in Shanghai with full military honors. He is considered the first American aviator killed in World War II—nine years before the attack on Pearl Harbor.

9. The Moscow-based Comintern was an organization founded by Lenin to fuel international Communist expansion.

10. Karen Gernant, "The Long March," 10–13.

Chapter 3: The Chosen

1. Lu Liping, "The Starting Point of the Long March," 159.

2. Much of Liu Ying's story told here comes from her brief *Autobiography.*

3. Young, 164–66, 185, 258 n. 19.

4. In the rest of China at the time, an unhappy bride had no recourse. Divorcing was called *chu qi*—"ousting a wife"—and could be done by either her husband or his parents. A woman had few defenses. She could not initiate the procedure and could fight it only under three conditions—the "Three Blocks to Divorce": if she had no place else to go, if her husband's family had become rich after she joined it, or if she had already mourned the death of a parent-in-law. If a man attempted to sell his wife or killed one of her relatives, a *yi jue,* or "divorce due to violation of propriety," might be granted. Otherwise, she was a prisoner of the ancient codes.

5. Wang Quanyuan, interview, May 14, 2006.

6. Young, 186–87; Xi Jun, *The Sad Melody of the Women Soldiers,* chap. 17.

7. In Guo Chen's list of the "thirty women" who joined the First Army's Long March (pp. 3–4), he actually names only twenty-eight, the first ten being those who did not have to undergo a physical: Deng Yingchao, Cai Chang,

Kang Keqing, Li Jianzhen, Little Sparrow, He Zizhen, Liu Qunxian, Jin Weiying, Qian Xijun, and Li Bozhao. These women passed their physicals: Deng Liujin, Wei Xiuying, Li Guiying, Wu Fulian, Wang Quanyuan, Liu Caixiang, Zhou Yuehua, Qiu Yihan, Wu Zhonglian, Han Shiying, Chen Huiqing, Xie Fei, Zeng Yu, Liao Siguang, Xiao Yuehua, Zhong Yuelin, Xie Xiaomei, and Yang Houzhen. "Recently," Guo notes, "comrade Li Jianzhen recalled that Cai Yuanxian also went on the Long March. Cai was a third-year graduate of Ruijin Central Party College and served as a member of the Peng Yang School. She did not survive the Long March, and her story is not well known" (p. 6). Guo does not name Li Jianhua or Wei Gongzhi. Wei had been denounced as a Trotskyite and walked of her own accord.

8. Salisbury, 81. On this subject, Agnes Smedley, who lived and traveled extensively with the Red troops shortly after the Long March, writes in *China Fights Back:*

> In this army are masses of men who entered its ranks when they were adolescents. They are virgins. They have never known sex experience. Once the American newspaperman Edgar Snow called this army a "virgin army." That is not exactly true. But it seems to me true that men who have never known sex experience and who live the rugged, active life of this army, do not find the need for sex expression as do other men. . . . I can tell you honestly that any woman could live in that army without the least fear of molestation. (pp. 248–49)

In *China Correspondent,* she notes that the Red Army "tried to absorb the energies of the soldiers in military training and various cultural activities which continued from reveille to taps" and that it was "so poor that it lacked even money for the essentials of existence; it had never heard of *French letters* [condoms]." She also points out that as "all Chinese women are married at an early age; a sex life for soldiers would automatically have meant the violation of married women . . . a criminal offence in the Army" (p. 130). Prostitution was also illegal.

Otto Braun was also impressed by the discipline of the troops. "During the year of my stay in the Soviet Area, I heard of only one gross violation of discipline," he writes in his memoir, *A Comintern Agent in China.* "Two scouts disguised as KMT [Nationalist] soldiers raped a woman behind the enemy's lines. When they returned from their mission, they were brought before a drumhead court-martial and executed. Let me repeat that this was a drastically exceptional case" (p. 38).

9. Wang Quanyuan, interview, May 14, 2006.

Chapter 4: Leaving Jiangxi

1. Originally named Li Weihan, Luo Mai was called Lo Man by Edgar Snow, Helen Foster Snow, and Harrison Salisbury.

   Dates used throughout the book should be regarded as best estimates. Frequently, different chroniclers give varying dates for the same events. Some of the confusion may be due to the use of the lunar calendar, but it is mostly due to the fact that many of the stories about the Long March were transmitted orally and written down years later. In this case, Xie Xiaomei says that they set out on October 14 (Young, p. 189).

2. Each army group also had medical and convalescent companies for its soldiers, but division-level officers and above and other cadres went to the cadre convalescent company, where the care and resources were better.

3. Mao was joined in the temple, which served both as a residence and an office, by Zhang Wentian.

4. Guo Chen, 4; Young, 189–90.

5. Dong Biwu served as a member of the Chinese Communist Party Politburo from 1945 to 1975. He also served as acting vice president of the People's Republic of China (PRC) jointly with Soong Chingling from 1959 to 1975 and as acting president of the PRC from 1968 to 1975 (jointly with Soong until 1972).

6. Salisbury, 13–14.

7. Some 14,000 soldiers of the Military Commission and central column departed from various points around Ruijin and Meikeng toward Yudu. But it is Meikeng that is generally considered the starting place of the exodus.

8. Lee and Wiles, 23.

9. Both sides were ruthless to leaders and used gory executions and displays of corpses as warnings. To give an example on the other side, in 1930 the Communists captured a Nationalist commander in Jiangxi. Chiang Kaishek offered an exchange of prisoners and a large supply of medicine, ammunition, and money for him. Instead, the Communists held a public trial of the commander, agitated the crowd, and executed him on the spot. They floated his head down the Gan River on a raft to the Nationalists in Nanchang.

10. Kang Keqing, interview by Harrison Salisbury, 1.

11. Helen Foster Snow, *Red Dust*, 214; Kang Keqing, *Memoir*, 121–42. Unless otherwise noted, all references to Kang Keqing come from her memoir.

12. Fleming, 246; Smedley, *China Fights Back*, 245–48. Smedley met Carlson at the headquarters of the Eighth Route Army in December 1937. Carlson was living with and observing the Eighth Route Army, which was largely derived from the Red Army, whose best soldiers were veterans of the Long March.

13. Fleming, 189; Salisbury, 14, 33; Dick Wilson, *The Long March 1935*, 68.

The Mexican dollar, with its snake-grasping eagle, began circulating in China as early as 1823. By 1910, the Mexican eagle dollar, as it was called, represented a third of all foreign currency and was preferred in the southern and central provinces. In 1928, the Communists on Jinggangshan started minting a "Jinggangshan workers silver dollar," using confiscated silver and the Mexican eagle dollar template and adding the character for "worker." Production of these silver dollars ceased when the Reds lost Jinggangshan in 1929. In 1932, they captured a set of coin templates and manufacturing machines in Fujian. The equipment went to Ruijin, where they resumed minting coins, including some with portraits of Sun Yatsen and Yuan Shikai for use in Nationalist areas and others with their portraits replaced by a hammer and sickle.

Oddly, Otto Braun would argue forcefully that the troop movement was not a movement of the state. "It was certainly not a 'nation emigrating' as Edgar Snow purported in *Red Star over China*," Braun writes in *A Comintern Agent in China* (p. 83). "Nor was it 'precipitate, panic-stricken flight,'" as Mao Tse-tung later alleged. It was a well thought out operation, painstakingly prepared over time."

14. Lee and Wiles, 186; Kang Keqing, 121–42.
15. These troop-strength estimates are taken from Braun (p. 81). Braun put the overall numbers at between 75,000 and 81,000 men. The standard count for those departing the Jiangxi Soviet on the Long March is 86,000 men and women.
16. Field Force report of October 8, 1934.
17. Lee and Wiles, 74; Young, 183. Two months before the thirty women and the rest of the First Army set out, the Red Sixth Army Group, 9,000 strong, had marched from its base on the Jiangxi-Guangdong border to seek out a relocation site for a new Central Soviet zone. Contrary to instructions, they joined up with the Second Army Group, 4,000 men under General He Long, in northwestern Hunan. The two army groups would connect on October 22 and eventually merge as the Second Army. Thus, the women were basically following in the Sixth Army Group's footsteps.

Chapter 5: No Tears
1. The term "Long March" was not used until about halfway into the journey, and it did not acquire broader use until even later.
2. Some parts of Ma Yixiang's story come from telephone interviews with Ma, who was eighty-three years old at the time, conducted for me by Elly Zhen on December 4 and 27, 2006. Much of Ma's story was first captured by Helen Praeger Young, who interviewed Ma for *Choosing Revolution*

(pp. 82–118). Young also generously provided me with a transcript of her interview with Ma.

3. Ma Yixiang would later write an autobiographical novel called *Sunflower*. The main character, a child named Wu Xiaolan ("Little Orchid" Wu), is beaten with a tea tree branch and a carrying pole. She calls her grandmother-in-law, who does most of the beating, "Grandmother with an Oily Mouth" and her equally mean grandfather-in-law "Grandfather with the Rotten Eye."

Chapter 6: Into Hunan and Guangdong

1. "Kang Keqing, interviews with Harrison Salisbury, October 24 and November 3, 1984, p. 4.
2. Guo Chen, 49; Kang Keqing, 121–42.
3. Guo Chen, 48–50.
4. Jonathan Fenby, *Generalissimo Chiang Kai-shek and the China He Lost*, 262.
5. Ibid., 258–63.
6. Cai Xiaoqian, *The Long March Records of a Taiwanese*, 184.
7. Li Guiying told this story to Helen Praeger Young, p. 140.
8. Salisbury, 36.
9. Mao had a wife prior to Yang Kaihui in a marriage arranged by his father. Mao never recognized that marriage.
10. Gernant, 58–61; Lee and Wiles, 53–54.
11. Ed Jocelyn and Andrew McEwen, *The Long March*, 61–62.
12. Cai Xiaoqian, 243; Lee and Wiles, 55, 89. The Reds used the doors to sleep on.
13. Kang Keqing, 121–42; Lee and Wiles, 272.
14. The *New York Times* (December 23, 1934, 11, col. 3) reported Chiang Kai-shek's description of conditions in the former Jiangxi Soviet. Chiang claimed that 6 million people had been rendered homeless and driven into exile by the Communists and that 1 million had been killed. "Sections of the people had developed a hardened conscience and insensibility to shame," he said.
15. Salisbury, 209–10; Cai Xiaoqian, 193; Smedley, *Battle Hymn of China,* 259; Guo Chen, 19. For the next three years, Chen Yi, a protégé of Zhu De and now military commander in the Jiangxi Soviet region, and crafty and austere Xiang Ying, a former Political Department head, led a band of guerrillas, whom the Nationalists hunted like animals, sometimes torching forests to flush them out of their hiding places. Finally, Chen, who was portly and known as "the Fat General," retreated south with several hundred Red soldiers to join up with Communist partisans on the Jiangxi-Guangdong border.

16. Gernant, 66–67; Salisbury, 91; Jocelyn and McEwen, 55; Cai Xiaoqian, 195–96; Chen Yun, "Chen Yun's Report on 15th October 1935." In 1957, the Yuehan Railroad was joined to the Jinghan (Beijing to Hankou) Railroad to form the Jingguang (Beijing to Guangzhou) Railroad, still in use today.

Chapter 7: Xiang River Debacle

1. Chronology and events in this section come from Gernant, pp. 67–68; Cai Xiaoqian, pp. 198–201; and Kang Keqing, pp. 121–42.
2. Young, 191.
3. Wang Quanyuan, interview, May 15, 2006.
4. Gernant, 70–81.
5. Salisbury, 98–99; Guo Chen, 123–24. Liu Bocheng's nickname is often misleadingly translated as "the One-Eyed Dragon," but that is actually Chinese slang for a one-eyed person and not a reflection of his demeanor or fighting prowess. It is more accurate to call him "the One-Eyed General."
6. Lee and Wiles, 51; Wang Quanyuan, interview, May 15, 2006.
7. Cai Xiaoqian, 186.
8. *Complete History of the Long March of the Chinese Workers and Peasants Red Army — Campaign Record of the Red 25th Army*, 34–35.
9. In *China's Red Army Marches* (p. 5), Agnes Smedley puts the relative value of the Chinese dollar at about a third or a fourth of the American dollar. Calculations for current comparative values vary greatly. The 100,000 silver coins, or Chinese dollars, would have been worth at least a half million U.S. dollars in today's money.
10. Edgar Snow, 298–302; Selden, *The Yenan Way*, 67; Salisbury, 52; Xi Jun, chap. 1; Liu Jinghuai, "Zhou Dongping: The Footprints of a Red Army Nurse."
11. This dialogue and the ensuing argument are taken from Liu Jinghuai, pp. 44–59, and Xi Jun, chap. 1, which both tell the same story.

Chapter 8: Thundergod Cliff

1. Lee and Wiles, 51, 87. Cai Xiaoqian, 225.
2. This situation still exists in some places, as the author Xinran points out in her 2003 book, *The Good Women of China*. When she visited a village in western China where the children seemed to be mostly boys, she found that one family's eight daughters shared a single pair of pants. Each girl went outside only when it was her turn to wear the pants and then went home and excitedly reported to her sisters what she had experienced that day.

3. Kang Keqing, 121–42.

4. Ibid., 129.

5. Guo Chen, 95–96.

6. Kang Keqing, 121–42; Lee and Wiles, 29.

7. Wang Quanyuan, interview, May 14, 2006.

8. Cai Xiaqian, part 2, chap. 3. Much of the account of crossing Laoshanjie is based on Kang Keqing (pp. 121–42) and on Cai Xiaoqian's memoir, which first appeared as twenty-four articles in *Communism Study* magazine from 1968 to 1970. Cai draws heavily on a May 1955 article titled "Laoshanjie," credited to Lu Dingyi, who at the time was director of propaganda. Cai admits to using Communist records to augment his faded memories, but in this case he seems to have reproduced Lu's version, which is now included in Chinese school texts, almost verbatim, a practice too common in Chinese historical accounts.

   Salisbury (p. 105) calls the mountain Laoshan and translates it as "Old" Mountain.

9. Li Bozhao, interview by Harrison Salisbury, October 31, 1984, 5.

10. Guo Chen, 98.

11. In a mountainous Miao area, Mao was said to have given a chief more than a thousand guns taken from the Nationalists. Although this seems improbable since the Reds were always short of weapons themselves, guns were heavy and only as good as their working condition and the availability of ammunition. Useless castoffs could well have been freely given as peace offerings.

12. Cai Xiaoqian, chap. 4.

13. Young, 200.

14. The *New York Times* (December 23, 1934, 11, col. 3, and December 28, 1934, 11, col. 2) reported that Western missionaries in northern Hunan had been advised to leave the area and were in a panic. Two missionary women from Iowa and Pennsylvania fled on the Yuan River in a small junk. About twenty miles south of Changde, a treaty port, a group of Communists commandeered their junk. The two women crouched belowdecks in a cramped hold for six days while the Communists used the craft as a pontoon in a bridge across the river. Finally, the junk was released, and the women made it to safety.

15. Guo Chen, 114–21; Salisbury, 109–13.

16. Ma Hongwei and Zhang Tiezhi, eds., *Women Soldiers of the Long March*, 197; Liu Jinghuai.

17. The dialogue is based on Xi Jun, chap. 3. Indeed, Xu's five-day rest was a nap compared to the last time he had been seriously injured. Then, he had

been galloping along a road when his horse's hoof struck a soldier. When Xu turned in the saddle to see if the soldier was all right, the horse shied and ran Xu into a tree, according to Edgar Snow (p. 296). Xu was knocked out and lay unconscious for two weeks.

18. Xi Jun, chaps. 3, 4; Liu Jinghuai, 44–59.

Chapter 9: Into Guizhou

1. Young, 196.
2. After repeatedly failing to stymie the opium trade by diplomacy and edict, the Chinese government had conspired to destroy a supply of opium in a British storehouse near Guangzhou (then Canton), resulting in the First Opium War in 1839. After British ships bombarded and seized Guangzhou and took other measures, a peace treaty concluded in 1842 (and supplemented in 1843) granted Britain the island of Hong Kong and established "treaty ports" in Shanghai, Guangzhou, and several other coastal cities, where Western nations could conduct free trade, including the importation of opium. In 1860, China lost the Second Opium War and was forced to open five more treaty ports. Unable to rid itself of the opium trade, China began its own massive cultivation of poppies. In many provinces, the most fertile soil was given over to the lucrative crop, squeezing out grain and other food sources and increasing the nation's vulnerability to famine. In 1907, as an epidemic of opium use gradually brought the country to its knees, China finally struck a deal with the British that reduced both the domestic crop and the importation of opium. Still, opium was far from eradicated in China, especially in the poor, remote provinces, where corrupt officials thrived on the trade.
3. Wang Quanyuan, interview, May 15, 2006; Jocelyn and McEwen, 79.
4. Young, 194–96; Lee and Wiles, 262; Jean Fritz, *China's Long March,* 25; Jocelyn and McEwen, 87.
5. Guo Chen, 22, 105; Wang Quanyuan interview, May 15, 2006; Gernant, 105; Cai Xiaoqian, part 2, chap. 4.
6. Kang Keqing, 121–42; Lee and Wiles, 28, 86, 278 n. 24; Guo Chen, 114.
7. Guo Chen, 48–50; Cai Xiaoqian, part 2, chap. 4; Gernant, 123.
8. Liao Siguang's story is adapted from a written account of her remembrances as translated by Young (pp. 152 and 195–96). "What were we to do?" she wrote. "At that time, our first aim was to keep alive in order to accomplish the revolution."
9. Liu Ying, interview by Harrison Salisbury, 5.

10. "Wei Xiuying," chap. 2, *My Long March;* Lee and Wiles, 251.
11. Fritz, 78; Jocelyn and McEwen, 87.
12. Young, 203–4, 215; Guo Chen, interview, May 10, 2006.
13. "Wei Xiuying," chap. 3, *My Long March.*
14. Before the Yuan dynasty (1279–1368), toilet paper was not commonly used. The upper classes preferred cloth. During the Han dynasty (206 BC–AD 220), the emperor used delicate damask dyed in yellow, while court officials used hemp cloth. Peasants wiped themselves with pieces of wood or bamboo, leaves, or even rocks. Early toilet paper was made of bamboo pulp, tree bark, or straw and was very coarse.
15. Li Guiying said that when they crossed rivers, menstrual blood sometimes flowed down their legs. In one famous if unlikely Long March anecdote, the convalescent company reached a river. As they were carrying the stretchers into waist-deep water, a young soldier saw blood staining the Cannon's pants and making the water red. "Deng Liujin," he shouted with alarm, "you're wounded!" She looked down to see what was the matter and then responded shyly, "I'm not hurt. This is the business of us female comrades."

    This story appears in a variety of forms in Long March lore. Guo Chen (p. 9) and the *People's Liberation Army Daily* (pladaily.com.cn) tell the story about the Cannon. Li Guiying told Young (p. 203) that it happened to her and that she found herself in the awkward position of having to explain it to the young soldier, who did not understand.
16. Smedley, *China Fights Back,* 21–22; Young, 193.
17. Wang Quanyuan, interview, May 15, 2006; Gernant, 123–24.
18. Young, 196; Guo Chen, 44.
19. Guo Chen, 128–29.
20. Ibid., 129–36. While Liu's miscarriage was probably due to poor nutrition and stress, she would have blamed it on the bite due to the popular belief that centipedes are especially venomous. Centipedes have poisonous fangs and in China can grow to more than six inches long. They are used in traditional Chinese medicine to treat lockjaw, seizures, convulsions, carbuncles, and snakebites. During the Duanwu Festival, in the fifth lunar month, when the Five Poisonous Creatures are supposedly most active, the Chinese drink special medicinal wine and wear scented sachets around their necks for protection.
21. Gernant, 118–20, 126–29; Cai Xiaoqian, part 2, chap. 4.
22. Cai Xiaoqian, part 2, chap. 4.
23. Liu Lili, *They,* 118–19; Helen Foster Snow, *Inside Red China,* 178.

Chapter 10: Love, Power, and Revolution in Zunyi

1. Kang Keqing, 121–42; Liu Lili, 19.
2. Cai Xiaoqian, part 2, chap. 6; Gernant, 150; Braun, 94; Chen Yun, part 3.
3. Guo Chen, 136; Young, 150, 198–99; Fritz, 44; He Diyu, "Mud Buddha"; Cai Xiaoqian, part 2, chap. 6.
4. Cai Xiaoqian says the meeting occurred on the third day after the Red Army's arrival, which would be January 12. He Diyu (pp. 148–52) says it took place on the sixth day. Kang Keqing (pp. 121–42) agrees with Cai, whose timing I have used. Harrison Salisbury does not mention the event, only noting the formation of the Zunyi revolutionary committee before moving on to a detailed account of the Zunyi Conference (pp. 119–26).
5. Fritz, 44.
6. Converting this goodwill into results was not easy. While the local students were eager to sign up, the Zunyi peasants were culturally myopic and wary of change. Kang Keqing (pp. 121–42) noticed how much more difficult recruiting was here than it had been in Wengan, just half a day's journey away. There both the Han and the Miao, whom they had feted at New Year's, had simply followed them out of town. By comparison, after recruiting eight shoeless young men in tattered clothes in the Zunyi market, Kang and Pan Kaiwen invited them to lunch back at their headquarters. As the men ate, they talked little, and afterward several of them excused themselves to go to the restroom and never returned.

   Kang realized that if they wanted to retain more recruits, they had to do more. From then on, she and Pan spoke with a recruit's family, helping the family resolve problems caused by a son or husband's departure — such as finding a helper for the farm — and emphasizing the benefits of army pay, perks, and status.
7. Wang Daojin, interview, May 19, 2006.
8. He Diyu, 148–50; Fritz, 44; Young, 198; Lee and Wiles, 52–53.
9. Cai Xiaoqian, 244; Young, 198; Lee and Wiles, 52–57, 90; Guo Chen, chap. 4; Smedley, *China Fights Back,* 91–92; Salisbury, 370 n. 14. A story that made the rounds in this area of heavy opium use was that one confiscated horse would not move until someone held opium under its nostrils for it to sniff. Although opium use was strictly forbidden among the soldiers, Red Army recruiters were not above luring new recruits with confiscated opium. Those who enlisted for the immediate gratification of the drug promptly received a dose of tough love from the army.
10. Liu Tong, ed., *Personal Experiences of the Long March,* 220; Lee and Wiles, 61, 69, 281 n. 3; Wang Quanyuan interview, May 14, 2006.
11. Wang Quanyuan, interview, May 14, 2006. This admission seems to be

contradicted by the fact that they soon spent nearly a month together apart from the main body of the army while helping to politically organize the Tibetans, though privacy would have been at a minimum. Lee and Wiles, 52–54, 280 n. 11; Young, 163, 200; Guo Chen, 76.

12. As told by Wei Xiuying to Young, 199; also from Lee and Wiles, 47–48, 266.

13. Kang Keqing, 142; Young, 196–97; Lee and Wiles, 32–33, 90; Fritz, 40; Sun Shuyun, *The Long March,* 122; Chen Yun, part 3.

Chapter 11: Little Devils

1. The dialogue and events in this section come primarily from Young, pp. 88–92.

2. Lin Yutang, *With Love and Irony,* 85.

3. Ma Yixiang, interview, December 27, 2006.

4. Xi Jun, chap. 4. Many events in this chapter and other sections on the Twenty-fifth Army are taken from Liu Jinghuai and Xi Jun.

5. Xue Shaohui (1855–1911), the editor in chief of the journal *Chinese Girls' Progress,* in Dorothy Ko, *Cinderella's Sisters,* 40.

6. Liu Jinghuai, 44–59.

7. Zhang Guotao, *The Rise of the Chinese Communist Party, 1928–1938,* vol. 2, 464.

Chapter 12: A New Year

1. Guan Qianxin, "Some Seniors in the 1st Route Army"; Cai Xiaoqian, part 2, chap. 6; Lee and Wiles, 90; Gernant, 188; Young, 201.

2. This scene and dialogue come from "Interview of Wei Xiuying About Jin Weiying" in *My Long March.*

3. Guo Chen, chap. 3; Gernant, 191; Sun Shuyun, 124; Lee and Wiles, 54, 260.

4. Information in this paragraph is from Gernant, pp. 193–95, 532 n. 26; Young, pp. 201–202; and Short, p. 322.

5. No one knows exactly where He Zizhen gave birth. Qian Xijun told Young that it was in a "remote place in Guizhou" (p. 202). Jocelyn and McEwen (pp. 141–52) argue convincingly that it was in Huafangzi (Flower House), a Qing dynasty wooden house with flowers engraved on its window panels, in the village of Shuitianzhai near Zhaxi. They met a woman in a mountain-top Miao village who they believed might have been Mao and He Zizhen's lost daughter. However, there is no way to prove this without DNA testing, which known Mao descendants refuse to undergo. (The woman, Xiong Huazhi, died in 2007.)

6. This account from Qian Xijun, Mao's sister-in-law, comes from Young (p. 202). Guo Chen (p. 84) notes that there has been some debate over whether He Zizhen gave birth to a boy or a girl on the Long March. According to Deng Yingchao, He Zizhen had a girl.

7. Liu Ying, interview by Harrison Salisbury, 5.

8. Historians quibble over the exact dates the Reds were in Zhaxi. Salisbury (p. 153) places their arrival on February 5. Cai Xiaoqian (chap. 6) says that it was February 6 and that they rested there for only a day, but later he says that they arrived on February 11. Gernant says that they reached Zhaxi between February 6 and 11 and that their arrival "coincided with lunar New Year" (pp. 196–97), though that actually fell on February 4. Jocelyn and McEwen (p. 141) suggest February 8, the date I have used because of their meticulous on-site research and corroborating chronology in other towns. Liu Ying (chap. 5) says that she attended a meeting in Zhaxi on February 10, which fits with this timing.

    Many factors contribute to the discrepancies and confusion of dates during the Long March. The many army groups within the First Army were moving together but separately, meaning that various groups might pass through the same town on different days. Most of the Long March histories have been related orally and recorded long after the fact, adding to the convolution and generalization of dates. The translation from lunar dates to Gregorian dates provides more opportunity for error.

9. Liu Ying, chap. 5; Jocelyn and McEwen, 153. Dissemination of the news of the change in leadership seems to have been somewhat haphazard. Three women cadres reported hearing about the change of leadership at three different meetings spanning more than a month.

10. Li Jianzhen describes these events in her memoir, *Reminiscences*, 84–5.

11. The Mao quote comes from Li Guiying, in Young (p. 201). According to Jocelyn and McEwen (p. 143), the X-ray machine now resides in the Zhaxi museum.

12. Cai Xiaoqian, part 2, chap. 6; Kang Keqing, 144–45.

13. Kang Keqing, 121–42.

14. Lee and Wiles, 57; Salisbury, 156–57, 370 n. 14; Guo Chen, 70. In 1980, Hu Yaobang became general secretary of the Chinese Communist Party. He was a reformer admired by students, and the lack of official reverence at his death in 1987 triggered the Tiananmen Square protests two years later.

15. Although Cai Xiaoqian (chap. 6) implies that the convalescent company reentered Zunyi on February 27, the same evening as the Third Army Group, the *Party History Document Newsletter of the Zunyi Government* says that the convalescent company did so on March 2. The newsletter also says that

when Dong Biwu arrived, he was called into a meeting to hear the results of the Zunyi Conference. Upon finding out that Mao had been elevated, Dong, it says, bought alcohol to drink in celebration. Other sources indicate that this news had already been widely disseminated via a mass meeting in Zunyi in January and other meetings. According to the newsletter, on March 4 Dong assembled the convalescent company beside a small temple and told them of the leadership change.

16. Otto Braun, 111; Fritz, 54; Salisbury, 156–57.

17. Guo Chen (p. 77) says that Zhang Wentian, who was thirty-four at the time, proposed later: "After the troops passed the Golden Sands River, Zhang proposed to Liu. Liu refused even though the leadership did not have to obey the 'Three Prohibitions' concerning dating and marriage. She simply did not want to become pregnant and make the journey even more difficult." I have relied on the timing given by Liu Ying (p. 67).

18. Liu Ying, 67.

19. Liu Lili, 136–39.

20. In 1990, a statue of the Red Army Pusa (*pusa* is Chinese for "bodhisattva"), a nurse giving medicine to an infant cradled in her arm, was erected on a hill in Zunyi. The nurse, citizens of Zunyi will tell you today, remained behind after the Red Army departed, to care for patients afflicted with dysentery. She was captured by the Nationalists and executed. When local partisans reverently buried her, the Nationalists exhumed her, only to have the locals retrieve her and this time bury her in a secret place. None of the accounts of the First Army women mentions nursing local citizens in Zunyi. In reality, the nurse was not a woman but the Third Army Group soldier Long Siquan, who was historically transformed into a woman because Buddhism ascribes the role of compassion to females. Since it is more fitting for a *pusa* to be a woman than a man, history was changed to fit the belief. So many people rub the Red Army Pusa each day for protection and good luck that her feet have been worn out and replaced several times.

Chapter 13: Where the Han Are Unwelcome

1. The March 2, 1935, London *Times* (p. 11) noted that the Communists had reached a crossroads and could "turn south into Yunnan, where large revenues are derived from opium, or cross Szechwan [Sichuan], and also make for Kansu [Gansu]." The *Times* reported that the choice would be determined by "the pressure the Government forces now coming up the Yangtze are able to apply at so difficult a point." It also mentioned that because of activity in the northern province of Shaanxi, "missionaries . . . are withdrawing to places of safety."

2. Now considered a national treasure, maotai is officially distilled by a state-run company under the name Moutai. It comes in a variety of forms, including the traditional 106 proof. According to one source (chinaculture.org), Moutai undergoes eight fermentations and nine distillations over the course of a year, is "beneficial to the health," and "won't [make you] feel dizzy, even if you drink too much." According to another (the Mandarin .blogspot.com), which calls the taste of Moutai "reminiscent of turpentine or cat urine," the price of a bout of drinking it is the "dreaded Moutai sweats." I can attest to the fact that its peculiar herbal flavor makes the mouth pucker, but it also has a salubrious, warming effect at night on the Long March trail.

3. Cai Xiaoqian, part 2, chap. 6.

4. *New York Times,* March 3, 1935, 18, col. 5.

5. Fenby, 265; Chen Yun, part 4; Lee and Wiles, 91.

6. Braun, 113. Cai Xiaoqian, part 2, chap. 7.

7. Cai Xiaoqian, chap. 7.

8. Guo Chen, 17, 78; Lee and Wiles, 34–35; Salisbury, 172–73, 374 n. 15; Young, 203; Jocelyn and McEwen, 195. No exact date is ever given for this attack. Lee and Wiles (p. 34) say it was two months after He Zizhen had her baby. Young (p. 203) says it was "within a month after giving birth." But even this birth date, which I have placed on February 5 based on the observations of Jocelyn and McEwen (147), remains a matter of speculation. Also, in Lee and Wiles, they are heading into "night camp." But in her article "The Long March," Liao Siguang implies that they were leaving a day camp to walk under the cover of darkness.

9. The account of Hou Zheng's plight comes from Li Jianzhen (pp. 92–94). Li notes with something akin to relish that "the comrade from the Political Security Bureau was later transferred elsewhere and died during the Long March."

10. Cai Xiaoqian, part 2, chap. 7.

11. Braun, 113.

12. Guo Chen, 163; Lee and Wiles, 57; Braun, 113–14; Salisbury, 370 n. 14.

13. Liu Ying, chap. 5. Liu Ying's exact position has been somewhat misconstrued over the years. She writes that in April 1935, the Central Committee had decided that she would take the place of Deng Xiaoping, the "general secretary of the Central Committee," but that chief leadership role belonged to Zhang Wentian at the time. Young (p. 152) quotes Liu Ying in an interview: "I was General Party Secretary for a while." Lee and Wiles (p. 262) say that she was "appointed secretary-general of the Central Committee." More accurately, Guo Chen (p. 77) says that Liu was

"appointed the Head Secretary of the Central Team." Salisbury (p. 193), who interviewed Liu Ying in 1984, uses similar wording, noting that after Deng Xiaoping was "relieved of his Central Committee secretarial duties," Liu Ying "became secretary to the 'Central Team.'"

14. Guo Chen, 77.

15. Otto Braun, 112–14; Lee and Wiles, 91.

16. Young, 216–17; Guo Chen, 150–55; Lee and Wiles, 170.

17. Guo Chen, 81–83; Lee and Wiles, 35–36. Guo Chen notes that according to Deng Yingchao, to make it easier to search for them later, she named both Chen Huiqing's and He Zizhen's baby girls "Shuang Feng," or "Twin Phoenix." (In China, a phoenix is considered a feminine creature, while a dragon is a masculine one.) The name did not help, however. Neither girl was ever found.

Some Fifth Army Group soldiers were outraged when they found out that they had fought the battle for a baby. "What a waste that so many soldiers died defending a little kid!" a soldier complained. "The purpose of the revolution and our struggle," the commander rejoined, "is to provide a future for the children!" Yet the child they risked their lives for was then abandoned, almost certainly to die. "Indeed, the blood and sacrifice of the revolutionaries allowed millions of Chinese children to enjoy the freedom that previous generations only dreamt of," wrote Guo Chen (p. 84). "Although most revolutionaries lost their own children during the war, their legacies live on in the smiling faces of children today." But for the mothers who had but moments to look at their babies and could easily imagine them alone in an abandoned home, crying out, starving to death, or falling prey to a hungry animal, such celebratory claims were likely insufficient compensation.

18. Chen Yun, chap. 5. Half a century later, when William Lindsey retraced the Long March, he visited a Ruijin apothecary shop to get medical supplies. The doctor suggested Yunnan Baiyao. "This panacea was a secret formula concocted from Yunnan province's abundant flora," wrote Lindsey in *Marching with Mao* (p. 69). "For internal or external use, the powder was prescribed for almost anything in anybody: from period pain to sore throats, from internal hemorrhage to gunshot wounds and animal bites. It was to be taken dry, with water or with wine. I had immediate faith in this wonderful stuff: it smelt like a walk in Kew Gardens." The medicine's ingredients are still considered a trade secret, but it is known that one of its active ingredients is *sanqi,* a ginseng-type herb. It is also said that pregnant women should not use the medicine because it can distress the uterus and cause spontaneous abortion.

19. Jocelyn and McEwen, 211–12. Some would later say that Mao had struck a deal with the warlord Long Yun. Long had no interest in fighting Mao and even less in bottling him up in Yunnan and having Chiang Kaishek's Nationalist Army duke it out with the Reds on his turf. Both armies presented a threat to his rule. Contrary to official accounts, the maps and medicine may have been gifts from Long Yun.

Chapter 14: Dead Child

1. Zhang Guotao, 316, 351; Lee and Wiles, 67–68; Luo Huilan, "Women on the Long March," 33.
2. Zhang Guotao, 316; author correspondence with Ed Jocelyn, September 3, 2009.
3. Xiao Yun, *My Mother*, 3–5.
4. Zhang Guotao, 317.
5. Xiao Yun, 21; Zhang Guotao, 351.
6. Zhang Guotao, 350–51.
7. Wang Xinlan, interview, November 18, 2006.
8. Xiao Yun, 25–26.
9. Ibid., 38–39.
10. Wang Xinlan's story is told in *My Mother* by her son, Xiao Yun. Much of Xinlan's story in this narrative comes from Xiao's book, as well as an interview with Wang Xinlan and two interviews with Xiao for this book. Xiao says (p. 51) that the crossing took place on the last day of March. Zhang Guotao (p. 367) says that it took place "one April evening."
11. Zhang Guotao, 351.
12. Xiao Yun, 29–30.
13. Ibid., 52.
14. Ibid.
15. Injured in China, Agnes Smedley wrote this harrowing description of what it was like to be carried by stretcher:

> My carriers had no food at all. They labored along over the mountains, and their heavy breathing sickened my heart. I am not accustomed to being carried on the shoulders of human beings. Once I took my eyes from the distant plateau and looked down the side of my stretcher. Below me yawned a vast, deep ravine. The sides had crumbled away. I turned to the other side, to avoid looking into this abyss, only to find that another abyss yawned on that side. I was swinging in space, with what seemed a bottomless ravine on either side of me. Only the carriers before and behind me showed

that the earth was there, under their feet. I closed my eyes and waited. (*China Fights Back,* pp. 11–12)

16. Zhang Guotao, 376.
17. Young, 92–95.
18. Ma Yixiang recounted this exchange to Young (p. 95).

Chapter 15: Two Raging Rivers

1. Braun, 109; Jocelyn and McEwen, 216; Cai Xiaoqian, 270.
2. At a wharf a bit upriver, called Luchedu, the Red Army seized two boats to use at Jiaopingdu. (A small band of soldiers also crossed here.) Sacrificing accuracy for convenience, some historians, including the Taiwanese chronicler Cai Xiaoqian (chap. 8), combined elements of both names — using the characters "jiao" from Jiaopingdu and "che" from Luchedu — to create the name Jiaochedu to refer to the place of the river crossing.
3. Cai Xiaoqian, 270–71; Chen Yun, part 5; Jocelyn and McEwen, 213–14.
4. Braun, 118; Gernant, 272; Cai Xiaoqian, part 2, chap. 8.
5. Cai Xiaoqian, 273.
6. Liu Lili tells this story in *They* (pp. 191–92).
   The Central Committee is technically the highest authority within the Chinese Communist Party, but between Party congresses, the real power and decision-making rest with the much smaller Politburo and especially its standing committee. The Politburo is appointed by the Central Committee but is responsible for calling Central Committee sessions. Thus, it is the de facto highest governing body of the CCP.
7. Elected in Ruijin in 1934, the Politburo standing committee at this time consisted of Bo Gu (Qin Bangxian), Zhang Wentian, Zhou Enlai, and Xiang Ying. The other members were Wang Ming, Chen Yun, Kang Sheng, Ren Bishi, Zhang Guotao, Mao Zedong, Gu Zuolin, and Zhu De. Alternate Politburo members included Liu Shaoqi, Wang Jiaxiang, Guan Xiangying, and Deng Fa (Kai Feng).
8. Chen Yun, part 6; Gernant, 272–73; Cai Xiaoqian, part 2, chap. 8; Jocelyn and McEwen, 226, 233–37.
9. Stephen Yu, "Zu De: The First Person to Use the Phrase 'Long March,'" *China Finance Net,* October 19, 2006.
10. Kang Keqing, 149–50.
11. Liu Lili, 183, 189–90.
12. Kang Keqing, 150; Liu Lili, 188.
13. From a wealthy landlord family, Shi Dakai joined the Christian cult started by Hong Xiuquan, who claimed to be the younger brother of Jesus and the

son of God. Shi, whose title was "the Wing King," was one of the five kings of the Heavenly Kingdom of Great Peace (the Taiping), established in 1851. Among the cult's revolutionary beliefs was that men and women are equal. It banned foot-binding and encouraged women to take part in politics and to become soldiers, which they did in large numbers for the first time in Chinese history. The Taiping leaders, however, clung to the practices of polygamy, concubinage, and female subservience. After establishing a capital in Nanjing, the cult tried to overthrow the Qing. In 1856, Shi, dubbed the seventh son of God, became embroiled in disputes within the cult, leading to the murder of his family in Nanjing and finally to his own demise at the Dadu River.

14. Jocelyn and McEwen, 255; Fritz, 66.

15. Cai Xiaoqian said that five Red Army soldiers were injured in the action and that all were awarded "Red Hero" status. He called the battle "a miracle of the Red Army's escape to the west" (p. 282).

16. The distance to Luding was actually about seventy-five miles. Gernant, 301; Jocelyn and McEwen, 240–51; Braun, 119; Chen Yun, part 6; Kang Keqing, 121–242.

17. Xi Jun, chap. 11. According to Xi, even five decades later, Li Jianzhen still remembered that soldier and often visited his family in Jiangxi.

18. Jocelyn and McEwen, 241, 256; Cai Xiaoqian, part 2, chap. 8; Chen Yun, part 6.

19. Jocelyn and McEwen, two British journalists who walked the entire Long March route beginning in October 2002, interviewed locals in Luding and reported this account of the actions (pp. 250–51). In his book *One's Company*, Peter Fleming, the London *Times* special correspondent who traveled across China in 1933, reported that "the Communist attack usually comprises a screen of . . . guerillas, supplemented by boys—occasionally women—armed with spears on whom the enemy expends much of his never very plentiful ammunition" (pp. 184–85).

20. Even now, the clash at Luding remains somewhat enshrouded in mystery. Kang Keqing, zealous woman warrior that she was, made no mention of the battle in her autobiography years later. "The Red Army vanguard had already secured the bridge," she recorded tersely. "We stopped to rest and called roll. To our surprise, after three days of intensive marching, not one person was lost from the group" (p. 152). Otto Braun's account largely supports the official account. He reported that "half a dozen fell into the raging waters" (pp. 119–20).

21. Braun, 119.

22. Cai Xiaoqian said that they reached Luding early on the morning of May 29 (chap. 8). According to Fei Kanru's *Diary of the First Army over* [sic] *Long March,* the Ninth Army Group, the rear guard of the Red Army, arrived at

the Luding Bridge on June 1. This was also the day the commanding unit made camp in Luding (246).

23. Kang Keqing, 152; Xi Jun, chap. 11; Young, 205; Liu Lili, 195.

24. Cai Xiaoqian, part 2, chap. 9.

Chapter 16: Hitting the Roof

1. Jocelyn and McEwen, 255; Wilson, 176; Liu Lili, 205; Cai Xiaoqian, part 2, chap. 9. No two histories report the progression through the Snowy Mountains or the number of Snowies crossed by the First Army in the same way. Some say that four were crossed, others five. Names vary. (Making the situation more difficult to decipher is the fact that the Chinese use the same name for the peaks as for the large massifs that the peaks lie in.)

   On my trek in the Snowies, led by Ed Jocelyn, we crossed these four mountains consecutively on the Long March route. Some of the First Army also crossed Changdeshan to reach Dagu Valley before crossing Dagushan. Most of the First Army took an easier route, going around Changdeshan and entering at the head of the valley.

2. Cai Xiaoqian (pp. 288–90) tells of the crossing of Baoxianggang (also seen elsewhere as Paotonggang or Baotonggang).

3. Gernant, 329; Kang Keqing, 161–62; Lee and Wiles, 36–37, 60.

4. Jing Li, *The Newly-Written Pictures and Files on the Long March,* "Part 2: The Women on the Journey."

5. Regarding the timing of Zeng Yu's childbirth, Lee and Wiles place it on Laoshan in Guizhou in November (p. 272) or December (pp. 29–30), based on Guo Chen (p. 80). However, Young (pp. 205–7) offers several corroborating interviews placing it later, in Sichuan. In a response to my query, Guo agreed that the later date makes more sense than the one in his book, because if Zeng gave birth on the border of Guizhou, she would have been seven months—and thus quite visibly—pregnant when she set out on the Long March, which is unlikely.

   Ma Hongwei and Zhang Tiezhi present an even more dramatic and perhaps more improbable version of Zeng's childbirth with some different details in *Women Soldiers of the Long March,* which says that with an involuntary thrust, she suddenly squatted on the trail and saw the baby's head emerge between her legs. The women rushed to her side and cupped the baby's head. Together they stumbled into camp like this. The next morning, Zeng put the naked infant on a straw bed. As the baby wailed and the enemy closed in, Zeng's Red sisters ushered her away. The baby's cry broke Zeng's heart.

6. Xikang province was short-lived. It was divided in 1950 along the Yangtze River. In 1965, parts of it were merged with the Tibetan Autonomous

Region, an administrative region of China comprising about half the territory of traditional Tibet, and parts with Sichuan province.

7. Braun, 120.

8. Vaccines against both typhoid and typhus had recently been developed in the United States and would be used extensively during World War II, but they were not available to the marchers.

9. Guo Chen, 52–53; Fritz, 79.

10. Lee and Wiles, 58–59.

11. Kang Keqing, 121–42. Chen Changfeng, in *The Long March: Eyewitness Accounts,* 128–29; Gernant, 325; Lee and Wiles, 98.

12. Braun, 120; Lee and Wiles, 60.

13. Smedley, *The Great Road,* 323; Fritz, 77.

14. Lee and Wiles, 98; Liu Lili, 197; Jocelyn and McEwen, 265.

15. Kang Keqing, 156. The village of Highland has been relocated uphill from its original position to make way for a reservoir. Many distant peaks are visible from the hillside, where a red marble monument has been positioned to commemorate the Long March.

16. A search of diaries and other writings composed during or around the time of the Long March turned up no use of the Chinese term for altitude sickness, *gao shan zheng,* literally "high mountain symptom."

17. Guo Chen, 10, 183; Lee and Wiles, 58–60.

18. Smedley, *The Great Road,* 325–26.

19. Kang Keqing, 155–60; Lee and Wiles, 98–99; Young 203.

20. Kang Keqing, 159.

21. Lin Wei, *The Footsteps of Strategic Cavalry,* 204–5; Liu Ying, 77.

22. Gernant, 346.

Chapter 17: A Meeting of Armies

1. Xiao Yun, 51–53.

2. Salisbury, 240; Short, 328–29; Liu Ying, chap. 5; Cai Xiaoqian, part 2, chap. 9.

3. Guo Chen, 56.

4. Fritz, 100.

5. This story comes from Guo Chen, 57. Bo Gu was originally named Qin Bangxian. His nickname, Ah Xian, meaning "spreading the message to the nations," came from the last part of his given name.

6. Jocelyn and McEwen, 269–70; Gernant, 347; Liu Ying, 78.

7. Kang Keqing, 162. Gift giving is an important part of maintaining proper relations in Chinese society. Between individuals of equal status, it is

traditionally customary to exchange gifts of equal value, although people of higher status can accept gifts from subordinates without reciprocating. As with other Chinese customs, superstitions abound. Gifts that are inappropriate include clocks, the Mandarin for "to give a clock" closely resembling the phrase "a deathbed farewell"; pears, because the word for pear, *li,* sounds like that for "leave"; and fans, because the word for fan sounds the same as the one for "depart."

8. Ibid.
9. Xiao Yun, 55.
10. In 1987, during the celebration of the sixtieth anniversary of the establishment of the People's Liberation Army, Wang Xinlan was interviewed by a television journalist and sang the song from memory.
11. Wang Quanyuan, interview, May 15, 2006; Lee and Wiles, 37, 60–61.
12. Zhang, 377; Short, 328–30.
13. Dong Hanhe, *Women Soldiers of the Western Route Army Fall into Enemy Hands,* chap. 20; Young, 210.
14. Salisbury, 252.

Chapter 18: Through the Tibetan Snowies

1. Cai Xiaoqian, part 2, chap. 10; Gernant, 357; Salisbury, 252–53. In Tibetan, Mengbishan is called Mengzhainuo, which means "the Great Path" or "the Path of 10,000 People." In the Qing dynasty, the mountain's Tibetan name was transliterated into Mandarin Chinese.

   Salisbury (pp. 252–53) puts Mengbishan at 14,000 feet and Jiajinshan at 14,200 feet. He names none of the other Snowy Mountains, noting only that once the Reds had crossed them, they had "broken through a geographic barrier." According to Salisbury, the Snowies were "unmapped, unexplored, uninhabited, uninhabitable. It was really not China. No Chinese felt at home in this landscape of the moon, snow mountains and barren wastes to the horizon," though the Tibetans "had for four centuries been inching their way into this unknown world."

2. Kang Keqing, 165.
3. Ibid.
4. One Zhuokeji native, a Tibetan trader who spoke Mandarin and was a child when the Reds passed through, gave Jocelyn and McEwen (pp. 276–79) quite a different version of events. He said that the residents had all fled to the hills or other towns in the area before the First Army arrived, except for one villager who shot at them and was killed. He claimed that the Fourth Army had already sacked and burned the fortress before the First Army arrived and that

the Fourth and First argued and fought each other in a bloody battle there. As a youth, he said, he and his friends dug up the bones of the dead and sold them to a fertilizer manufacturer. He also said that he once heard his mother say that the Reds burned their houses and stole their possessions. While elements of his account may be true, there is no evidence to support it.

5. Liu Tong, 380.

6. Guo Chen, 58; Cai Xiaoqian, part 2, chap. 10.

7. Guo Chen, 73.

8. Cai Xiaoqian, part 2, chap. 10.

9. Guo Chen, 72–73; Kang Keqing, 165–66.

10. Jocelyn and McEwen, 263, 277, 280–81; Gernant, 361; Liu Ying, chap. 5.

11. Gernant, 364, 373–74; Kang Keqing, 165–66.

12. Kang Keqing, 165–66; Liu Ying, chap. 5.

13. Kang Keqing, 165–67.

14. This account comes from Guo Chen (pp. 72–73).

15. Liao Siguang, "The Long March."

16. This story is originally found in Guo Chen (p. 58).

17. Mo Wenhua, "Life at Dagu," 384.

18. They had also caused panic among the Westerners there. The United States legation had notified Gansu and Shaanxi authorities that they expected American interests to be protected and had warned Americans in these provinces to prepare to evacuate. The *New York Times* reported, "Britons residing in Shaanxi have already evacuated except those already held by the Reds" (March 2, 1935, 4). The same edition carried an Associated Press report that 25,000 Communist troops passing through southwestern Shaanxi had created a "reign of terror, accompanied by wholesale executions and looting of towns." According to the account, twenty-five Christian missionaries, some carrying babies, had fled east on foot through snow-covered mountains.

19. Liu Jinghuai, 44–59.

20. Gansu Province website.

21. Xi Jun, chap. 4; *Gansu Daily* website.

22. Xi Jun, chap. 5.

23. Young, 95–97.

Chapter 19: Beyond the Snowies

1. Kang Keqing, 167–68; Salisbury, 256. In her book *China Fights Back,* Agnes Smedley, who traveled with elements of the former First Army during the Second Sino-Japanese War in 1937, corroborates such policies, noting that the military tried not to force the peasants to contribute supplies, labor, or

the use of their animals involuntarily and always took great care to remunerate them.

2. Guo Chen, 59–60.

3. Several versions of this story exist. One, taken from Guo Chen (pp. 58–60), appears in Wei Xiuying's *My Long March* profile. In it, Shorty returned to camp to the terrible sight of her prostrate friends and three male soldiers and at once realized that they had eaten poisonous mushrooms. She reached Liu first and put her fingers down her throat to make her vomit. In Liao Siguang's "The Long March—Magnificent Historical Feat," it is Liao who saved them. She says, "Fortunately, I grew up in the country, so I told them to put their fingers down their throats to make themselves vomit, and then drink lots of water."

4. Guo Chen, 77.

5. Ibid., 76.

6. Ibid.

7. Most histories confuse the place names and geography of the Maoergai River valley, referring to the village of Shawo and the town of Maoergai and not to Wodeng and Shanbazhai. However, Maoergai Town is an administrative district, encompassing numerous villages and not a town as we know it in the West. Shanbazhai, where I stayed on my 2009 Snowies trek, is the largest village in the area. Likewise, though many accounts make reference to a place called Shawo, as I discovered on the same journey, there is no such town. Shawo is a simple Tibetan house, now a registered historic landmark, in the village of Wodeng. As I explored the interior and sat on a tree stump in a back room said to be Mao's seat during the meeting, my friend and fellow trekker Gordon Wallace assembled his fishing rod, cast a fly into the Maoergai River, and caught a fourteen-inch carp to the cheers of the villagers.

8. Kang Keqing, 167–68; Salisbury, 256–60; Gou Chen, 77.

9. Salisbury, 256–60; Liu Ying, 81; Wei Bihai, *The Battle Record of the Fourth Front Army*, 88–136; Kang Keqing, 167–68. The Left Column was made up of the First Army's Fifth and Ninth army groups (the latter renamed the Thirty-second Army), along with the Fourth Army's Ninth, Thirty-second, and Thirty-third armies. The Right Column consisted of the Fourth Army's Fourth and Thirtieth armies and the First Army's First and Third army groups.

10. Young, 217–18; Guo Chen, 150–55.

11. Young, 226–27; Guo Chen, 160–63.

12. Lee and Wiles, 267–68; Salisbury, 260–62, 384 n. 22; Short, 331.

13. Salisbury, 257–58.

14. Zhang Guotao, 420.

15. Wei Bihai, 88–136; Zhang Guotao, 420; Lee and Wiles, 69, 169, 268.
16. Wang Quanyuan, interview, May 14, 2006.
17. Ibid., May 15, 2006. Young, 229.

Chapter 20: The Caodi

1. Xiao Yun, 60.
2. Chen Changfeng, 62; Young, 212–13; Gernant, 427–28, 431, 473–74.
3. This story comes originally from Guo Chen (p. 82). Guo asks the reader, "How can Deng Fa not look gaunt eating only wild grass, mushrooms, and roots boiled in water?" And this was just the first day on the Caodi.
4. Liu Ying, 84–85; Guo Chen, 92; Young, 212; Fritz, 95, 100; Gernant, 429, 436.
5. Wang Quanyuan, interview, May 15, 2006.
6. Gernant, 427; Chen Changfeng, 62.
7. Liao Siguang; Fritz, 94; Guo Chen, 93.
8. Young, 213–15; Wilson, chap. 19; Short, 331; Liu Ying, chap. 5.
9. Gernant, 430–34; Salisbury, 268.
10. Gernant, 430–42; Salisbury, 268–70; Liu Ying, chap. 5.
11. Liu Ying, 85; Guo Chen, 92.
12. Xiao Yun, 60.
13. Salisbury, 252.

Chapter 21: Life After Death

1. Salisbury, 271.
2. Gernant, 436–39.
3. Information on this battle comes from the commemorative monument at Upper Baozuo. Oddly, Harrison Salisbury reports that only "a small stock of biscuits, canned goods, and cigarettes was captured" (p. 274).
4. Smedley, *The Great Road,* 337–40; Salisbury, 263, 270; Gernant, 441–42.
5. Liu Ying, chap. 5; Guo Chen, 137.
6. China's remote villages are, to this day, not well mapped. Whereas Salisbury (p. 273) puts Banyou and Baxi at four miles apart, Jocelyn and McEwen (p. 307) place Baxi "10 miles east" of Banyou. The sign that Cai Xiaoqian (pp. 371–72) reports seeing places Baxi at fifty *li,* or about seventeen miles, from Banyou.
7. Cai Xiaoqian, 371–72; Gernant, 443–44; Guo Chen, 92.
8. An historical marker at the Banyou Monastery (not Banyou village) above the village of Baxi in Axi Valley commemorates the Long March stay of the Communist leaders and the meetings held here.
9. Guo Chen, 92.

10. Xiao Yun, 62.

11. Zhang Guotao (p. 421) calls it the upper reaches of the Black (Maqu) River, but most other sources, including Salisbury (p. 271), agree that it was the White (Gaqu) River.

12. Zhang Guotao, 421.

13. Wei Bihai, 88–136; Fritz, 89, 110–11; Salisbury, 271–74.

14. These dates correspond to those on official monuments at the Banyou Monastery and in the village of Yalong. Ruined walls of the original temple still remain next to the buildings constructed after the devastation of the Cultural Revolution.

15. According to Wei Bihai (pp. 88–136), some historians believe that Mao left in a hurry after he intercepted a secret telegram from Zhang Guotao ordering Chen Changhao to use force if Mao failed to comply with Zhang's decision to move the Right Column southward. In Zhang's account *The Rise of the Chinese Communist Party, 1928–1938,* he does not mention any directives sent to Chen but says that he received "an urgent radio message . . . reporting that the First and Third armies had secretly marched forward, in defiance of the order from General Headquarters to stop advancing temporarily" (422). Zhang accuses Mao of abandoning his duty.

16. Liu Ying, 85; Salisbury, 275–77; Jocelyn and McEwen, 307–10; Lee and Wiles, 40; Guo Chen, 125; Young, 213.

17. Liu Ying, 86. Zhang Wentian added that the Thirtieth Army, loyal to Zhang Guotao, had found out and was pursuing them and that they had to continue on rapidly to a hill to the north. In fact, however, the Thirtieth Army did not pursue them.

18. Xiao Yun, 62–63.

19. Salisbury, 277; Lee and Wiles, 61–69, 256, 281 n. 3, n. 21.

20. Xiao Yun (p. 64), quoting from Wang Xinlan's confession during the Cultural Revolution. In 1966, Mao launched the Cultural Revolution to regain control of the Party after his failing policies brought his regime to the brink of collapse. During a decade of terror, targets of the Party included politicians, religious leaders, and the social, artistic, and intellectual elite, and thus the Long March survivors. Many were forced to write confessions and were publicly humiliated, abused, exiled to the countryside, or killed by the Red Guard, a Maoist youth militia.

21. Kang Keqing, 172–89.

22. Zhang Guotao, 425; Xiao Yun, 65; Kang Keqing, 187. The Women's Independent Regiment went by various names at different times, and the name varies according to different translators. Although often called a "division" (10,000 to 20,000 soldiers), it was the size of a regiment (2,000 to 3,000 soldiers).

23. Kang Keqing, 189.

24. Now one entity, in a narrow gorge in Gansu, both the Maya Lamasery and the Cirina are in the administrative district of the town of Wangzang and are often referred to by that name.

25. Salisbury, 282–84; Jocelyn and McEwen, 309; Chang Jenchu, in *Stories of the Long March,* 124–33; Gernant, 455–66.

26. Lee and Wiles, 141; Gernant, 337; Jocelyn and McEwen, 309.

27. Smedley, *Battle Hymn of China,* 133–34. Even today, in the poorest remotes of China, some children share clothes and go outside only when it is their turn.

28. Salisbury (p. 285) says that each soldier received two silver dollars. He also reports, improbably, that some of the famished Red soldiers ate so much that their stomachs burst. Also Fleming, p. 189.

29. Salisbury, 286; Young, 214; Gernant, 471.

30. Salisbury, 286. In 1935, reports of Xu Haidong and Liu Zhidan and movements of their Red forces appear in the August 1 and 28 and September 13 editions of *Dagongbao,* which brands them "Shaanxi bandits."

    Salisbury has perhaps been misinterpreted as implying that Mao and the First Army officials had no idea that there was a North Shaanxi Soviet. However, he continues: "The papers revealed that Liu Zhidan, the daring commander of the Twenty-fifth Army, a friend of Mao's, a great folk hero, was alive and leading his army," which implies simply that Mao and the other leaders were overjoyed to hear that this group had not been defeated and still controlled their territory. In *Mao,* Jung Chang and Jon Halliday argue that "Mao and the core leaders had known about this base before the Long March, and Moscow had told them it was a possible destination as far back as 3 May 1934, well before the March set off" (171). This is probably true (see also Gernant, pp. 388–89). Nonetheless, after having been evicted from their own soviet and run ragged by enemy forces for the better part of a year, Mao and his First Army cohorts certainly had to be greatly pleased at the confirmation that *any* Communist stronghold still existed.

31. Liu Ying, chap. 5. Fenby (p. 271) says six hundred miles. A straight line on a map from Hadapu to Wuqi in Shaanxi runs a little under three hundred miles. However, Ed Jocelyn told me that, on his retracing of the Long March in 2002, it was almost exactly five hundred miles between the two towns.

Chapter 22: A Five-Hundred-Mile Sprint

1. Mark Selden (p. 67) says that when Xu Haidong learned from the newspaper *Dagongbao* that the First Army was heading north from Sichuan, he guessed

that it might be heading for the North Shaanxi Soviet, corroborating the fact that the Shaanxi Soviet was common knowledge among the Communists.

2. Xi Jun, chap. 6.

3. The Twenty-fifth Army's Long March has been estimated at "nearly ten-thousand *li*" (news.xinhuanet.com).

4. Jocelyn and McEwen, 319; Selden, 67–68.

5. Xi Jun, chap. 4; Liu Jinghuai, 44–59. Of the Twenty-fifth Army nurses, Three-Inch Lotus Feet was already married to Dai Jiying. Three others soon married in North Shaanxi, all to medical men: Tian Xilan to Qian Xinzhong, who had established the Twenty-fifth Army's hospital and cared for the wounded Xu Haidong; Yu Guoqing (later Yu Guang) to Li Ziping, a First Army convalescent company leader; and Dai Juemin to Rao Zhengxi of the Third Army Group.

6. Jocelyn and McEwen were stunned at the pace at which the Reds traveled at the end. "We didn't expect that . . . the Reds would sprint off faster and further than ever before," they wrote. To match their tempo, the modern-day authors note, "from the border of Gansu to the end, we will walk 620 miles in 35 days, with one day's rest" (p. 311).

7. Gernant, 471–73. Much of the chronology in this chapter derives from Gernant (pp. 471–93) and Salisbury (pp. 285–89). Also, Liu Ying, chap. 5; Fei Kanru interview, May 20, 2006.

8. Liu Ying, chap. 5; Salisbury, 286–87.

9. Gernant, 475–77, 480–82.

10. Jocelyn and McEwen, 303, 315–16; Gernant, 483–85; Salisbury, 285.

11. Lovell, 60–61, 322; Helen Foster Snow, *Inside Red China,* 79.

12. Helen Foster Snow.

13. Gernant, 487–88.

14. Salisbury, 288.

15. Salisbury, 311; Xi Jun, 65.

16. Gernant, 489–90.

17. Jocelyn and McEwen, 319; Liu Ying, chap. 5; Salisbury, 288. Estimates range from 3,000 to 5,000 survivors. A photograph of the formerly strapping German adviser Otto Braun in *A Comintern Agent in China* (facing p. 181) tells it all. Braun looks a decade older, gaunt with his gums exposed. Despite their vastly diminished ranks, Little Sparrow later said, "The Long March of the First Army was finished successfully" (Braun, p. 89).

18. Gernant, 491–93; Salisbury, 289; Jocelyn and McEwen, 319; Liu Ying, chap. 5; Young, 215.

19. Selden, 72. This is the official version of the story, but questions remain about the chain of events. By some accounts, Liu Zhidan had already been

imprisoned in a mid-September purge. He was released in November after the First Army's arrival and would die fighting the Japanese in 1936. One conspiracy theory holds that Mao, to consolidate his hold on the region, questioned Liu's loyalty to the Party, had him arrested to preempt a rivalry with him, and then had him killed on the battlefield. In June 1936, the city of Baoan changed its name to Zhidan in Liu's honor. In 1959, Liu's brother and widow wrote a biography of him that discussed the sensitive topic of relations between the First Army and Liu's troops. During the Cultural Revolution, those associated with the book were tortured or killed.

Chapter 23: The Fourth Army Hunkers Down

1. Xiao Yun, 65–69; Wei Bihai, 206; Zhang Guotao, 432.
2. Wang Xinlan, interview, November 18, 2006; Xiao Yun, 68–69; Wei Bihai, 206.
3. "On Tactics against Japanese Imperalism," December 27, 1935; works of Mao Zedong by date; Marxists Internet Archive, marxists.org.
4. Smedley, *Battle Hymn of China*, 133; Edgar Snow, 205; Spence, 294; Jocelyn and McEwen, 327. McEwen missed 320 miles while being treated for health issues. "Even though it was only 12,000 *li*, half what Mao promised, it has taken us fifteen days longer than it took the Red Army to reach this point," Ed Jocelyn wrote. "I reach the end of the Long March trail with my respect for the Reds' accomplishment not just intact, but increased."
5. Wei Bihai, 211–14.
6. Helen Foster Snow, *Inside Red China,* 192–93.
7. Ibid., 194–95.
8. Zhang Guotao, 443–44.
9. Kang Keqing, 192–93; Zhang, 438.
10. Xiao Yun, 70; Kang Keqing, 194–95; Helen Foster Snow, *Inside Red China,* 187; Zhang Guotao, 441.

Chapter 24: A Union of Forces

1. Young, 97.
2. R. A. Bosshardt, *The Restraining Hand: Captivity for Christ in China,* 130–44; *New York Times,* March 2, 1935, 4, col. 3. Duplicity in prisoner ransoming was not unusual in China. In 1931, the Red Army captured Yue Weijun, a Nationalist division commander. In exchange for Yue's release, his family and the Nationalists sent the Communists gasoline, uniforms, Western medicine, and a large sum of money. On the eve of Yue's release in August 1932, Zhang Guotao decided to execute Yue while keeping the ransom.

3. Young, 32–34.
4. The information on Xiang Jingyu comes from the *UXL Encyclopedia of World Biography* (2003) and Donald W. Klein and Anne B. Clark's *Biographic Dictionary of Chinese Communism, 1921–1965*.
5. Young, 98–99.
6. Bosshardt, 149.
7. Kang Keqing, 195–97; Young, 229.
8. Zhang Guotao, 239, 439–41.
9. Guo Chen, 184; Young, 229–31.
10. Kang Keqing, 196–99.
11. Guo Chen, 184–85; Young, 230–31.
12. Zhang Guotao, 434, 440.
13. Young, 108–9, 230–31; Zhang Guotao, 452–53; Xiao Yun, 70; Kang Keqing, 199–206.
14. The Japanese occupation of Manchuria, which lasted until the end of World War II, started with the Mukden Incident, the dynamiting of a section of Japan's South Manchuria Railway lines near present-day Shenyang in 1931. The explosion was perhaps perpetrated by Japan, which used it as an excuse to invade Manchuria and establish the puppet state of Manchukuo in 1932.
15. Kang Keqing, 201; Zhang Guotao, 444, 451, 456.
16. Zhang Guotao, 456.
17. Kang Keqing, 201–2; Young, 111.
18. Young, 110, 111. Ma Yixiang would later base a character on Qing in her 1961 autobiographical novel, *Sunflower*. Also Wolf, 155–56.
19. Dong Hanhe, chap. 20; Xiao Yun, 71.
20. Luo Huilan, 33.
21. Kang Keqing, 202.
22. Luo Huilan, 34.
23. Kang Keqing, 203–4; Guo Chen, 126.

Chapter 25: In the Throat

1. Selden, 5–6; Edgar Snow, 93–96.
2. Kang Keqing, 207–8.
3. Edgar Snow, 122–30, 349, 510; Lee and Wiles, 264–69.
4. Lee and Wiles, 256–58. The Eight Elders were a group of senior Party members who were consulted on matters of national importance during the 1980s and 1990s.
5. Young, 219; Guo Chen, 150–55.

6. Wang Xinlan interview, November 18, 2006.
7. Edgar Snow, 365–68.
8. Dong Hanhe, chap. 20.
9. Dong Hanhe, chap. 2. Much of the chronology and many of the events in this chapter are from Dong, chapters 2, 3, and 5. This book is not currently available in English.
10. Young, 229–231; Lee and Wiles, 69–71.
11. Salisbury, 320. For Salisbury, who was a guest of the Communist government, as for other Long March historians, the tragic events that befell the Women's Regiment were too remote, too marginal, and yet at the same time too controversial to pursue. Salisbury uses the standard head count of 2,000 for the Women's Regiment, which actually numbered closer to 1,300 at this point.
12. Wei Bihai, 376–78.
13. This information is from Wang Dingguo's profile in *My Long March,* chap. 3.
14. Dong Hanhe, chaps. 3, 5; Wang Dingguo, interview, May 11, 2006. Lee and Wiles, 70.
15. Dong Hanhe, chaps. 3, 5, and 22; Sun Shuyun, 253.
16. Fenby, 1–11.
17. Young, 219–20.

Chapter 26: The Destruction of the West Route Army

1. Braun, 190; Helen Foster Snow, *Inside Red China,* 75–78.
2. Kang Keqing, 207–8; Braun, 190.
3. Smedley, *Battle Hymn of China,* 171.
4. Helen Foster Snow, *Inside Red China,* 78–81.
5. Dong Hanhe, chaps. 2, 20.
6. Wei Bihai, 360–64. This and much of the West Route Army chronology in this chapter comes from Wei Bihai and especially from Dong Hanhe (chaps. 1, 2, 7, 14, 18, 19).
7. Dong Hanhe, 362–64.
8. Wei Bihai, 368–69; Dong Hanhe, chap. 18; Lee and Wiles, 69, 267–68. Several sources say that Wu Zhonglian gave birth to a boy in January 1937 at Linze and left the infant there. Other sources, however, hold that Wu brought a toddler son with her to Linze.
9. Dong Hanhe, chaps. 2, 18; Wei Bihai, 369–70.
10. Dong Hanhe, chap. 18; Sun Shuyun, 254.
11. Dong Hanhe, chap. 18.
12. Ibid., based on the 1958 report of the Zhangye Crackdown on

Counterrevolutionaries Team. When the Red Army cemetery in Xining was rebuilt in 1988, 517 skulls were discovered. The Ma dug "10,000-person pits" in Zhangye, Gulang, and some remote valleys.

Several months after escaping this appalling execution, Li Guizhen was picked up by Ma public security officers in Xining, and the security chief's wife took her in as a servant. Three years later, Li married their stable hand.

13. Ibid., 217.
14. Wei Bihai, 371–74.
15. Ibid., 375.
16. Ibid., 387–88.
17. Dong Hanhe, chaps. 1, 2, 7, 14, 19, 20.

Chapter 27: Prisoners of the Ma

1. Dong Hanhe, chaps. 6, 7, 9. Of the First Army women in the West Route Army, the newlywed wireless operator Li Jianhua had been missing since January and was presumed dead. Wu Zhonglian, who had left her son in Linze in January and whose husband was killed in April, had been captured.
2. Ibid., chap. 2; Lee and Wiles, 63, 72.
3. In her book *The Long March,* Sun Shuyun raises questions about Wang Quanyuan's conduct during this time. According to Sun, one Ma guard commander claimed in a forced confession that "Wang slept with him and worked with him to manage the 130 women prisoners" (p. 247). To substantiate this claim, Sun cites a Red Army woman prisoner she interviewed who deemed Wang a "witch" (p. 259). In 2006, when I asked Wang about the allegations, she became furious and called them a "fart." Given her record of courage both during and after the Long March (and the dubious nature of the guard's confession), I find it hard to believe that Wang deliberately did anything to improve her own circumstances at the expense of her comrades.
4. Dong Hanhe, chap. 4.
5. Ibid.; Wang Dingguo, interview, May 11, 2006.
6. From Wang Dingguo's profile in *My Long March,* chap. 3; Dong Hanhe, chap. 12; and Lee and Wiles, 169–70.
7. Helen Foster Snow, *Inside Red China,* 167.
8. Ibid., 193.
9. Salisbury, 335; Lee and Wiles, 260–62; Edgar Snow, 460.
10. Smedley, *China Correspondent,* 131.
11. Dong Hanhe, 31.
12. Young, 219–22.

Epilogue

1. Helen Foster Snow, *Inside Red China,* caption, photo insert after p. 184; Lee and Wiles, 51, 249–59; Young, 89–90, 163–66; Guo Chen, 28–34.

2. Lee and Wiles, 266–70; Guo Chen, 77–78; Young, 138–39; Wei Xiuying's profile in *My Long March*, chap. 5.

3. Xiao Yun, 38–49.

4. Young, 118.

5. From "Zhang Qinqiu's Memorial Meeting Held in Beijing," *People's Daily,* June 24, 1979, found in Dong Hanhe, chap. 12.

6. Guo Chen, 77–81; Lee and Wiles, 269.

7. Lee and Wiles, 253.

8. Ibid., 256–57.

9. Guo Chen, 70–71; Lee and Wiles, 268–69.

10. Lee and Wiles, 262. Qian Xijun, who died in 1990, was also influential in creating a history of the Long March women. She remained in touch with her fellow Long Marchers throughout her life, visiting Wei Gongzhi in a hospital during the Cultural Revolution and helping Beijing journalist Guo Chen interview survivors in the 1980s.

    Xie Fei is still living in Beijing, where I met with her in the spring of 2006. Though she could still sing revolutionary songs, Xie was mentally unable to discuss events. I also interviewed Wang Dingguo, who marched with the Fourth Army, at her home in Beijing.

11. Guo Chen, 187–88.

12. Ibid., 188.

13. Young, 143.

14. Guo Chen, 189.

INTERVIEWS CONDUCTED
FOR THIS BOOK

Chen Chixuan, interview by author and Elly Zhen at his home near Zunyi, Guizhou, May 20, 2006.

Fei Kanru, interview by author and Elly Zhen at his home in Zunyi, Guizhou, May 20, 2006.

Guo Chen, interview by author and Elly Zhen at his home in Beijing, May 10, 2006, and by Sharon Meng at his home, February 27, 2007.

Ma Yixiang, telephone interviews by Elly Zhen, December 4 and 27, 2006.

Nie Zhiqun, telephone interviews by Sharon Meng, August 13, 2007, and March 27, 2008.

Wang Daojin, interview by author and Elly Zhen at the Zunyi Long March Museum, Zunyi, Guizhou, May 19, 2006.

Wang Dingguo, interview by author and Elly Zhen at her home in Beijing, May 11, 2006.

Wang Quanyuan, interviews by author and Elly Zhen at her home in Taihe County, Jiangxi, May 14 and 15, 2006.

Wang Xinlan, interview by Elly Zhen at her home in Beijing, November 18, 2006.

Xiao Yun, telephone interviews by Elly Zhen, September 19 and 21, 2006.

BIBLIOGRAPHY

Bashford, James W. *China: An Interpretation*. New York: Abingdon Press, 1916.

Bosshardt, R. A. *The Restraining Hand: Captivity for Christ in China*. London: Hodder & Stoughton, 1936.

Braun, Otto. *A Comintern Agent in China, 1932–1939*. London: C. Hurst, 1982.

Cai Xiaoqian. *Taiwan ren de changzheng jilu* [The Long March Records of a Taiwanese]. Taipei: Study Publisher of the Communist Party, 2002.

Chang Jenchu. "Red Flag over Latsekou," in *Stories of the Long March*, 124–133. Peking: Foreign Language Press, 1960.

Chen Changfeng. *Gensui Maozhuxi Changzheng* [On the Long March with Chairman Mao]. Beijing: Cultural Liberation Army Publisher, 1986.

Chen Yue. *Shaanxi*. Beijing: China Great Encyclopedia Publisher, 2003.

Chen Yun. "Chen Yun's Report on 15th October 1935." *The Documents of the Party*, no. 4 (2001). In a sophisticated propaganda ploy, Chen wrote *Suijun xixing jianwen lu* [Experiences of the March Westward] in Shanghai in 1935 under an assumed identity—that of Lian Chen, a Nationalist Army doctor and prisoner of the First Army, who paints a heroic picture of the Red Army and the Long March. His account ends after the First and Fourth armies met up, when he was sent to Shanghai to oversee the Communist underground there. A member of the Politburo since 1931, Chen was a representative of the CCP assigned to the Fifth Army Group during the march. After writing his account, he attended the Third Congress of the Comintern in Moscow, where he presented a report, which was published in 1936 as *The Heroic March to the West* under the name Shi Ping. Though lean, Chen's account was the best available until Edgar Snow's *Red Star over China* (1938). In the 1990s, Chen was considered one of China's Eight Elders, to be consulted on important Party matters.

Bibliography

*Complete History of the Long March of the Chinese Workers and Peasants Red Army —
Campaign Record of the Red 25th Army.* Edited by the Academy of Military
Science Historical Research Bureau. Beijing: Military Science Publishing,
2006.

Dong Hanhe. *Xilujun Nuzhanshi Mengnan ji* [Women Soldiers of the Western
Route Army Fall into Enemy Hands]. Beijing: Cultural Liberation Army
Publisher, 2001.

Fairbank, John King. *China: A New History.* Cambridge, MA: Belknap Press of
Harvard University Press, 1992.

Fei Kanru. *Hong yifangmianjun Changzheng Rizhi* [The Diary of the First Front
Army over [*sic*] Long March]. Shanghai: Eastern Publishing, 2006.

Fenby, Jonathan. *Generalissimo Chiang Kai-shek and the China He Lost.* London:
Free Press, 2005.

Fleming, Peter. *One's Company: A Journey to China in 1933.* London: Jonathan
Cape, 1934. Reprint, London: Pimlico, 2004.

Fritz, Jean. *China's Long March: 6,000 Miles of Danger.* New York: G. P. Putnam's
Sons, 1988.

Gascoigne, Bamber. *A Brief History of the Dynasties of China.* London: Robinson,
2003.

Gernant, Karen. "The Long March." Ph.D. diss., University of Oregon, 1980.

Guan Qianxin, "Some Seniors in the 1st Route Army." In *The Party History
Document of the Zunyi Government,* n.d.

Guo Chen. *Jinguo Liezhuan: Hongyifangmianjun Sanshiwei Changzheng Nuhongjun
Shengping Shiji* [The Biographies of the Heroines: Thirty Women Soldiers of
the First Front Red Army]. Beijing: Rural Reading Publisher, 1986.

He Diyu. "Mud Buddha." In *Personal Experiences of the Long March,* edited by
Liu Tong, 148–50. Beijing: Central Archives Publisher, 2006. Articles and
accounts by Red Army cadres composed at Mao's request in August 1936
as part of the Red Army's international fundraiser.

Honig, Emily. *Sisters and Strangers: Women in the Shanghai Cotton Mills, 1919–
1949.* Stanford, CA: Stanford University Press, 1986.

Hsiao Peng et al. *The Long March: Eyewitness Accounts.* Beijing: Foreign Languages
Press, 1963.

Hu Guohua. "Li Kaifen: A Woman Supported by Belief." In *Biographies of the Red
Army Heroines,* 116–34. Beijing: Xinhua Publishing, n.d.

Jing Li. *The Newly-Written Pictures and Files on the Long March.* Beijing: China
Social Sciences Publishing House, 2002.

Jocelyn, Ed, and Andrew McEwen. *The Long March: The True Story Behind the
Legendary Journey That Made Mao's China.* London: Robinson, 2006.

Jung Chang. *Wild Swans: Three Daughters of China.* New York: Simon & Schuster, 1991.

Jung Chang and Jon Halliday. *Mao: The Unknown Story.* London: Jonathan Cape, 2005.

Kang Keqing, interview by Harrison Salisbury, November 2, 1984. New York: Harrison Salisbury Archives, Columbia University Rare Book and Manuscript Library.

Kang Keqing. *Memoir of Kang Keqing.* Beijing: People's Liberation Army Publishing, 1993.

Ko, Dorothy. *Cinderella's Sisters: A Revisionist History of Footbinding.* Berkeley: University of California Press, 2005.

Lawrence, Anthony. *China: The Long March; The World's Great Photographers Retrace the Route on the Fiftieth Anniversary.* Hong Kong: Intercontinental Publishing, 1986.

Lee, Lily Xiao Hong, and Sue Wiles. *Women of the Long March.* St. Leonards, Australia: Allen & Unwin, 1999.

Li Bozhao, interviews by Harrison Salisbury, June 15 and October 31, 1984. New York: Harrison Salisbury Archives, Columbia University Rare Book and Manuscript Library.

Li Haiwen. *Zhongguo Gongnong Hongjun Changzheng Qinliji* [The Personal Experiences of China's Peasant and Laborer's Red Army on the Long March]. Chengdu: Sichuan People's Publisher, 2005.

Li Jianzhen. *Li Jianzhen Huiyilu* [The Reminiscences of Li Jianzhen]. Beijing: Chinese Communist Party Historic Publisher, 1991.

Li Jing. *The Newly Written Pictures and Files on the Long March.* Beijing: China Social Sciences Publishing, 2002.

Liao Siguang. "The Long March — Magnificent Historical Feat." *Party History Document Newsletter of the Zunyi Government* (1988).

Lin Wei. *Zhanlue Qibing de Zuji* [The Footsteps of Strategic Cavalry]. Beijing: Warrior Publisher, 1983.

Lin Yutang. *With Love and Irony.* New York: John Day, 1940.

Lindsey, William. *Marching with Mao: A Biographical Journey.* London: Hodder & Stoughton, 1993.

Liu Jinghuai. "Zhou Dongping: The Footprints of a Red Army Nurse." In *Biographies of Red Army Heroines,* 44–59. Beijing: Xinhua Publishing, n.d.

Liu Lili. *Tamen: Sanshierge Nurende Changzheng* [They: The Long March of the 32 Women]. Beijing: Central Archives Publisher, 2006.

Liu Tong, ed. *Personal Experiences of the Long March.* Beijing: Central Archives Publisher, 1986.

Liu Ying, interview by Harrison Salisbury, June 14, 1984. New York: Harrison Salisbury Archives, Columbia University Rare Book and Manuscript Library.

Liu Ying. *Liu Ying Zi Shu* [The Autobiography of Liu Ying]. Beijing: People's Publishing, 2005.

The Long March: Eyewitness Accounts. Peking: Foreign Languages Press, 1963.

"The Long March in Zunyi." *Beijing Morning Post,* October 19, 2006.

Lovell, Julia. *The Great Wall: China Against the World, 1000 BC–AD 2000.* New York: Grove Press, 2006.

Lu Liping. "The Starting Point of the Long March." In *The Long March Started Here,* edited by Li Yun, 159–60. Beijing: Chinese Communist Party Historic Publisher, 2004.

Luo Huilan. "Women on the Long March." *Women of China,* n.d.: 33–35. Harrison Salisbury Archives, Columbia University Rare Book and Manuscript Library.

Ma Hongwei and Zhang Tiezhi, eds. *Changzhengzhong de Nuhongjun* [Women Soldiers of the Long March]. Beijing: Military Science Publishing, 2004.

Ma Yixiang. *Chaoyang Hua* [Sunflower]. Reprint. Beijing: China Youth Publishing, 2006.

Miles, Rosalind. *Who Cooked the Last Supper? The Women's History of the World.* New York: Three Rivers Press, 1988.

Mo Wenhua. "Life at Dagu." In *Personal Experiences of the Long March,* edited by Liu Tong, 384–86. Beijing: Central Archives Publisher, 2006.

Salisbury, Harrison E. *The Long March: The Untold Story.* New York: Harper & Row, 1985.

Selden, Mark. *The Yenan Way in Revolutionary China.* Cambridge, MA: Harvard University Press, 1971.

Short, Philip. *Mao: A Life.* London: John Murray, 2004.

Siao-yu. *Mao Tse-Tung and I Were Beggars.* London: Hutchinson, 1961.

Smedley, Agnes. *Battle Hymn of China.* New York: Knopf, 1943. Reprinted as *China Correspondent.* London: Pandora Press, 1984.

———. *China Fights Back: An American Woman with the Eighth Route Army.* New York: The Vanguard Press, 1938.

———. *China's Red Army Marches.* New York: The Vanguard Press, 1934.

———. *The Great Road: The Life and Times of Chu Teh.* New York: Monthly Review Press, 1956.

———. *Portraits of Chinese Women in Revolution.* Edited by Jan and Steve MacKinnon. New York: Feminist Press, 1976.

Snow, Edgar. *Red Star over China.* Rev. ed. New York: Grove Press, 1968.

Snow, Helen Foster. *Inside Red China.* New York: Da Capo, 1979.

————[Nym Wales, pseud.]. *Red Dust: Autobiographies of Chinese Communists.* Stanford, CA: Stanford University Press, 1952.

Spence, Jonathan. *The Gate of Heavenly Peace: The Chinese and Their Revolution, 1895–1980.* New York: Penguin, 1981.

————. *Mao Zedong: A Life.* New York: Penguin, 1999.

————. *The Search for Modern China.* New York: W. W. Norton, 1990.

Sun Shuyun. *The Long March.* London: HarperCollins, 2006.

Sun-tzu. *The Art of War.* Translated by Ralph D. Sawyer. New York: Barnes & Noble, 1994.

Tao Jie, Zheng Bijun, et al. *Holding Up Half the Sky: Chinese Women Past, Present, and Future.* New York: Feminist Press, 2004.

Tsai Hsaio-Chien. *My Recollections of the Kiangsi Soviet and the Westward Flight of the Chinese Red Army.* Taipei: Institute for the Study of Chinese Communist Problems, 1970.

Wang Xia. *Suffering: The Legend of the Commander of the Women's Regiment.* Beijing: Military Science Publishing House, 1999.

Wei Bihai. *Hong Sifang Mianjun Zhengzhan Jishi* [The Battle Record of the Fourth Front Army]. Beijing: Cultural Liberation Army Publisher, 2002.

Wertz, Richard R. *Exploring Chinese History.* <www.ibiblio.org/chinesehistory>. 1998–2009.

Wilson, Dick. *The Long March 1935: The Epic of Chinese Communism's Survival.* London: Hamilton, 1971.

Wolf, Margery. *Women and the Family in Rural Taiwan.* Stanford, CA: Stanford University Press, 1972.

Wu Chengen. *Monkey.* Translated by Arthur Waley. New York: Grove Press, 1943.

Xi Jun. *Jinguo Beige* [The Sad Melody of the Women Soldiers]. Chengdu: Sichuan People's Publishing, 1995.

Xiao Yun. *My Mother: The Youngest Woman Soldier on the Long March.* Beijing: China Literature and Art Federation Publishing, 2004.

Xinhua News Agency and *Beijing Youth Daily,* eds. *My Long March.* Beijing: People's Liberation Army Publishing, 2003. Includes interviews of Wang Dingguo, Wei "Shorty" Xiuying, and Wei Xiuying about Jin Weiying.

Xu Guangqiu. *War Wings: The United States and Chinese Military Aviation, 1929–1949.* Westport, CT: Greenwood Press, 2001.

Yang, Benjamin. *From Revolution to Politics: Chinese Communists on the Long March.* Boulder, CO: Westview, 1990.

Young, Helen Praeger. *Choosing Revolution: Chinese Women Soldiers on the Long March.* Urbana: University of Illinois Press, 2001.

Zhang Enhua. "Cartography of Revolution: Space, Politics, and Cultural Representations in Modern China, 1919–1969." Ph.D. diss., in progress, Columbia University, 2006.

Zhang Guotao. *The Rise of the Chinese Communist Party, 1928–1938.* Vol. 2, *Autobiography of Chang Kuo-t'ao.* Lawrence: University Press of Kansas, 1972.

The websites of the following organizations have been helpful in providing background information for this book.

English Language:

Chinese Historical and Cultural Project (CHCP), a Santa Clara County, California-based nonprofit organization to preserve Chinese American and Chinese history and culture (chcp.org); godchecker.com; Marxist Internet Archive (marxists.org); MayoClinic.com; MDidea (mdidea.com); MotherNature.com; Naked Scientists, a media-savvy group of physicians and researchers from Cambridge University (nakedscientist.com); Secret China (secretchina.com); Sportdoctor.com; Traditional Chinese Medicine and Acupuncture Health Information Organization (tcm.health-info.org); Travel China Guide (travelchinaguide.com); Yi Ethnic Group Website (yizuren.com/english/Index.asp).

Chinese Language:

Abatrip.com; Aba County Travel Administration (ab.abzta.gov.cn); ATA Cooperate Formation & Management (investing-china.net); Chengdu International Tour Cooperation (youyou-tour.com); China Beijing TV (btv.org); China Central TV (cctv.com); China Gansu Website, published by the Gansu Government News Office (gscn.com.cn); China Internet Information Center, published by the State Council Information Office and the China International Publishing Group, Beijing (china.com .cn); China Jingniu Maozhedong Thoughts (mzdthought.com); China Tibet Information Center (en.tibet.cn); Chinese Academy of Sciences, Computer Network Information Center (kepu.net.cn); Chinese People's Political Conference, Hangzhou Committee (hzzx.gov.cn); Chinese Scientific Information Center (engine.cqvip.com); Communist Party History Research Office, Beijing, "History of the Communist Party" (bjds.bjdj.gov .cn); Comsenz, a military forum (calf.cn); Division of Districts in China (xzqh.org); Dongshuangqiao Community, Shaoxing, Zhejiang (dsqsq.gov .cn); Dongwan Library, Guangdong (dglib.cn); Dreams Travel, China's first government-licensed online tour planner and operator, Chengdu (dreams-travel.com); Fangzhi Office, Zunyi Government, Guizhou Province (fzb .zunyi.gov.cn); Feet Walking Culture Media, Fuzhou (pigtour.com); Fugu County Government, Yulin, Shanxi (fg.gov.cn); Gansu County Government (yongchang.gov.cn); Gansu Provincial Government, China (gs.gov.cn); Hangzhou Daily Newspaper (hangzhou.com.cn); Hangzhou Freshes, Zhejiang (freshes.com/en/mushinfo/pompon); Hebei Journals and Newspapers, Hebei Daily Newspaper Group (skb.hebnews.cn); Hebei Provincial Price Bureau's Price Information Center (hebwj .gov.cn); Holy City Makuielys (makuielys.info); HometownChina .com; Huachi County Government, Gansu (hcx.gov.cn); Hubei Second Normal College (hubce.edu.cn); Hudong.com; Hunan Chenzhou Water Conservancy Bureau (czwr.gov.cn); Hunan Library (library .hn.cn); Hunan Xiang Culture Promotion Organization (hnmrw .net); Jiange County Government (cnjmg.gov); Jiangxi Family Building Association, Wedding Committee (nchqw.com); Jiangxi Provincial Library (share.jxlib.gov.cn); Jichang Government, Xinjiang (xjcj.gov .cn); Jinqian Online (zt.gog.com.cn); Junxian Tea House (2499cn .com/majiajunf); Kunming Holiday Travel Agency (kmholiday .com); Lanzhou Morning Post (lzcb.gansudaily.com.cn); Liexun Military Information Website (1no.net); Lvren Travel Information Website (world.lvren.cn); Maerkang County government, Sichuan (mek.abzta.gov.cn); Maoer Mountain National Nature Preserve, Guangxi (gxmes.com); Military and Politics Online (ourzg.com); Min le Government, Gansu (gsml.gov.cn); News of the Communist Party of China (cpc.people.com.cn); New Zealand Investment Consultancy (huachengnz.com); HanMedi (okmedi.net); Pengyang County Commercial Administration, Guyuan city, Ningxia (pengyang.mofcom .gov.cn); People's Daily Online, a division of *People's Daily Newspaper,* published by the Chinese government (book.people.com.cn); *People's Liberation Army Newspaper,* published by the Chinese Department of Defense (chinamil.com.cn); Qinghai Oyuan Travel Agency (qhtravel.cn); Seeing Doctors Online (big5.91.cn); Senior History Education Website in China, ed. Zhou Jianding (lsfyw.net); Shanghai Rongshuxia Computer (article .rongshuxia.com); Shanghai Technology Information Center (yf.net .cn); Shanxi Cultural Information Website (Shanxi snwh.gov.cn); Shanxi Info (shaanxi.cn); Shanxi News Online (pic.cnwest); Shanxi Province Government (news.shaanxi.gov.cn); Sichuan Committee of Chinese People's Political Consultative Conference (sczx.gov.cn); Sichuan

Daily Network Media Development Company (sconline.com.cn); Sichuan Rural Information Website (scnjw.gov.cn); Shiyan Archives Bureau (sydaxxw.com); SINA Corporation (mil.news.sina.com.cn); Tom Online (army.news.tom.com); Taihe County Government, Jian, Jiangxi (jxth.gov.cn); Taiwan Golden Swallow (swallow.com.tw); Taiwan Huayi Digital (ceps.com.tw); Warsawto.com; Weixin County Government, Yunnan (weixin.gov.cn); Weixin County News Center, Yunnan (wxnews.org); Women's Original Literary Website (article .hongxiu.com); Wuhan Broadcast and TV (whbc.com.cn); Xian Education Bureau (xaeduhelp.com); Xiaojin County Government, Sichuan (xjsc .gov.cn); Xinhuanet, the online news service of Xinhua News Agency, the official news agency of China (xinhuanet.com); Xingdao Global Website, a portal news website for Chinese people all over the world (stnn.ccYongchang); Za shui County Government, Shanxi (snzs.gov.cn); Zhaotong Foreign Propaganda Office and Municipal News Center (ztnews .net); Zhidan County Government, Shanxi (zhidan.gov.cn).

INDEX

Page numbers in *italic* refer to maps and photographs.

ABOUT THE AUTHOR

Dean King is the author of the national bestseller *Skeletons on the Zahara* and the critically acclaimed biography *Patrick O'Brian: A Life Revealed,* as well as the Aubrey-Maturin companion books *A Sea of Words* and *Harbors and High Seas.* His adventures tracking down history have taken him from the sands of the Sahara to the snowy peaks of the Tibetan Plateau in northwestern China. A former contributing editor to *Men's Journal,* he has written for many publications, including *Esquire, National Geographic Adventure, New York* magazine, the *Daily Telegraph,* and the *New York Times.* You can read more about his works at his website, deanhking.com.

WOMEN

OF THE

LONG MARCH

1933–1937

CAI CHANG, 34
First Army. From distinguished political family.
Joined the Chinese Communist Party (CCP) in
1923. Beautiful and polished, she was often called
"Eldest Sister."

DENG "THE CANNON" LIUJIN, 22
First Army. So called for her booming voice. Almost
expelled from CCP after leaving behind Fourth
Army family unit.

DENG YINGCHAO, 30
First Army. From fallen gentry. Student activist.
Married Zhou Enlai, the future premier of the
People's Republic of China, in 1925. Ill with
tuberculosis and stretcher-bound for part of
the march.

HE ZIZHEN, 24
First Army. From Jiangxi intellectual class. Joined
CCP at sixteen. Married Mao Zedong in 1928.
Pregnant but increasingly estranged from Mao
during the march.

JIN "AH JIN" WEIYING, 30
First Army. From progressive family. Joined
CCP at twenty-two. Respected leader in Ruijin.
Briefly married to the future leader of the CCP,
Deng Xiaoping.

KANG KEQING, 23

First Army. Fisherman's daughter. Given to childless family. Married Zhu De in 1929. Embraced military life and often called "Director" or "Little Commander."

LI BOZHAO, 23

First Army. Married Yang Shangkun, future director of CCP, at eighteen. Her songs, dances, and skits were primary tools for entertaining and boosting morale.

LI JIANZHEN, 28

First Army. Guangdong peasant. Rose to head Women's Department. Supervised making of food sacks, straw shoes, clothing.

LIU "PORTER GIRL" CAIXANG, 19

First Army. Jiangxi *tongyangxi*. Carried stretchers and was one of three women chosen to lead doomed Fourth Army family unit when the two armies were briefly joined.

LIU "LITTLE SPARROW" YING, 29

First Army. Political fighter. In May 1935, succeeded Deng Xiaoping as Central Committee secretary.

MA YIXIANG, 11

Second Army. Tongyangxi from rural Hunan. Joined Red Army to escape her in-laws' abuse.

WANG QUANYUAN, 21

First Army. Admired for her beauty. Head of Women's Regiment of ill-fated West Route Army.

WANG XINLAN, 10

Fourth Army. From wealthy but progressive Sichuan family. Youngest woman on march.

WEI "SHORTY" XIUYING, 22

First Army. Joined Red Army in 1930 to escape abuse by her adoptive family. A favorite of all the women.

WU ZHONGLIAN, 26

First Army. Literate and capable. Joined CCP at age nineteen. Secretary of her cadres unit. Gave birth on march.

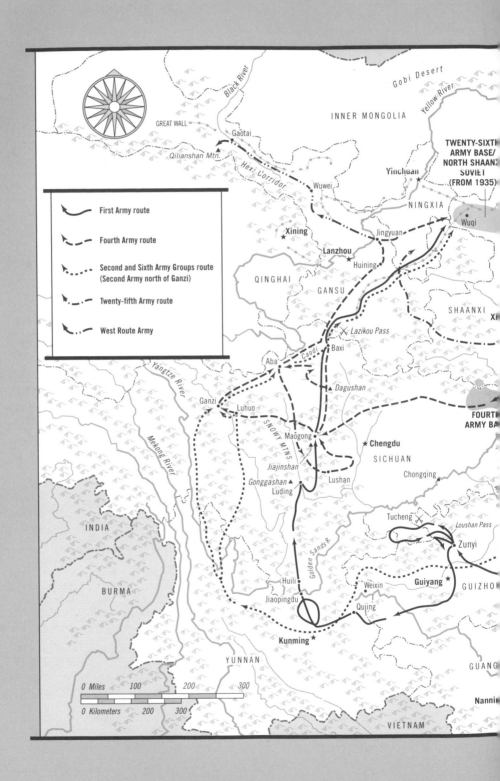